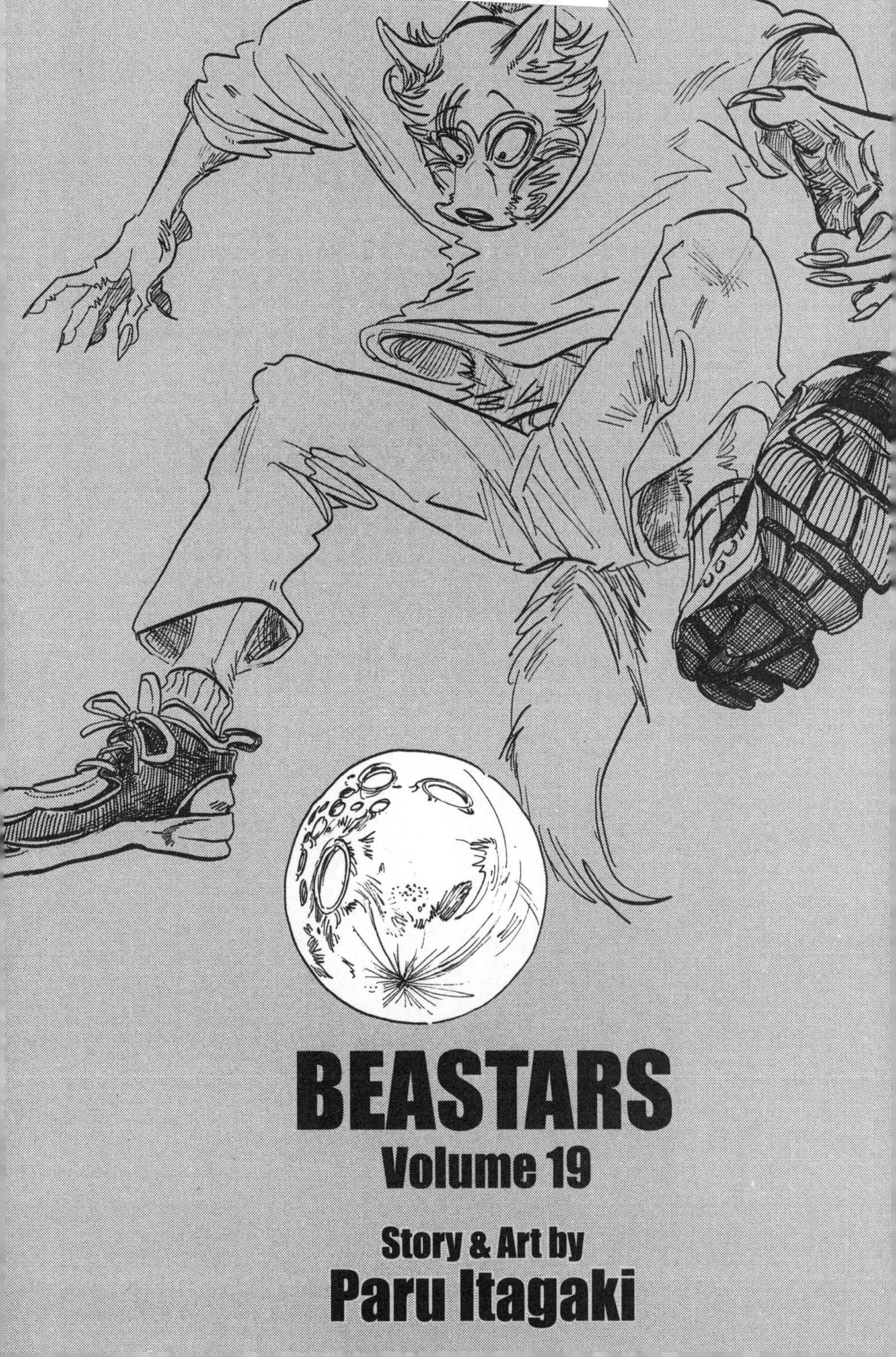

BEASTARS

Volume 19

Story & Art by

Paru Itagaki

STORY & CAST OF CHARACTERS

Legoshi has been designated a registered meat offender after consensually eating his friend Louis's leg to give him the strength to defeat the bear who murdered their friend. Now, while Legoshi's girlfriend Haru and Louis attend college, Legoshi works at an udon noodle shop. He is currently on the trail of mixed-species psychopath Melon, who tried to kill Legoshi twice but reminds him of the offspring Legoshi might someday have with Haru.

Melon's brutality on Happy Meat Day at the Black Market sends the tantalizing scent of fresh blood throughout the area. When the ensuing chaos spreads to the outside world and civilized society, it becomes clear that the black market is growing more dangerous and becoming a serious liability.

Legoshi runs into Louis in the streets of the black market, and together they go to the building where Louis was imprisoned as a fawn, kept as a "product" to be sold and devoured alive. The run-down building collapses with the two friends inside, and they find Louis's childhood comrades still living there. They too spent their childhoods awaiting their doom, but somehow managed to survive on their own.

Legoshi

★ Gray wolf ♂
★ Former Cherryton Academy student
★ Ate his friend Louis's leg to defeat Riz
★ Lives alone at Beast Apartments

Legoshi's five Canidae friends and former roommates. The Labrador in front is Jack, Legoshi's best friend.

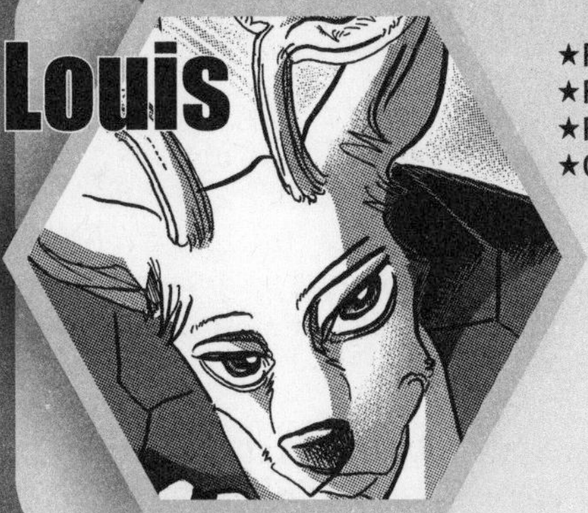

Louis

★Red deer ♂
★Former leader of the Drama Club actors poo
★Former leader of the Shishi-gumi lion gang
★Offered his leg to Legoshi so he could defea

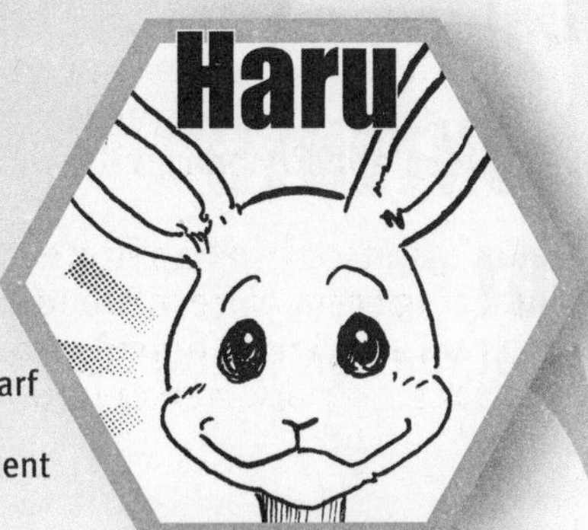

Haru

★Netherland dwarf rabbit ♀
★University student

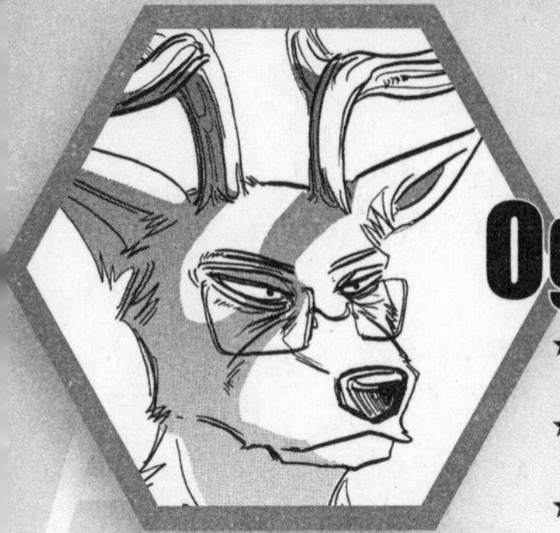

Ogma

★Louis's adoptive father ♂
★Head of the Horns Conglomerate
★Can't express his feelings, but loves his son

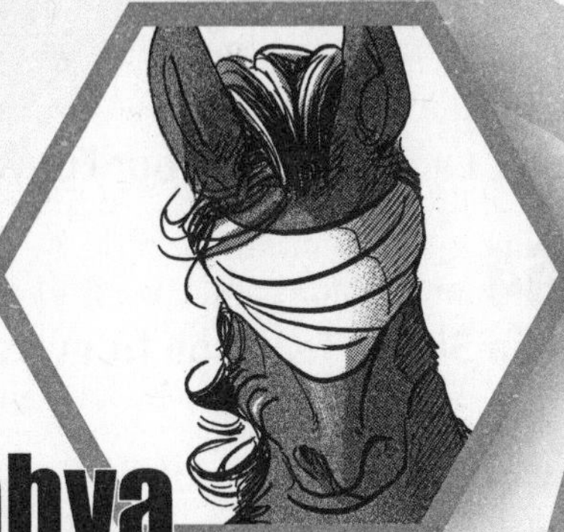

Yahya

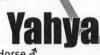

★Horse ♂
★Current Beastar
★Powerful combatant

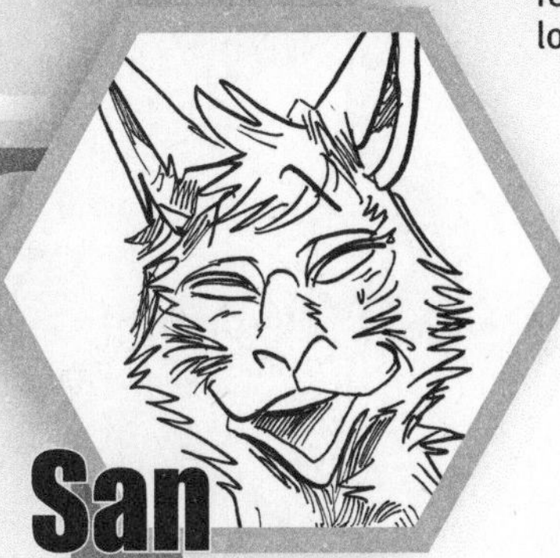

San

★Was once on sale at the black market with Louis and Kyu ♂
★Lacks combat skills
★Excels at detecting an opponent's weaknesses

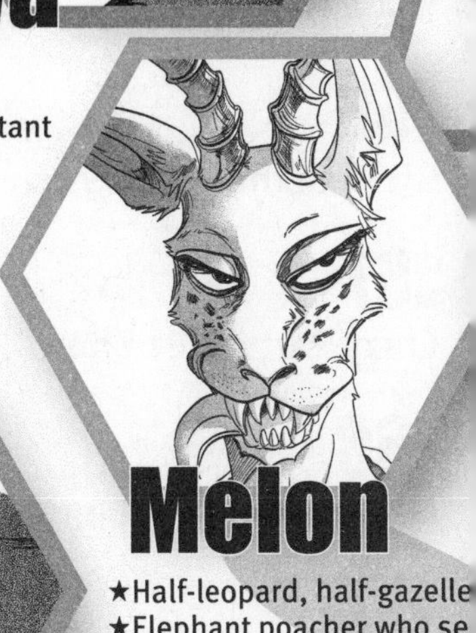

Melon

★Half-leopard, half-gazelle
★Elephant poacher who se tusks on the black markef

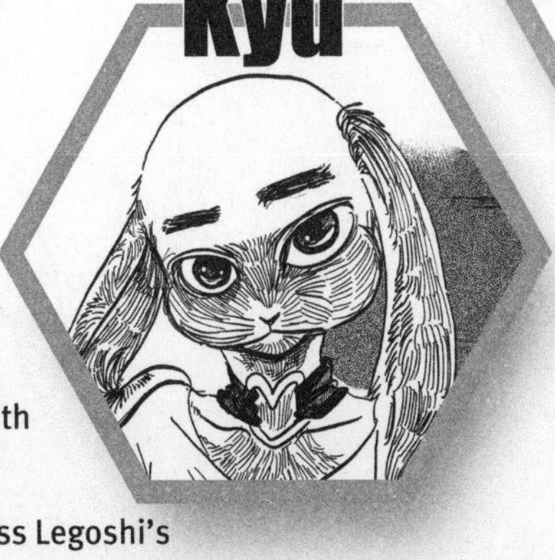

Kyu

★Was once on sale at the black market with Louis and San ♀
★Lop-eared rabbit
★Combat skills surpass Legoshi's

BEASTARS
Volume 19
CONTENTS

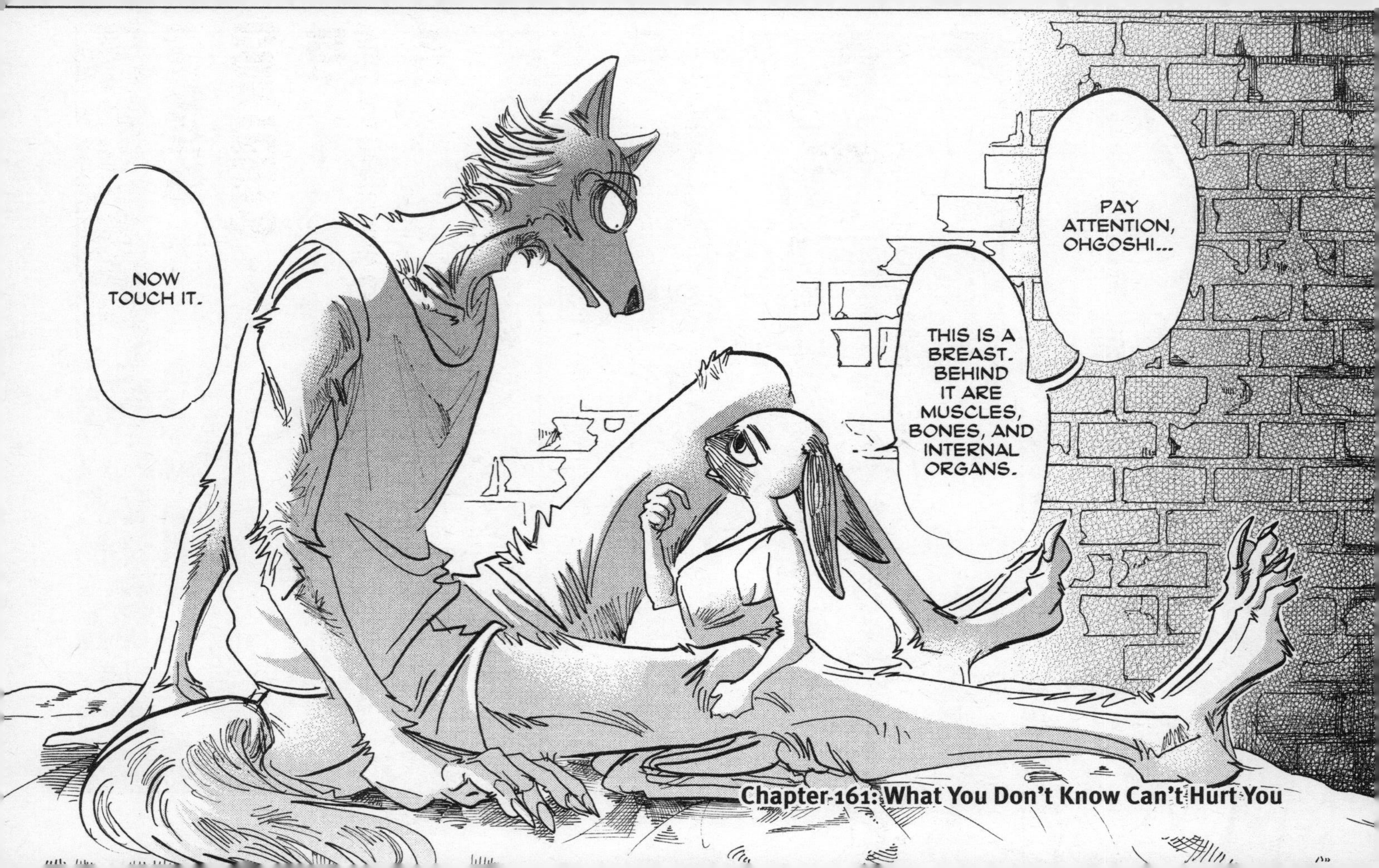
PAY ATTENTION, OHGOSHI...
THIS IS A BREAST. BEHIND IT ARE MUSCLES, BONES, AND INTERNAL ORGANS.
NOW TOUCH IT.

Chapter 161: What You Don't Know Can't Hurt You

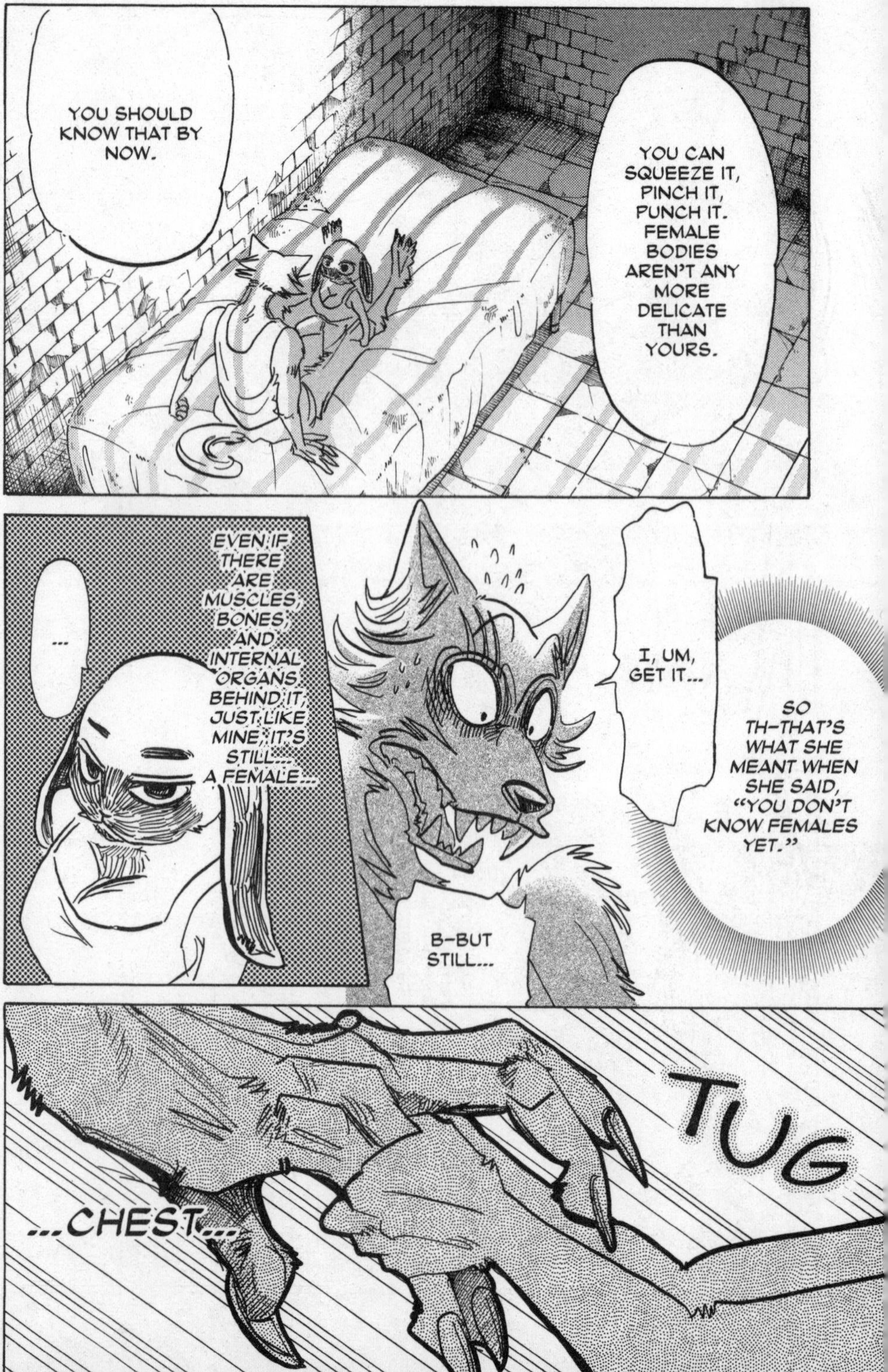
YOU CAN SQUEEZE IT, PINCH IT, PUNCH IT. FEMALE BODIES AREN'T ANY MORE DELICATE THAN YOURS.
YOU SHOULD KNOW THAT BY NOW.
SO TH-THAT'S WHAT SHE MEANT WHEN SHE SAID, "YOU DON'T KNOW FEMALES YET."
I, UM, GET IT...
B-BUT STILL...
EVEN IF THERE ARE MUSCLES, BONES, AND INTERNAL ORGANS BEHIND IT, JUST LIKE MINE, IT'S STILL... A FEMALE...
...
TUG
...CHEST...

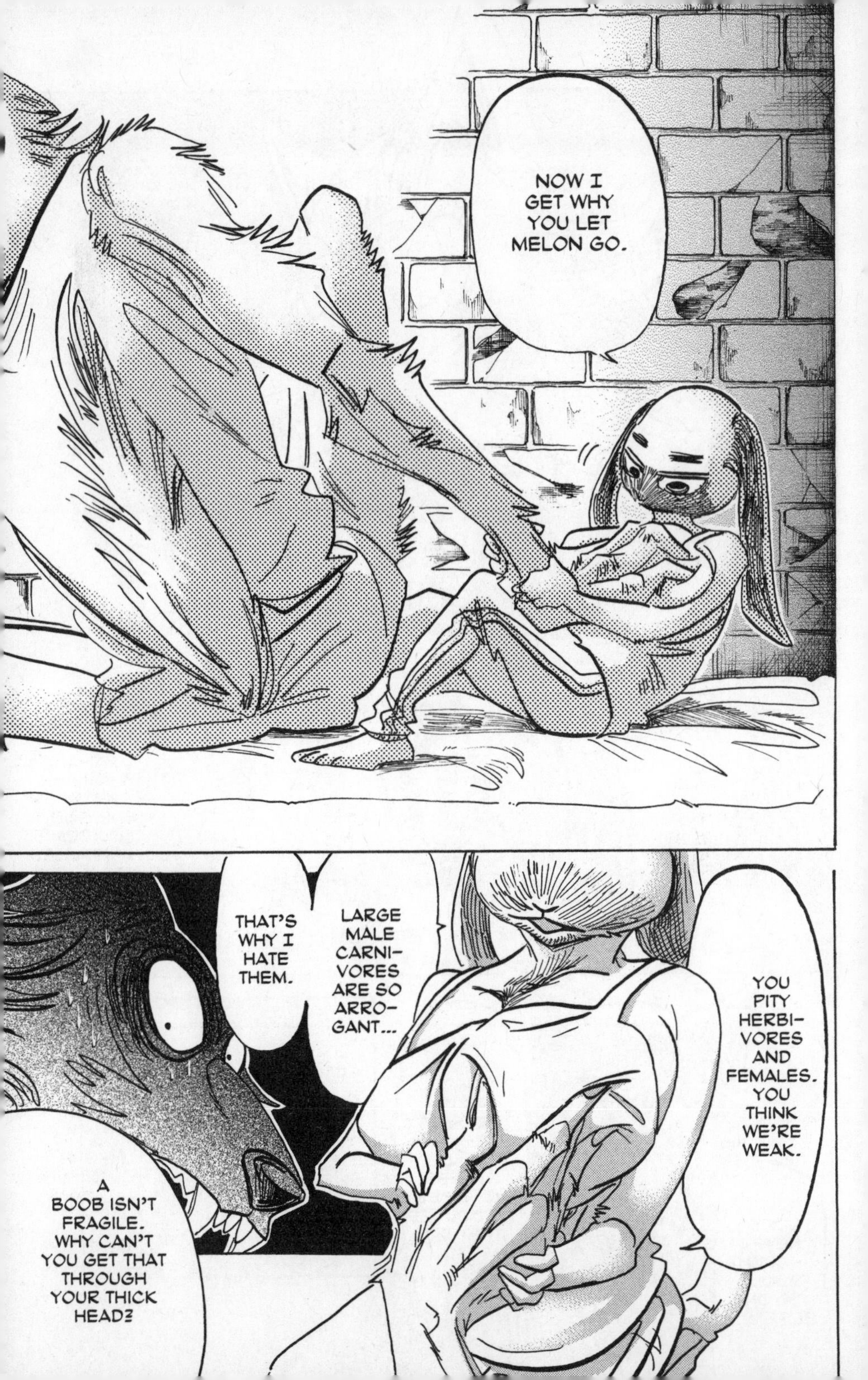
NOW I GET WHY YOU LET MELON GO.
YOU PITY HERBIVORES AND FEMALES. YOU THINK WE'RE WEAK.
LARGE MALE CARNIVORES ARE SO ARROGANT...
THAT'S WHY I HATE THEM.
A BOOB ISN'T FRAGILE. WHY CAN'T YOU GET THAT THROUGH YOUR THICK HEAD?

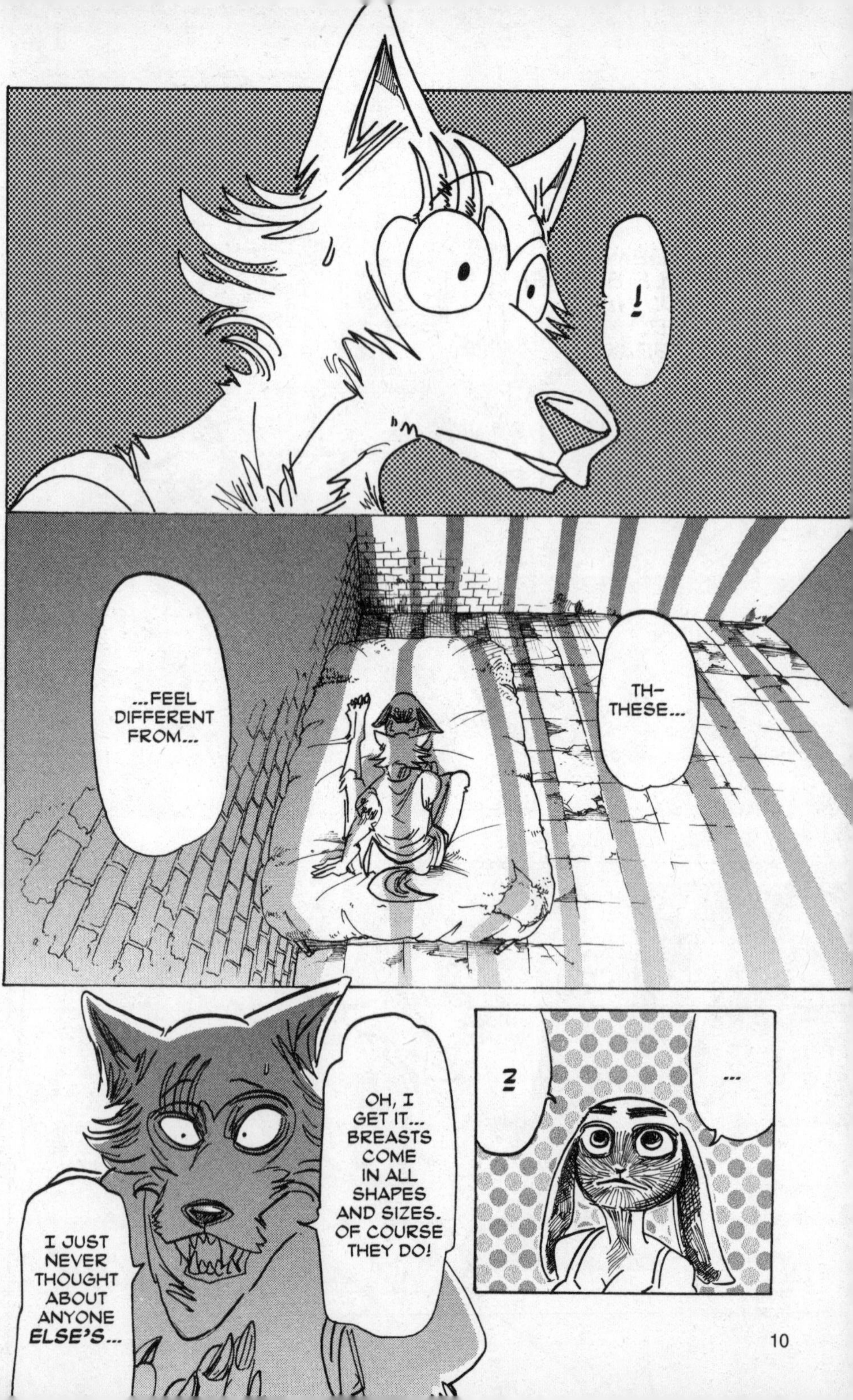
!
TH-THESE...
...FEEL DIFFERENT FROM...
...
?
OH, I GET IT... BREASTS COME IN ALL SHAPES AND SIZES. OF COURSE THEY DO!
I JUST NEVER THOUGHT ABOUT ANYONE *ELSE'S*...

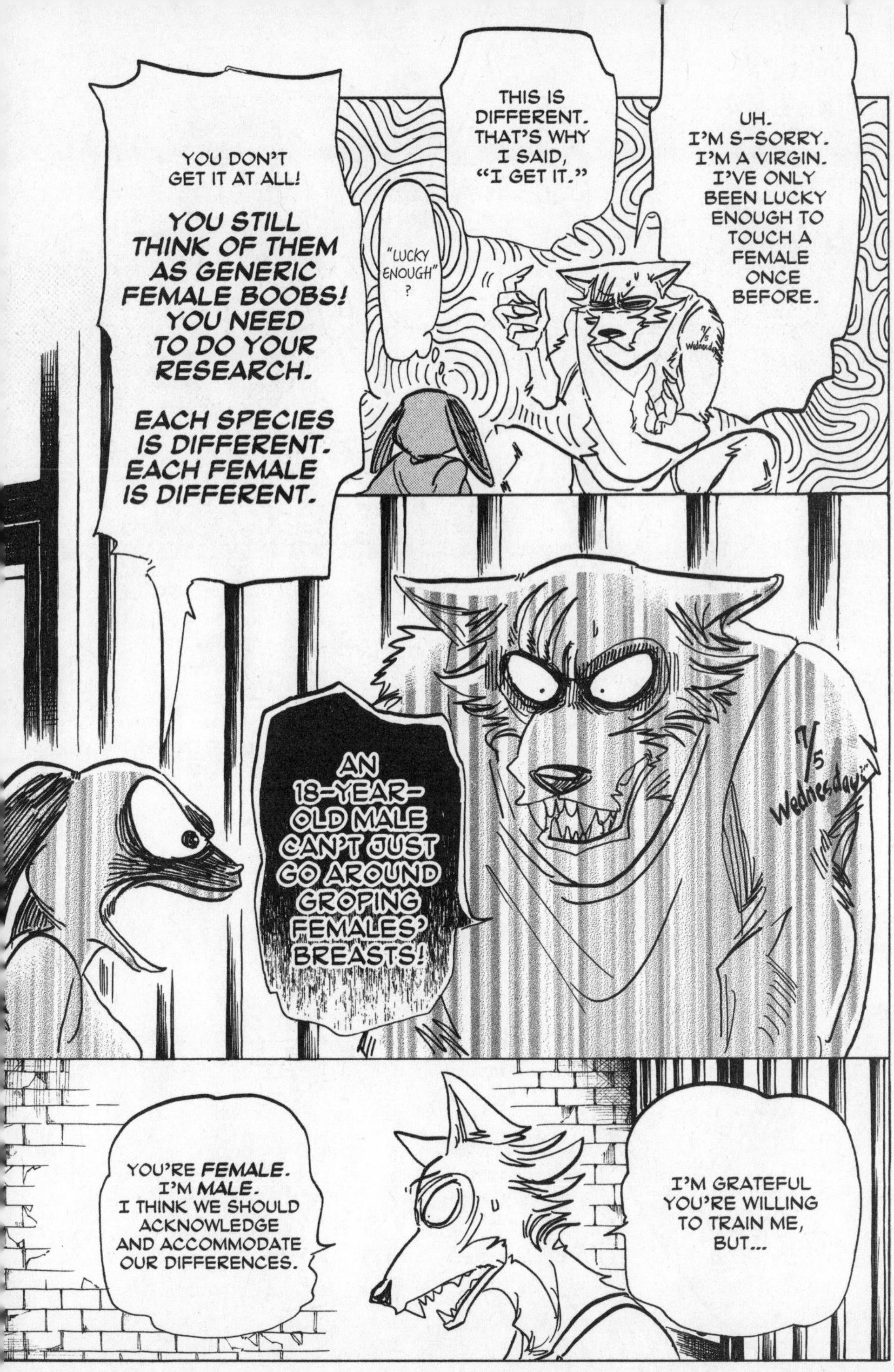
UH. I'M S-SORRY. I'M A VIRGIN. I'VE ONLY BEEN LUCKY ENOUGH TO TOUCH A FEMALE ONCE BEFORE.
THIS IS DIFFERENT. THAT'S WHY I SAID, "I GET IT."
"LUCKY ENOUGH"?
YOU DON'T GET IT AT ALL!
YOU STILL THINK OF THEM AS GENERIC FEMALE BOOBS! YOU NEED TO DO YOUR RESEARCH.
EACH SPECIES IS DIFFERENT. EACH FEMALE IS DIFFERENT.
7/5 Wednesday
AN 18-YEAR-OLD MALE CAN'T JUST GO AROUND GROPING FEMALES' BREASTS!
I'M GRATEFUL YOU'RE WILLING TO TRAIN ME, BUT...
YOU'RE FEMALE. I'M MALE. I THINK WE SHOULD ACKNOWLEDGE AND ACCOMMODATE OUR DIFFERENCES.

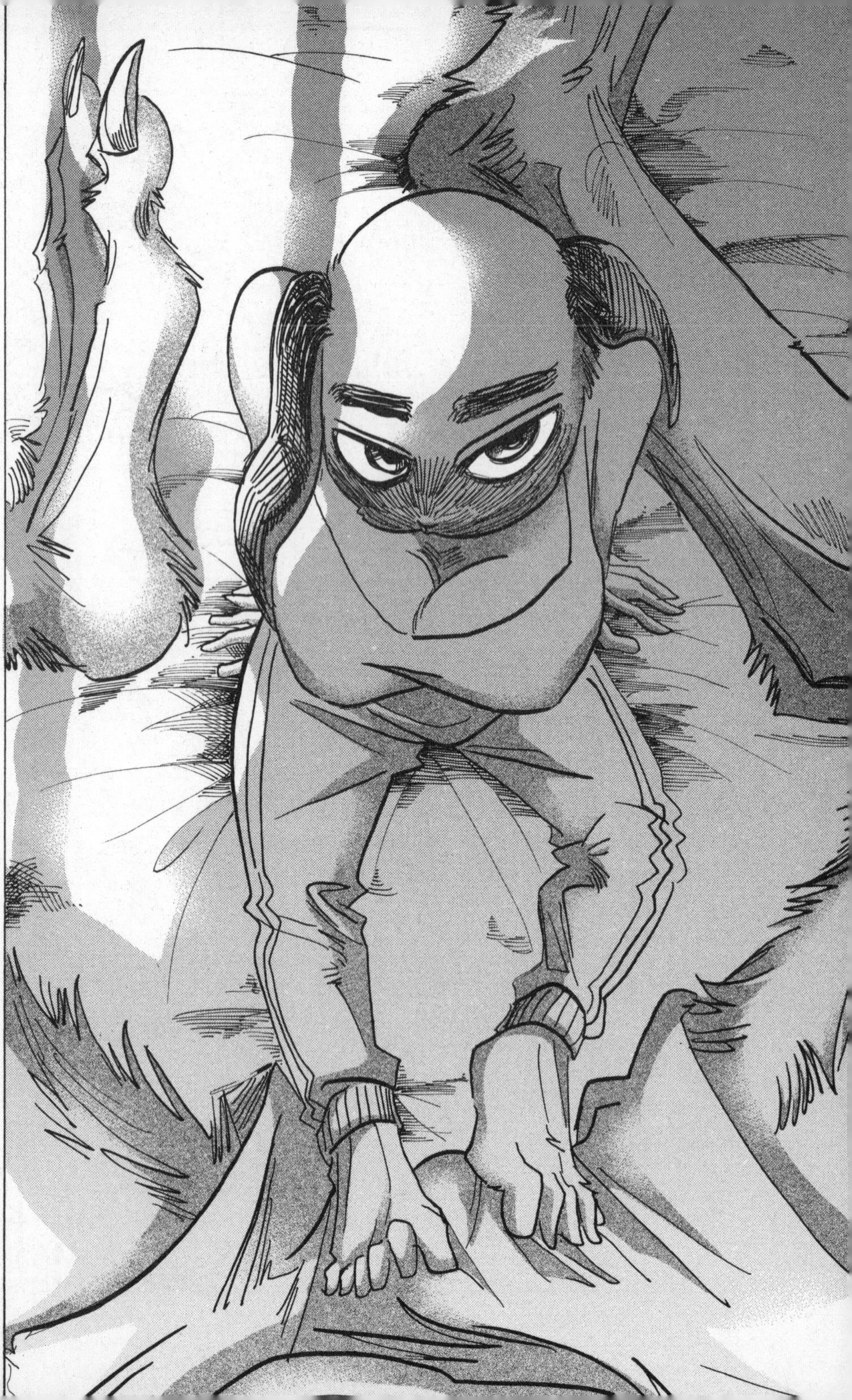

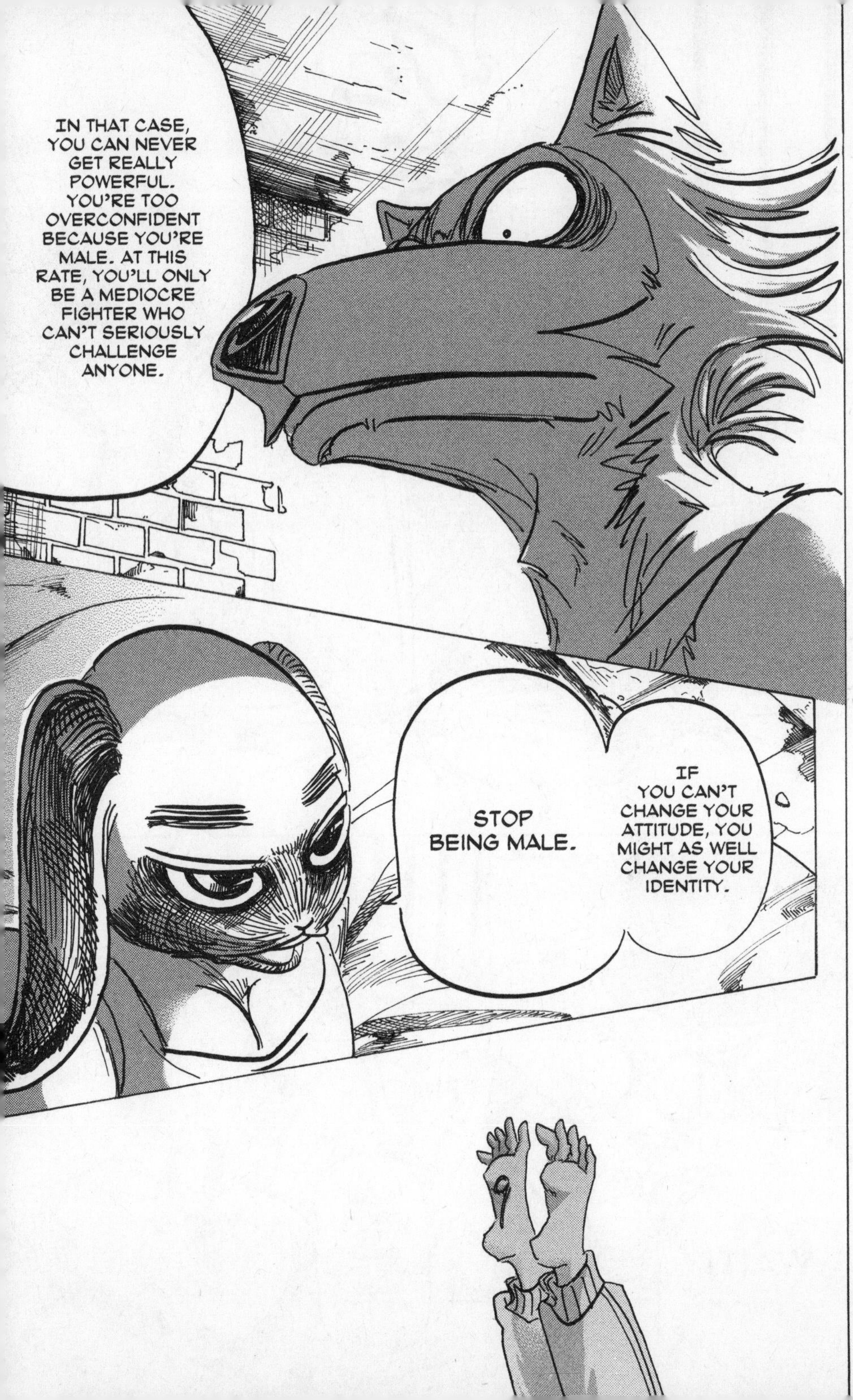
IN THAT CASE, YOU CAN NEVER GET REALLY POWERFUL. YOU'RE TOO OVERCONFIDENT BECAUSE YOU'RE MALE. AT THIS RATE, YOU'LL ONLY BE A MEDIOCRE FIGHTER WHO CAN'T SERIOUSLY CHALLENGE ANYONE.
IF YOU CAN'T CHANGE YOUR ATTITUDE, YOU MIGHT AS WELL CHANGE YOUR IDENTITY.
STOP BEING MALE.

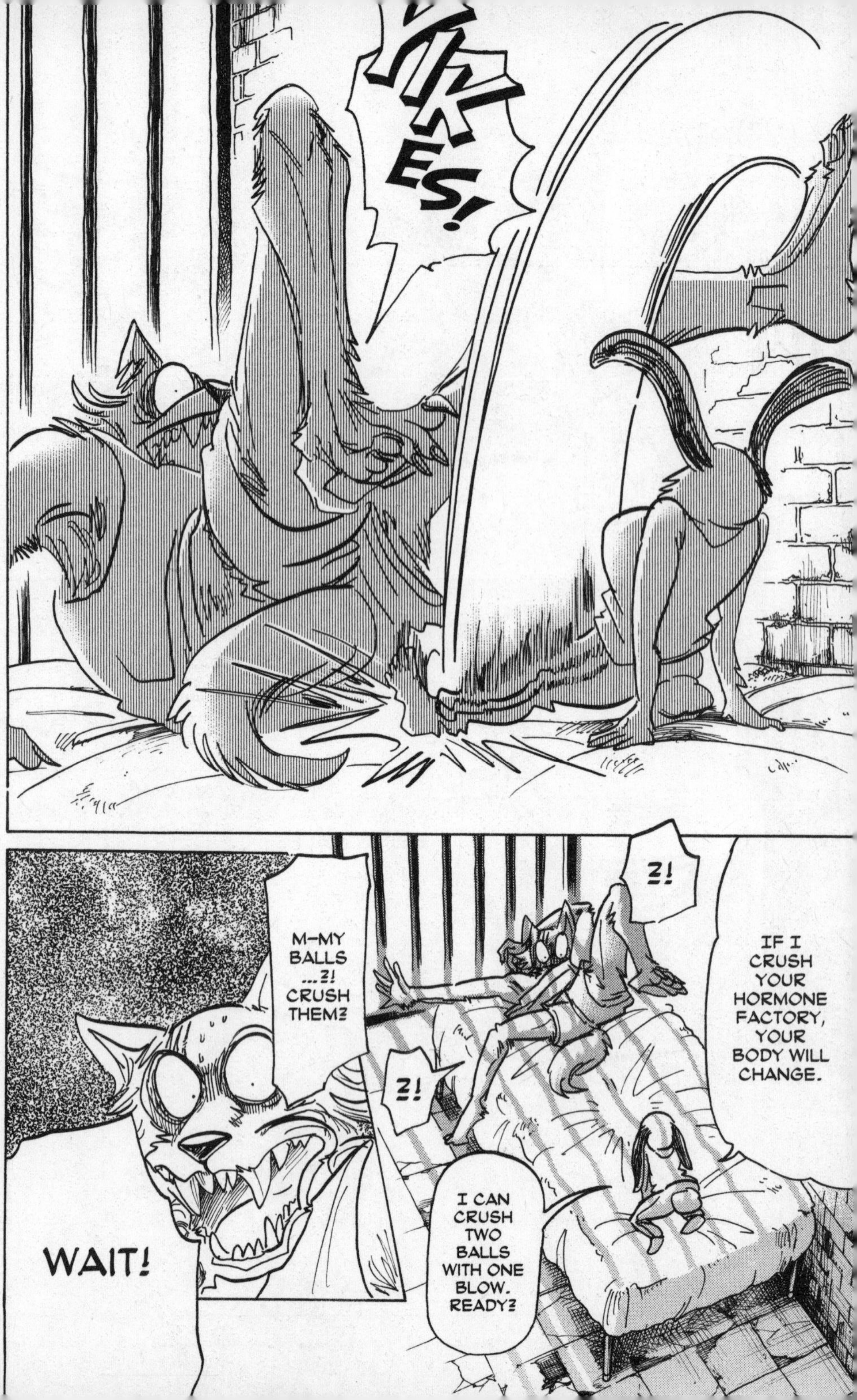
YIKES!
?!
IF I CRUSH YOUR HORMONE FACTORY, YOUR BODY WILL CHANGE.
M-MY BALLS ...?! CRUSH THEM?
?!
I CAN CRUSH TWO BALLS WITH ONE BLOW. READY?
WAIT!

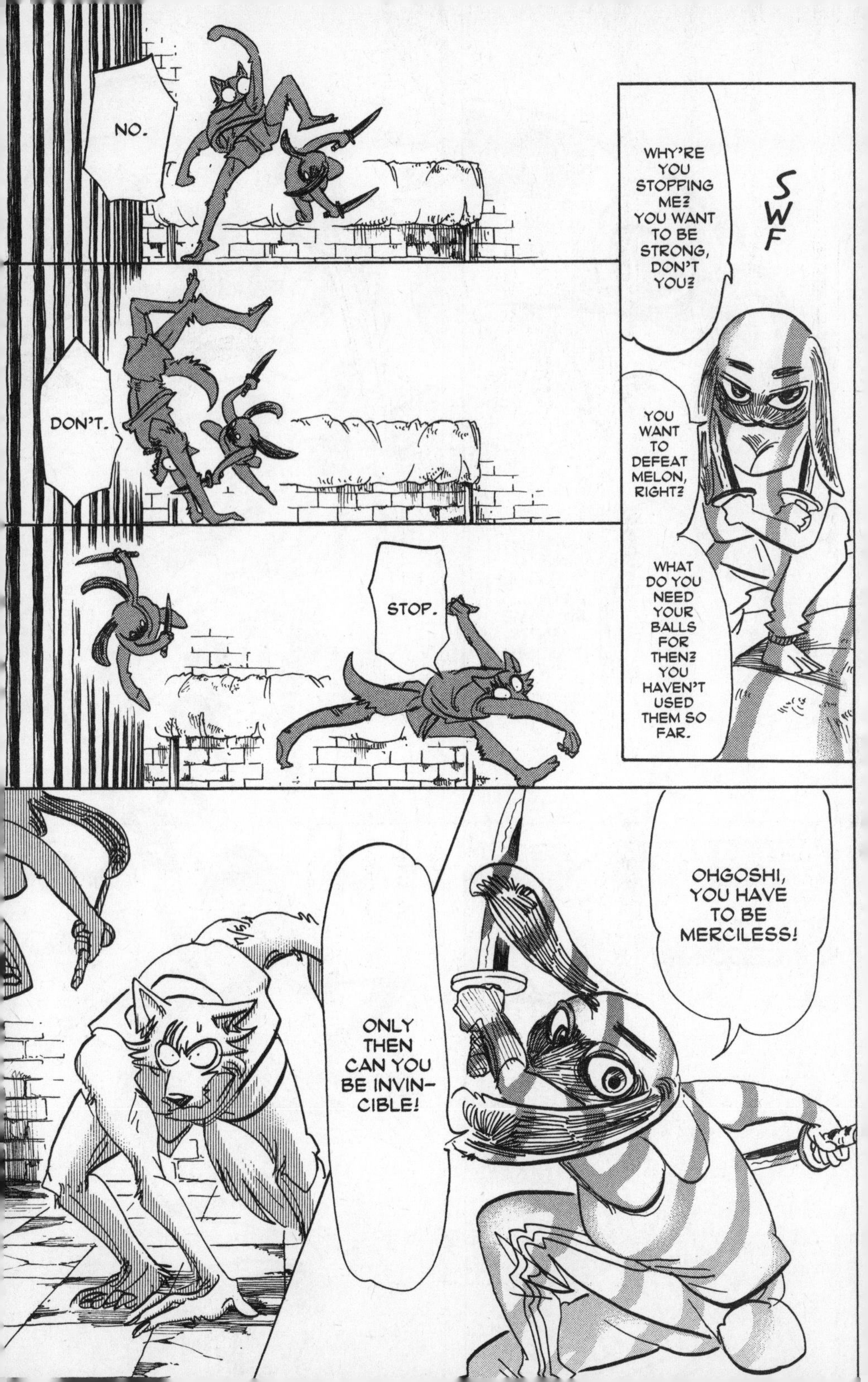
WHY'RE YOU STOPPING ME? YOU WANT TO BE STRONG, DON'T YOU?
SWF
YOU WANT TO DEFEAT MELON, RIGHT?
WHAT DO YOU NEED YOUR BALLS FOR THEN? YOU HAVEN'T USED THEM SO FAR.
NO.
DON'T.
STOP.
OHGOSHI, YOU HAVE TO BE MERCILESS!
ONLY THEN CAN YOU BE INVINCIBLE!

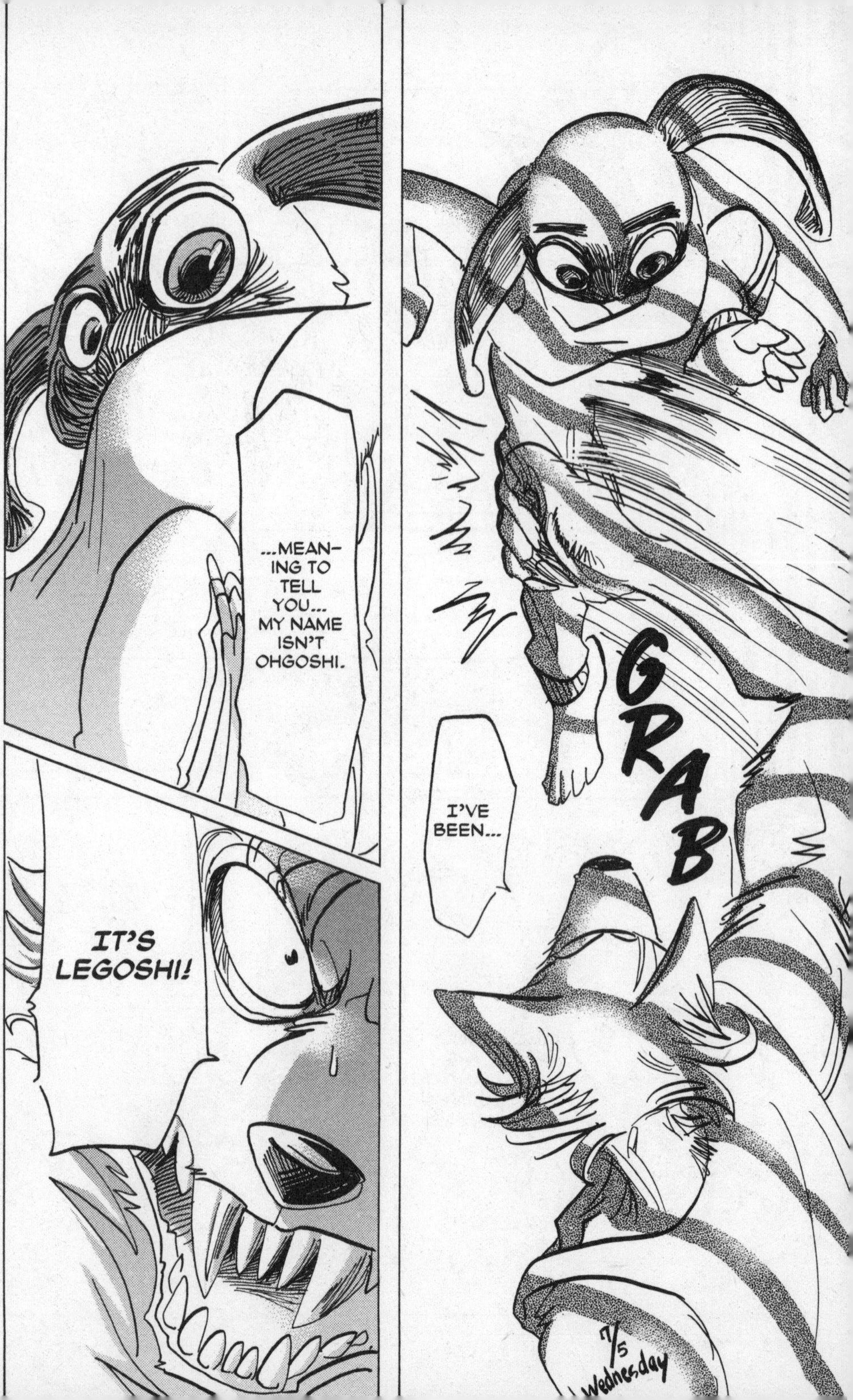
I'VE BEEN...
GRAB
7/5 Wednesday
...MEAN-ING TO TELL YOU... MY NAME ISN'T OHGOSHI.
IT'S LEGOSHI!

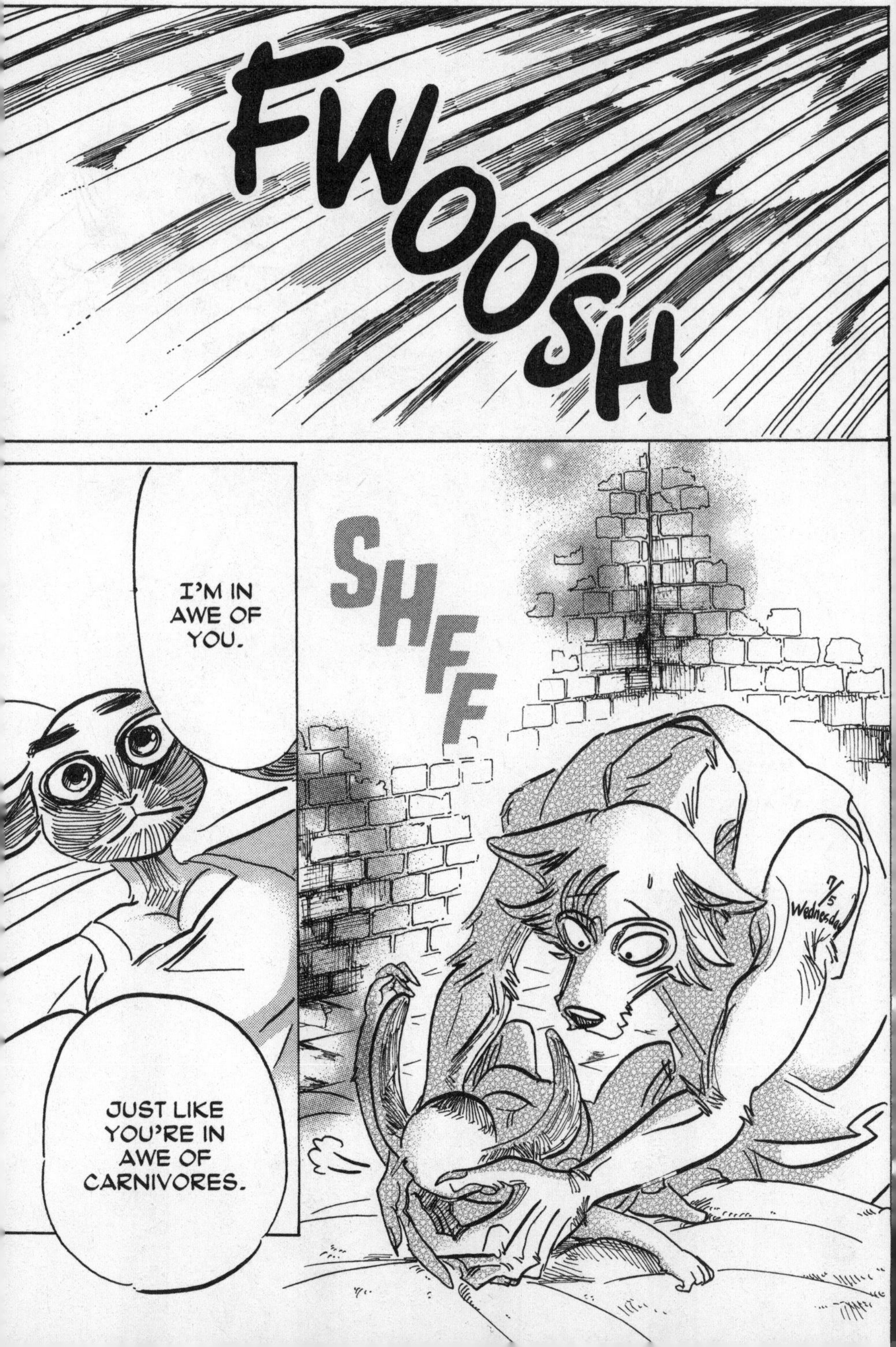
FWOOSH
SHFF
7/5 Wednesday
I'M IN AWE OF YOU.
JUST LIKE YOU'RE IN AWE OF CARNIVORES.

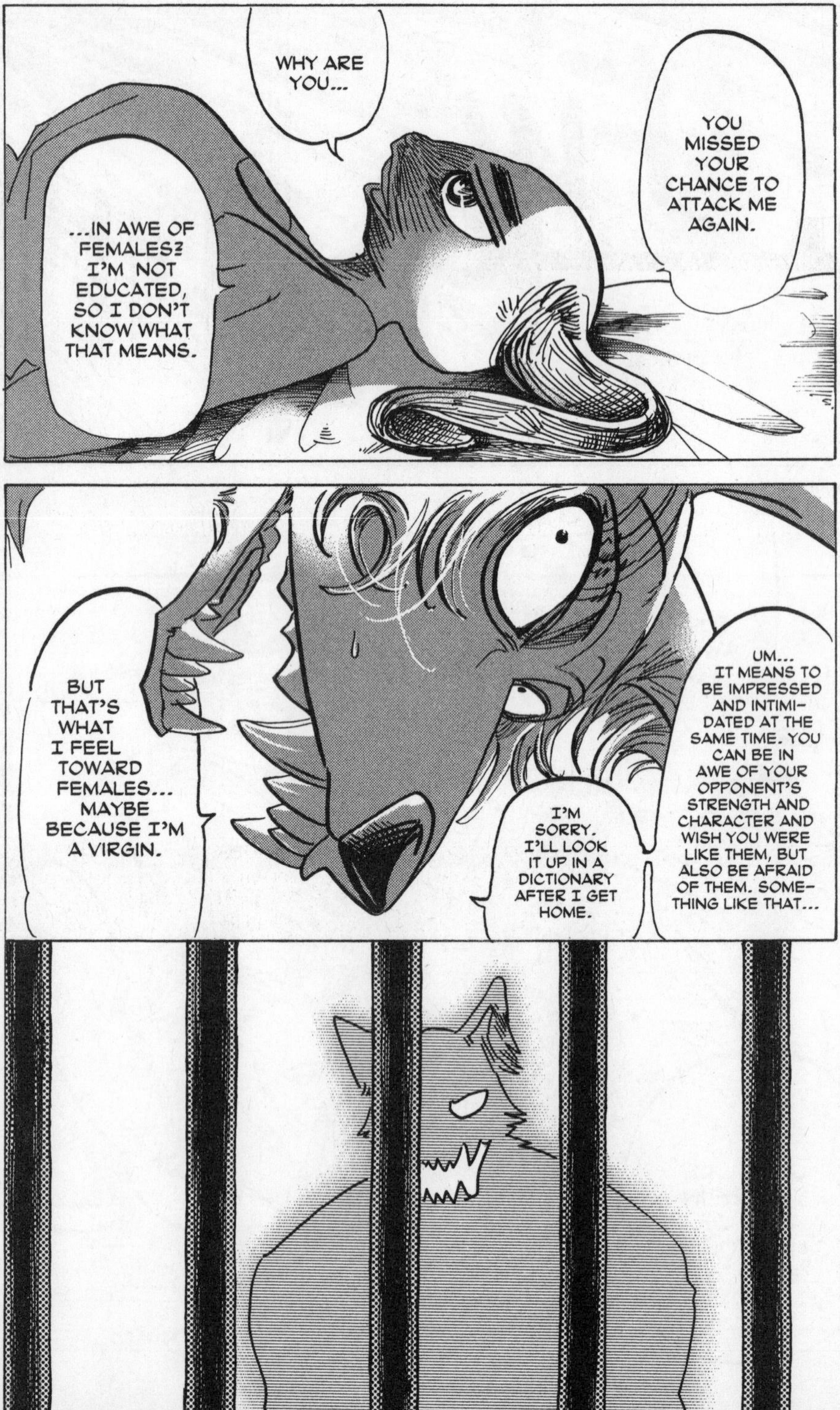
YOU MISSED YOUR CHANCE TO ATTACK ME AGAIN.
WHY ARE YOU...
...IN AWE OF FEMALES? I'M NOT EDUCATED, SO I DON'T KNOW WHAT THAT MEANS.
UM... IT MEANS TO BE IMPRESSED AND INTIMI-DATED AT THE SAME TIME. YOU CAN BE IN AWE OF YOUR OPPONENT'S STRENGTH AND CHARACTER AND WISH YOU WERE LIKE THEM, BUT ALSO BE AFRAID OF THEM. SOME-THING LIKE THAT...
I'M SORRY. I'LL LOOK IT UP IN A DICTIONARY AFTER I GET HOME.
BUT THAT'S WHAT I FEEL TOWARD FEMALES... MAYBE BECAUSE I'M A VIRGIN.

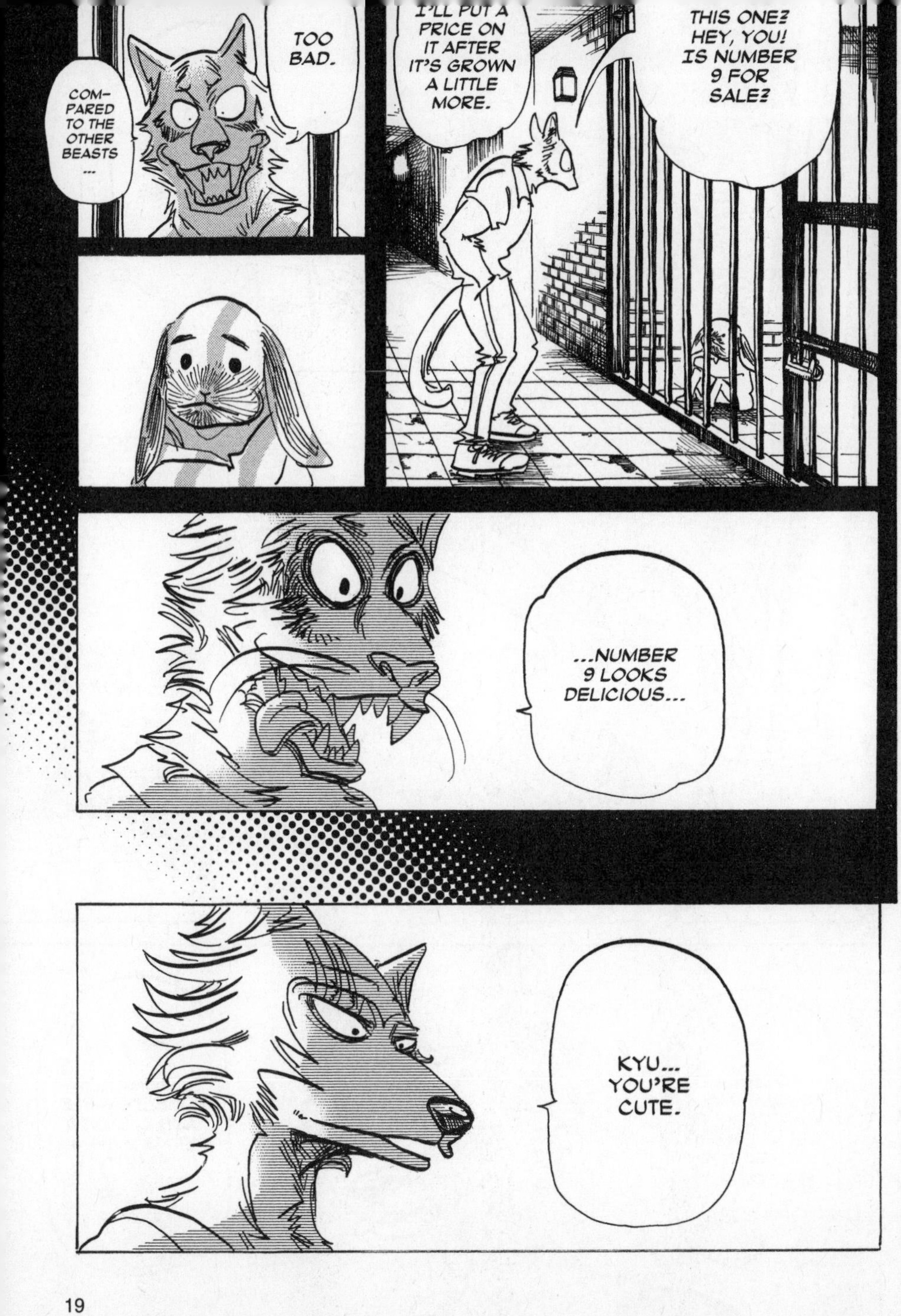
THIS ONE? HEY, YOU! IS NUMBER 9 FOR SALE?
I'LL PUT A PRICE ON IT AFTER IT'S GROWN A LITTLE MORE.
TOO BAD.
COMPARED TO THE OTHER BEASTS ...
...NUMBER 9 LOOKS DELICIOUS...
KYU... YOU'RE CUTE.

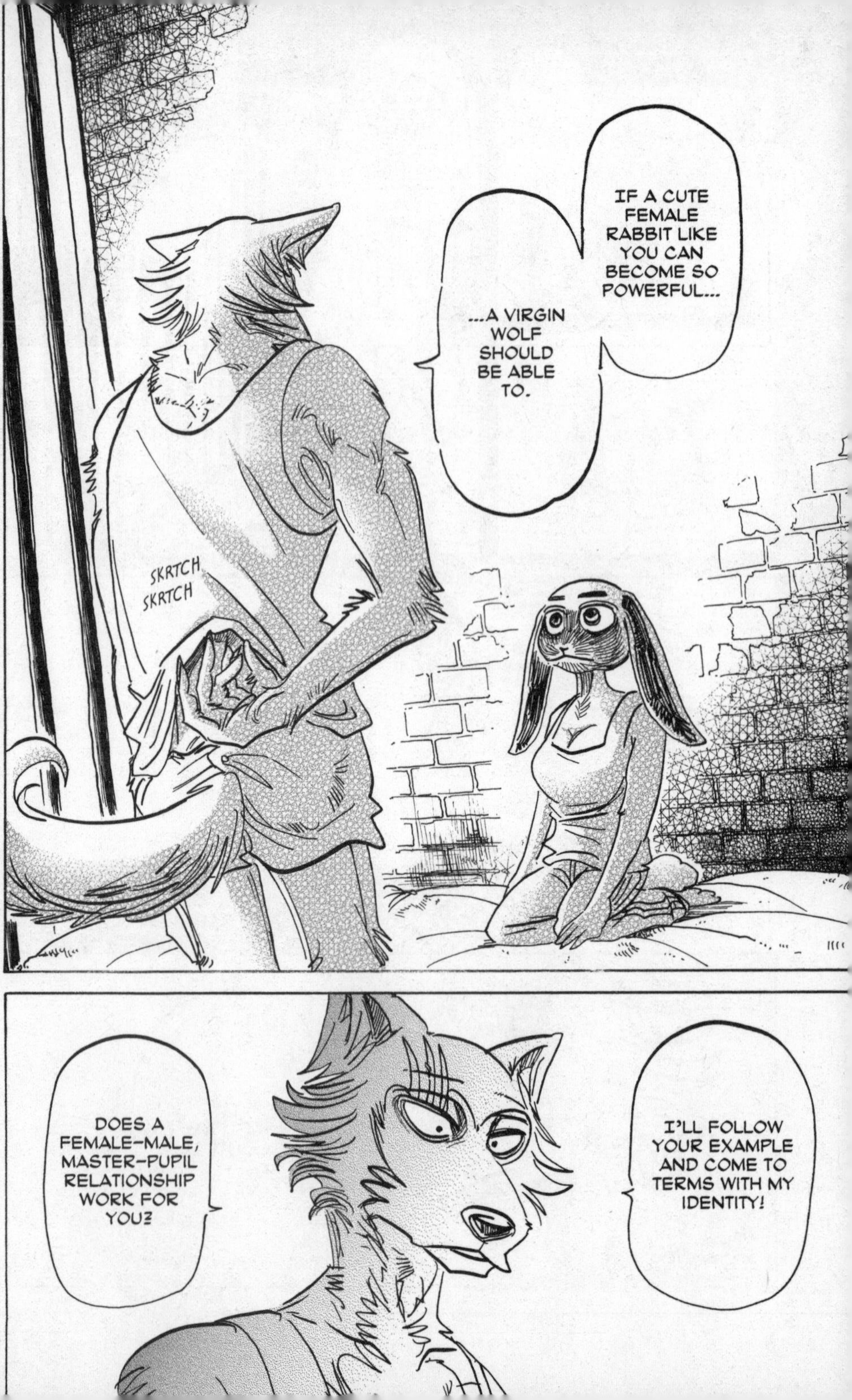
IF A CUTE FEMALE RABBIT LIKE YOU CAN BECOME SO POWERFUL...
...A VIRGIN WOLF SHOULD BE ABLE TO.
SKRTCH SKRTCH
I'LL FOLLOW YOUR EXAMPLE AND COME TO TERMS WITH MY IDENTITY!
DOES A FEMALE-MALE, MASTER-PUPIL RELATIONSHIP WORK FOR YOU?

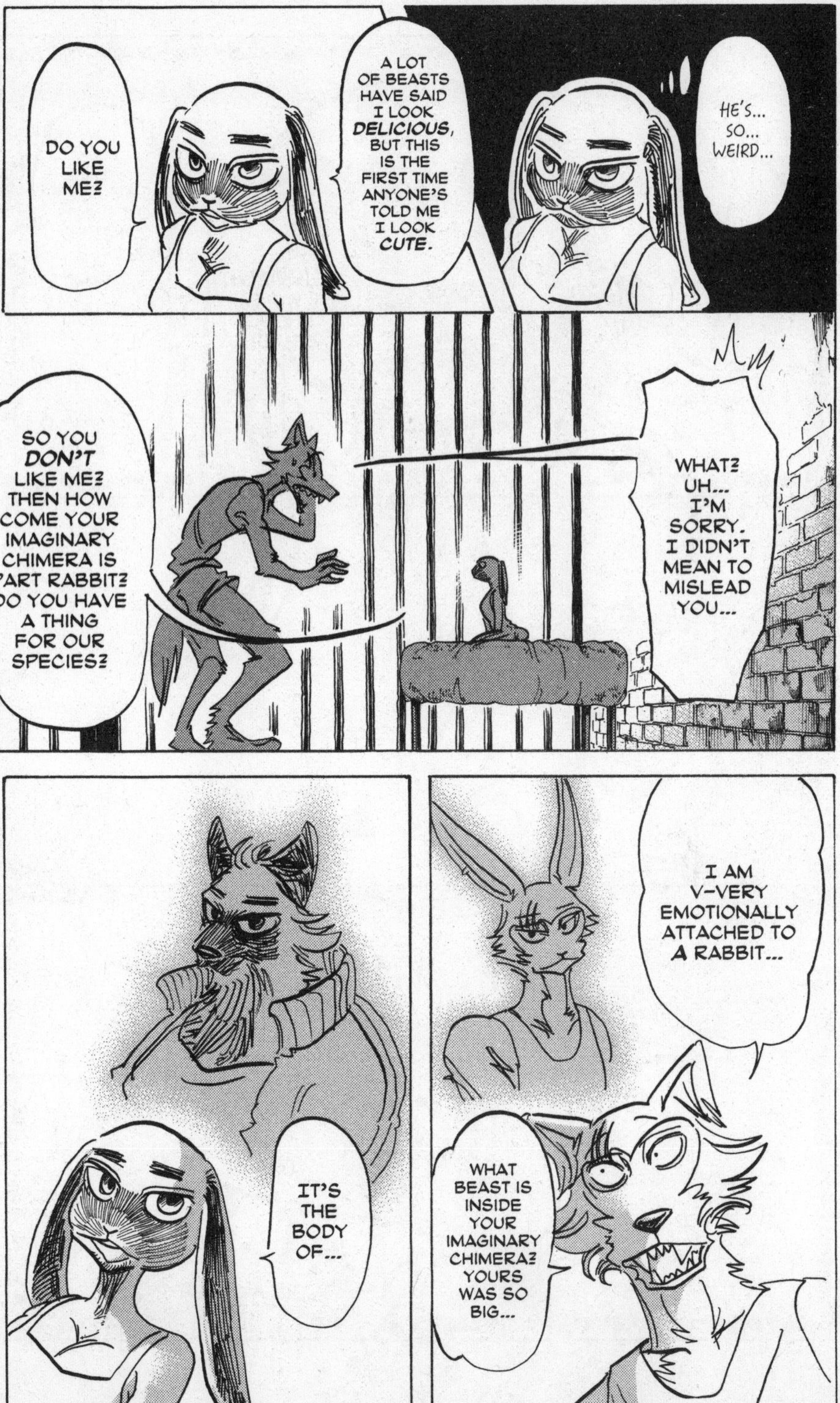
HE'S... SO... WEIRD...
A LOT OF BEASTS HAVE SAID I LOOK **DELICIOUS**, BUT THIS IS THE FIRST TIME ANYONE'S TOLD ME I LOOK **CUTE**.
DO YOU LIKE ME?
WHAT? UH... I'M SORRY. I DIDN'T MEAN TO MISLEAD YOU...
SO YOU **DON'T** LIKE ME? THEN HOW COME YOUR IMAGINARY CHIMERA IS PART RABBIT? DO YOU HAVE A THING FOR OUR SPECIES?
I AM V-VERY EMOTIONALLY ATTACHED TO A RABBIT...
WHAT BEAST IS INSIDE YOUR IMAGINARY CHIMERA? YOURS WAS SO BIG...
IT'S THE BODY OF...

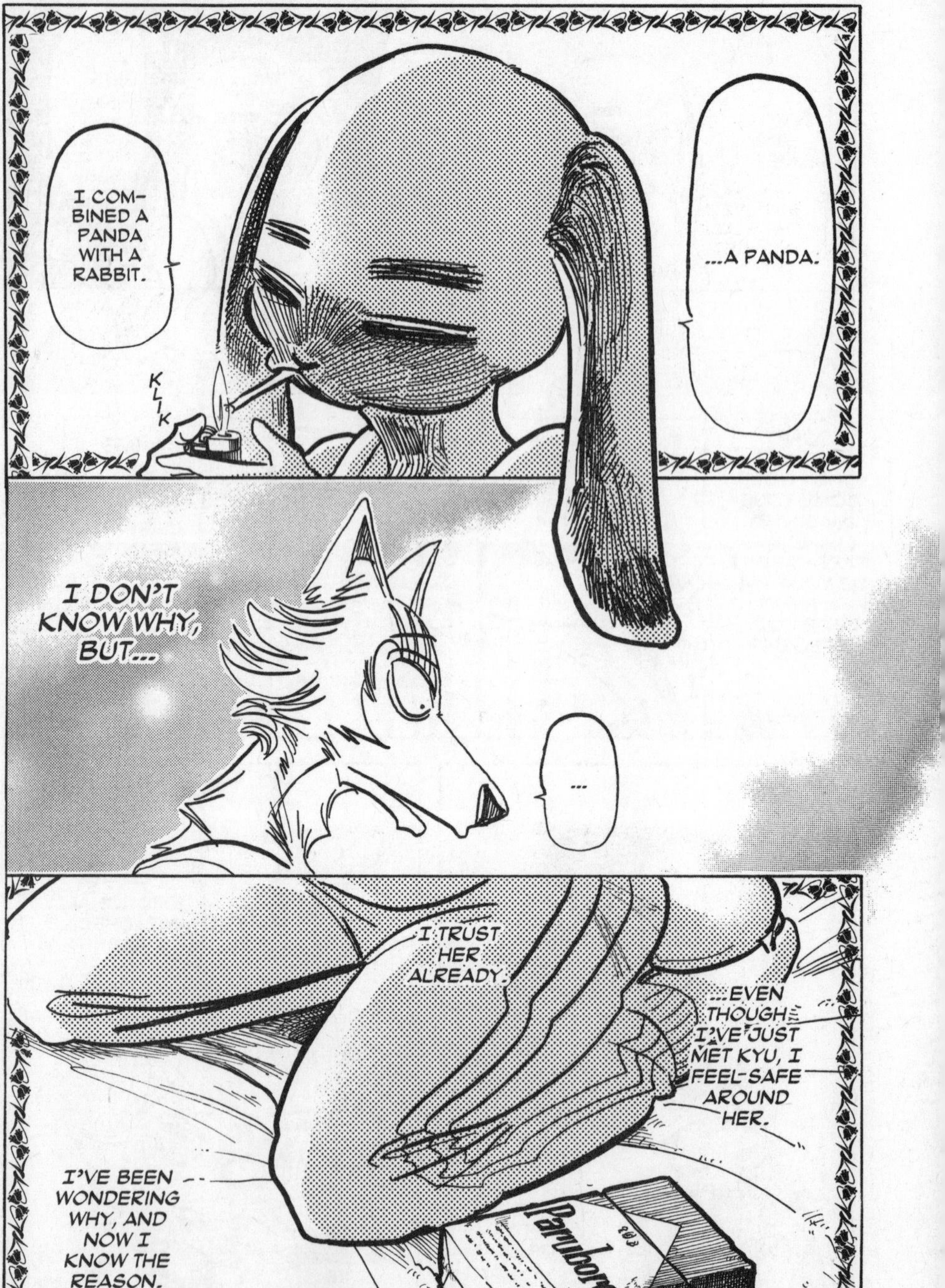
...A PANDA.
I COMBINED A PANDA WITH A RABBIT.
KLIK
I DON'T KNOW WHY, BUT...
...
I TRUST HER ALREADY.
...EVEN THOUGH I'VE JUST MET KYU, I FEEL SAFE AROUND HER.
I'VE BEEN WONDERING WHY, AND NOW I KNOW THE REASON.
Paruboro

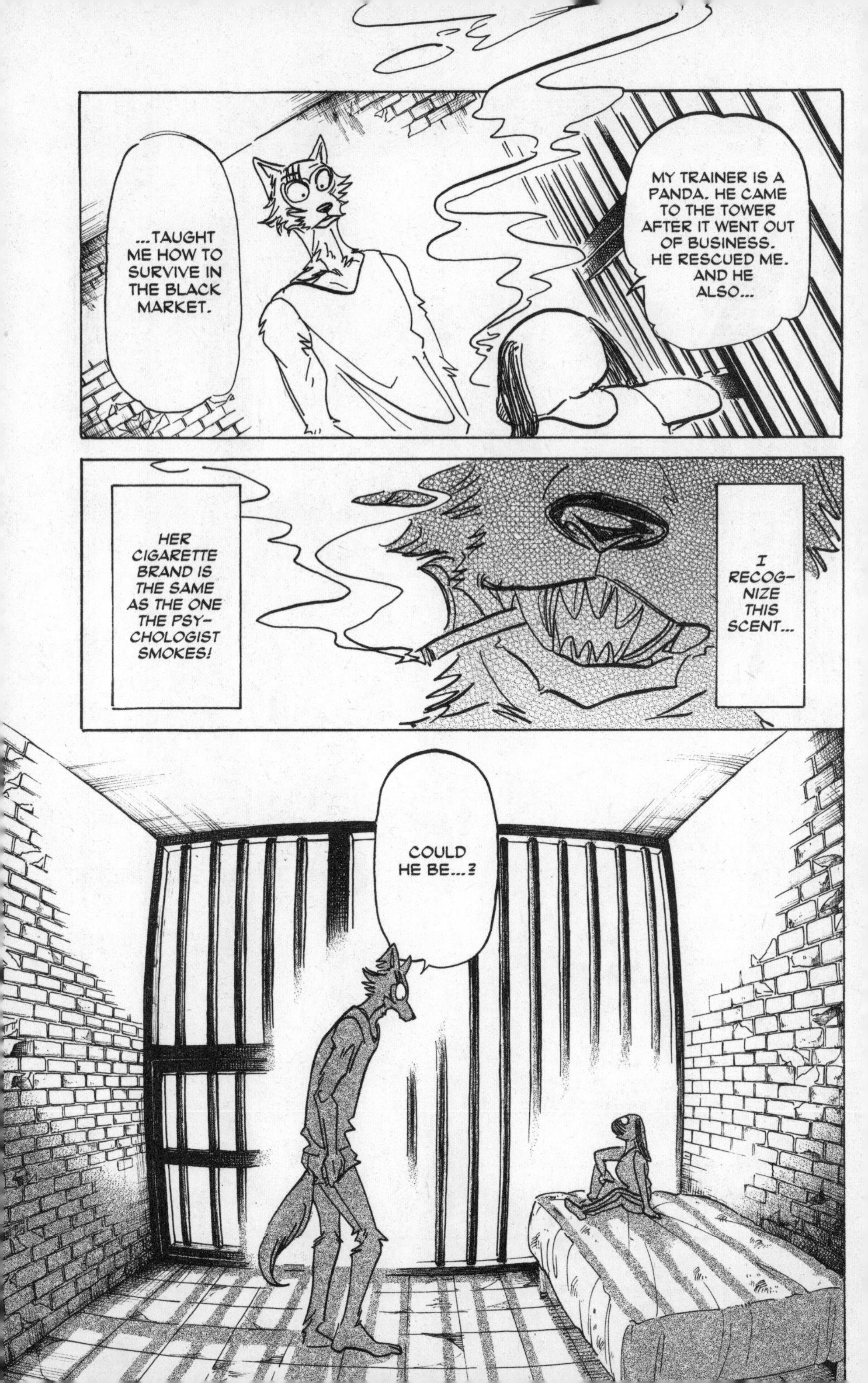
MY TRAINER IS A PANDA. HE CAME TO THE TOWER AFTER IT WENT OUT OF BUSINESS. HE RESCUED ME. AND HE ALSO...
...TAUGHT ME HOW TO SURVIVE IN THE BLACK MARKET.
I RECOG-NIZE THIS SCENT...
HER CIGARETTE BRAND IS THE SAME AS THE ONE THE PSY-CHOLOGIST SMOKES!
COULD HE BE...?

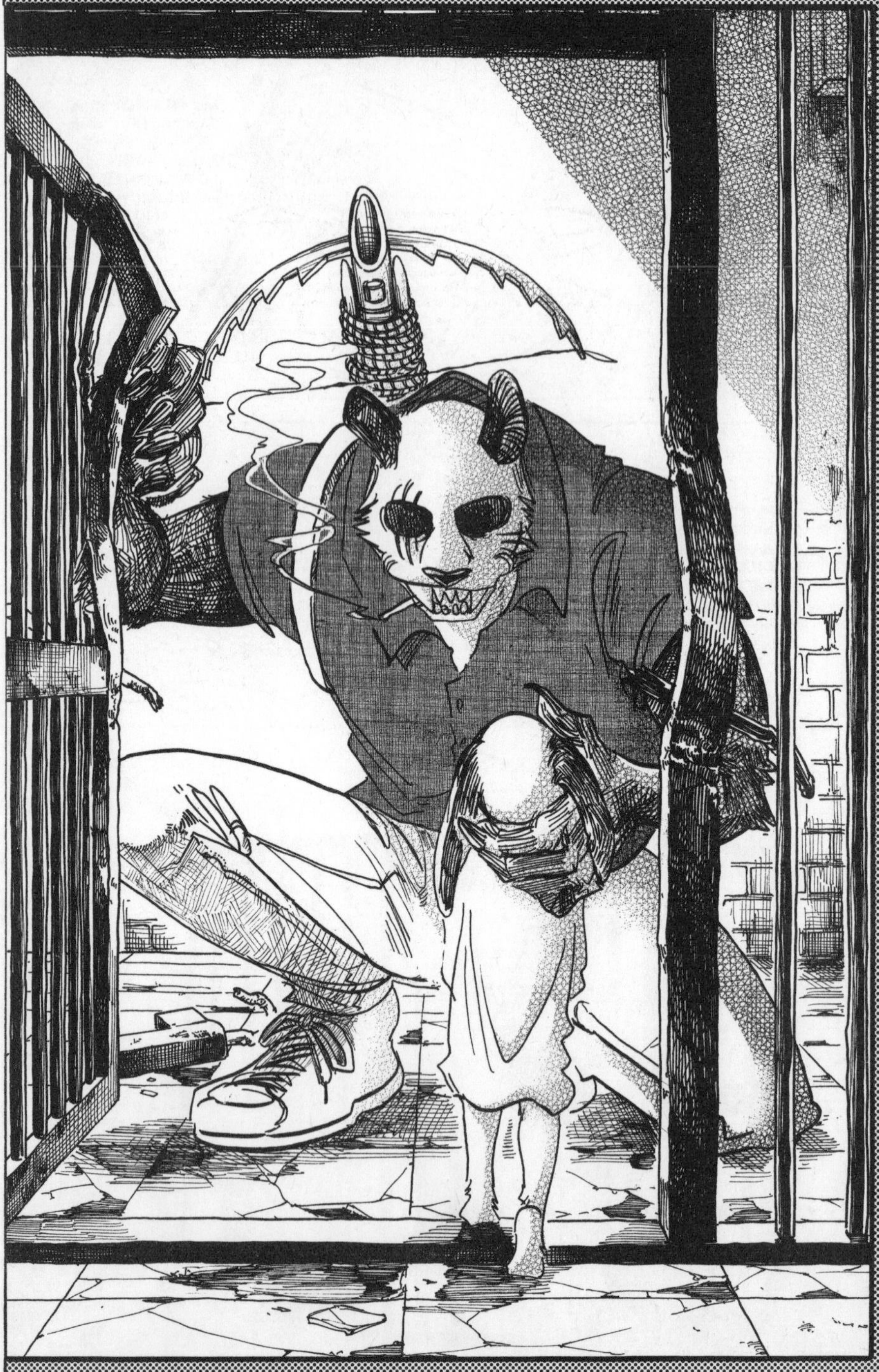

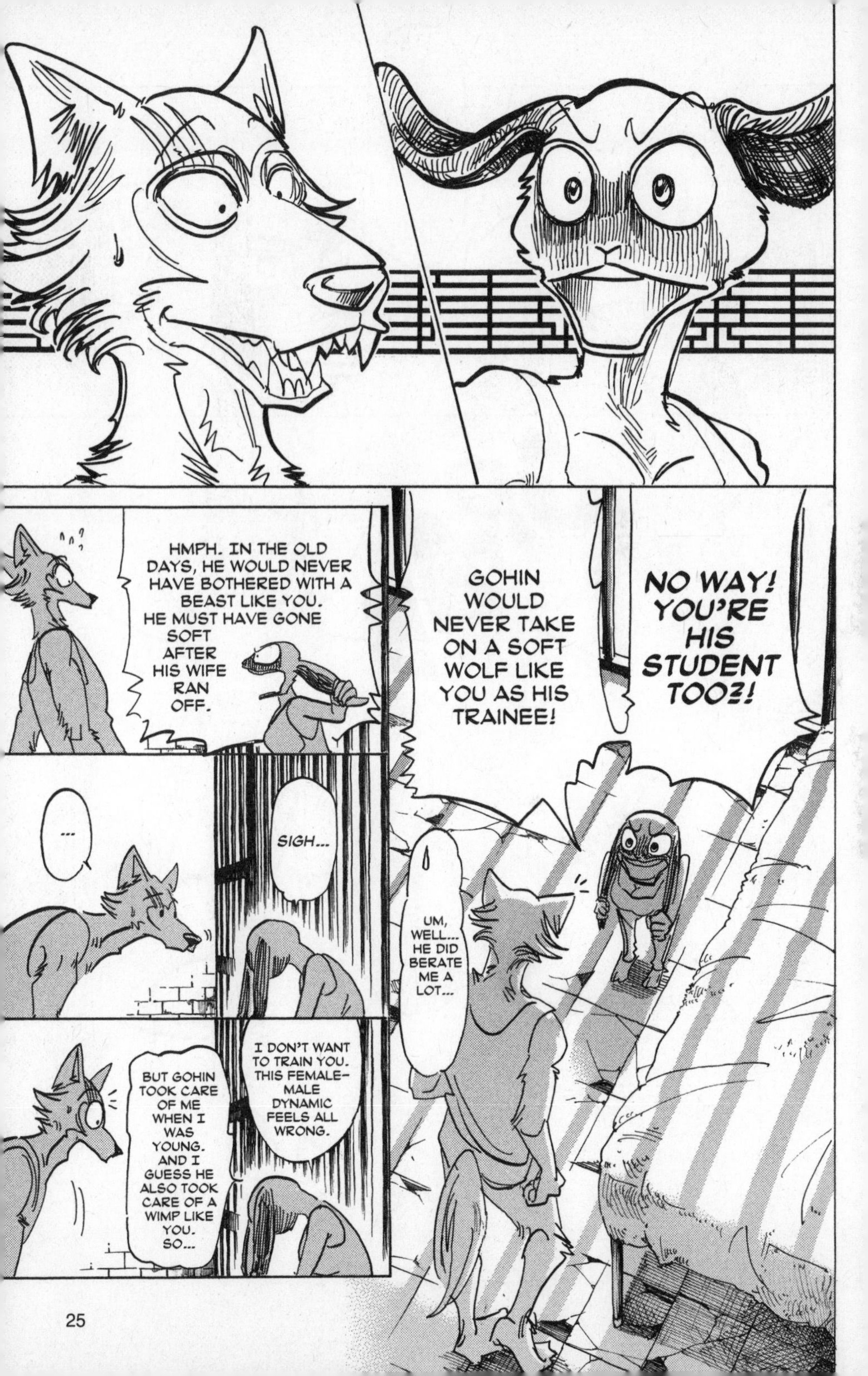

NO WAY! YOU'RE HIS STUDENT TOO?!
GOHIN WOULD NEVER TAKE ON A SOFT WOLF LIKE YOU AS HIS TRAINEE!
UM, WELL... HE DID BERATE ME A LOT...
HMPH. IN THE OLD DAYS, HE WOULD NEVER HAVE BOTHERED WITH A BEAST LIKE YOU. HE MUST HAVE GONE SOFT AFTER HIS WIFE RAN OFF.
SIGH...
...
I DON'T WANT TO TRAIN YOU. THIS FEMALE-MALE DYNAMIC FEELS ALL WRONG.
BUT GOHIN TOOK CARE OF ME WHEN I WAS YOUNG. AND I GUESS HE ALSO TOOK CARE OF A WIMP LIKE YOU. SO...

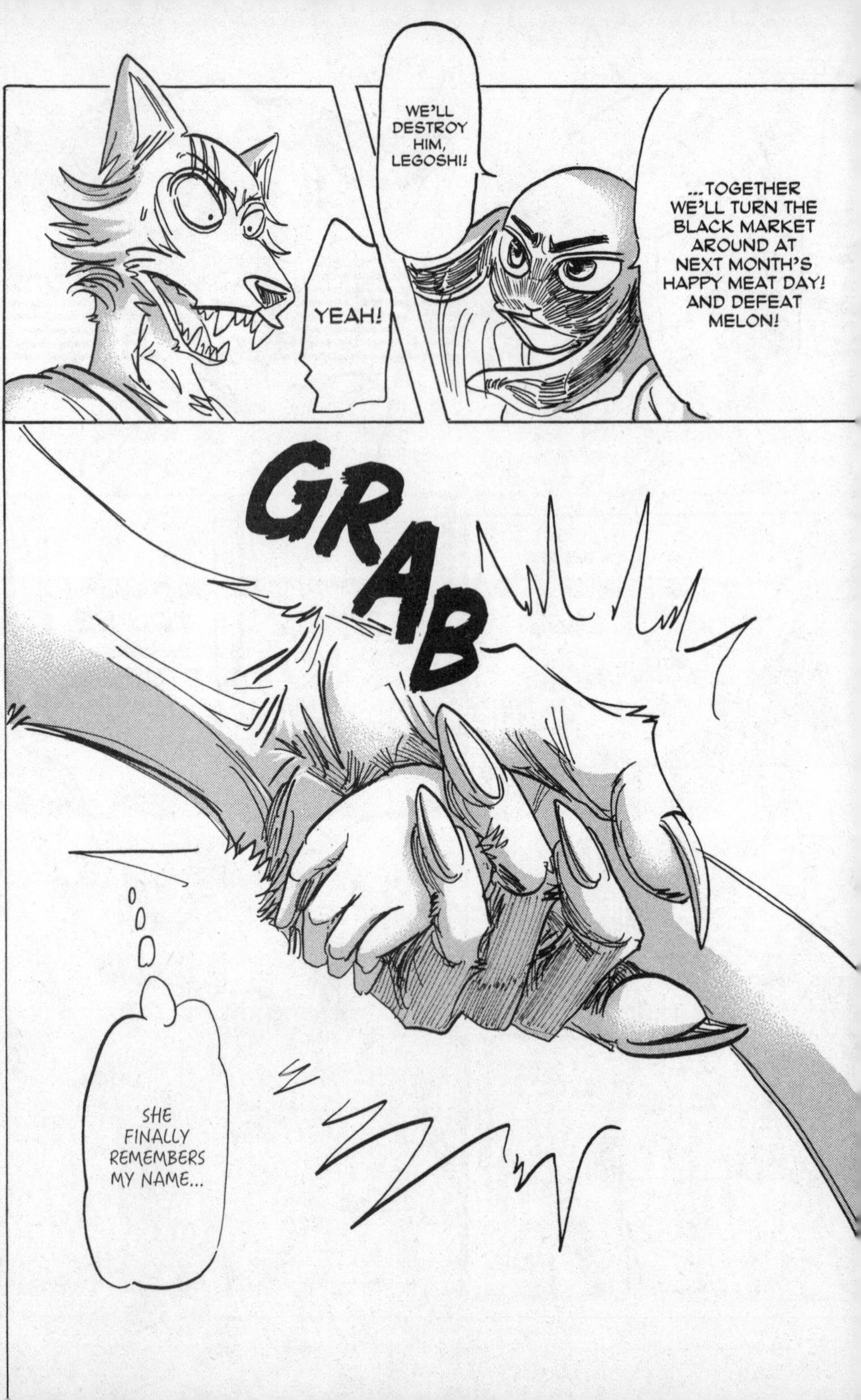
...TOGETHER WE'LL TURN THE BLACK MARKET AROUND AT NEXT MONTH'S HAPPY MEAT DAY! AND DEFEAT MELON!
WE'LL DESTROY HIM, LEGOSHI!
YEAH!
GRAB
SHE FINALLY REMEMBERS MY NAME...

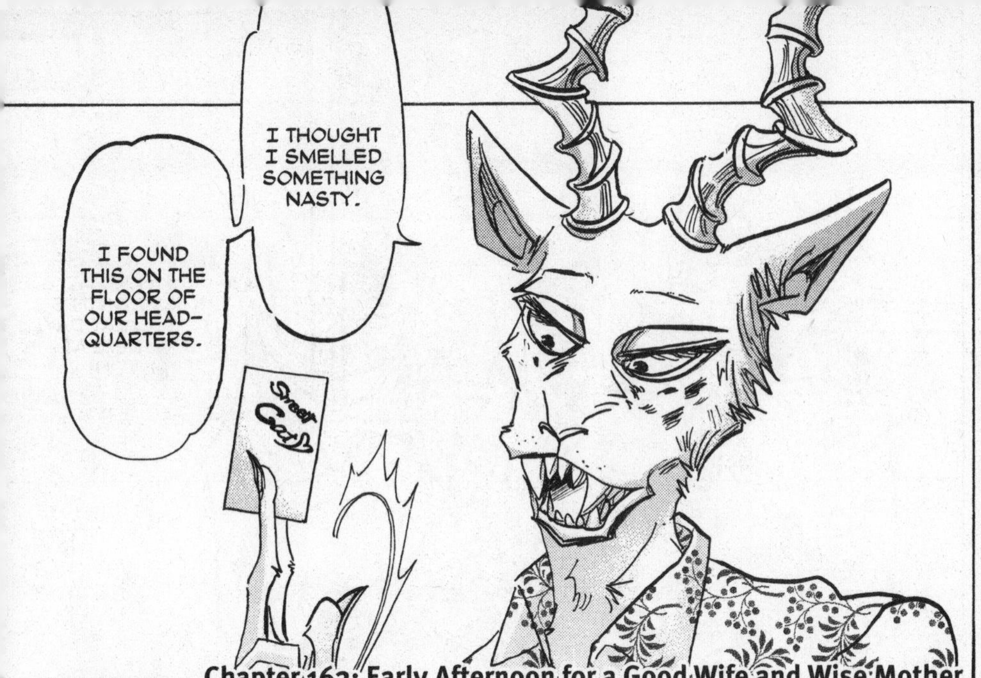
I THOUGHT I SMELLED SOMETHING NASTY.
I FOUND THIS ON THE FLOOR OF OUR HEAD-QUARTERS.

Chapter 162: Early Afternoon for a Good Wife and Wise Mother

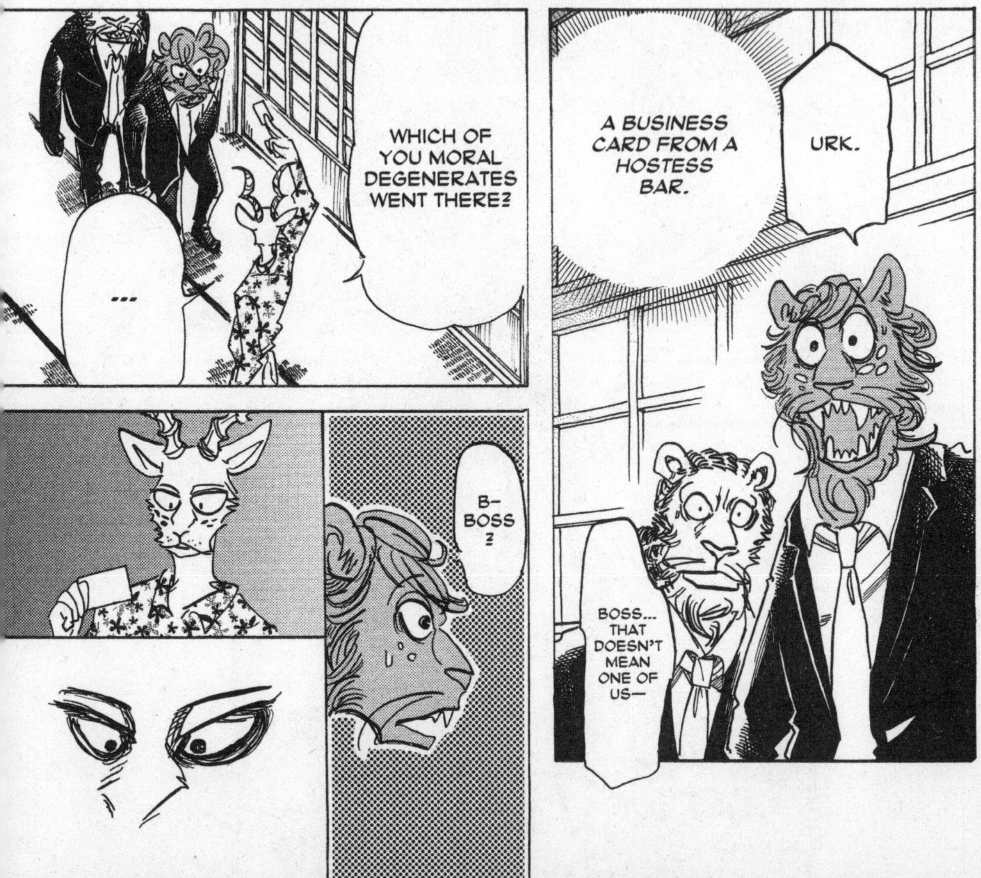
URK.
A BUSINESS CARD FROM A HOSTESS BAR.
BOSS... THAT DOESN'T MEAN ONE OF US—
WHICH OF YOU MORAL DEGENERATES WENT THERE?
...
B-BOSS?

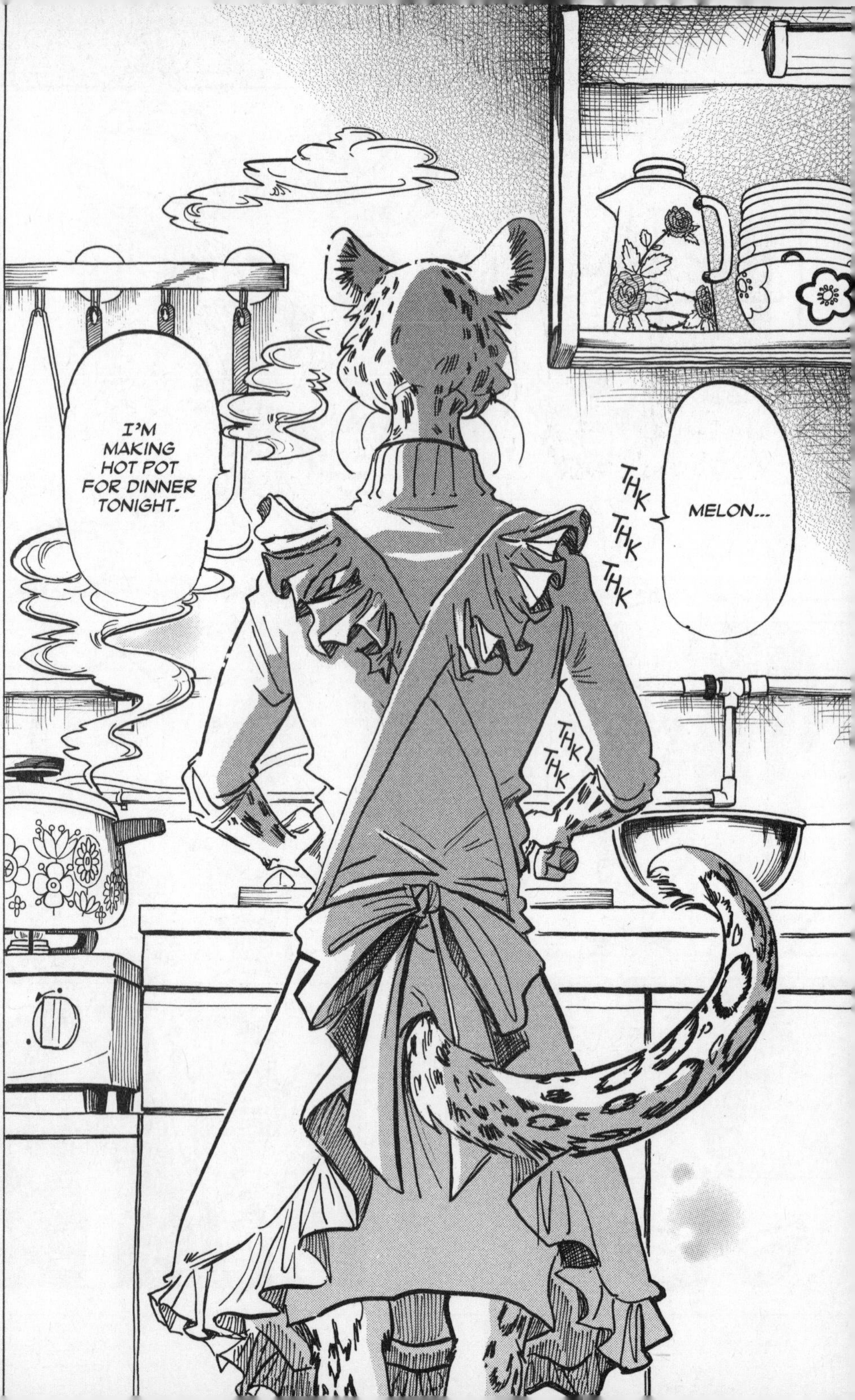
MELON...
THK THK THK
THK THK
I'M MAKING HOT POT FOR DINNER TONIGHT.

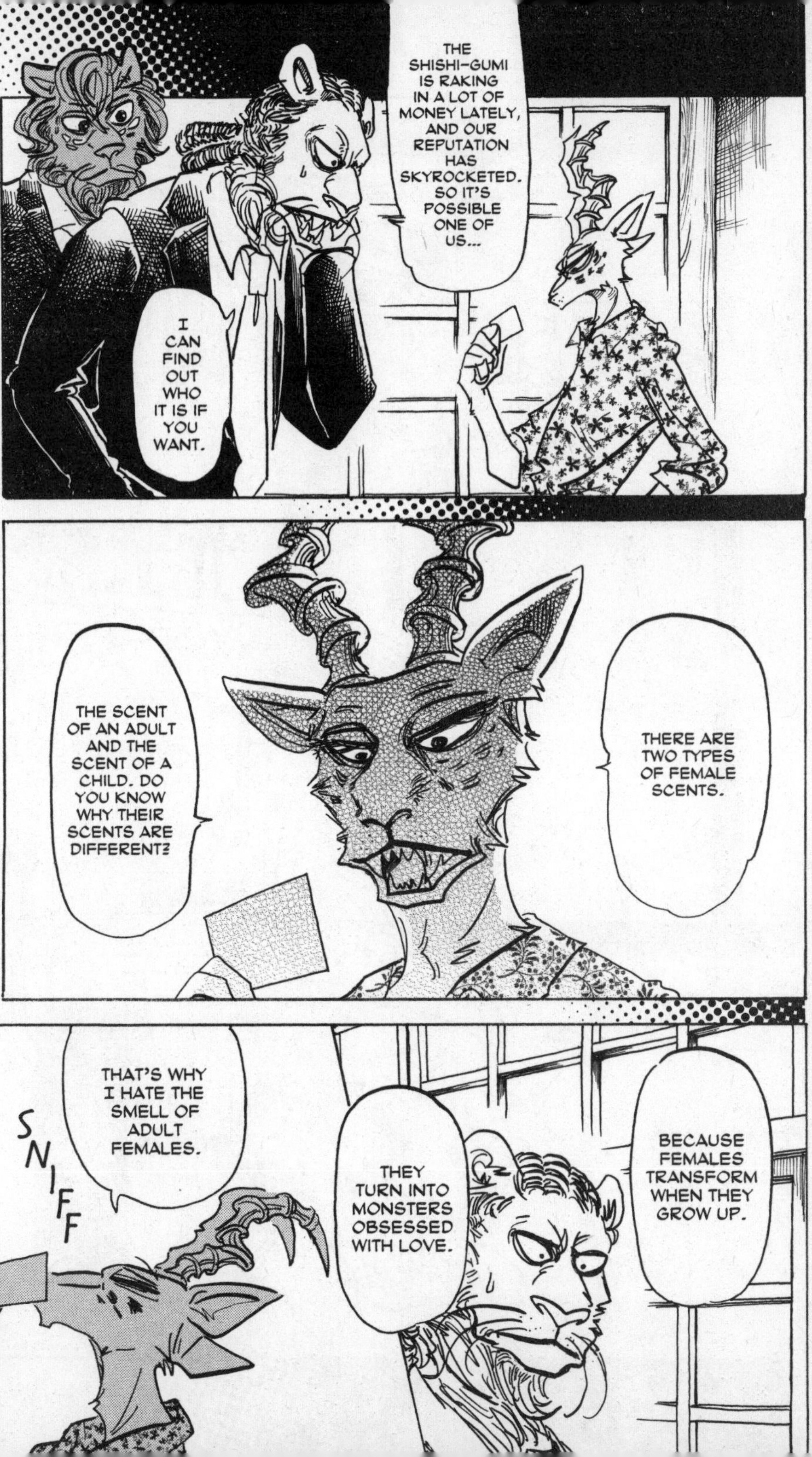
THE SHISHI-GUMI IS RAKING IN A LOT OF MONEY LATELY, AND OUR REPUTATION HAS SKYROCKETED. SO IT'S POSSIBLE ONE OF US...
I CAN FIND OUT WHO IT IS IF YOU WANT.
THERE ARE TWO TYPES OF FEMALE SCENTS.
THE SCENT OF AN ADULT AND THE SCENT OF A CHILD. DO YOU KNOW WHY THEIR SCENTS ARE DIFFERENT?
BECAUSE FEMALES TRANSFORM WHEN THEY GROW UP.
THEY TURN INTO MONSTERS OBSESSED WITH LOVE.
THAT'S WHY I HATE THE SMELL OF ADULT FEMALES.
SNIFF

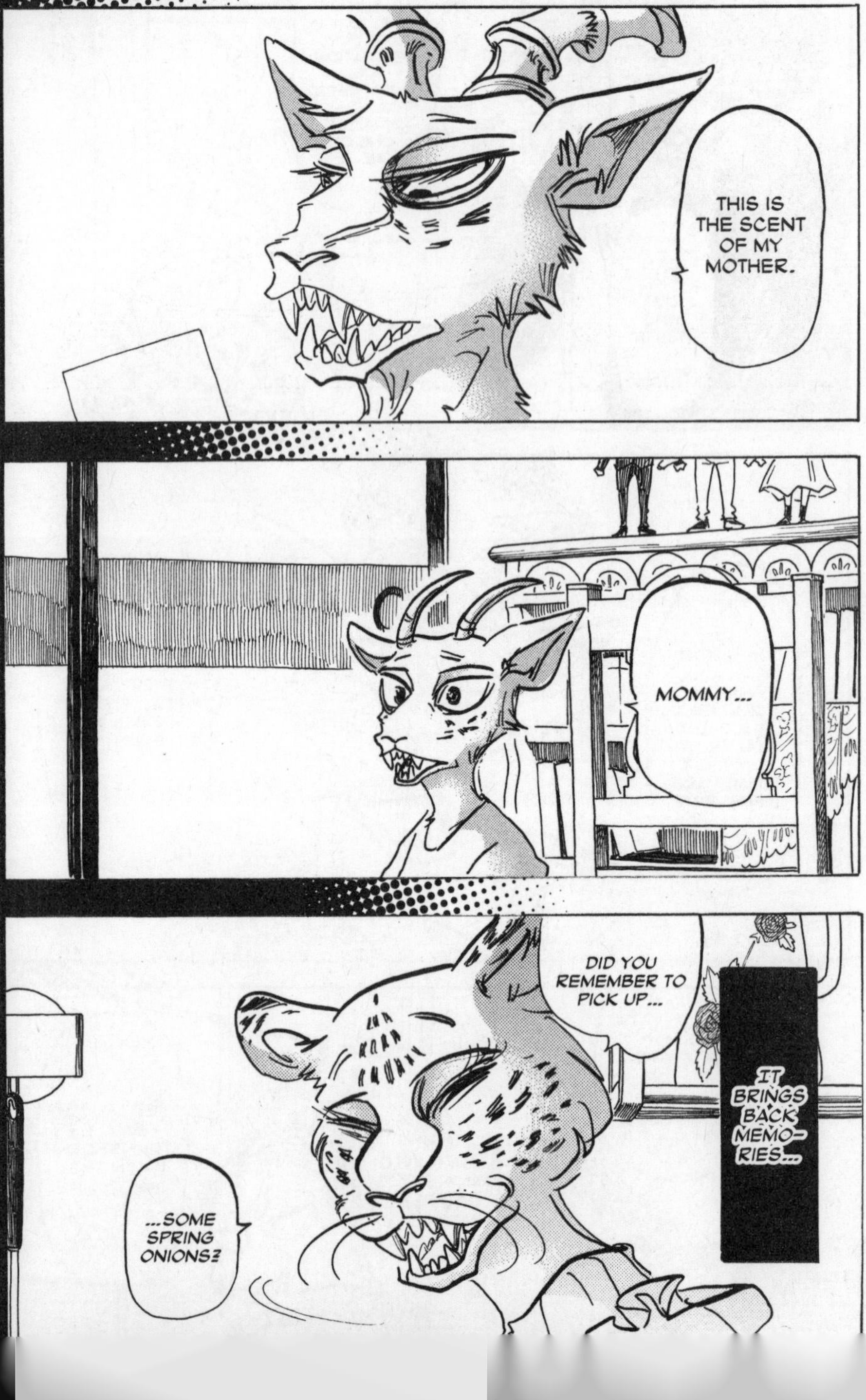
THIS IS THE SCENT OF MY MOTHER.
MOMMY...
IT BRINGS BACK MEMORIES...
DID YOU REMEMBER TO PICK UP...
...SOME SPRING ONIONS?

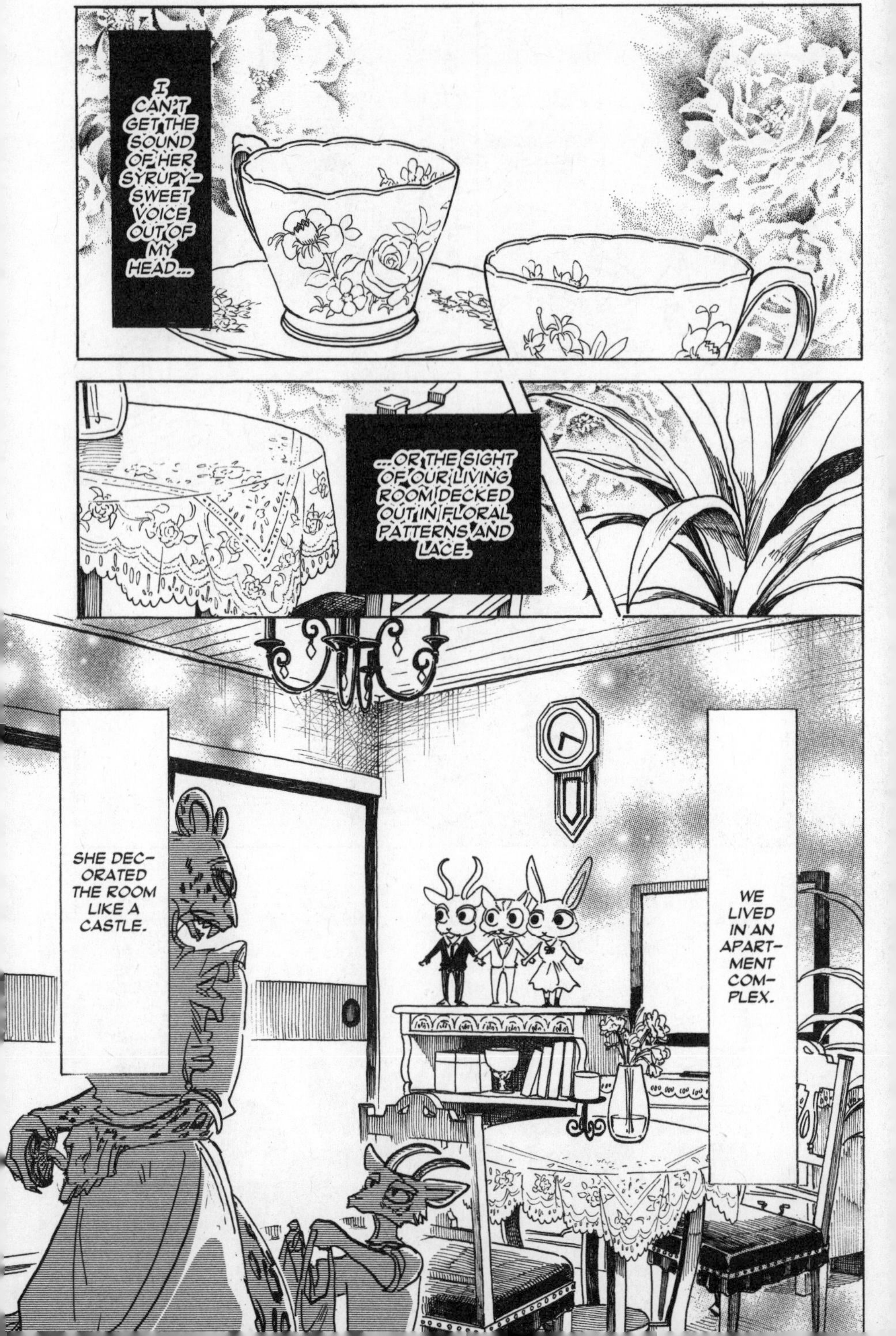
I CAN'T GET THE SOUND OF HER SYRUPY-SWEET VOICE OUT OF MY HEAD...
...OR THE SIGHT OF OUR LIVING ROOM DECKED OUT IN FLORAL PATTERNS AND LACE.
WE LIVED IN AN APARTMENT COMPLEX.
SHE DECORATED THE ROOM LIKE A CASTLE.

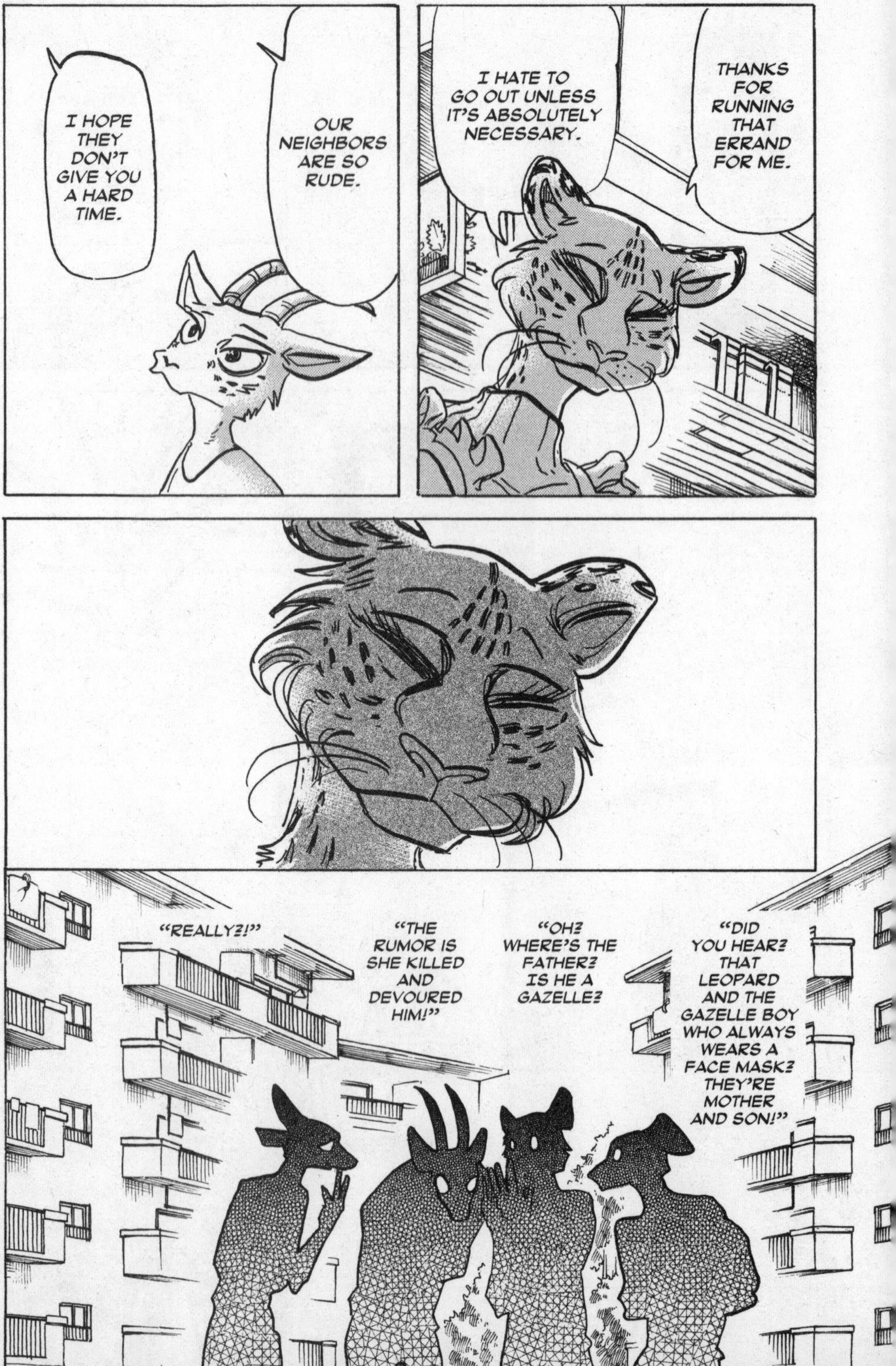
THANKS FOR RUNNING THAT ERRAND FOR ME.
I HATE TO GO OUT UNLESS IT'S ABSOLUTELY NECESSARY.
OUR NEIGHBORS ARE SO RUDE.
I HOPE THEY DON'T GIVE YOU A HARD TIME.
"DID YOU HEAR? THAT LEOPARD AND THE GAZELLE BOY WHO ALWAYS WEARS A FACE MASK? THEY'RE MOTHER AND SON!"
"OH? WHERE'S THE FATHER? IS HE A GAZELLE?
"THE RUMOR IS SHE KILLED AND DEVOURED HIM!"
"REALLY?!"

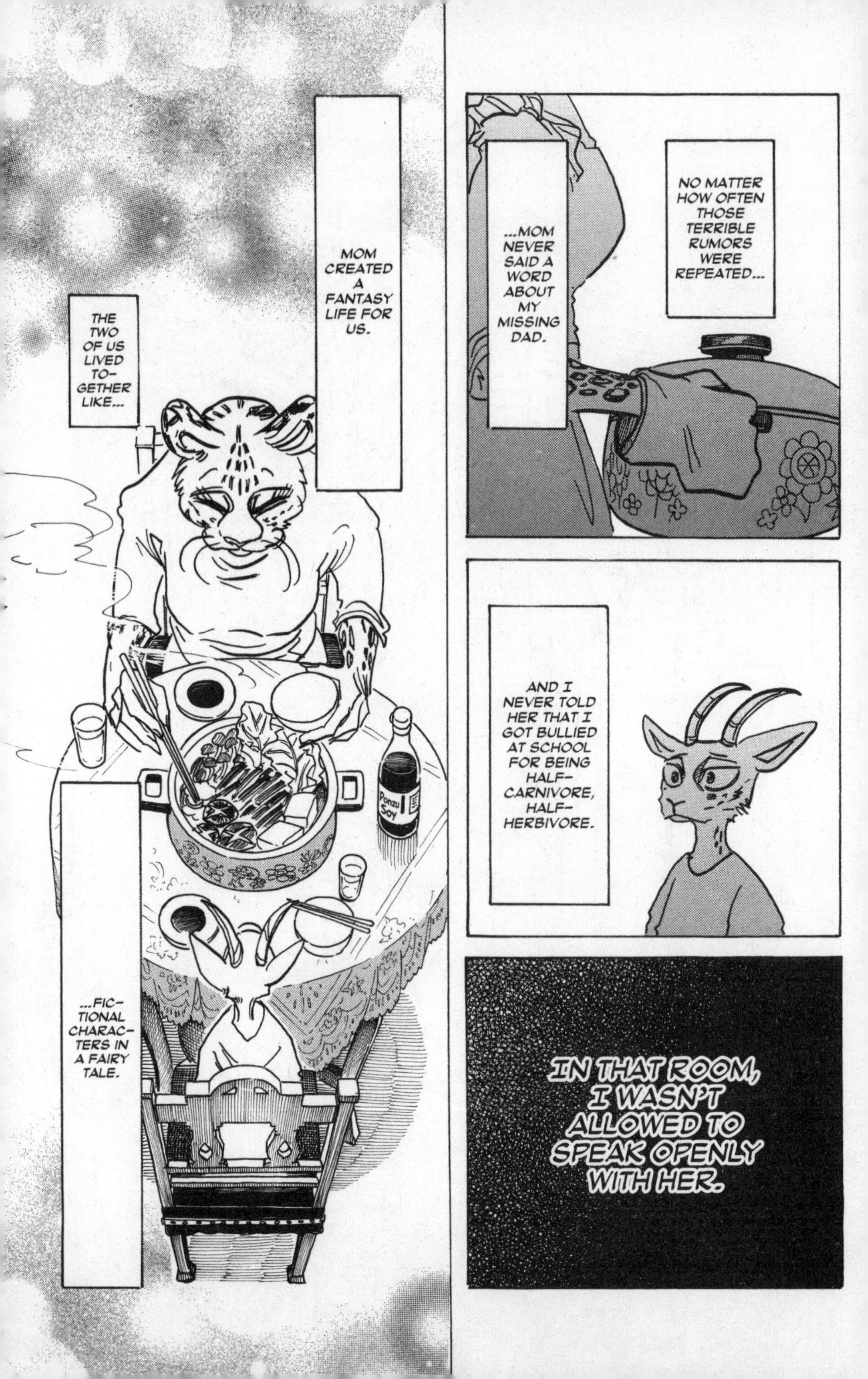
NO MATTER HOW OFTEN THOSE TERRIBLE RUMORS WERE REPEATED...
...MOM NEVER SAID A WORD ABOUT MY MISSING DAD.
AND I NEVER TOLD HER THAT I GOT BULLIED AT SCHOOL FOR BEING HALF-CARNIVORE, HALF-HERBIVORE.
IN THAT ROOM, I WASN'T ALLOWED TO SPEAK OPENLY WITH HER.
MOM CREATED A FANTASY LIFE FOR US.
THE TWO OF US LIVED TOGETHER LIKE...
Ponzu Soy
...FICTIONAL CHARACTERS IN A FAIRY TALE.

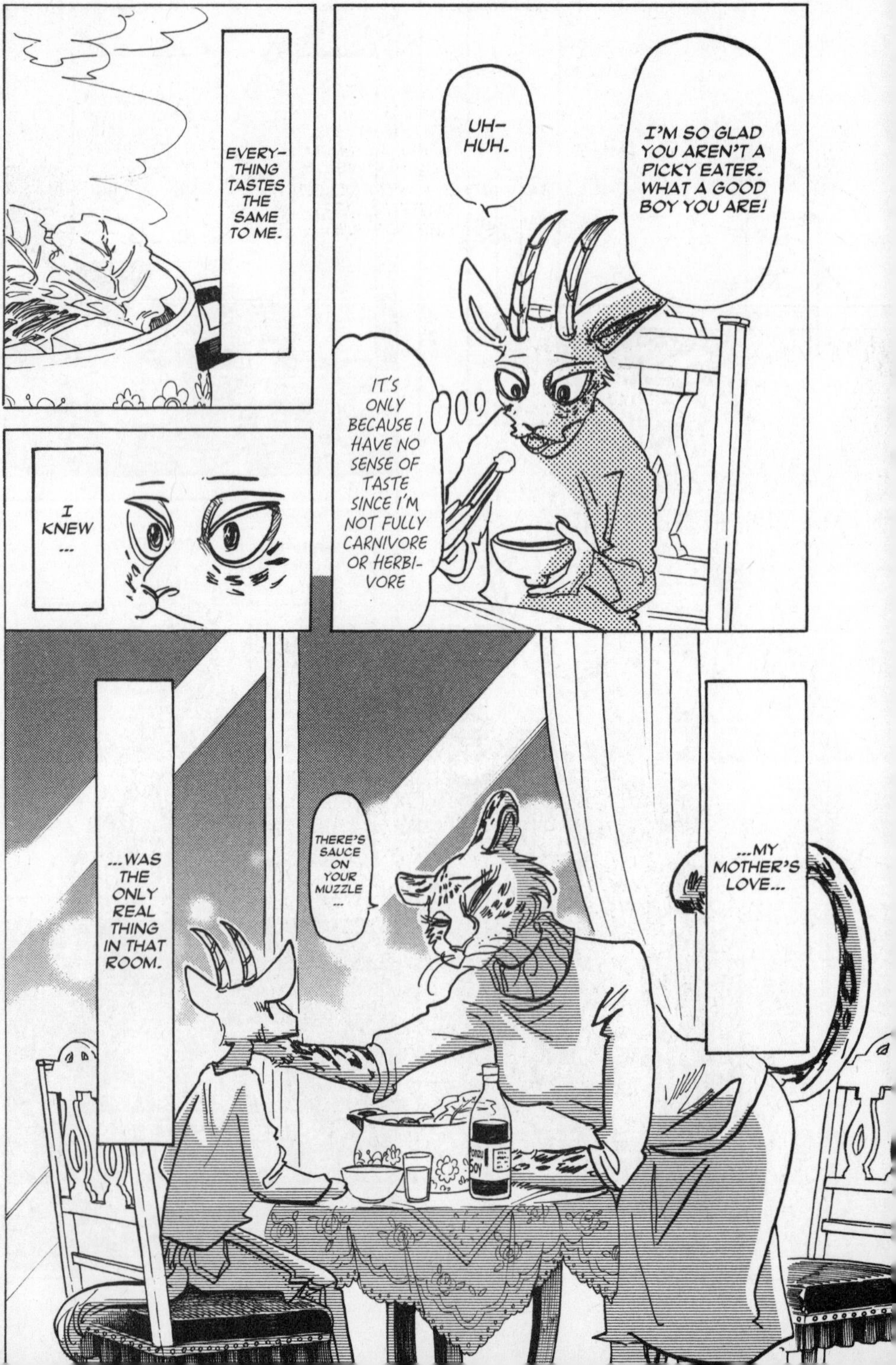
I'M SO GLAD YOU AREN'T A PICKY EATER. WHAT A GOOD BOY YOU ARE!
UH-HUH.
IT'S ONLY BECAUSE I HAVE NO SENSE OF TASTE SINCE I'M NOT FULLY CARNIVORE OR HERBIVORE
EVERYTHING TASTES THE SAME TO ME.
I KNEW...
...MY MOTHER'S LOVE...
THERE'S SAUCE ON YOUR MUZZLE...
...WAS THE ONLY REAL THING IN THAT ROOM.

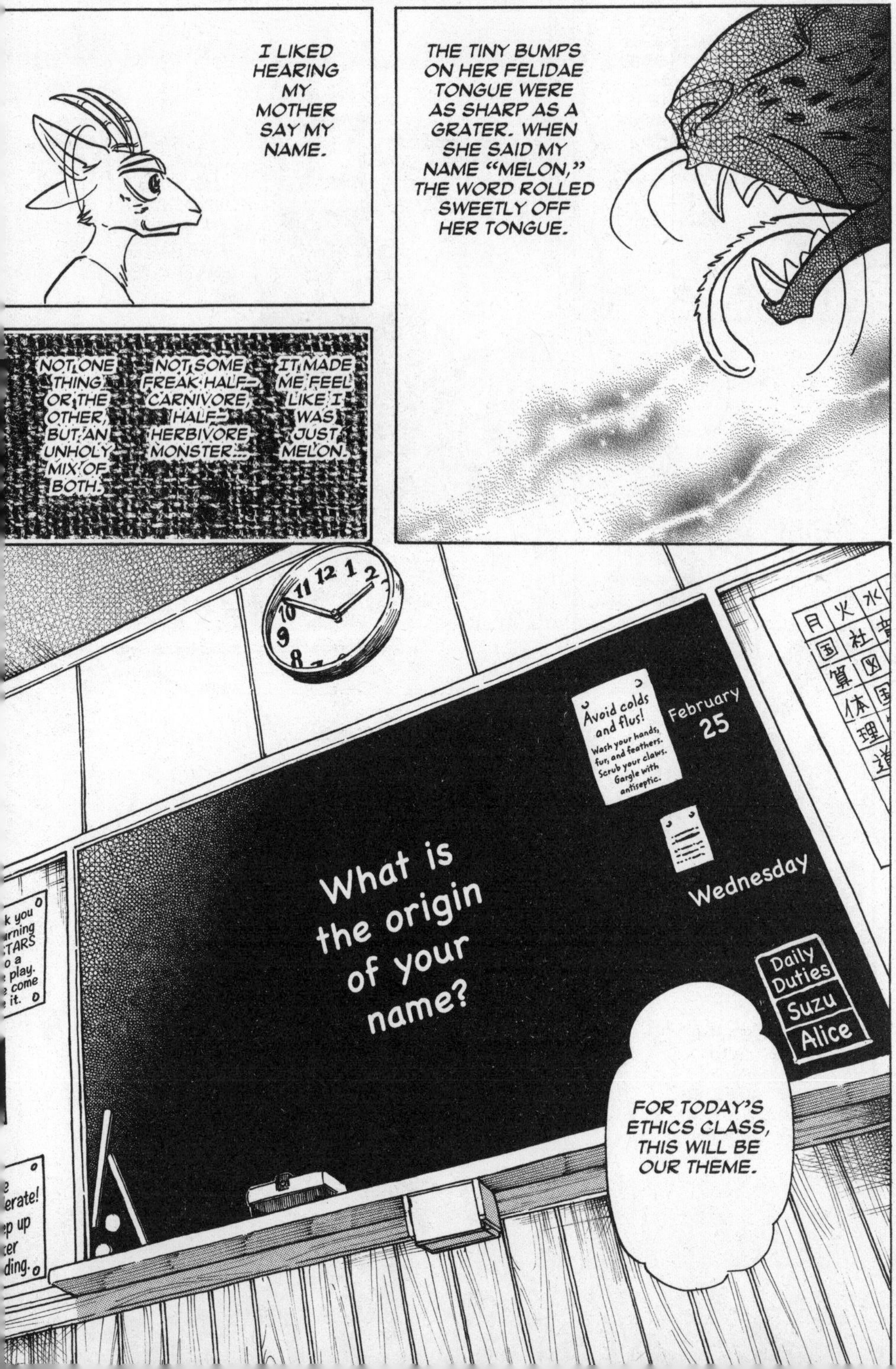
THE TINY BUMPS ON HER FELIDAE TONGUE WERE AS SHARP AS A GRATER. WHEN SHE SAID MY NAME "MELON," THE WORD ROLLED SWEETLY OFF HER TONGUE.
I LIKED HEARING MY MOTHER SAY MY NAME.
IT MADE ME FEEL LIKE I WAS JUST MELON.
NOT SOME FREAK HALF-CARNIVORE, HALF-HERBIVORE MONSTER...
NOT ONE THING OR THE OTHER, BUT AN UNHOLY MIX OF BOTH.
February 25
Avoid colds and flus! Wash your hands, fur, and feathers. Scrub your claws. Gargle with antiseptic.
Wednesday
What is the origin of your name?
Daily Duties
Suzu
Alice
FOR TODAY'S ETHICS CLASS, THIS WILL BE OUR THEME.

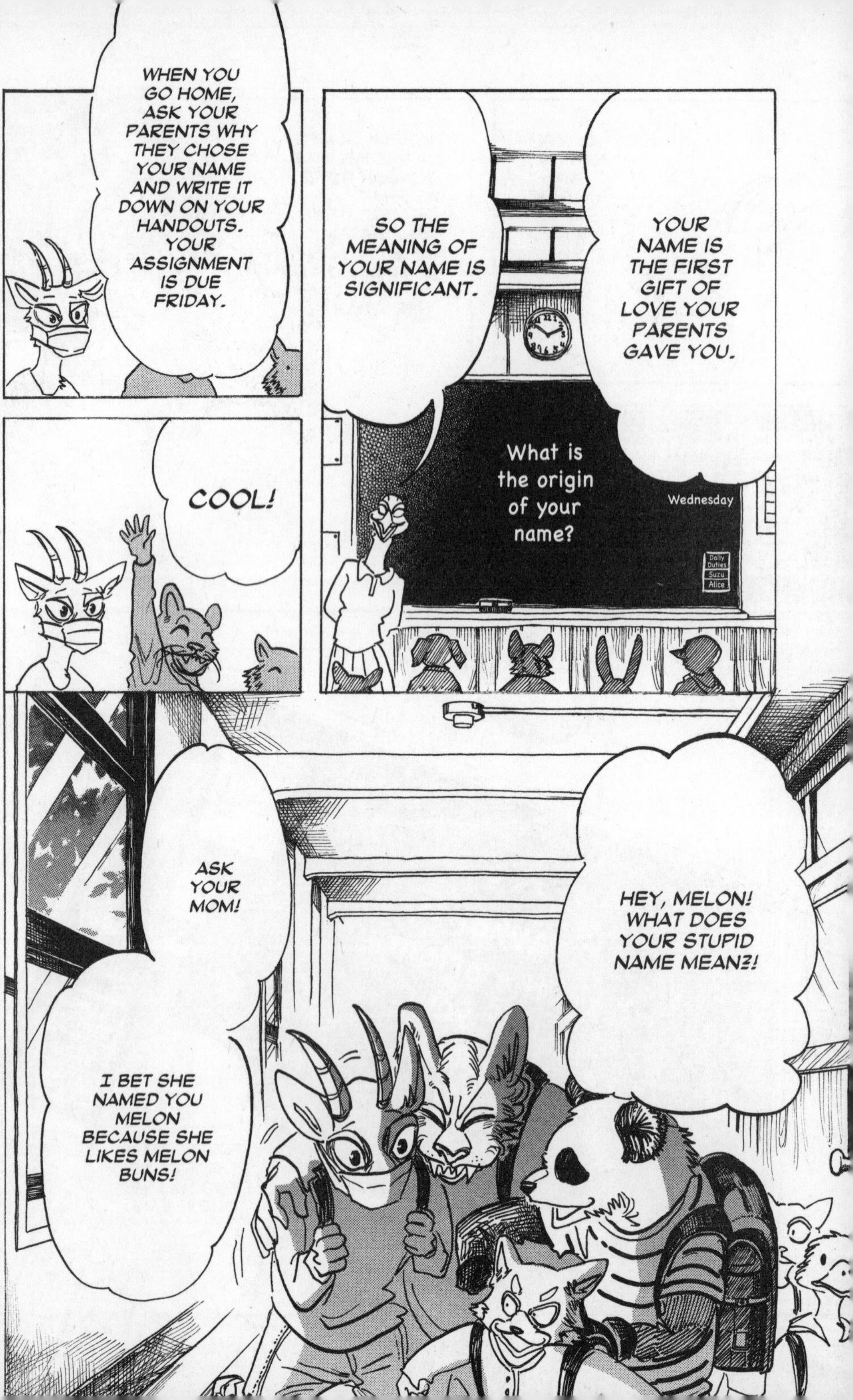
YOUR NAME IS THE FIRST GIFT OF LOVE YOUR PARENTS GAVE YOU.
SO THE MEANING OF YOUR NAME IS SIGNIFICANT.
What is the origin of your name?
Wednesday
Daily Duties
Suzu
Alice
WHEN YOU GO HOME, ASK YOUR PARENTS WHY THEY CHOSE YOUR NAME AND WRITE IT DOWN ON YOUR HANDOUTS. YOUR ASSIGNMENT IS DUE FRIDAY.
COOL!
HEY, MELON! WHAT DOES YOUR STUPID NAME MEAN?!
ASK YOUR MOM!
I BET SHE NAMED YOU MELON BECAUSE SHE LIKES MELON BUNS!

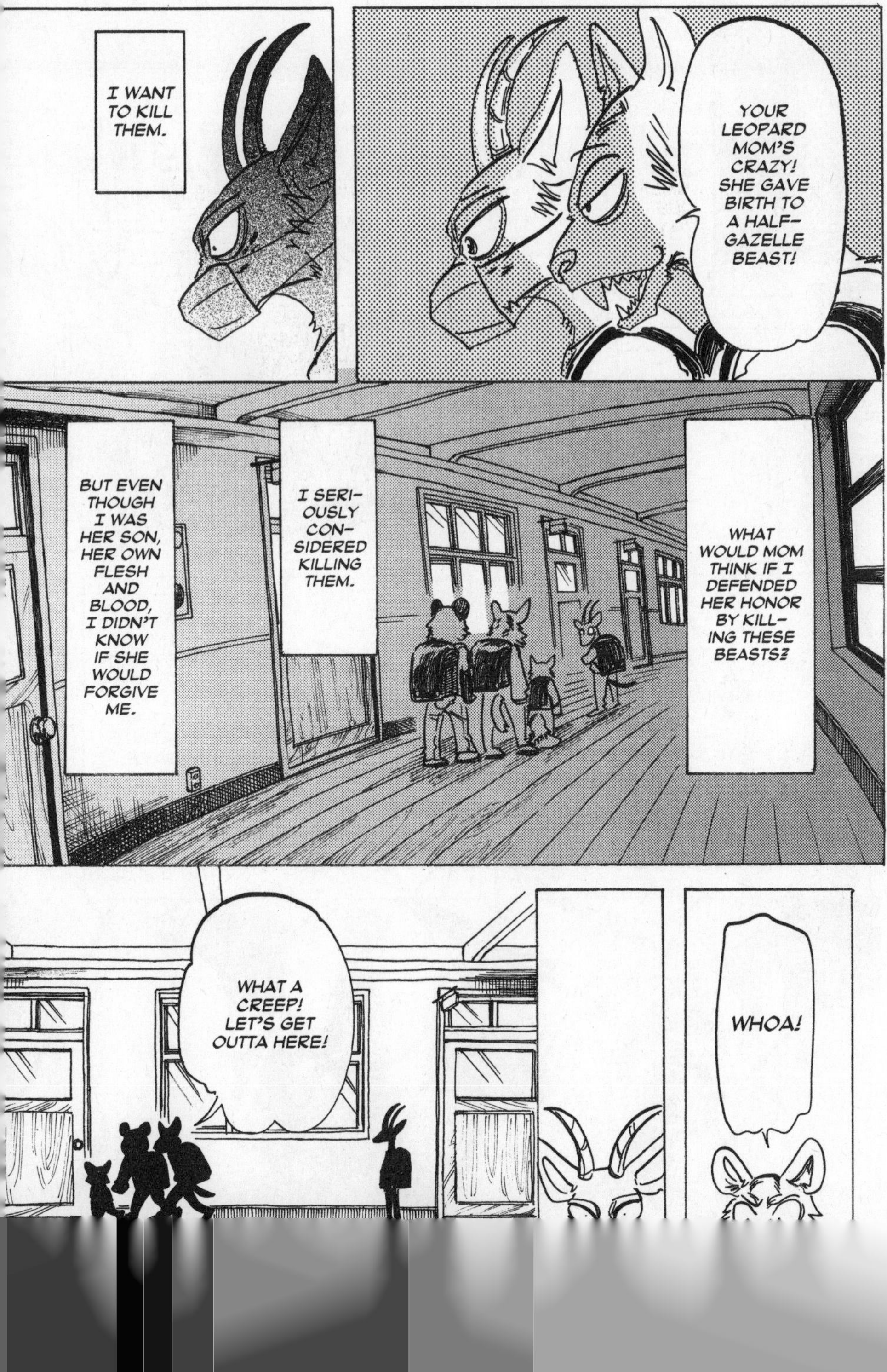
YOUR LEOPARD MOM'S CRAZY! SHE GAVE BIRTH TO A HALF-GAZELLE BEAST!
I WANT TO KILL THEM.
WHAT WOULD MOM THINK IF I DEFENDED HER HONOR BY KILLING THESE BEASTS?
I SERIOUSLY CONSIDERED KILLING THEM.
BUT EVEN THOUGH I WAS HER SON, HER OWN FLESH AND BLOOD, I DIDN'T KNOW IF SHE WOULD FORGIVE ME.
WHOA!
WHAT A CREEP! LET'S GET OUTTA HERE!

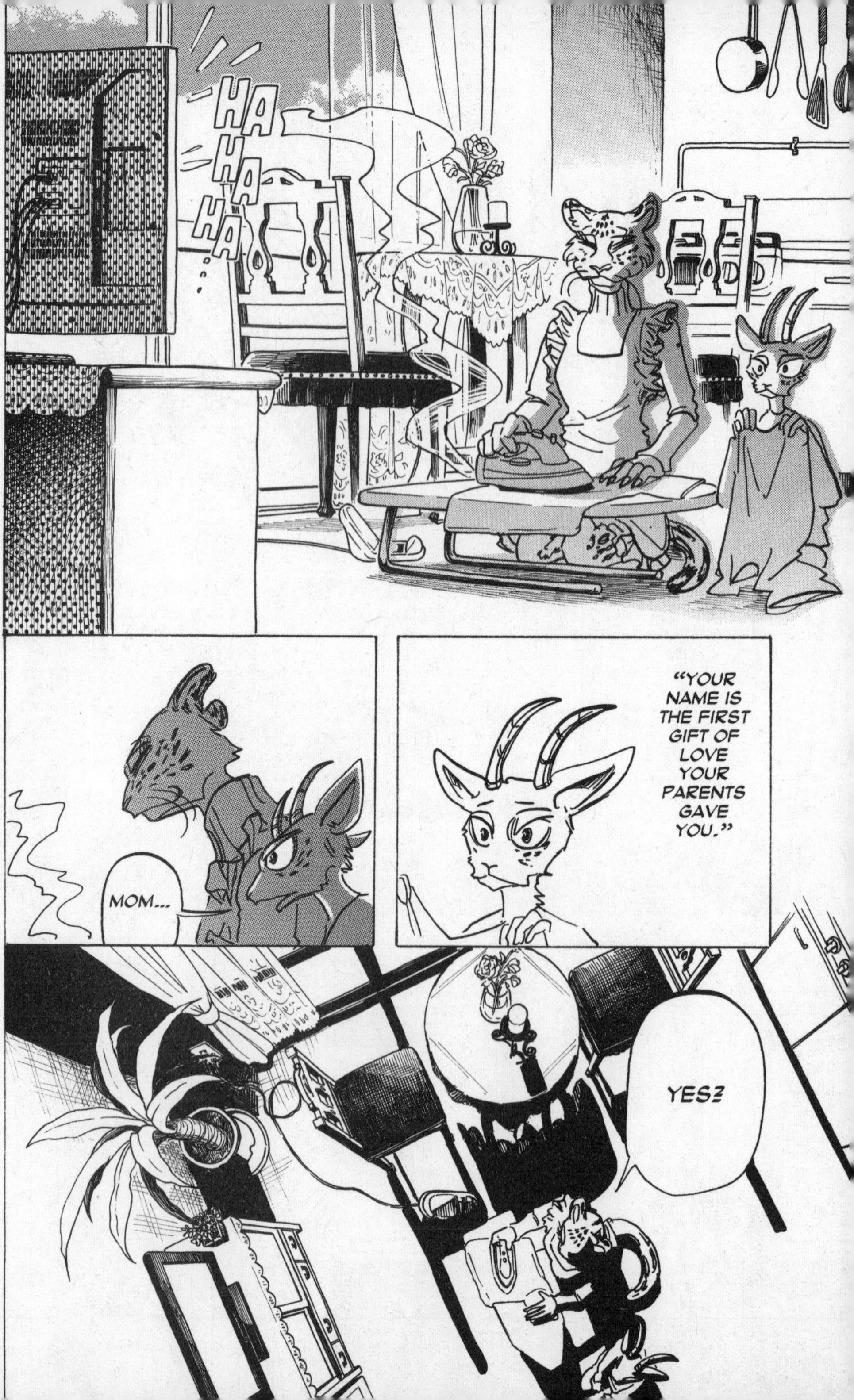
HA HA HA HA
"YOUR NAME IS THE FIRST GIFT OF LOVE YOUR PARENTS GAVE YOU."
MOM...
YES?

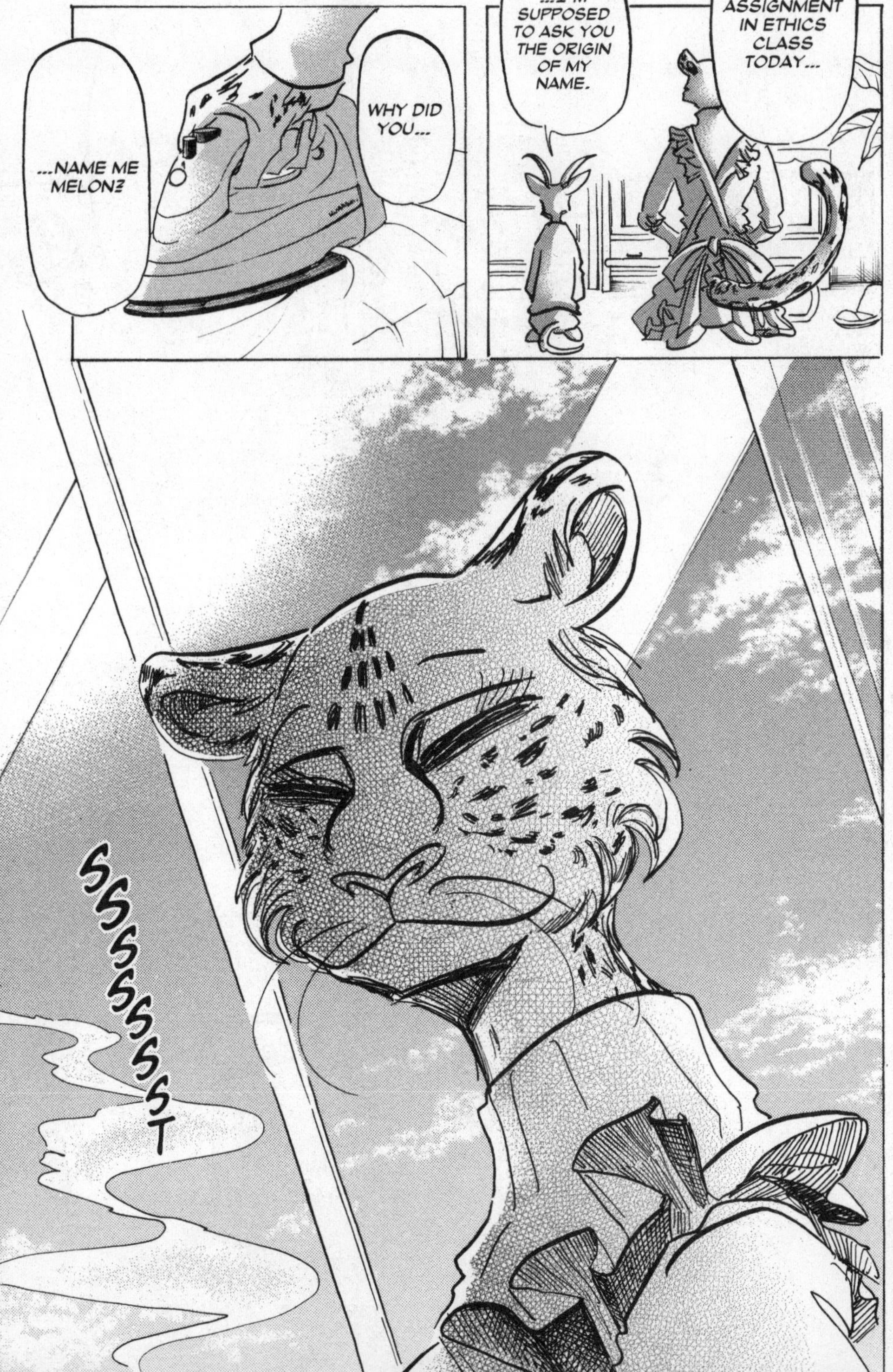
FOR MY ASSIGNMENT IN ETHICS CLASS TODAY...
...I'M SUPPOSED TO ASK YOU THE ORIGIN OF MY NAME.
WHY DID YOU...
...NAME ME MELON?
SSSSSSST

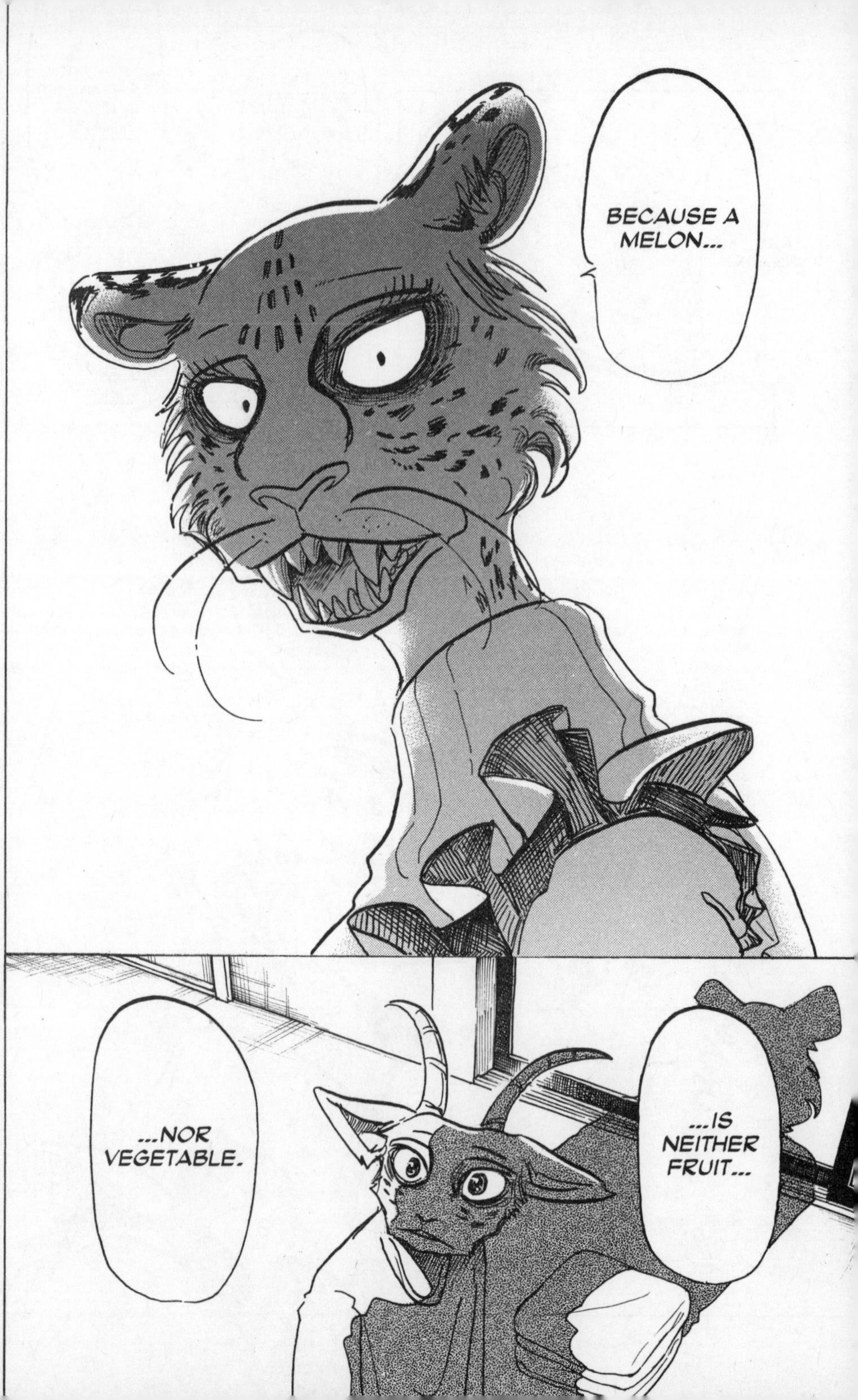
BECAUSE A MELON...
...IS NEITHER FRUIT...
...NOR VEGETABLE.

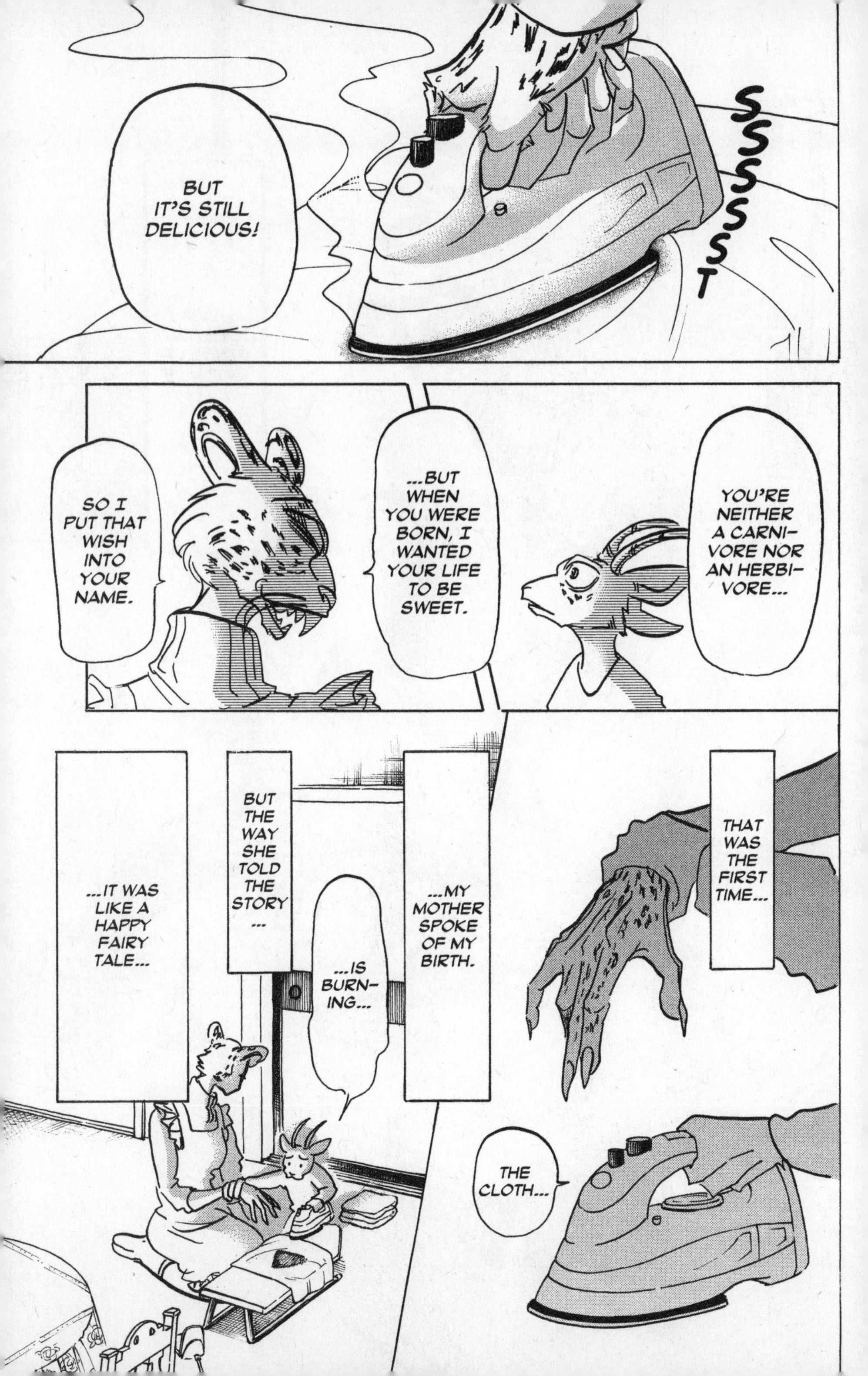
SSSSST
BUT IT'S STILL DELICIOUS!
YOU'RE NEITHER A CARNIVORE NOR AN HERBIVORE...
...BUT WHEN YOU WERE BORN, I WANTED YOUR LIFE TO BE SWEET.
SO I PUT THAT WISH INTO YOUR NAME.
THAT WAS THE FIRST TIME...
THE CLOTH...
...MY MOTHER SPOKE OF MY BIRTH.
...IS BURNING...
BUT THE WAY SHE TOLD THE STORY...
...IT WAS LIKE A HAPPY FAIRY TALE...

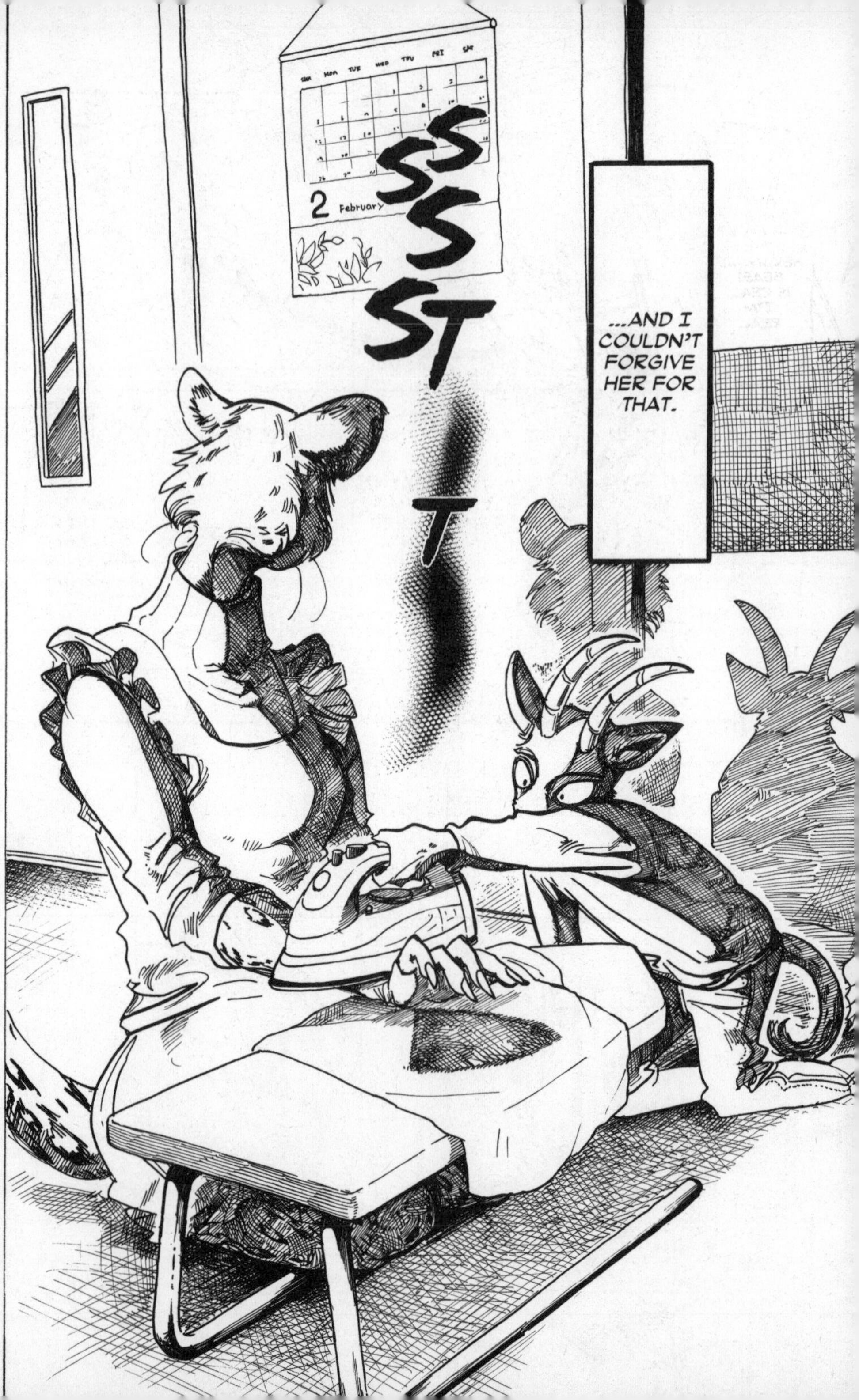
...AND I COULDN'T FORGIVE HER FOR THAT.
SSSST
T
2 February

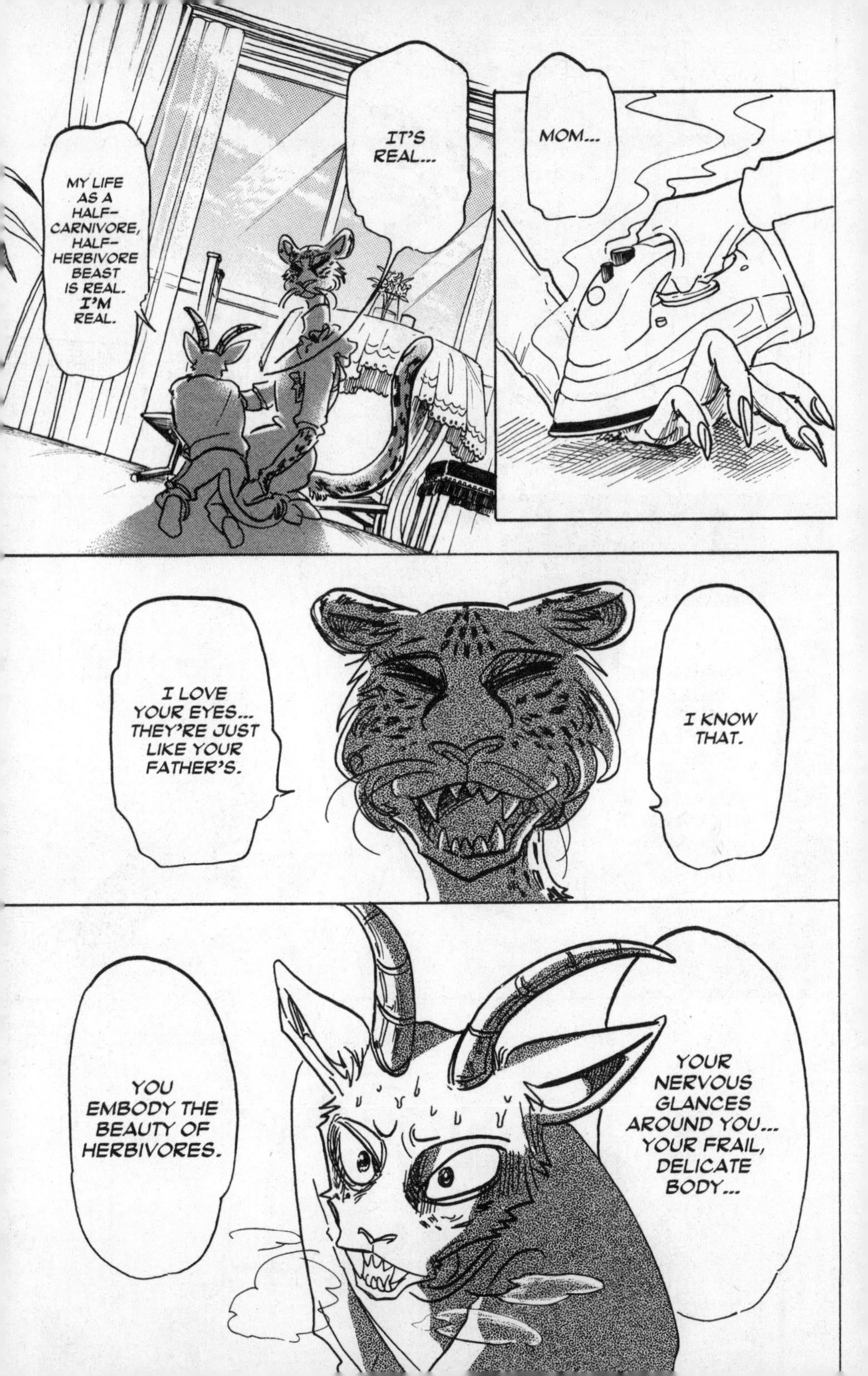
MOM...
IT'S REAL...
MY LIFE AS A HALF-CARNIVORE, HALF-HERBIVORE BEAST IS REAL. I'M REAL.
I KNOW THAT.
I LOVE YOUR EYES... THEY'RE JUST LIKE YOUR FATHER'S.
YOUR NERVOUS GLANCES AROUND YOU... YOUR FRAIL, DELICATE BODY...
YOU EMBODY THE BEAUTY OF HERBIVORES.

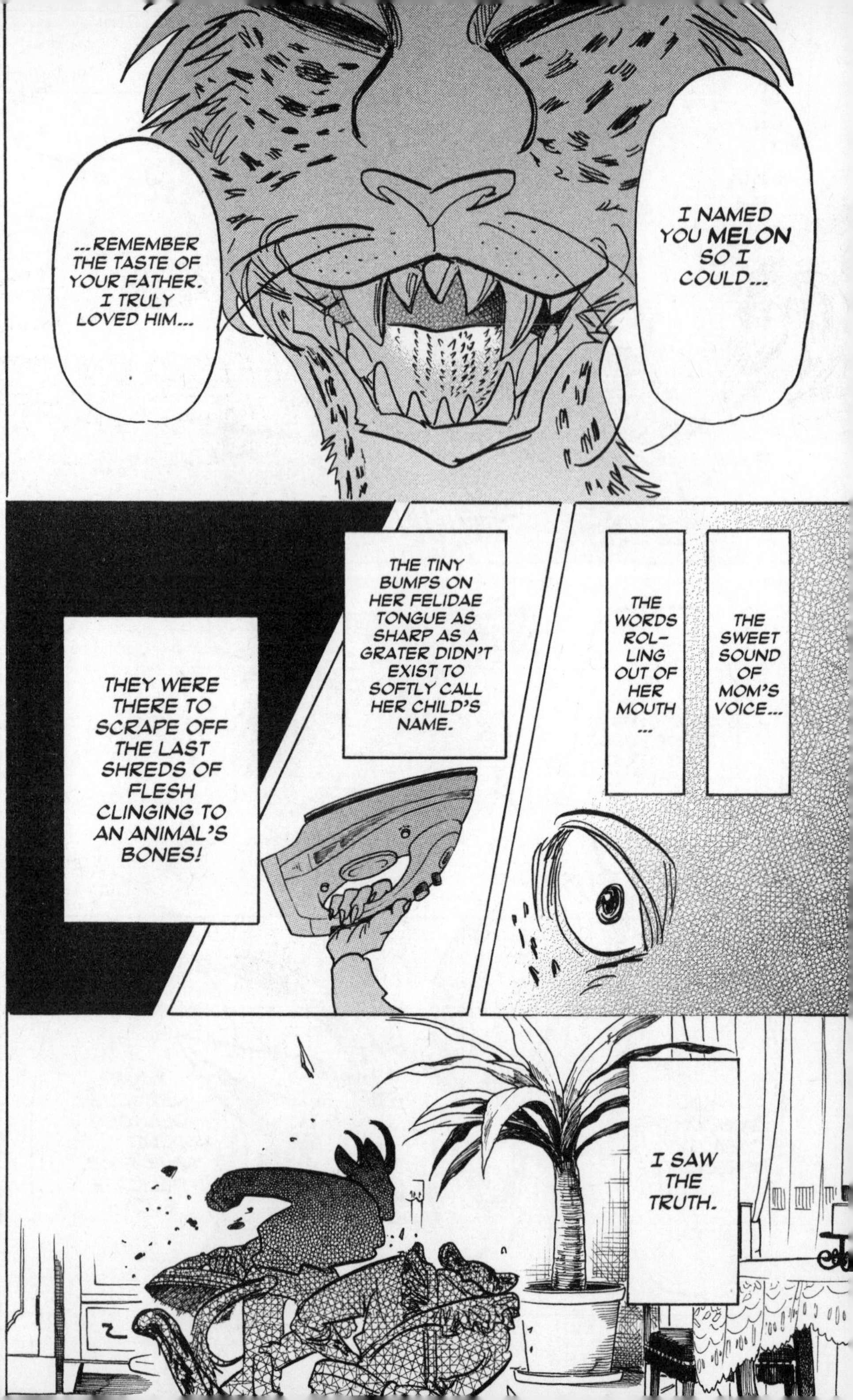
I NAMED YOU MELON SO I COULD...
...REMEMBER THE TASTE OF YOUR FATHER. I TRULY LOVED HIM...
THE SWEET SOUND OF MOM'S VOICE...
THE WORDS ROL-LING OUT OF HER MOUTH ...
THE TINY BUMPS ON HER FELIDAE TONGUE AS SHARP AS A GRATER DIDN'T EXIST TO SOFTLY CALL HER CHILD'S NAME.
THEY WERE THERE TO SCRAPE OFF THE LAST SHREDS OF FLESH CLINGING TO AN ANIMAL'S BONES!
I SAW THE TRUTH.

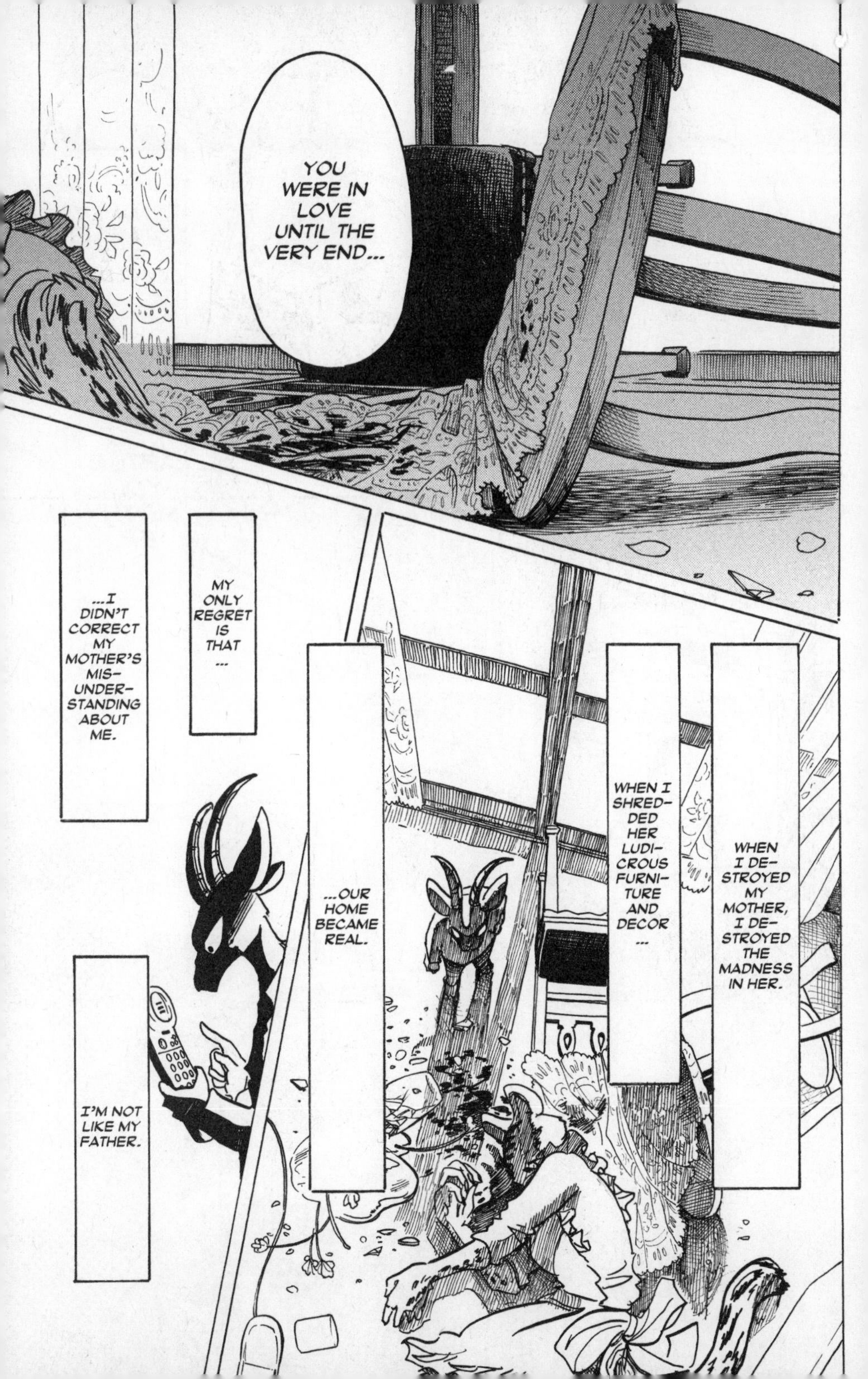
YOU WERE IN LOVE UNTIL THE VERY END...
WHEN I DESTROYED MY MOTHER, I DESTROYED THE MADNESS IN HER.
WHEN I SHREDDED HER LUDICROUS FURNITURE AND DECOR...
...OUR HOME BECAME REAL.
MY ONLY REGRET IS THAT...
...I DIDN'T CORRECT MY MOTHER'S MISUNDERSTANDING ABOUT ME.
I'M NOT LIKE MY FATHER.

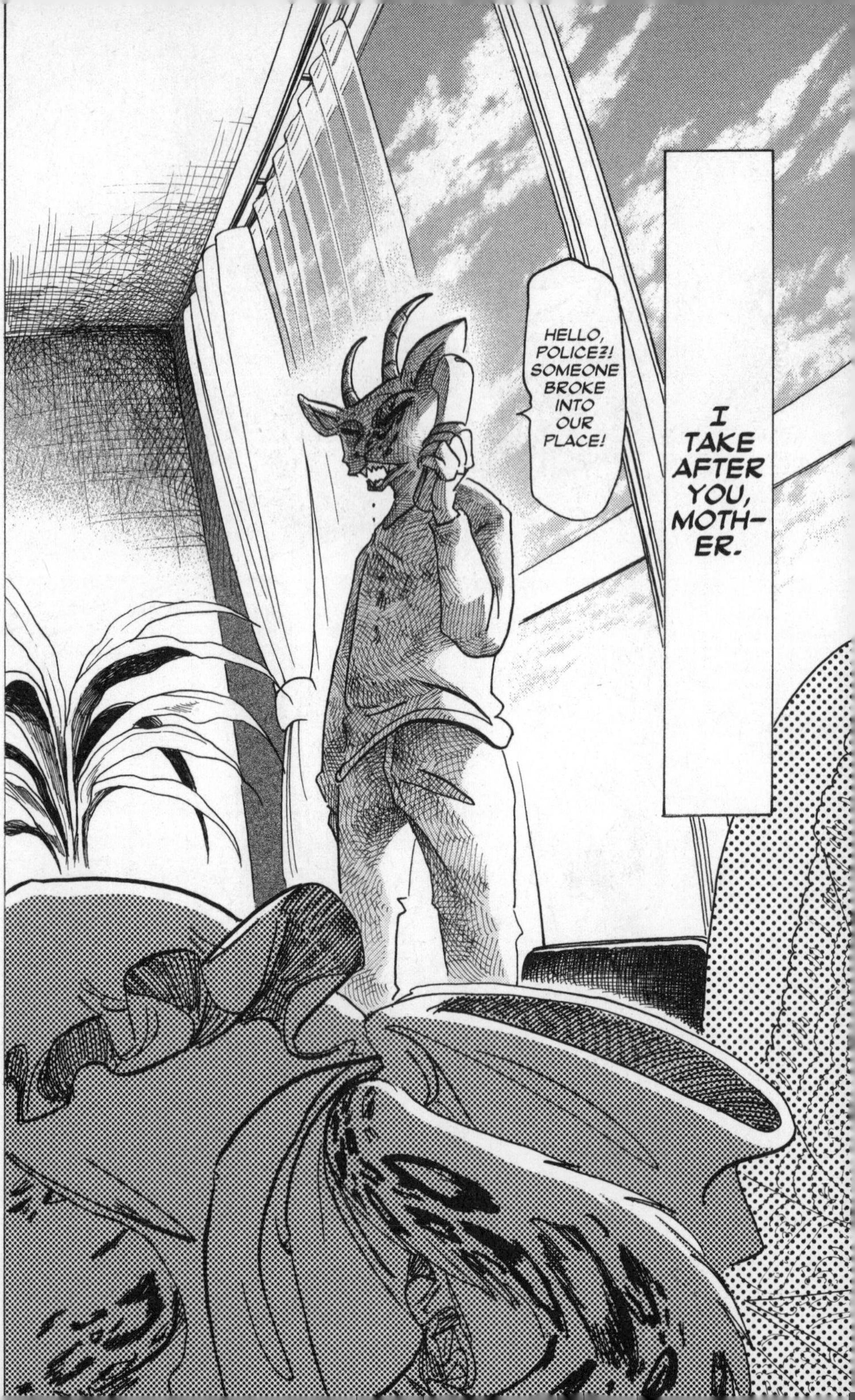
I TAKE AFTER YOU, MOTH- ER.
HELLO, POLICE?! SOMEONE BROKE INTO OUR PLACE!

Chapter 163: Don't Look Down or Your Fur Will Fall in Your Eyes

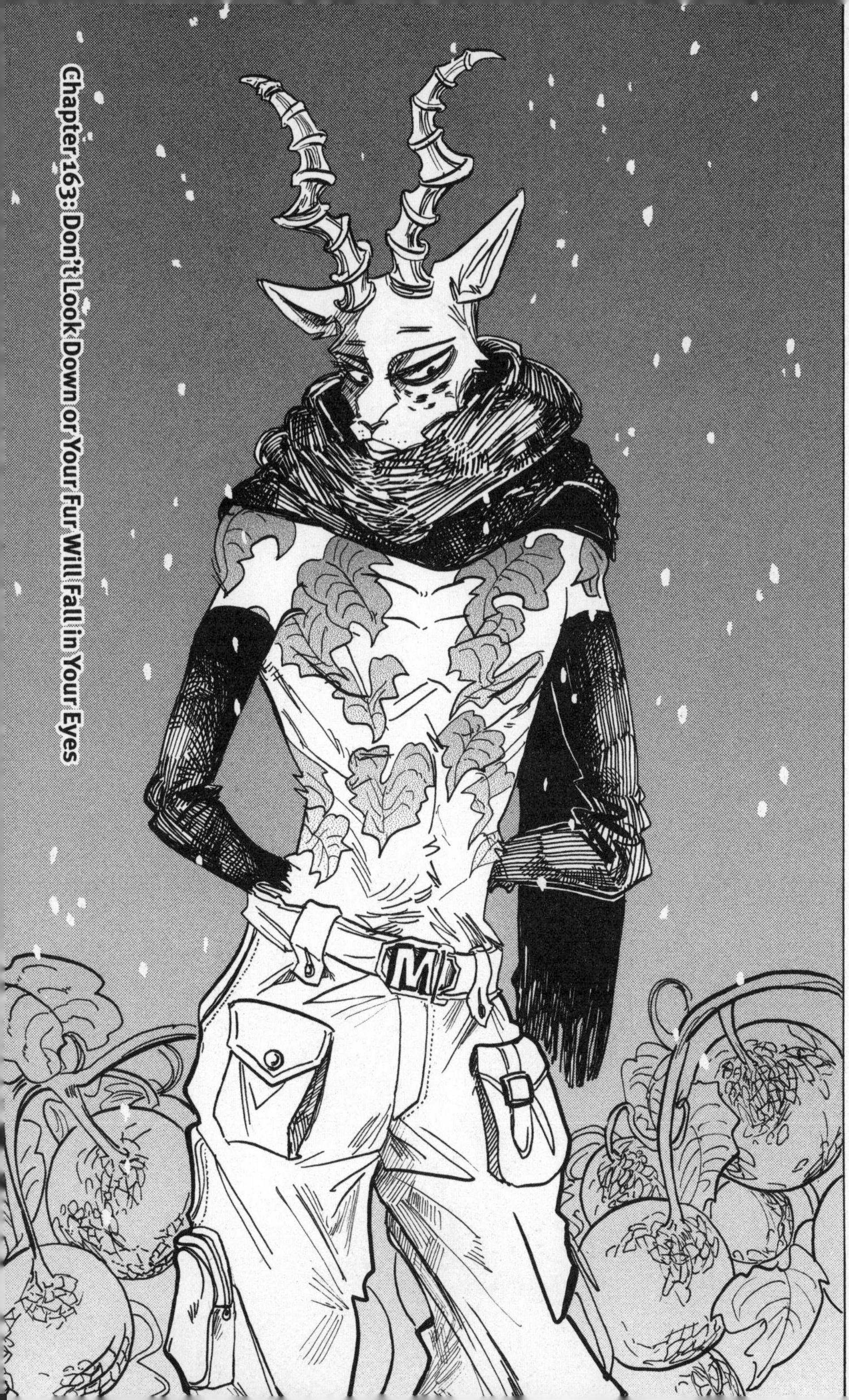

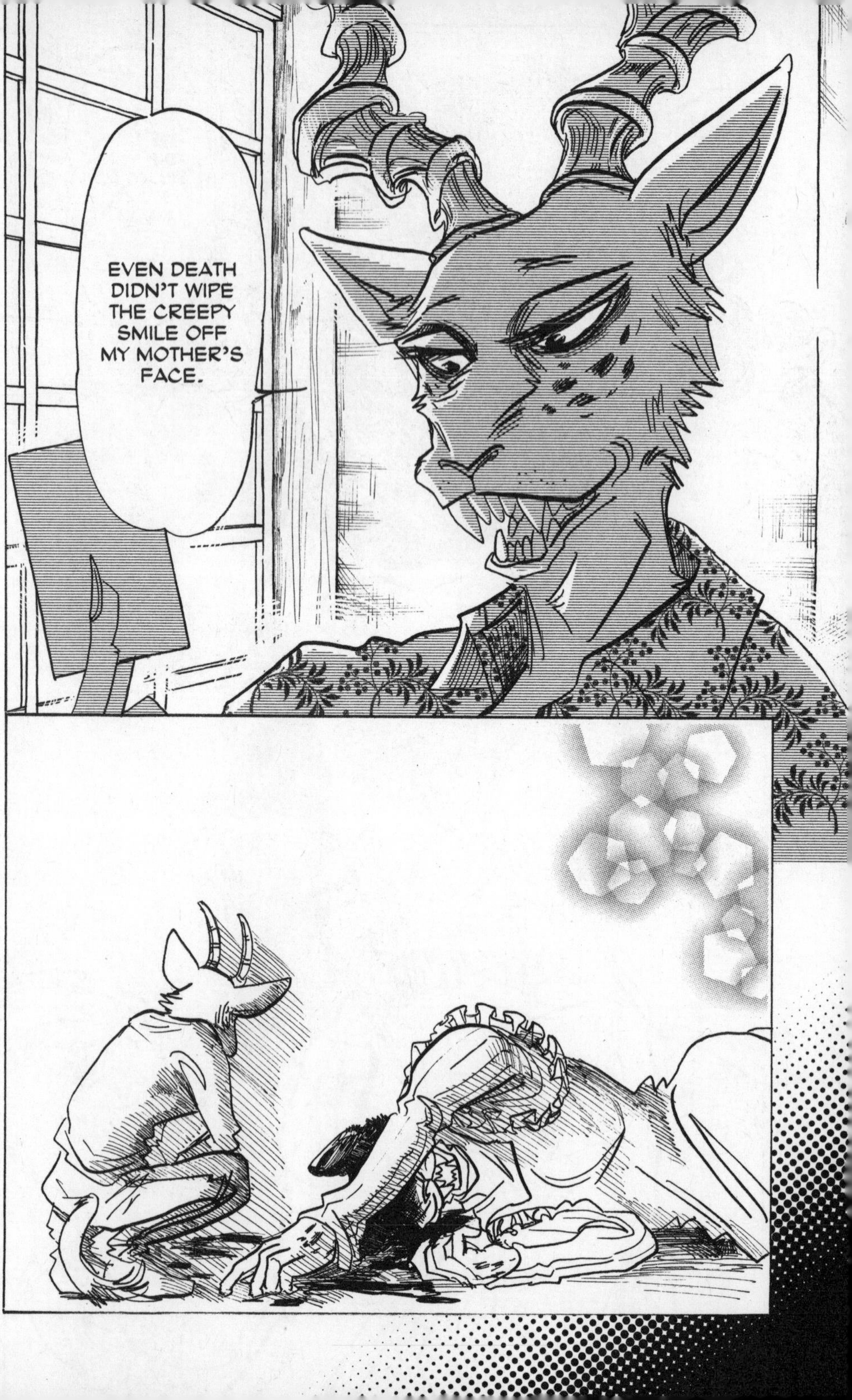
EVEN DEATH DIDN'T WIPE THE CREEPY SMILE OFF MY MOTHER'S FACE.

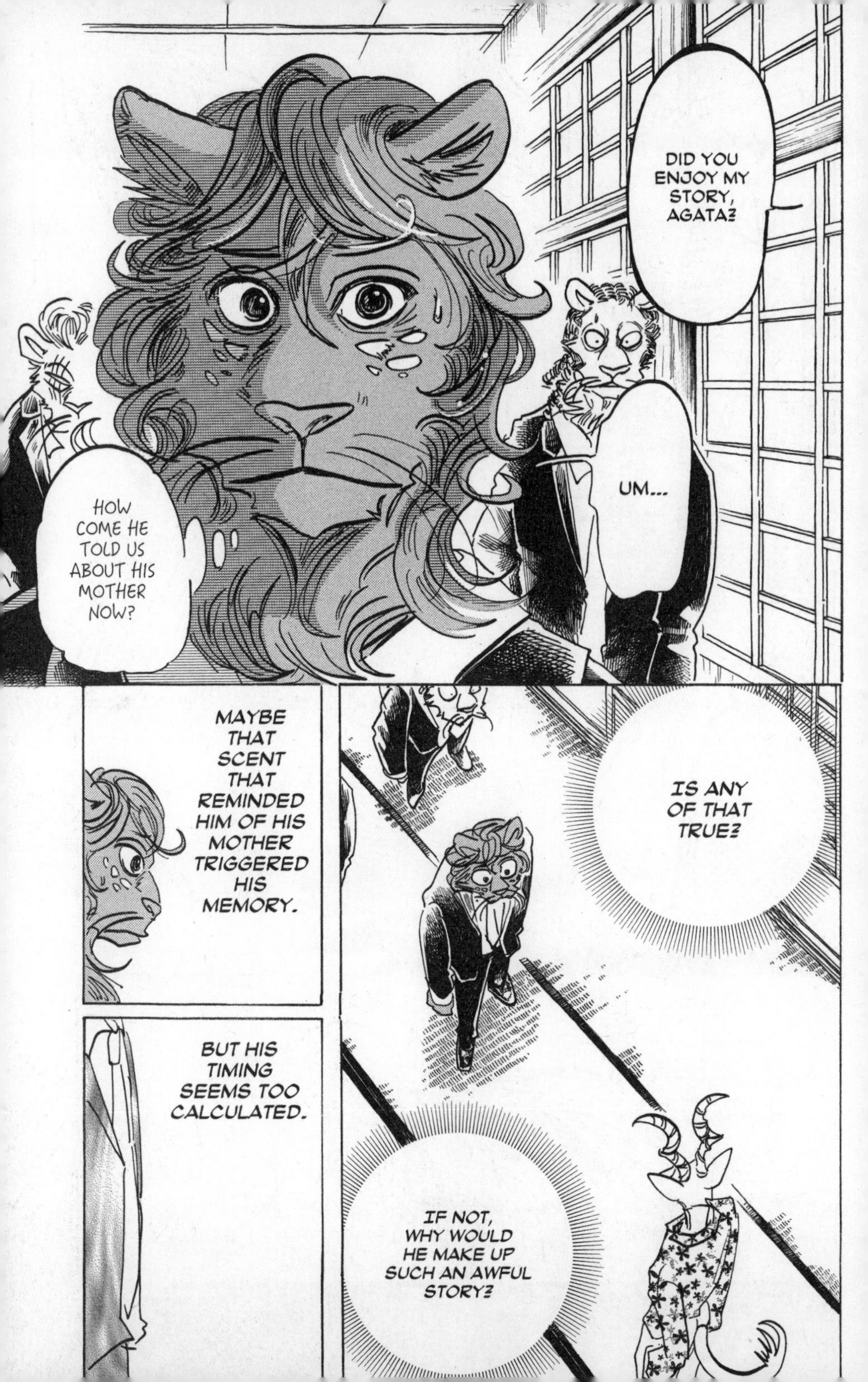
DID YOU ENJOY MY STORY, AGATA?
UM...
HOW COME HE TOLD US ABOUT HIS MOTHER NOW?
IS ANY OF THAT TRUE?
IF NOT, WHY WOULD HE MAKE UP SUCH AN AWFUL STORY?
MAYBE THAT SCENT THAT REMINDED HIM OF HIS MOTHER TRIGGERED HIS MEMORY.
BUT HIS TIMING SEEMS TOO CALCULATED.

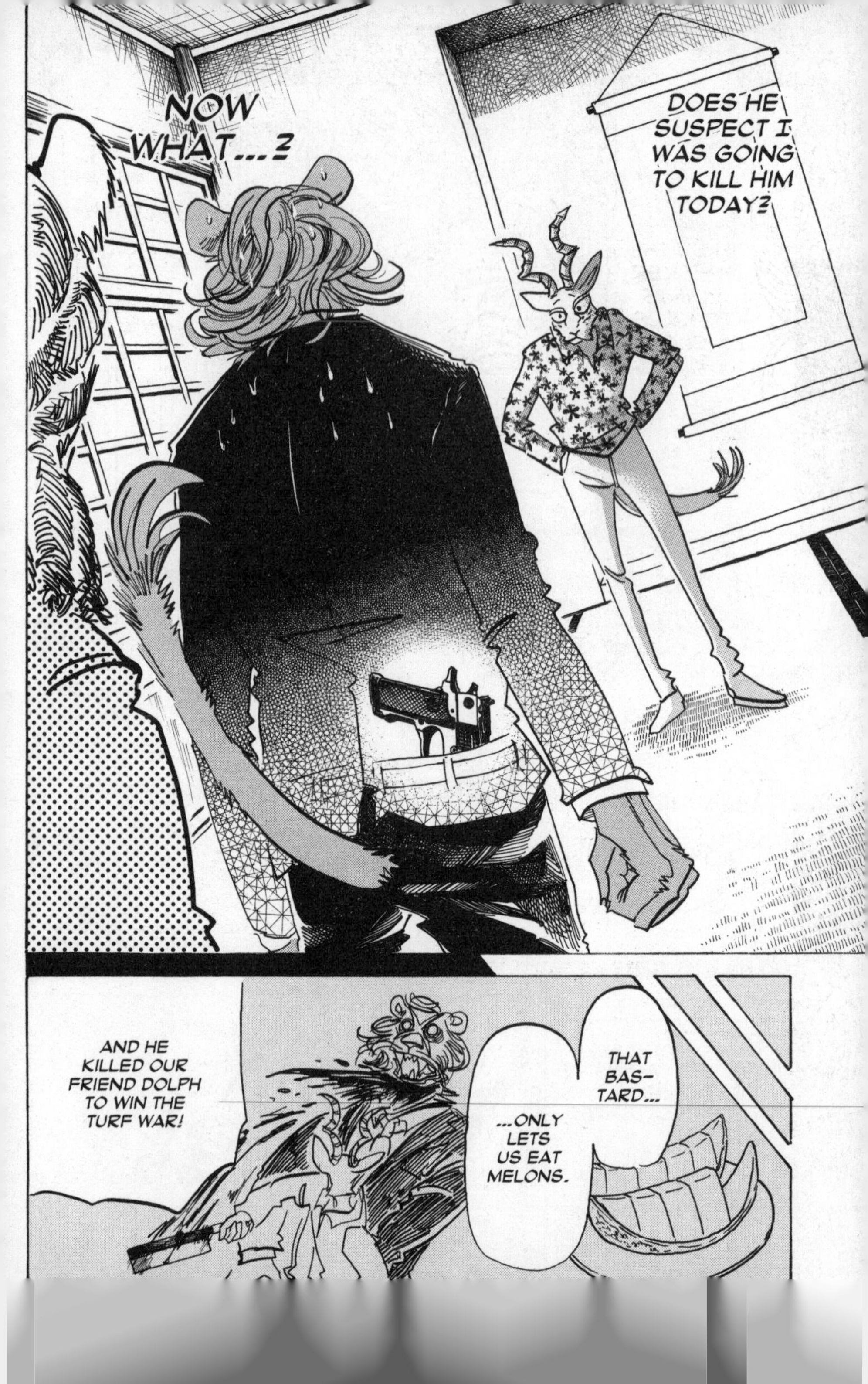

DOES HE SUSPECT I WAS GOING TO KILL HIM TODAY?
NOW WHAT...?
THAT BAS-TARD...
...ONLY LETS US EAT MELONS.
AND HE KILLED OUR FRIEND DOLPH TO WIN THE TURF WAR!

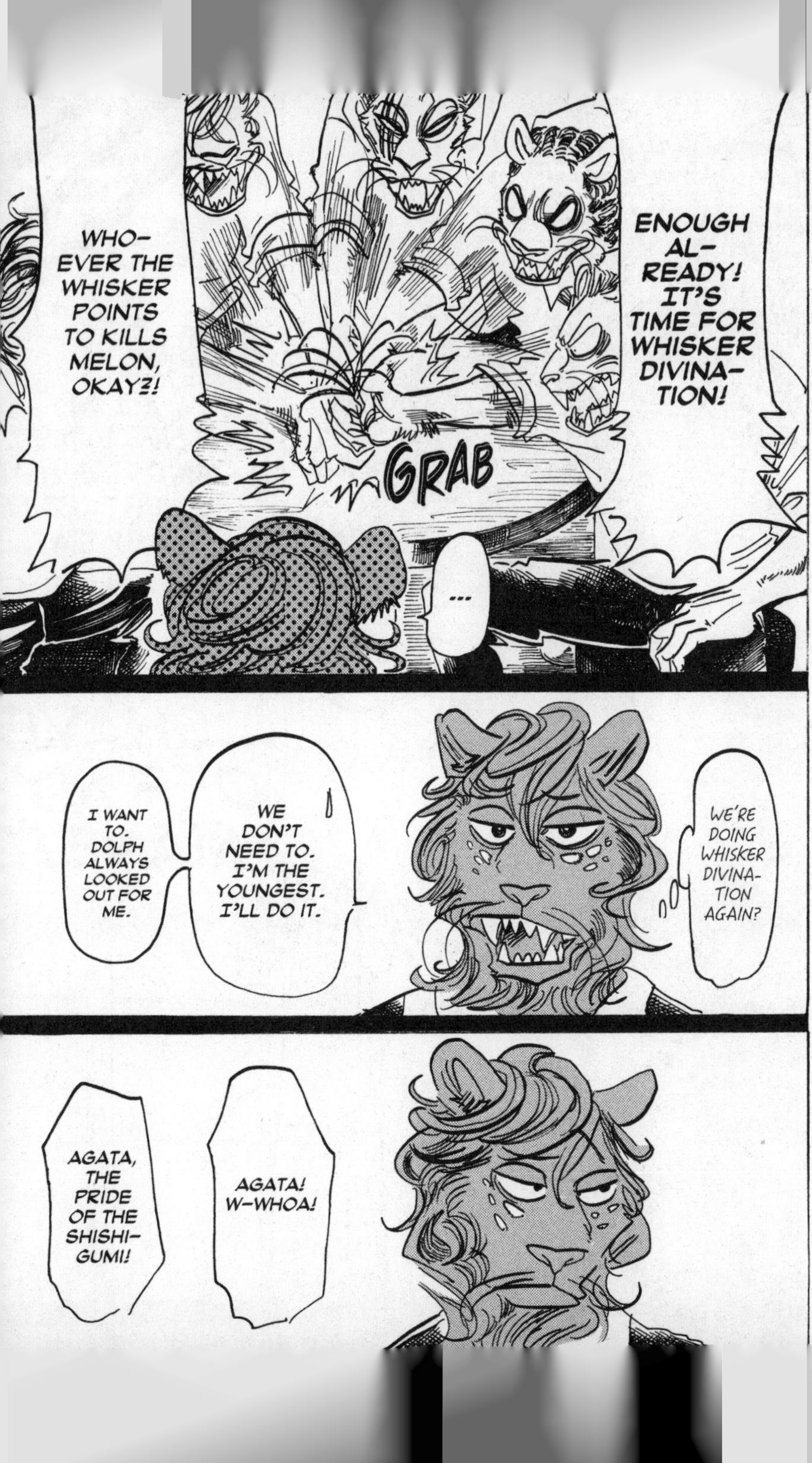
ENOUGH ALREADY! IT'S TIME FOR WHISKER DIVINATION!
WHOEVER THE WHISKER POINTS TO KILLS MELON, OKAY?!
GRAB
...
WE'RE DOING WHISKER DIVINATION AGAIN?
WE DON'T NEED TO. I'M THE YOUNGEST. I'LL DO IT.
I WANT TO. DOLPH ALWAYS LOOKED OUT FOR ME.
AGATA! W-WHOA!
AGATA, THE PRIDE OF THE SHISHI-GUMI!

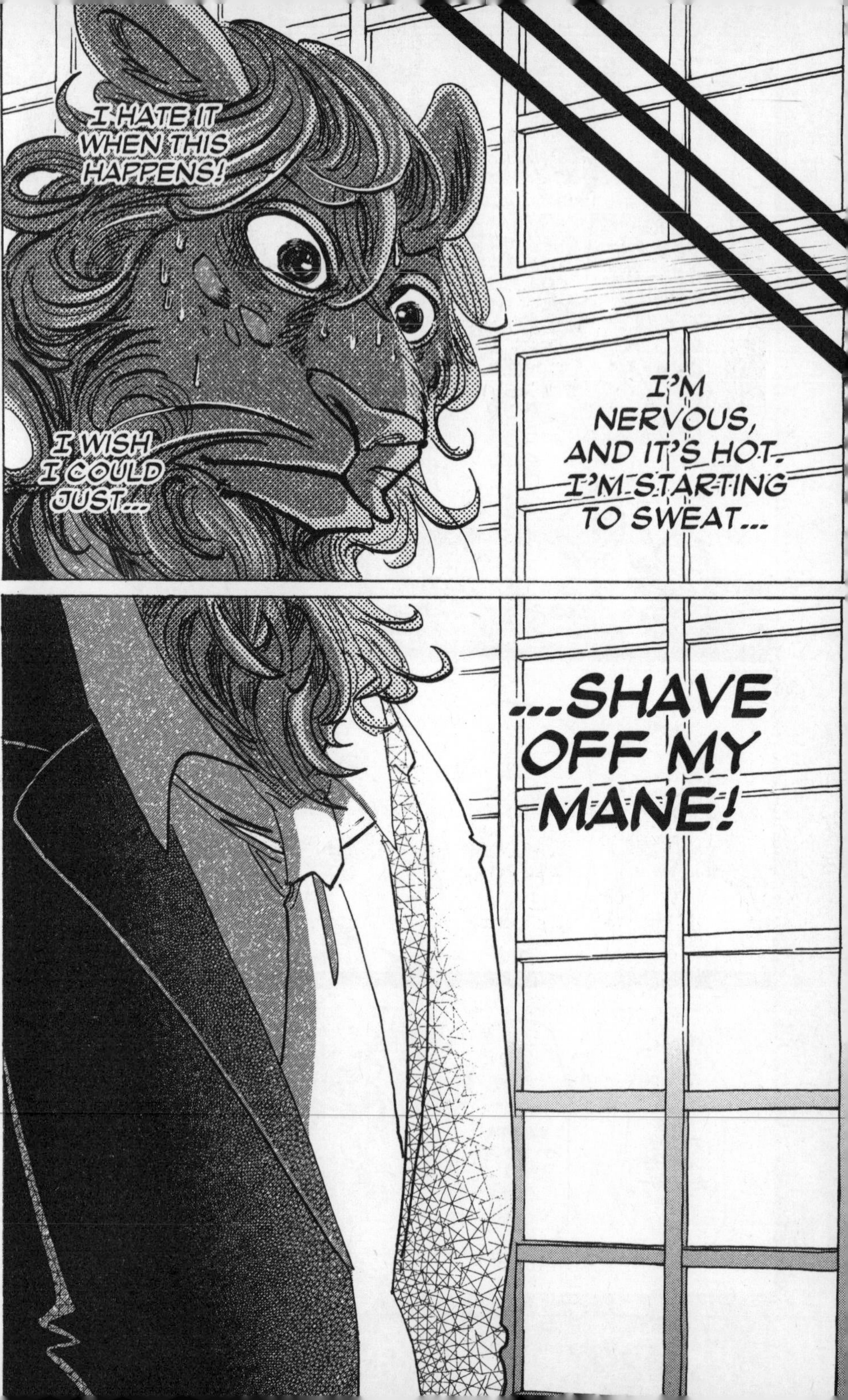
I'M NERVOUS, AND IT'S HOT. I'M STARTING TO SWEAT...
I HATE IT WHEN THIS HAPPENS!
I WISH I COULD JUST...
...SHAVE OFF MY MANE!

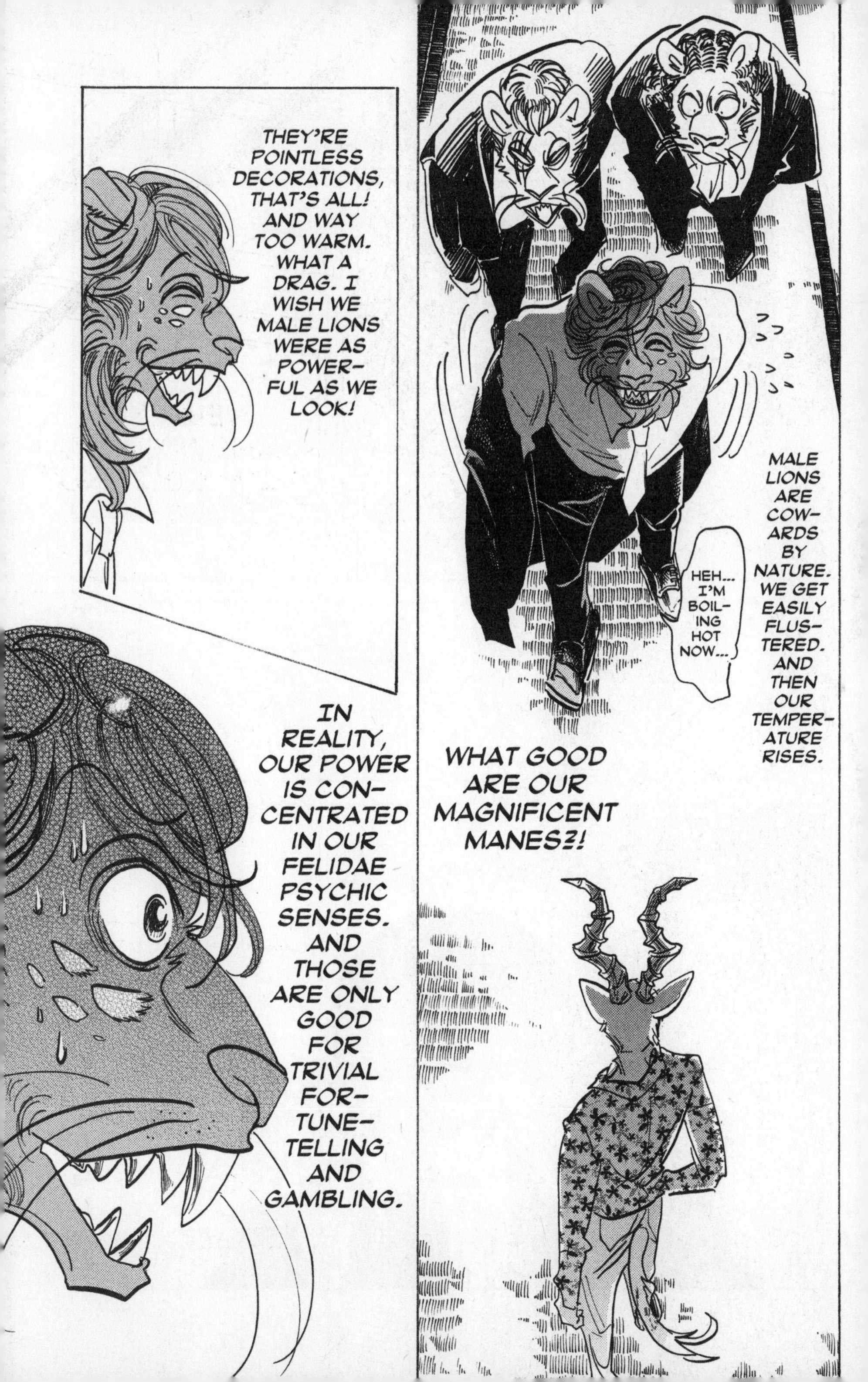
MALE LIONS ARE COWARDS BY NATURE. WE GET EASILY FLUSTERED. AND THEN OUR TEMPERATURE RISES.
HEH... I'M BOILING HOT NOW...
WHAT GOOD ARE OUR MAGNIFICENT MANES?!
THEY'RE POINTLESS DECORATIONS, THAT'S ALL! AND WAY TOO WARM. WHAT A DRAG. I WISH WE MALE LIONS WERE AS POWERFUL AS WE LOOK!
IN REALITY, OUR POWER IS CONCENTRATED IN OUR FELIDAE PSYCHIC SENSES. AND THOSE ARE ONLY GOOD FOR TRIVIAL FORTUNE-TELLING AND GAMBLING.

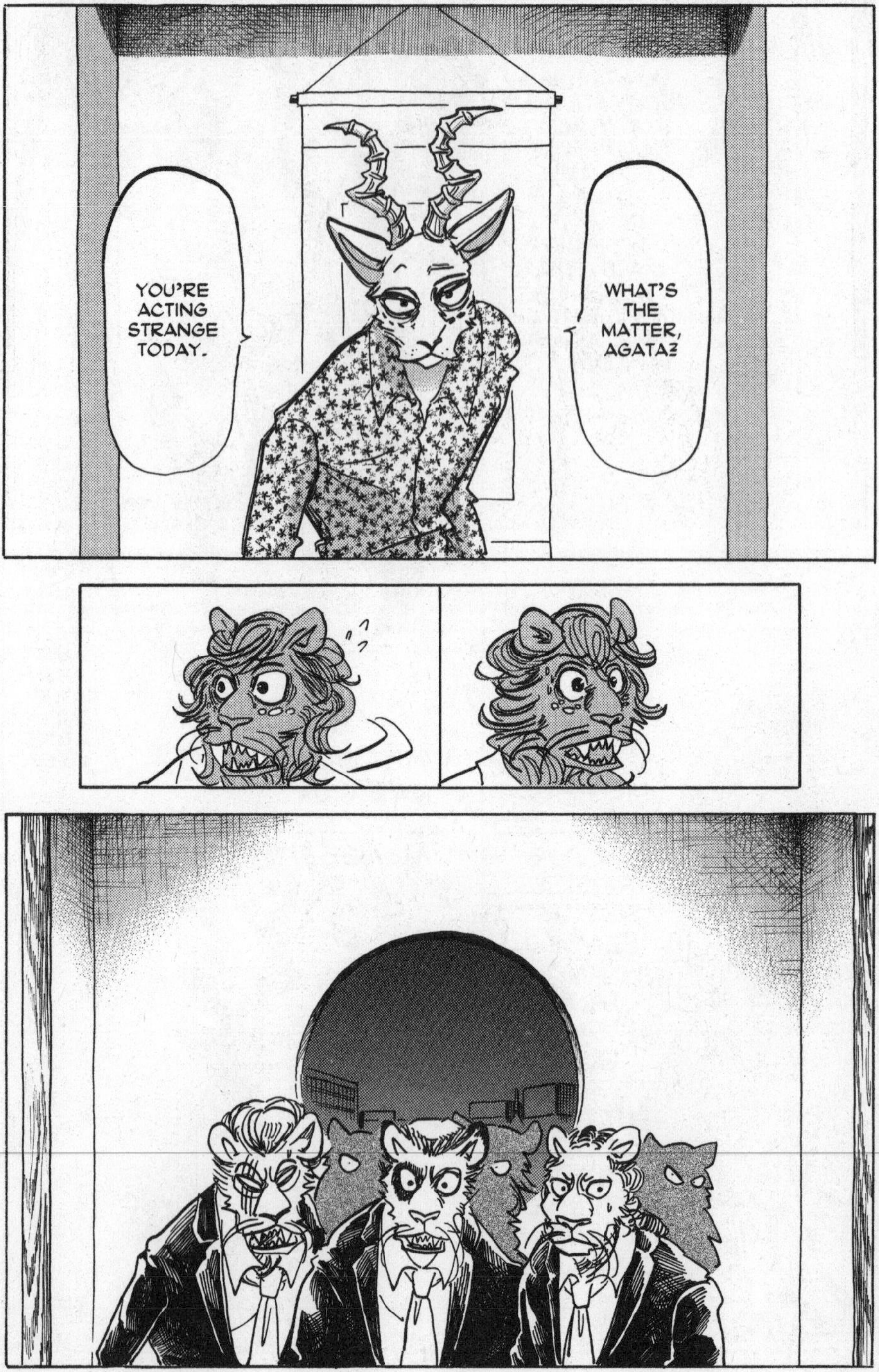
WHAT'S THE MATTER, AGATA?
YOU'RE ACTING STRANGE TODAY.

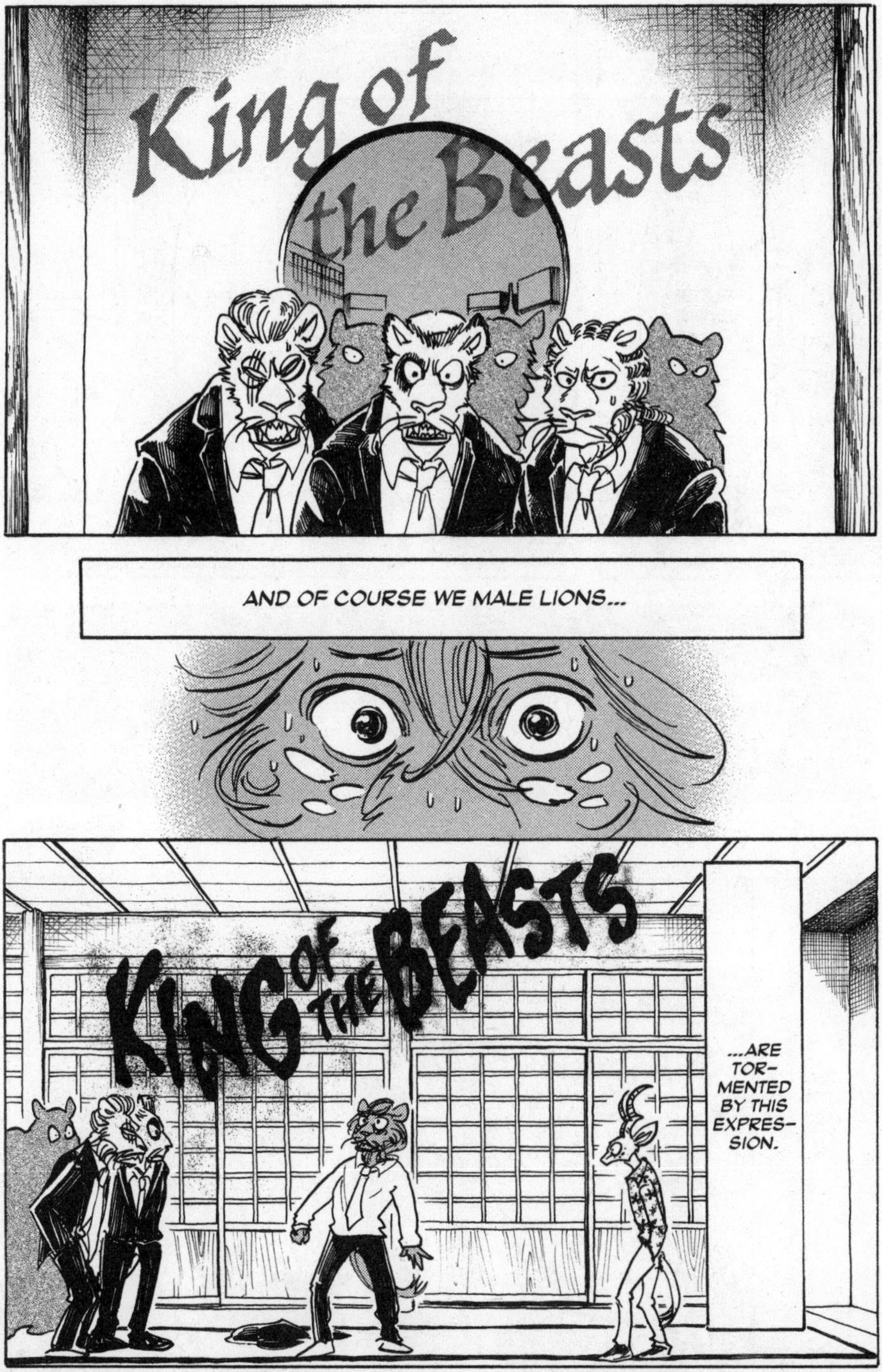
King of the Beasts
AND OF COURSE WE MALE LIONS...
KING OF THE BEASTS
...ARE TORMENTED BY THIS EXPRESSION.

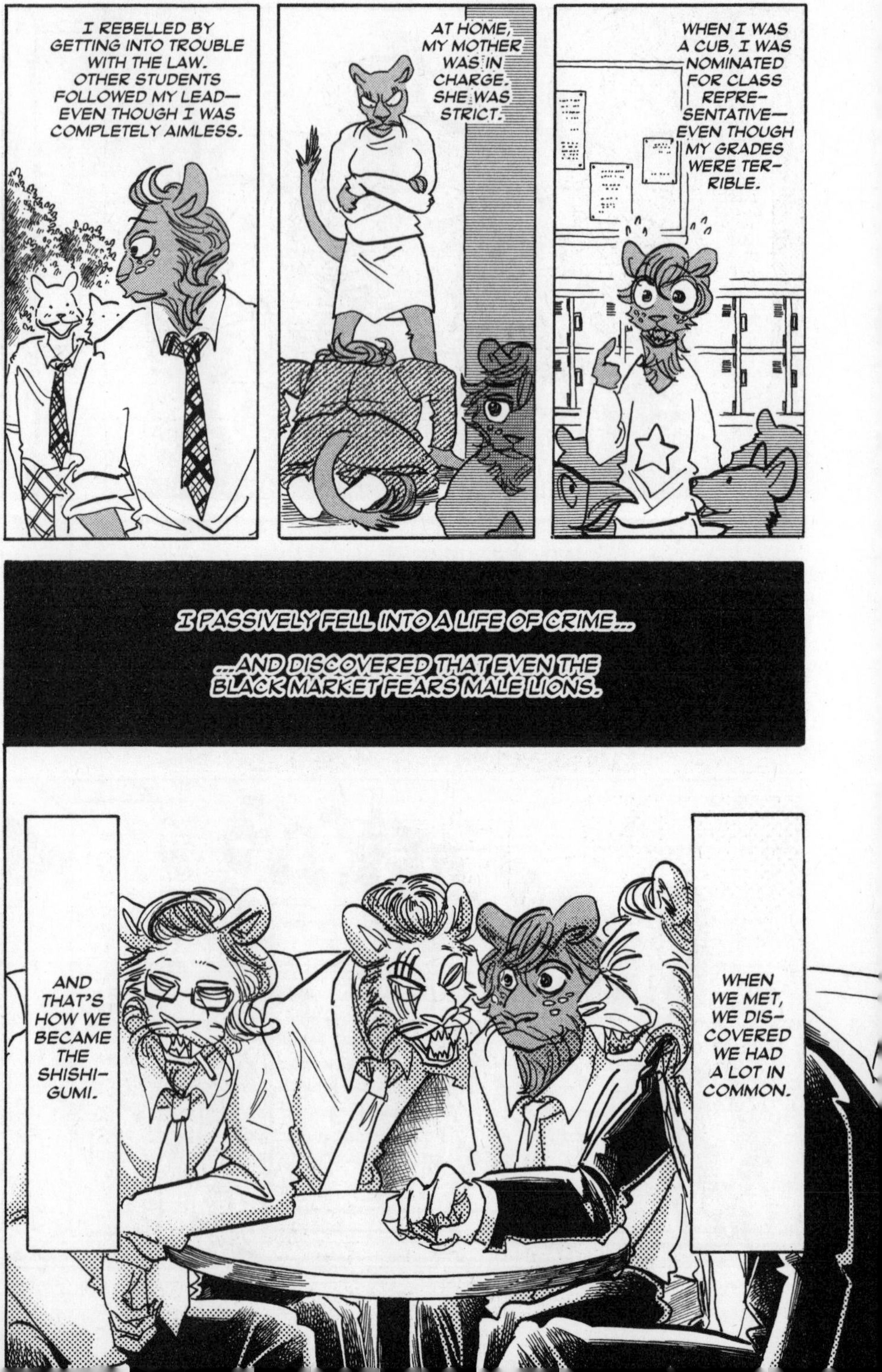
WHEN I WAS A CUB, I WAS NOMINATED FOR CLASS REPRE-SENTATIVE—EVEN THOUGH MY GRADES WERE TER-RIBLE.
AT HOME, MY MOTHER WAS IN CHARGE. SHE WAS STRICT.
I REBELLED BY GETTING INTO TROUBLE WITH THE LAW. OTHER STUDENTS FOLLOWED MY LEAD—EVEN THOUGH I WAS COMPLETELY AIMLESS.
I PASSIVELY FELL INTO A LIFE OF CRIME...
...AND DISCOVERED THAT EVEN THE BLACK MARKET FEARS MALE LIONS.
WHEN WE MET, WE DIS-COVERED WE HAD A LOT IN COMMON.
AND THAT'S HOW WE BECAME THE SHISHI-GUMI.

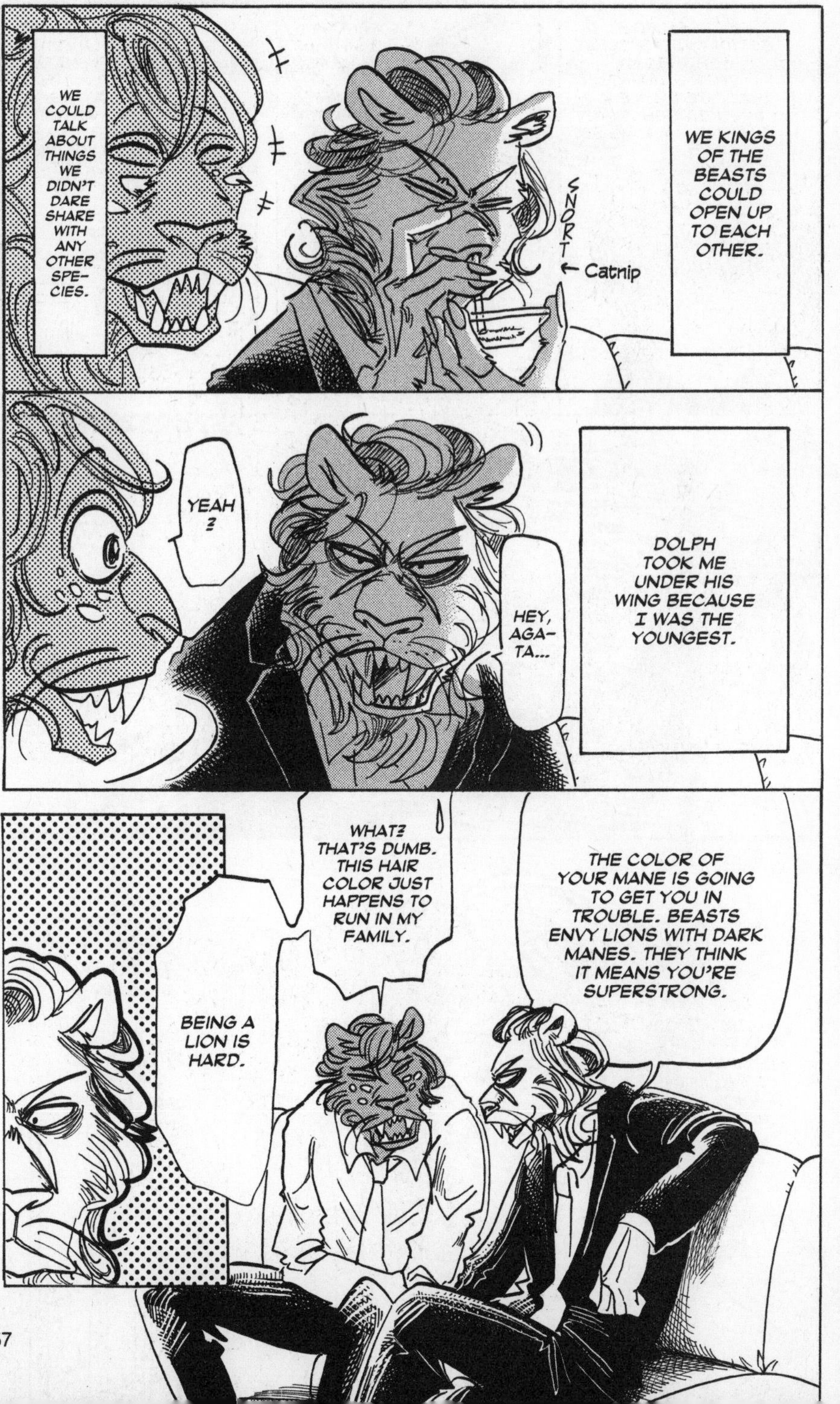
WE KINGS OF THE BEASTS COULD OPEN UP TO EACH OTHER.
SNORT
← Catnip
WE COULD TALK ABOUT THINGS WE DIDN'T DARE SHARE WITH ANY OTHER SPE-CIES.
DOLPH TOOK ME UNDER HIS WING BECAUSE I WAS THE YOUNGEST.
HEY, AGA-TA...
YEAH?
THE COLOR OF YOUR MANE IS GOING TO GET YOU IN TROUBLE. BEASTS ENVY LIONS WITH DARK MANES. THEY THINK IT MEANS YOU'RE SUPERSTRONG.
WHAT? THAT'S DUMB. THIS HAIR COLOR JUST HAPPENS TO RUN IN MY FAMILY.
BEING A LION IS HARD.

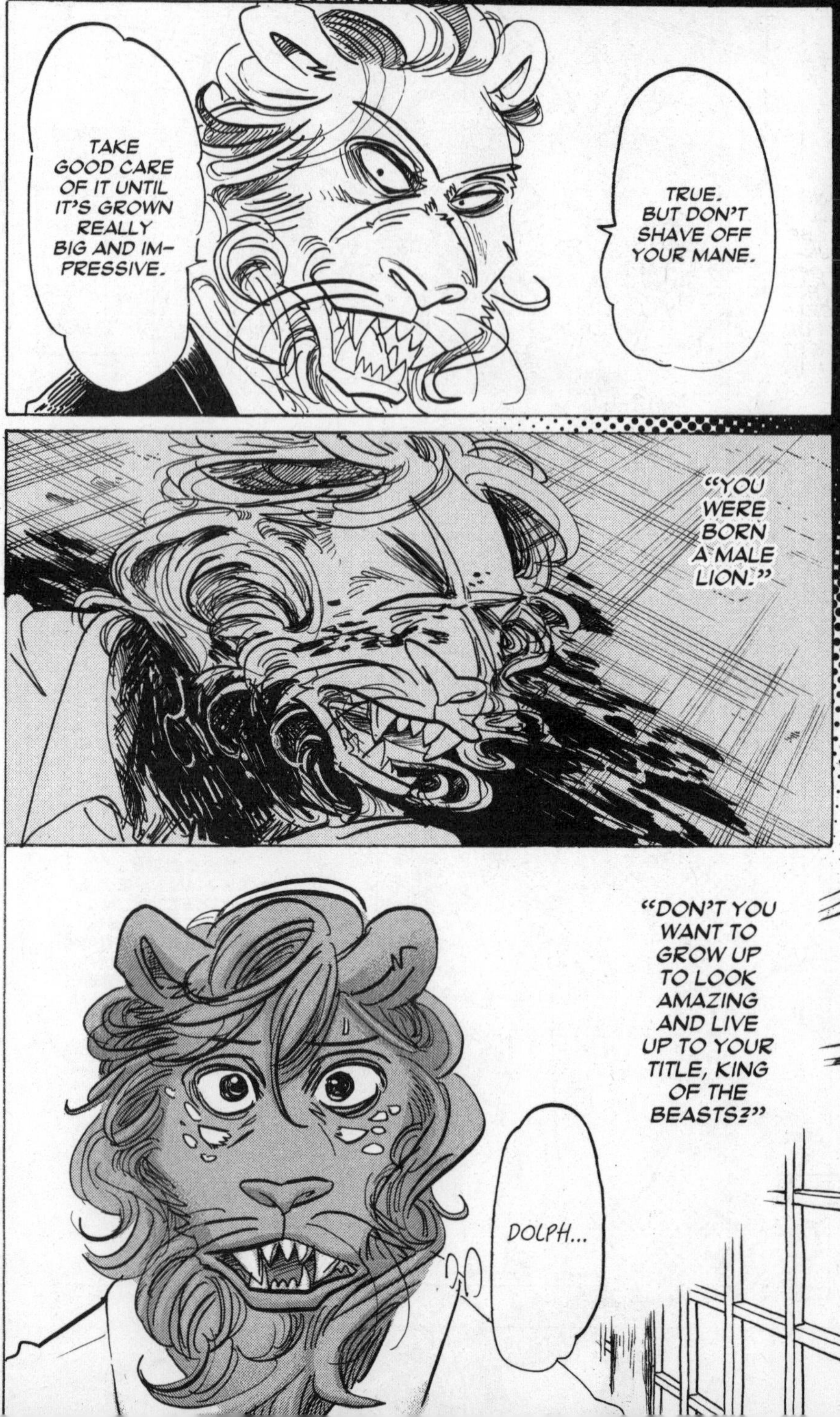
TRUE. BUT DON'T SHAVE OFF YOUR MANE.
TAKE GOOD CARE OF IT UNTIL IT'S GROWN REALLY BIG AND IM-PRESSIVE.
"YOU WERE BORN A MALE LION."
"DON'T YOU WANT TO GROW UP TO LOOK AMAZING AND LIVE UP TO YOUR TITLE, KING OF THE BEASTS?"
DOLPH...

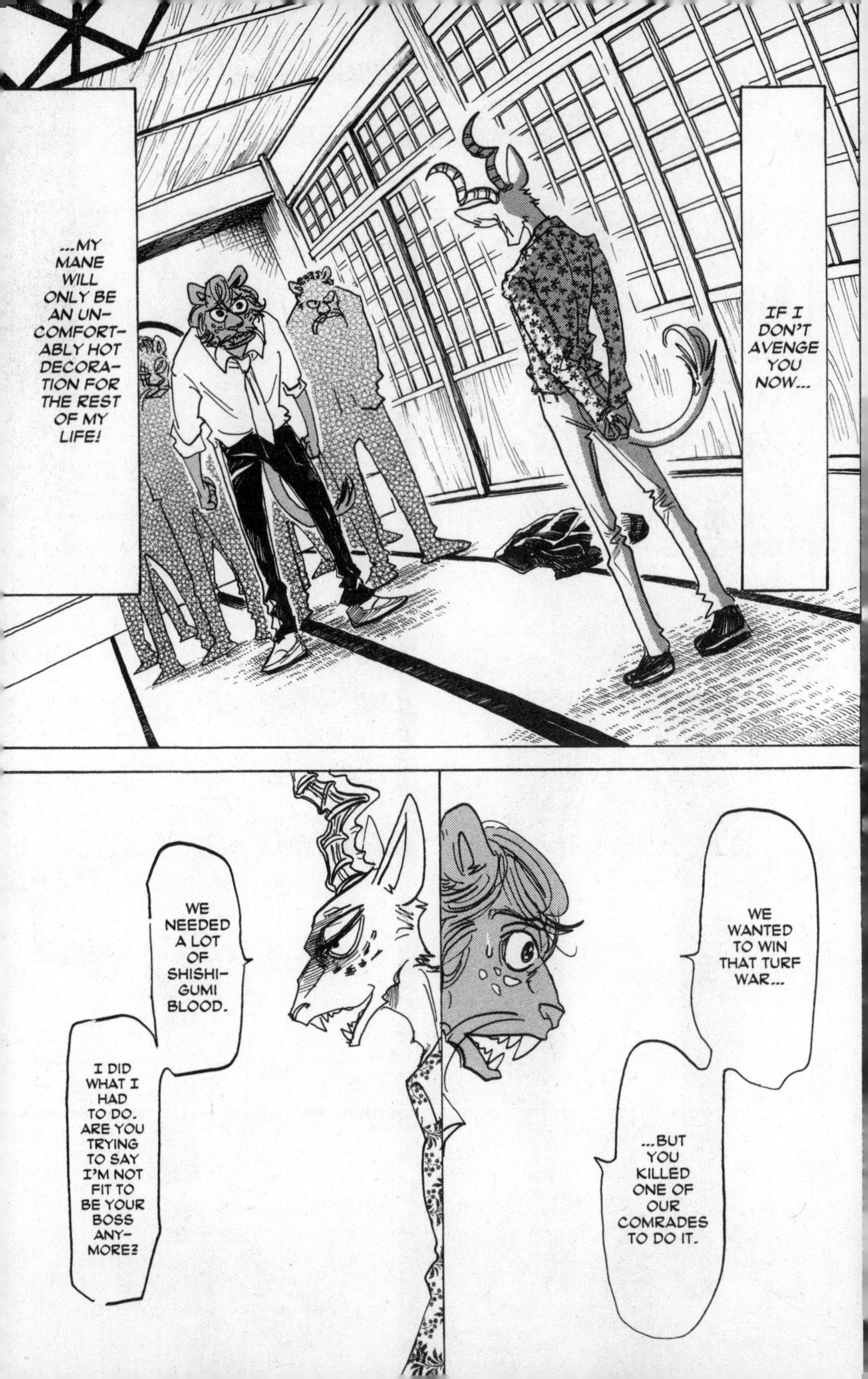
IF I DON'T AVENGE YOU NOW...
...MY MANE WILL ONLY BE AN UN-COMFORT-ABLY HOT DECORA-TION FOR THE REST OF MY LIFE!
WE WANTED TO WIN THAT TURF WAR...
...BUT YOU KILLED ONE OF OUR COMRADES TO DO IT.
WE NEEDED A LOT OF SHISHI-GUMI BLOOD.
I DID WHAT I HAD TO DO. ARE YOU TRYING TO SAY I'M NOT FIT TO BE YOUR BOSS ANY-MORE?

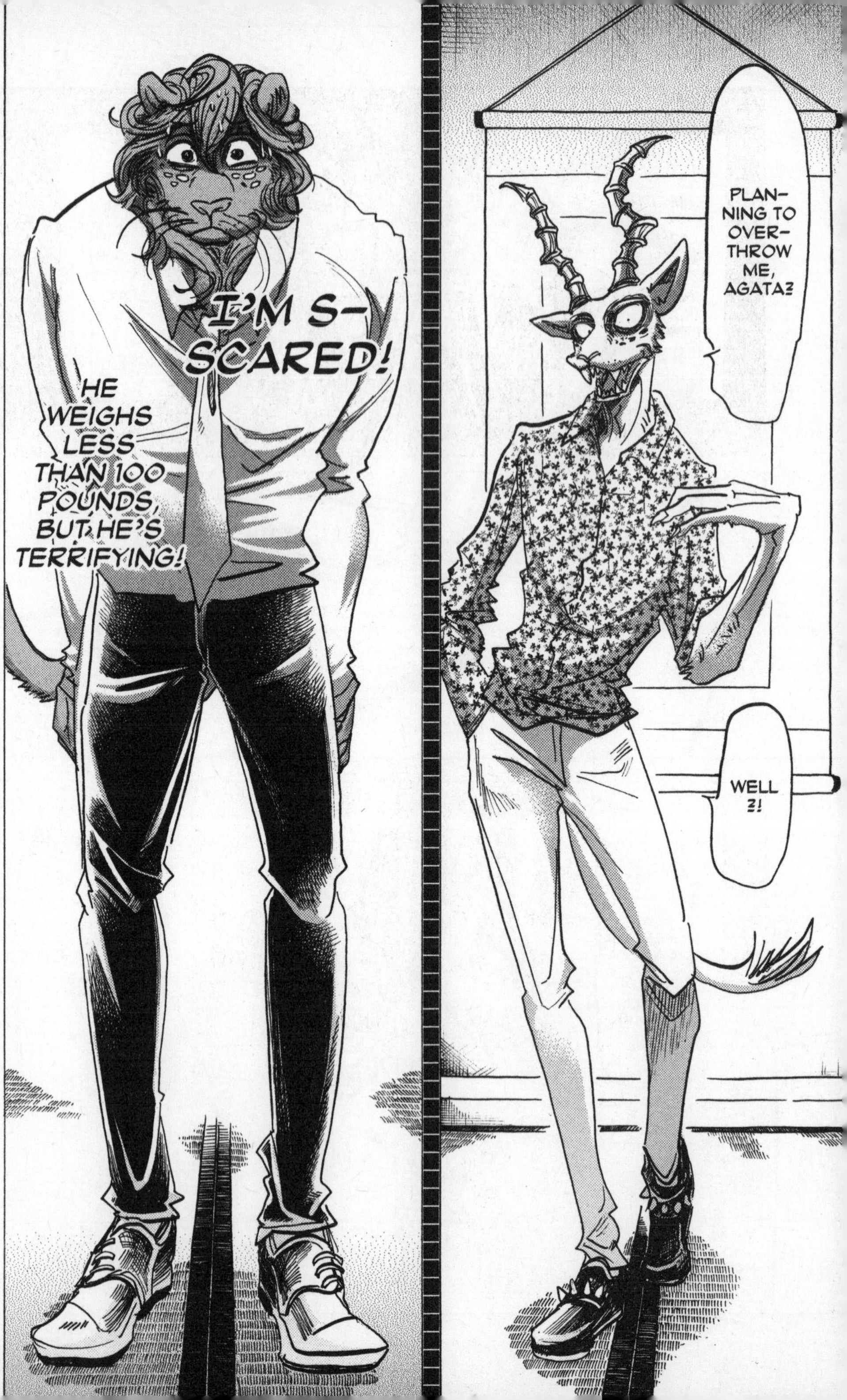
PLAN-NING TO OVER-THROW ME, AGATA?
WELL ?!
I'M S-SCARED!
HE WEIGHS LESS THAN 100 POUNDS, BUT HE'S TERRIFYING!

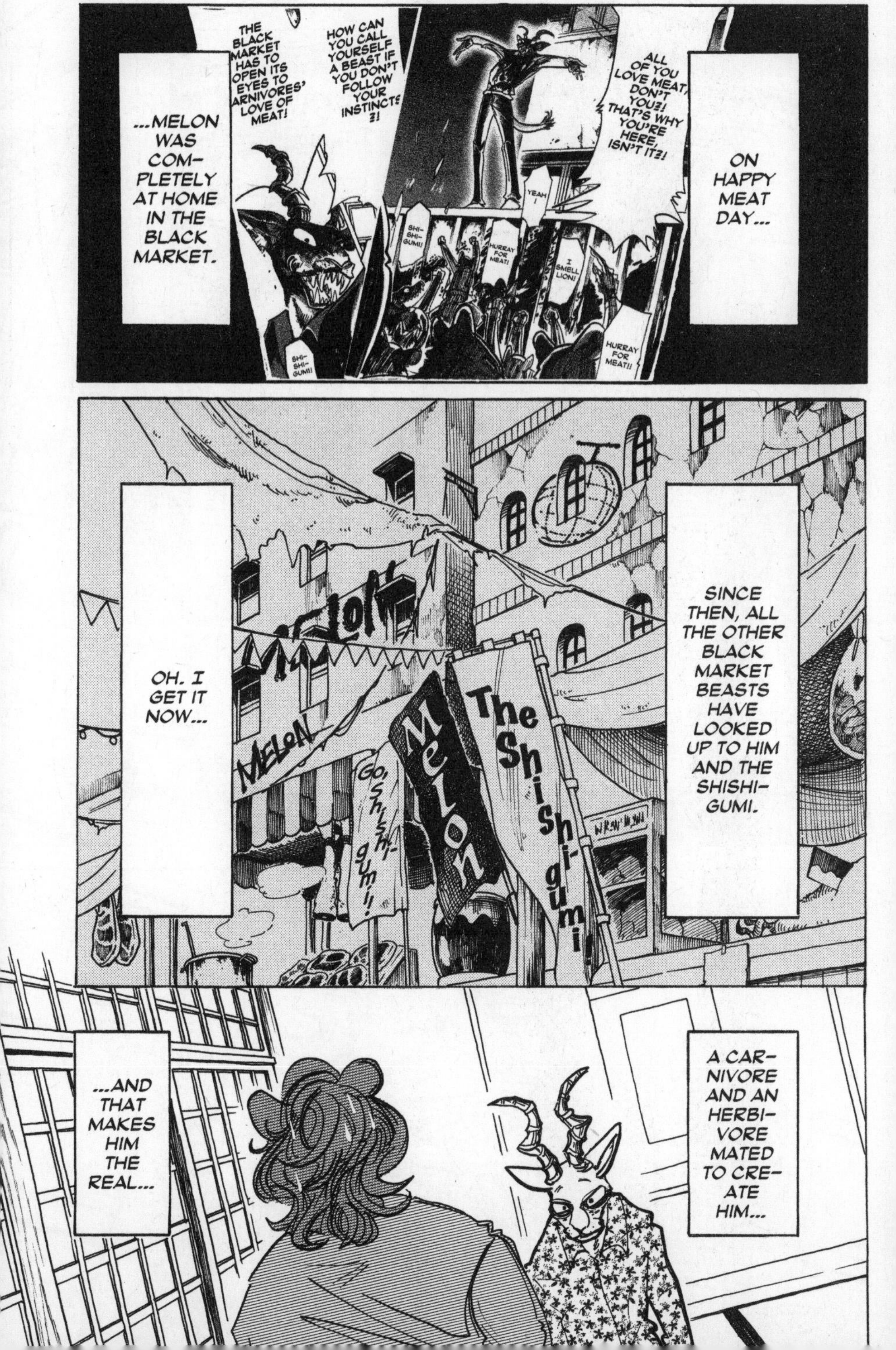
ON HAPPY MEAT DAY...
ALL OF YOU LOVE MEAT, DON'T YOU?! THAT'S WHY YOU'RE HERE, ISN'T IT?!
HOW CAN YOU CALL YOURSELF A BEAST IF YOU DON'T FOLLOW YOUR INSTINCTS?!
THE BLACK MARKET HAS TO OPEN ITS EYES TO ARNIVORES' LOVE OF MEAT!
YEAH!
I SMELL LION!
HURRAY FOR MEAT!
SHI-SHI-GUMI!
HURRAY FOR MEAT!!
SHI-SHI-GUMI!
...MELON WAS COMPLETELY AT HOME IN THE BLACK MARKET.
SINCE THEN, ALL THE OTHER BLACK MARKET BEASTS HAVE LOOKED UP TO HIM AND THE SHISHI-GUMI.
The Shishi-gumi
Melon
Go, Shishi-gumi!!
MELON
OH. I GET IT NOW...
A CARNIVORE AND AN HERBIVORE MATED TO CREATE HIM...
...AND THAT MAKES HIM THE REAL...

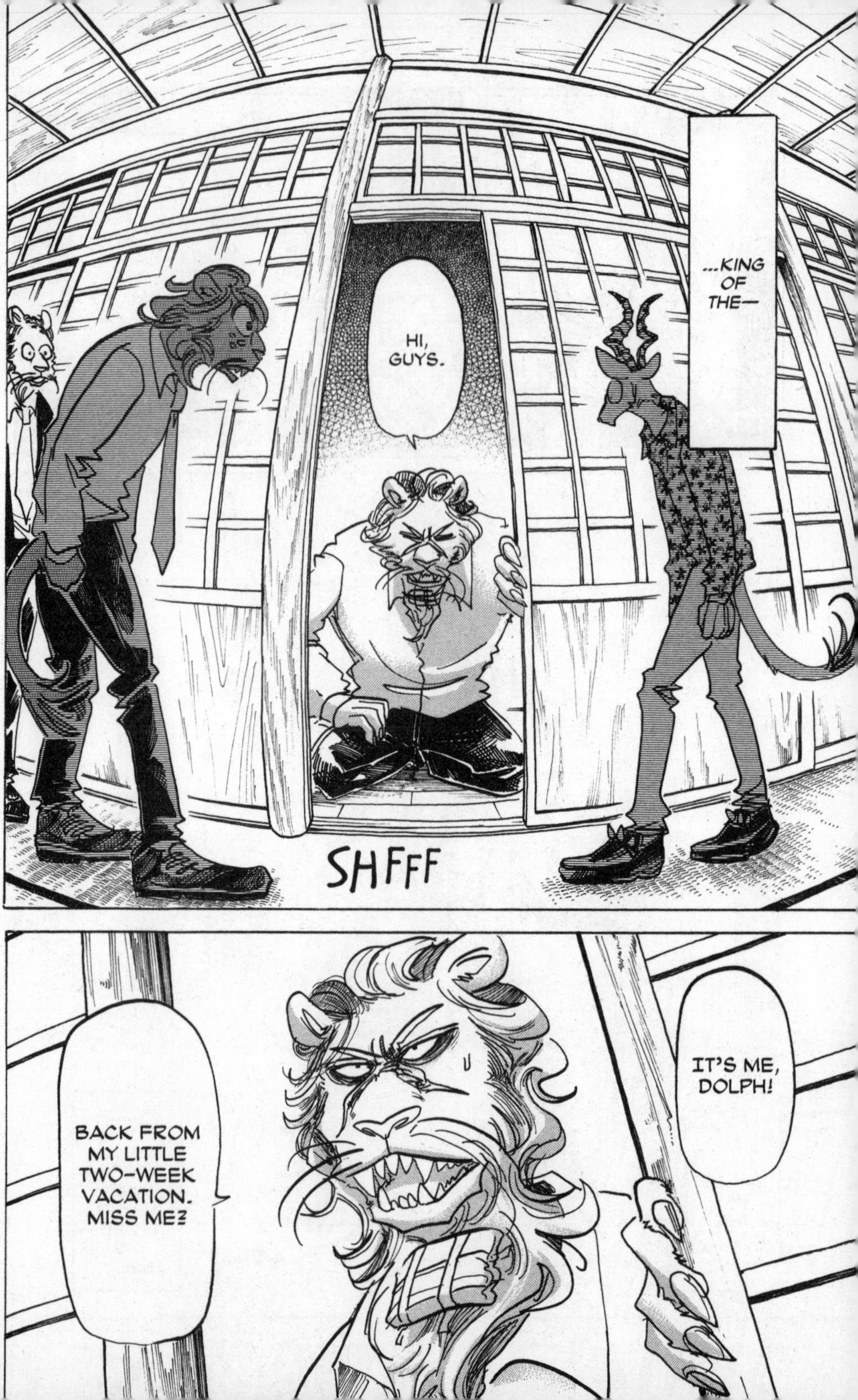
...KING OF THE—
HI, GUYS.
SHFFF
IT'S ME, DOLPH!
BACK FROM MY LITTLE TWO-WEEK VACATION. MISS ME?

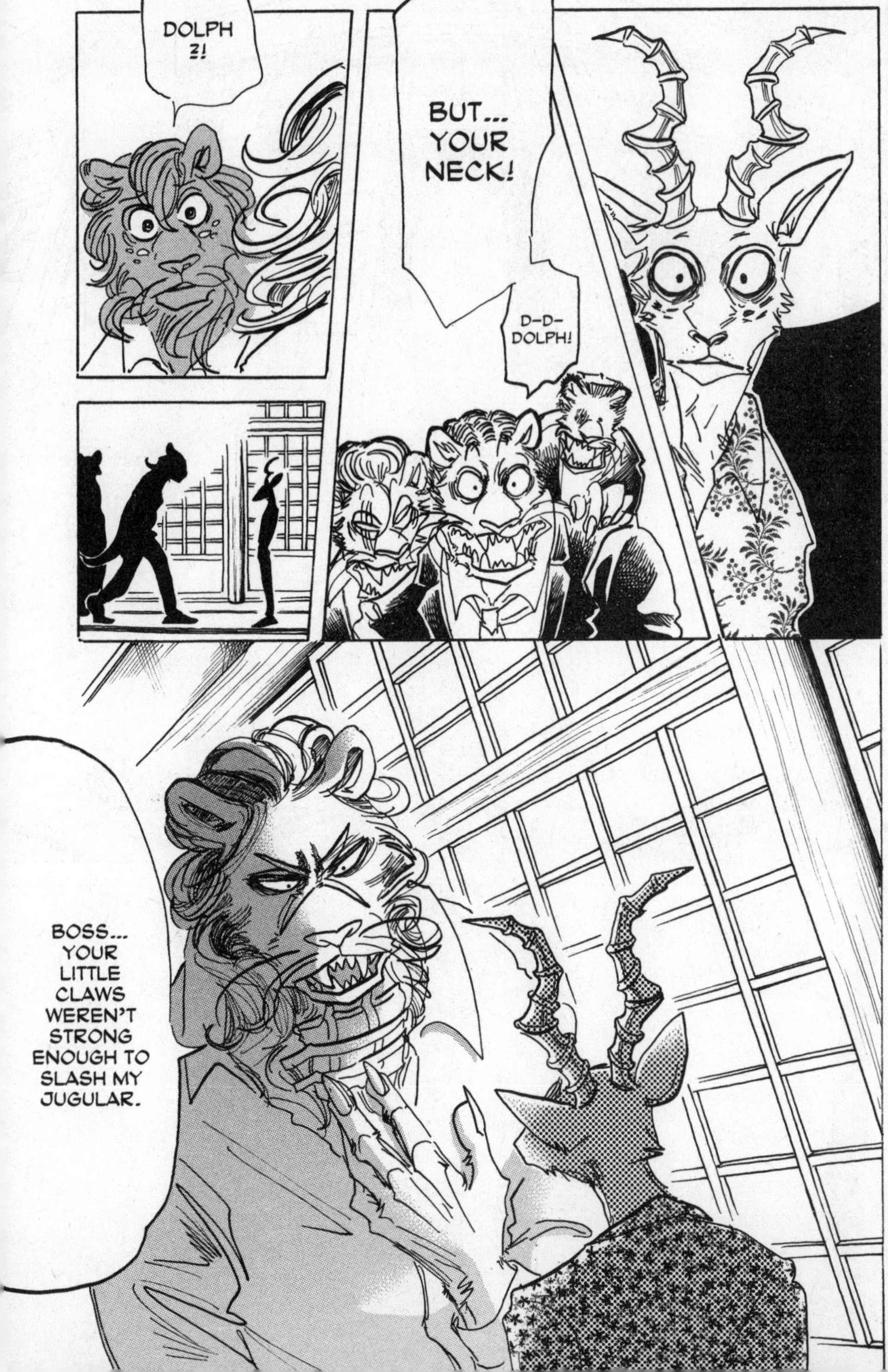
BUT... YOUR NECK!
D-D-DOLPH!
DOLPH?!
BOSS... YOUR LITTLE CLAWS WEREN'T STRONG ENOUGH TO SLASH MY JUGULAR.

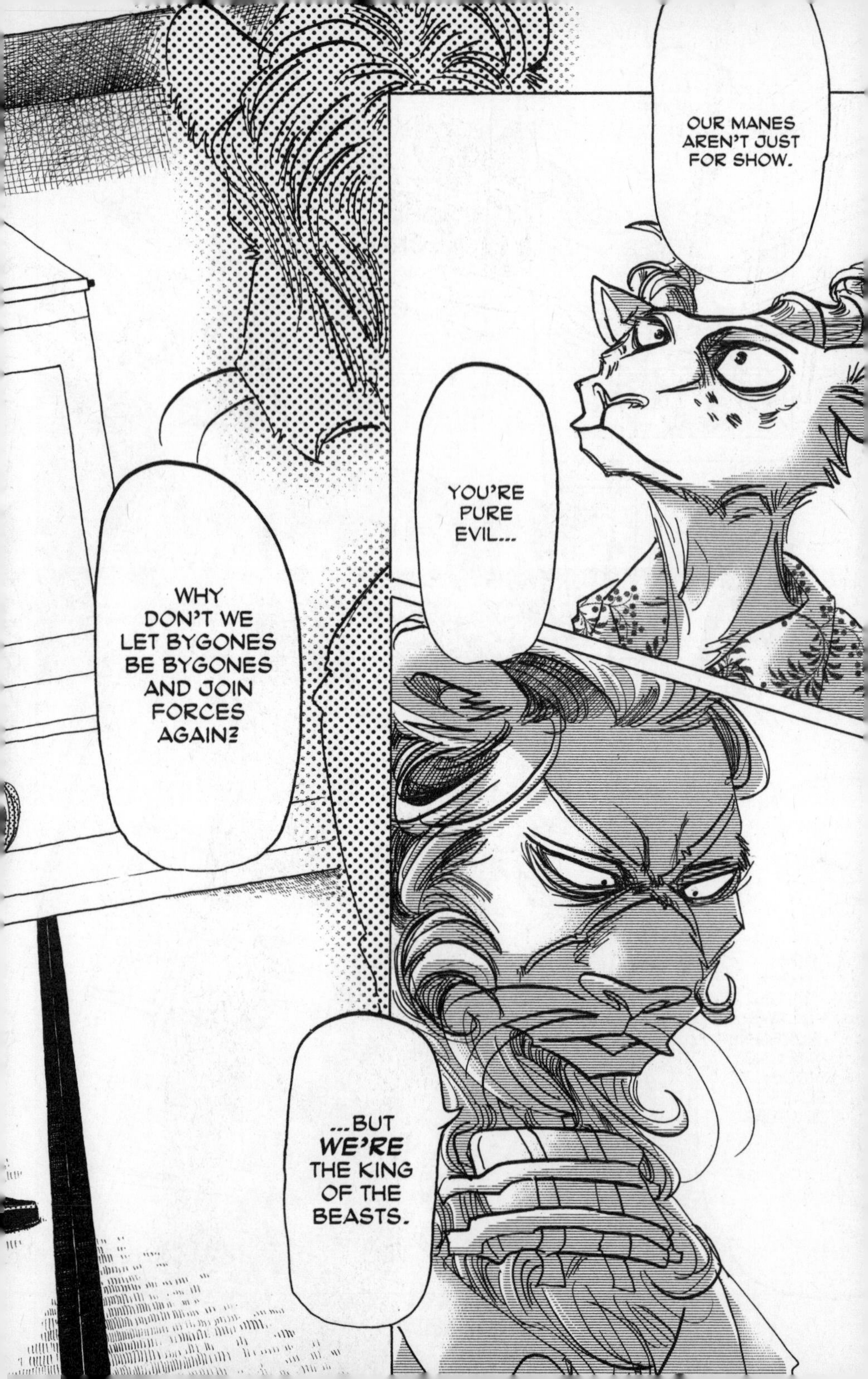
OUR MANES AREN'T JUST FOR SHOW.
YOU'RE PURE EVIL...
...BUT ***WE'RE*** THE KING OF THE BEASTS.
WHY DON'T WE LET BYGONES BE BYGONES AND JOIN FORCES AGAIN?

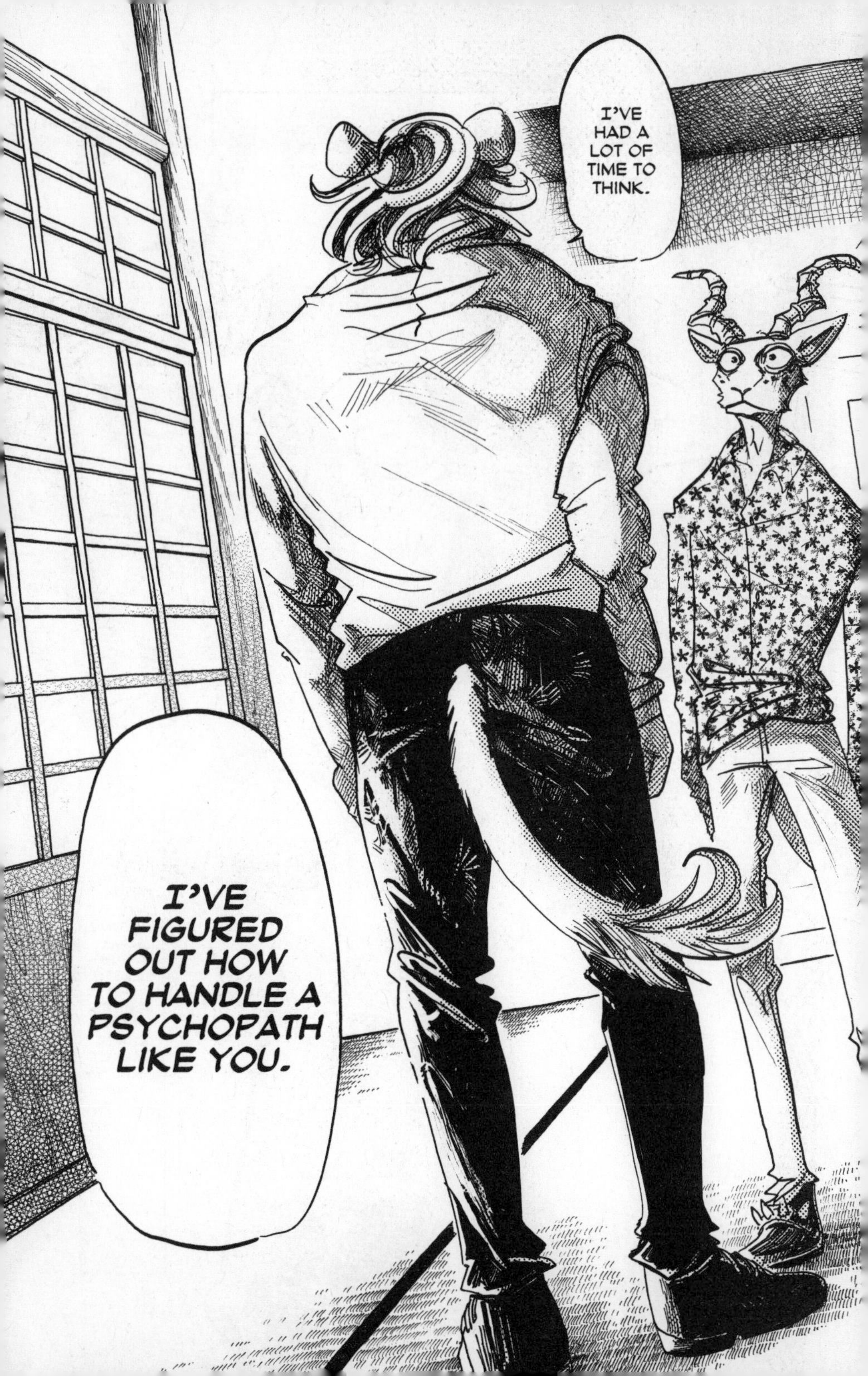
I'VE HAD A LOT OF TIME TO THINK.
I'VE FIGURED OUT HOW TO HANDLE A PSYCHOPATH LIKE YOU.

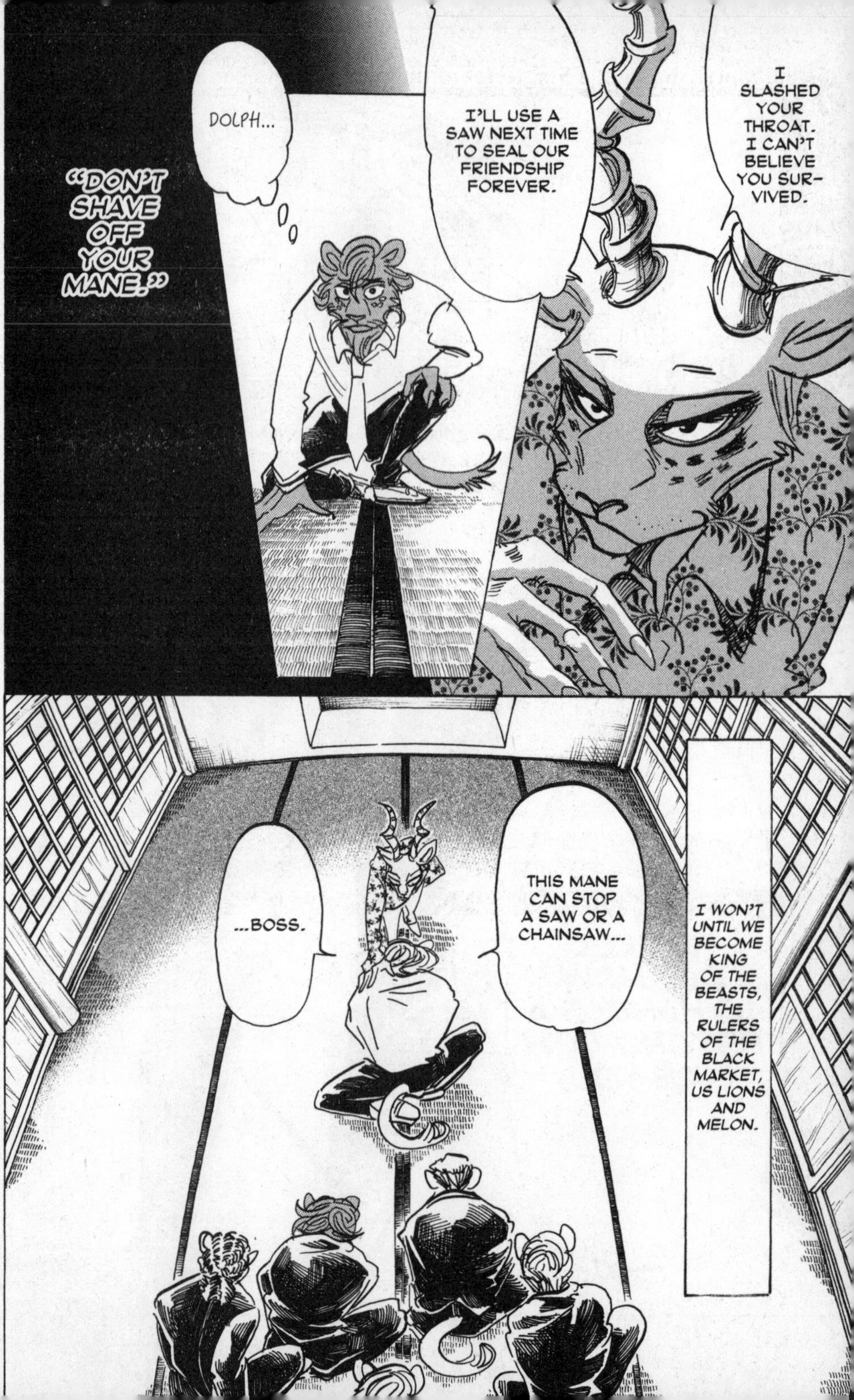
I SLASHED YOUR THROAT. I CAN'T BELIEVE YOU SURVIVED.
I'LL USE A SAW NEXT TIME TO SEAL OUR FRIENDSHIP FOREVER.
DOLPH...
"DON'T SHAVE OFF YOUR MANE."
I WON'T UNTIL WE BECOME KING OF THE BEASTS, THE RULERS OF THE BLACK MARKET, US LIONS AND MELON.
THIS MANE CAN STOP A SAW OR A CHAINSAW...
...BOSS.

Chapter 164: Just a Single Teardrop from Asura Is Enough

WHY DO I KEEP SELLING OUT OF MELONS LATELY?
Akita Shopping Street Vegetable Shop Owner
Melons Sold Out!
We don't know when the next shipment will arrive.
Spinach 177
197
Tomatoes 87 each
Spring onions 177
This has never happened before. Just melons. I can't get enough of them.
BEASTS KEEP ORDERING MELON PARFAITS...
Fruit Shack Employee
Melon Parfait
SOLD OUT!
These days, melon parfaits and melon cakes sell out before noon. However, only carnivores order them.
A MYSTERIOUS NEW EXPRESSION IS ALL THE RAGE WITH HIGH SCHOOL STUDENTS.
Students on Center Street
NEW ALBUM!
"Melo Melo Melooon!" That's how carnivores greet each other nowadays.

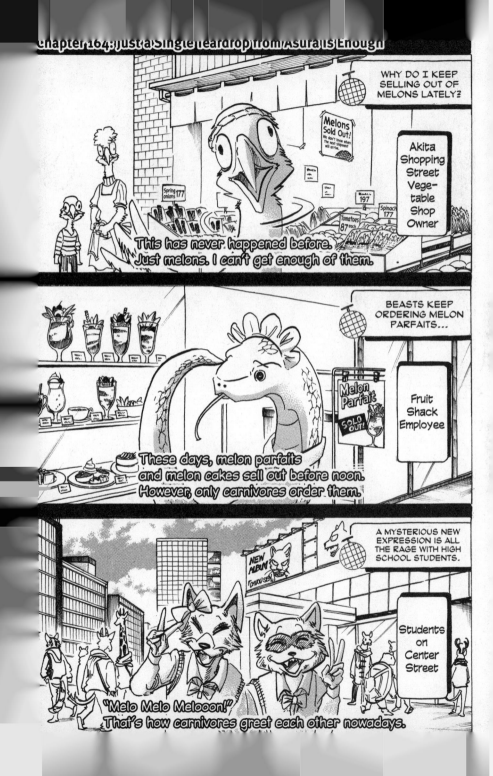

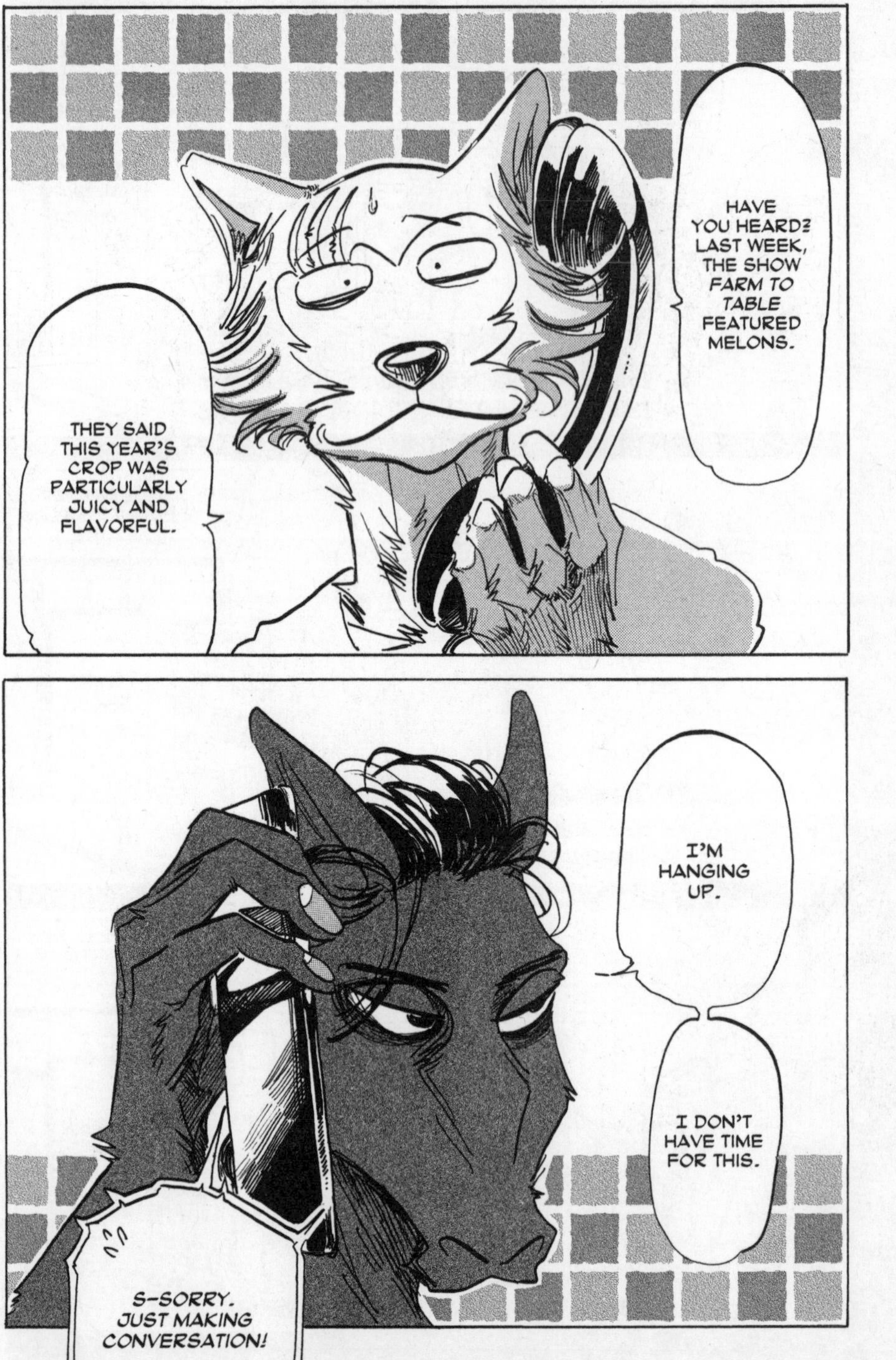
HAVE YOU HEARD? LAST WEEK, THE SHOW *FARM TO TABLE* FEATURED MELONS.
THEY SAID THIS YEAR'S CROP WAS PARTICULARLY JUICY AND FLAVORFUL.
I'M HANGING UP.
I DON'T HAVE TIME FOR THIS.
S-SORRY. JUST MAKING CONVERSATION!

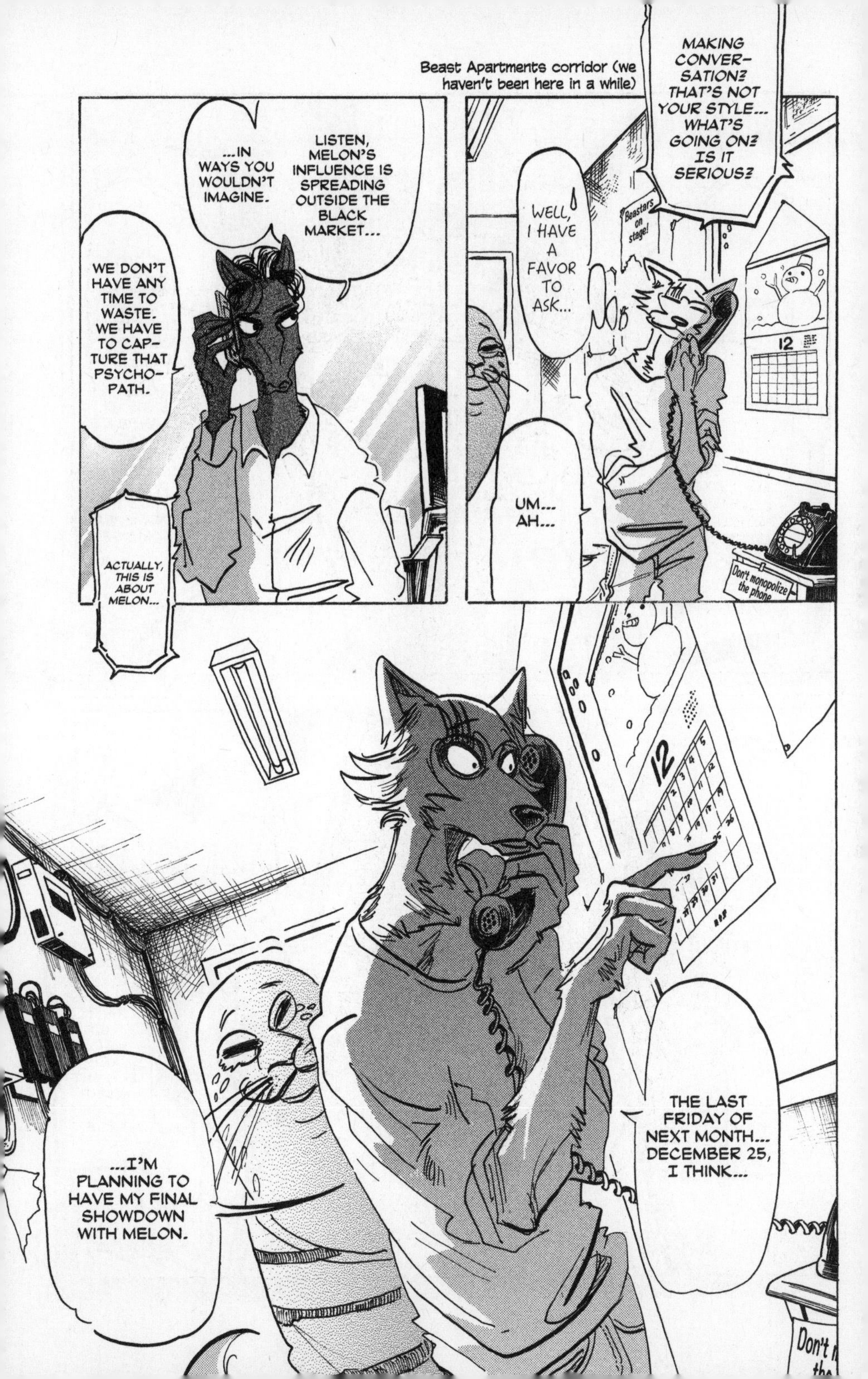
Beast Apartments corridor (we haven't been here in a while)
MAKING CONVER-SATION? THAT'S NOT YOUR STYLE... WHAT'S GOING ON? IS IT SERIOUS?
Beastars on stage!
WELL, I HAVE A FAVOR TO ASK...
UM... AH...
Don't monopolize the phone
LISTEN, MELON'S INFLUENCE IS SPREADING OUTSIDE THE BLACK MARKET...
...IN WAYS YOU WOULDN'T IMAGINE.
WE DON'T HAVE ANY TIME TO WASTE. WE HAVE TO CAP-TURE THAT PSYCHO-PATH.
ACTUALLY, THIS IS ABOUT MELON...
THE LAST FRIDAY OF NEXT MONTH... DECEMBER 25, I THINK...
...I'M PLANNING TO HAVE MY FINAL SHOWDOWN WITH MELON.

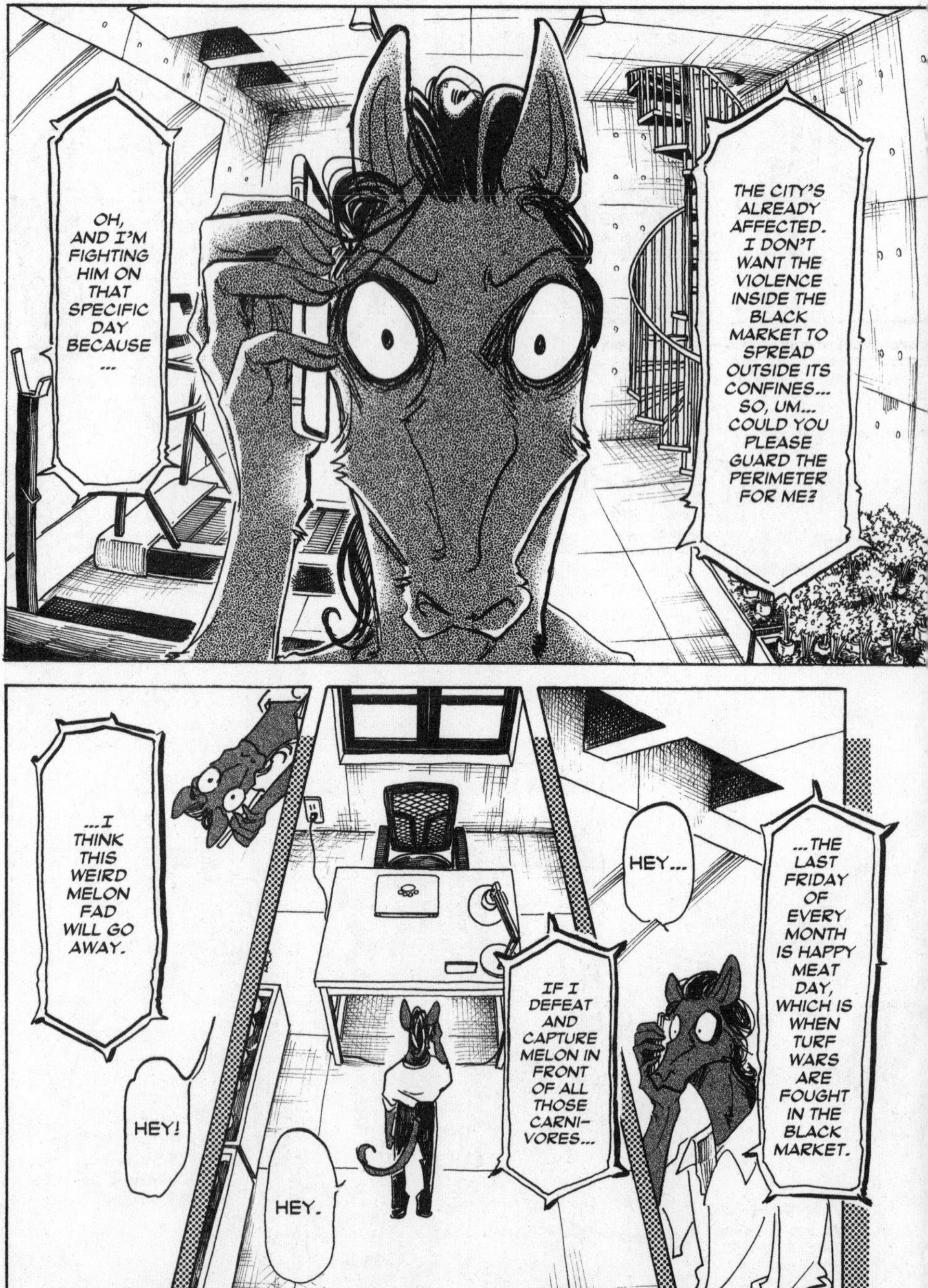
THE CITY'S ALREADY AFFECTED. I DON'T WANT THE VIOLENCE INSIDE THE BLACK MARKET TO SPREAD OUTSIDE ITS CONFINES... SO, UM... COULD YOU PLEASE GUARD THE PERIMETER FOR ME?
OH, AND I'M FIGHTING HIM ON THAT SPECIFIC DAY BECAUSE ...
...THE LAST FRIDAY OF EVERY MONTH IS HAPPY MEAT DAY, WHICH IS WHEN TURF WARS ARE FOUGHT IN THE BLACK MARKET.
HEY...
IF I DEFEAT AND CAPTURE MELON IN FRONT OF ALL THOSE CARNI-VORES...
HEY.
HEY!
...I THINK THIS WEIRD MELON FAD WILL GO AWAY.

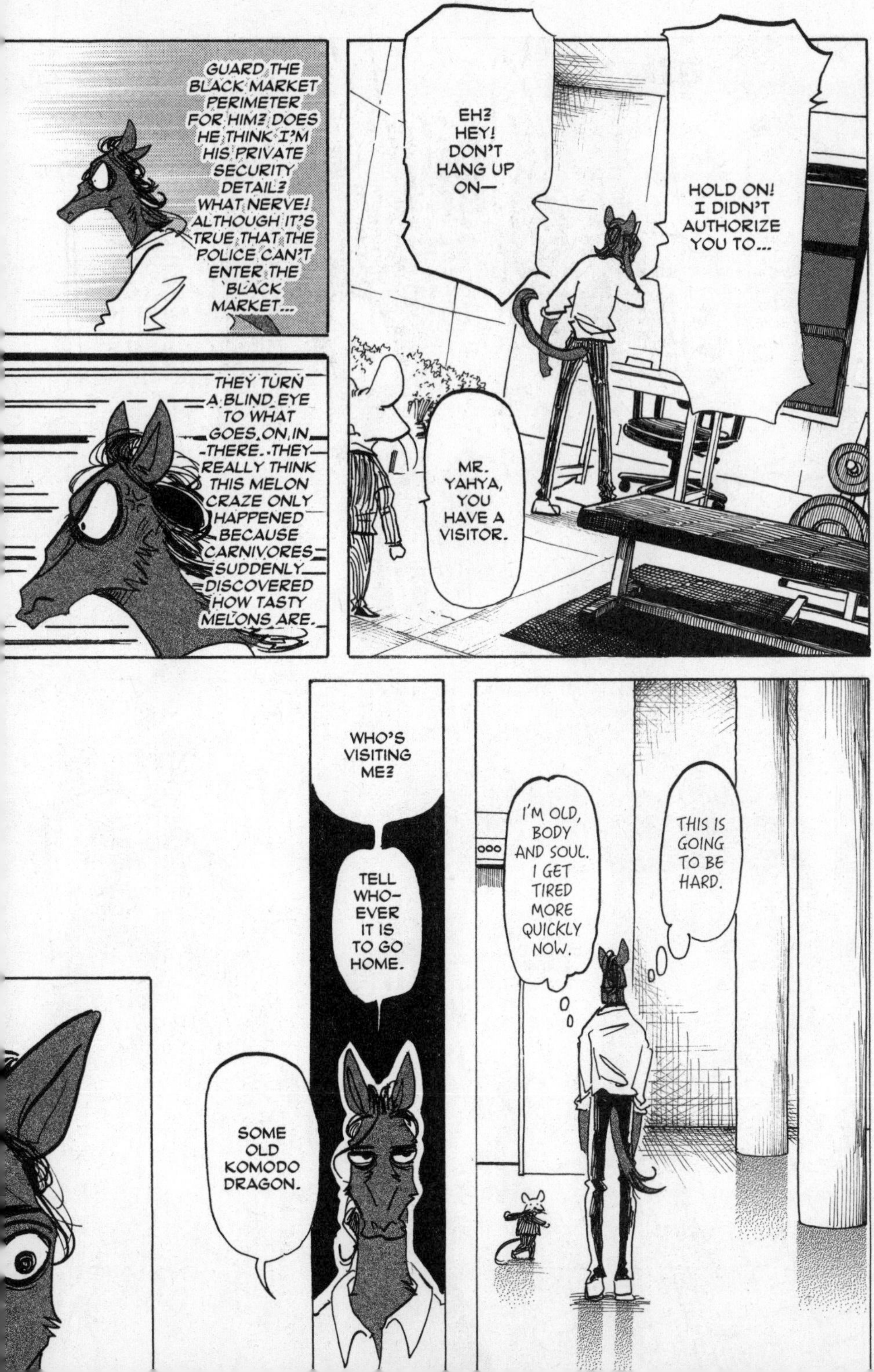
HOLD ON! I DIDN'T AUTHORIZE YOU TO...
EH? HEY! DON'T HANG UP ON—
MR. YAHYA, YOU HAVE A VISITOR.
GUARD THE BLACK MARKET PERIMETER FOR HIM? DOES HE THINK I'M HIS PRIVATE SECURITY DETAIL? WHAT NERVE! ALTHOUGH IT'S TRUE THAT THE POLICE CAN'T ENTER THE BLACK MARKET...
THEY TURN A BLIND EYE TO WHAT GOES ON IN THERE. THEY REALLY THINK THIS MELON CRAZE ONLY HAPPENED BECAUSE CARNIVORES SUDDENLY DISCOVERED HOW TASTY MELONS ARE.
THIS IS GOING TO BE HARD.
I'M OLD, BODY AND SOUL. I GET TIRED MORE QUICKLY NOW.
WHO'S VISITING ME?
TELL WHO-EVER IT IS TO GO HOME.
SOME OLD KOMODO DRAGON.

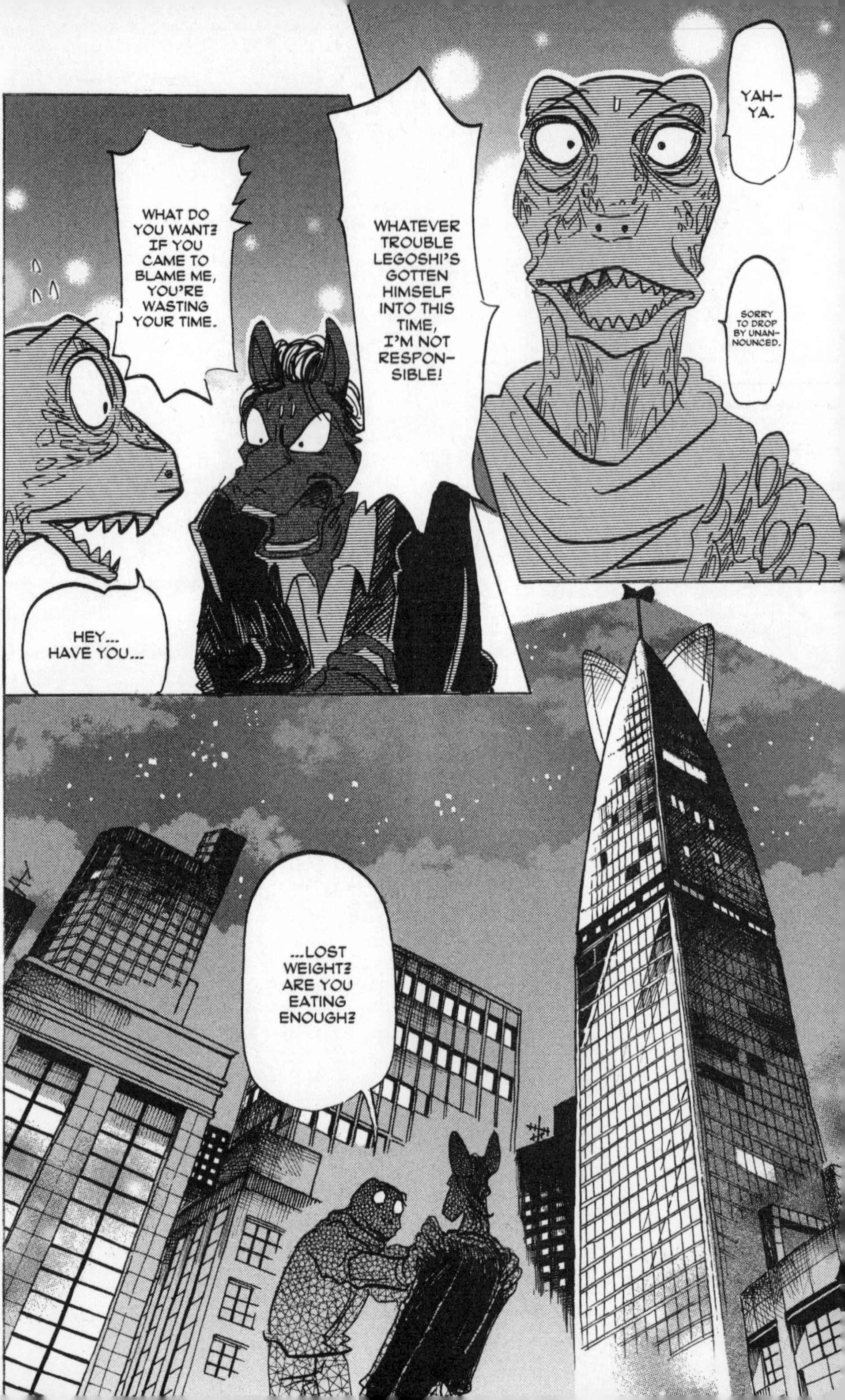
YAH-YA.
SORRY TO DROP BY UNANNOUNCED.
WHATEVER TROUBLE LEGOSHI'S GOTTEN HIMSELF INTO THIS TIME, I'M NOT RESPONSIBLE!
WHAT DO YOU WANT? IF YOU CAME TO BLAME ME, YOU'RE WASTING YOUR TIME.
HEY... HAVE YOU...
...LOST WEIGHT? ARE YOU EATING ENOUGH?

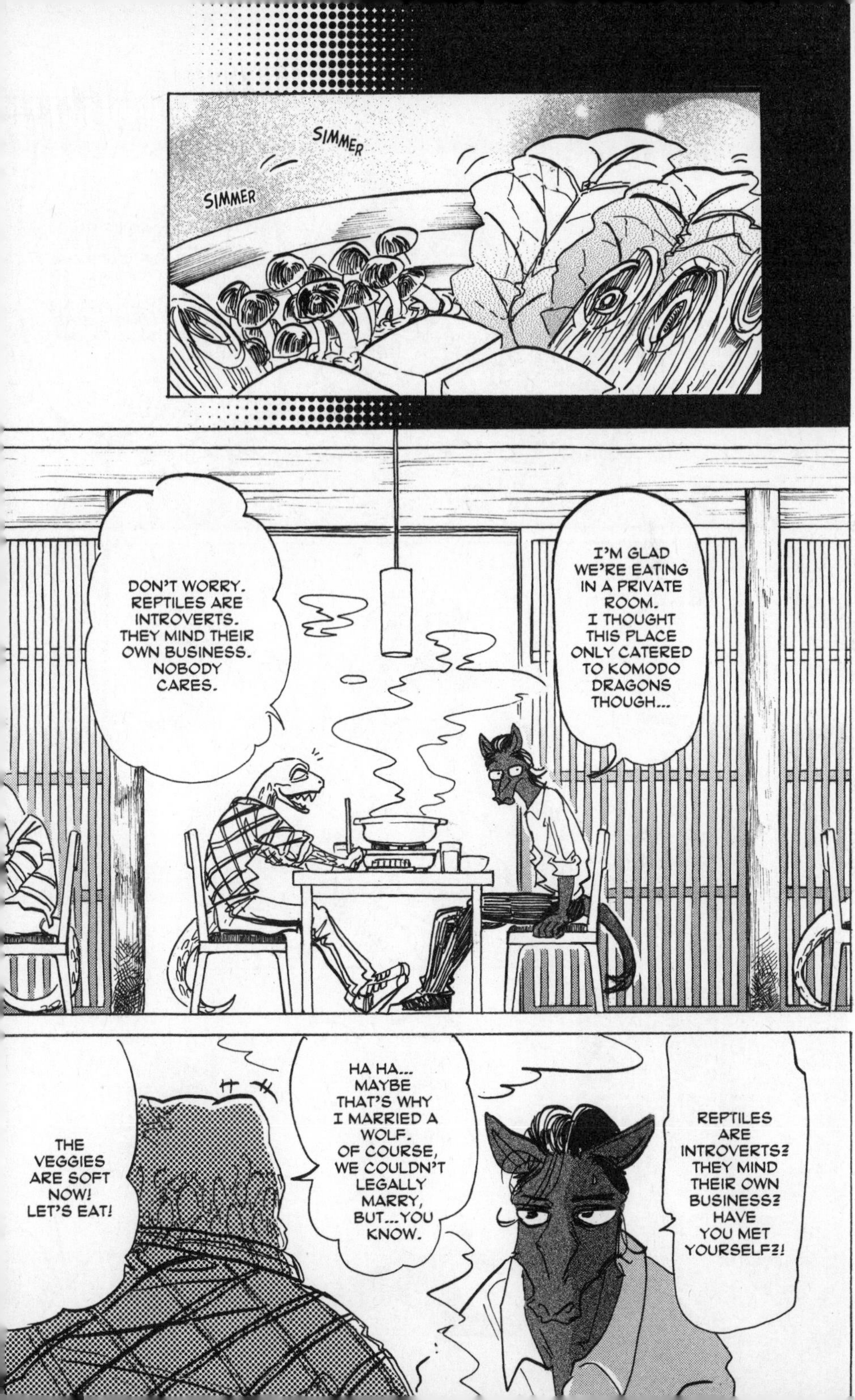
SIMMER
SIMMER
I'M GLAD WE'RE EATING IN A PRIVATE ROOM. I THOUGHT THIS PLACE ONLY CATERED TO KOMODO DRAGONS THOUGH...
DON'T WORRY. REPTILES ARE INTROVERTS. THEY MIND THEIR OWN BUSINESS. NOBODY CARES.
REPTILES ARE INTROVERTS? THEY MIND THEIR OWN BUSINESS? HAVE YOU MET YOURSELF?!
HA HA... MAYBE THAT'S WHY I MARRIED A WOLF. OF COURSE, WE COULDN'T LEGALLY MARRY, BUT... YOU KNOW.
THE VEGGIES ARE SOFT NOW! LET'S EAT!

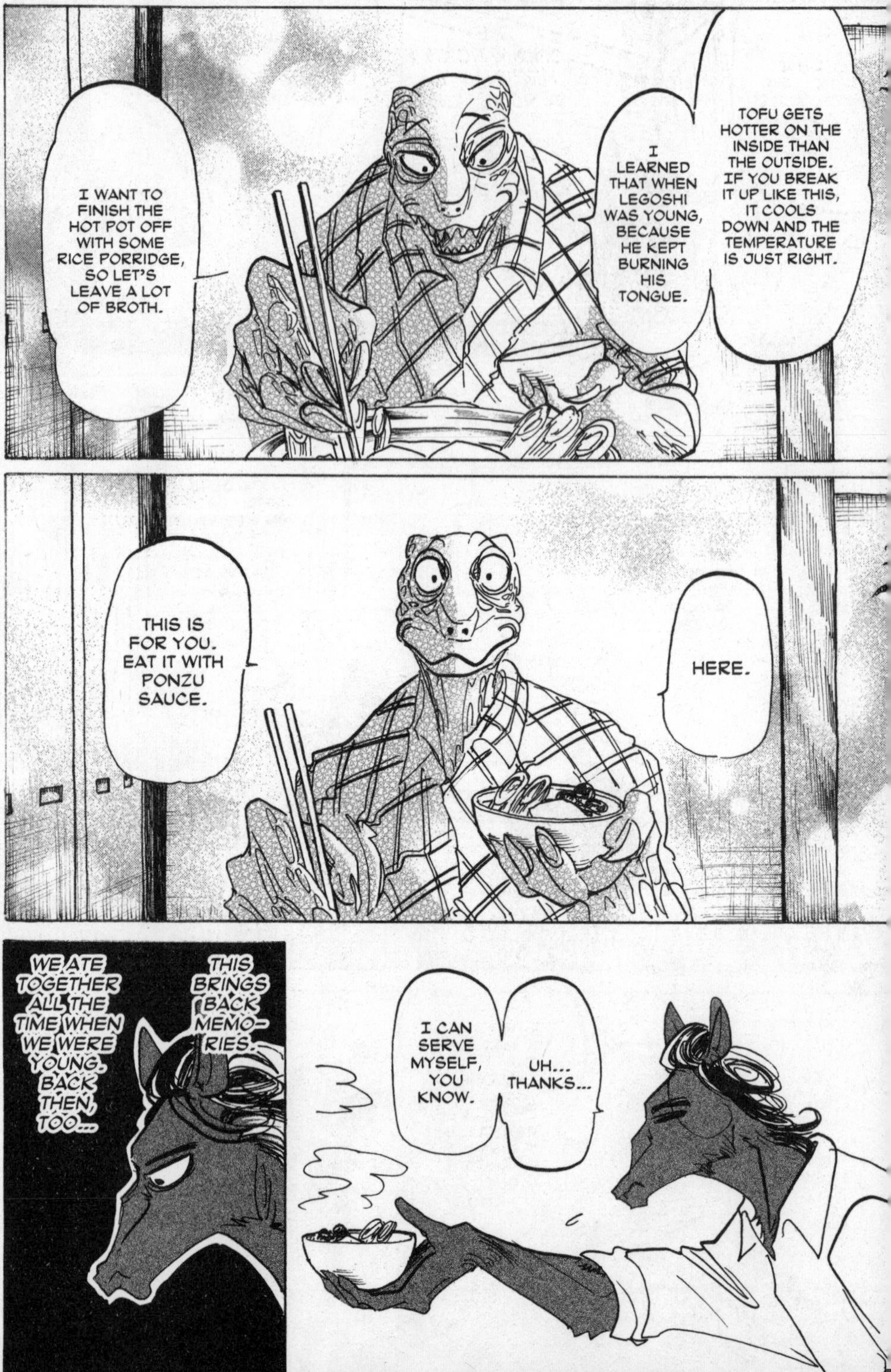
TOFU GETS HOTTER ON THE INSIDE THAN THE OUTSIDE. IF YOU BREAK IT UP LIKE THIS, IT COOLS DOWN AND THE TEMPERATURE IS JUST RIGHT.
I LEARNED THAT WHEN LEGOSHI WAS YOUNG, BECAUSE HE KEPT BURNING HIS TONGUE.
I WANT TO FINISH THE HOT POT OFF WITH SOME RICE PORRIDGE, SO LET'S LEAVE A LOT OF BROTH.
HERE.
THIS IS FOR YOU. EAT IT WITH PONZU SAUCE.
UH... THANKS...
I CAN SERVE MYSELF, YOU KNOW.
THIS BRINGS BACK MEMO-RIES.
WE ATE TOGETHER ALL THE TIME WHEN WE WERE YOUNG. BACK THEN, TOO...

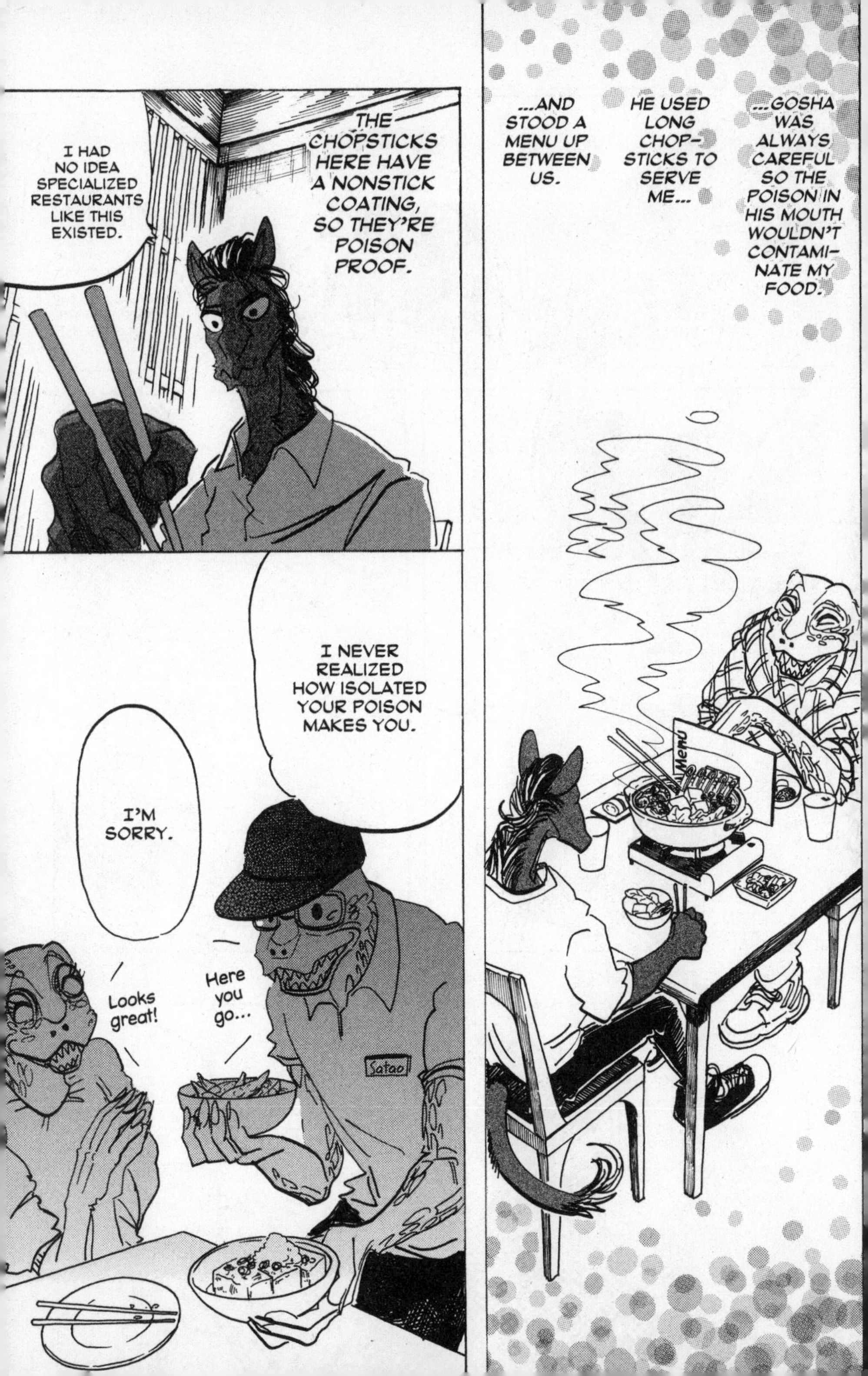
...GOSHA WAS ALWAYS CAREFUL SO THE POISON IN HIS MOUTH WOULDN'T CONTAMINATE MY FOOD.
HE USED LONG CHOPSTICKS TO SERVE ME...
...AND STOOD A MENU UP BETWEEN US.
Menu
THE CHOPSTICKS HERE HAVE A NONSTICK COATING, SO THEY'RE POISON PROOF.
I HAD NO IDEA SPECIALIZED RESTAURANTS LIKE THIS EXISTED.
I NEVER REALIZED HOW ISOLATED YOUR POISON MAKES YOU.
I'M SORRY.
Here you go...
Satao
Looks great!

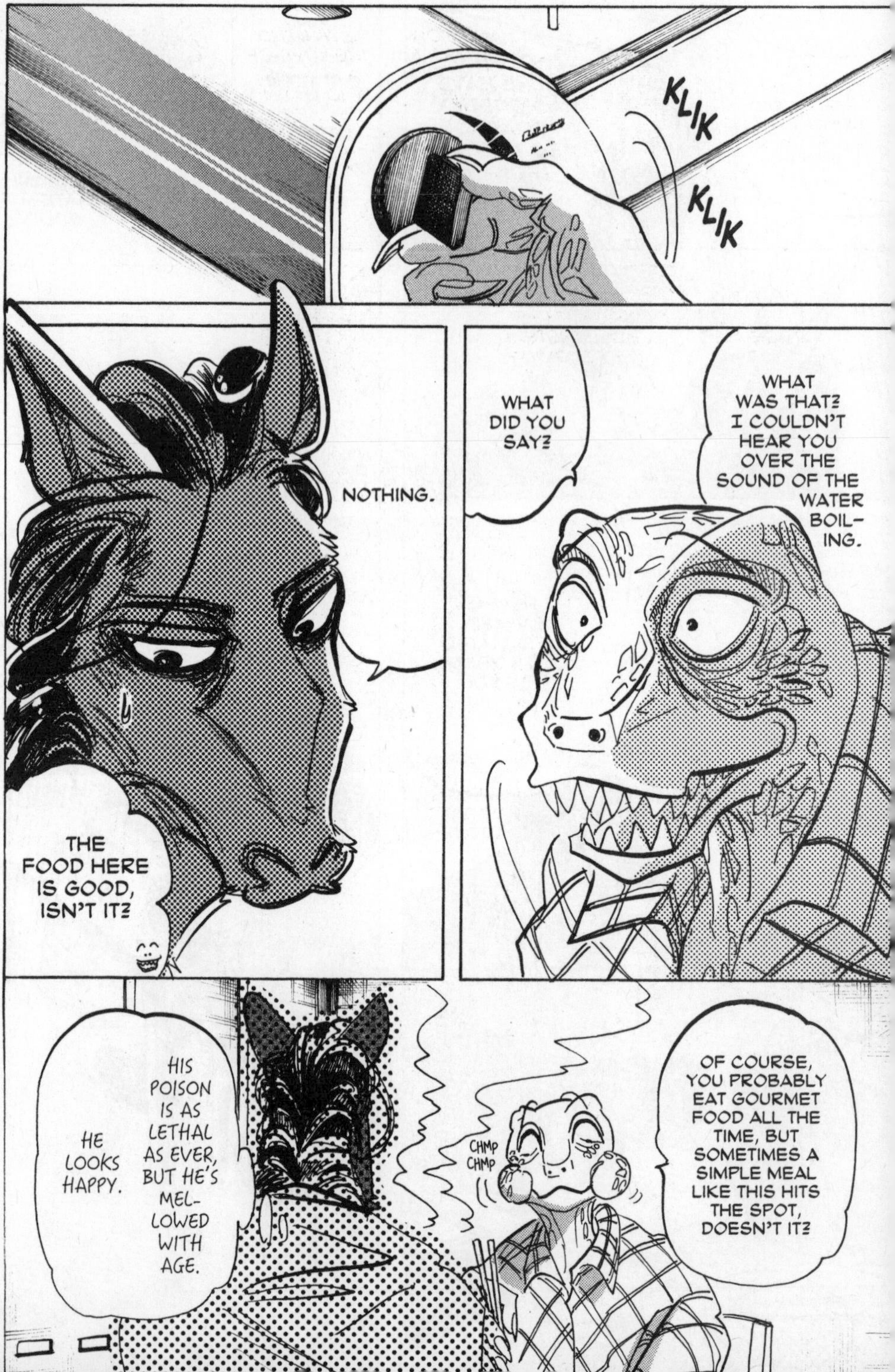
KLIK
KLIK
WHAT WAS THAT? I COULDN'T HEAR YOU OVER THE SOUND OF THE WATER BOILING.
WHAT DID YOU SAY?
NOTHING.
THE FOOD HERE IS GOOD, ISN'T IT?
OF COURSE, YOU PROBABLY EAT GOURMET FOOD ALL THE TIME, BUT SOMETIMES A SIMPLE MEAL LIKE THIS HITS THE SPOT, DOESN'T IT?
CHMP CHMP
HIS POISON IS AS LETHAL AS EVER, BUT HE'S MEL-LOWED WITH AGE.
HE LOOKS HAPPY.

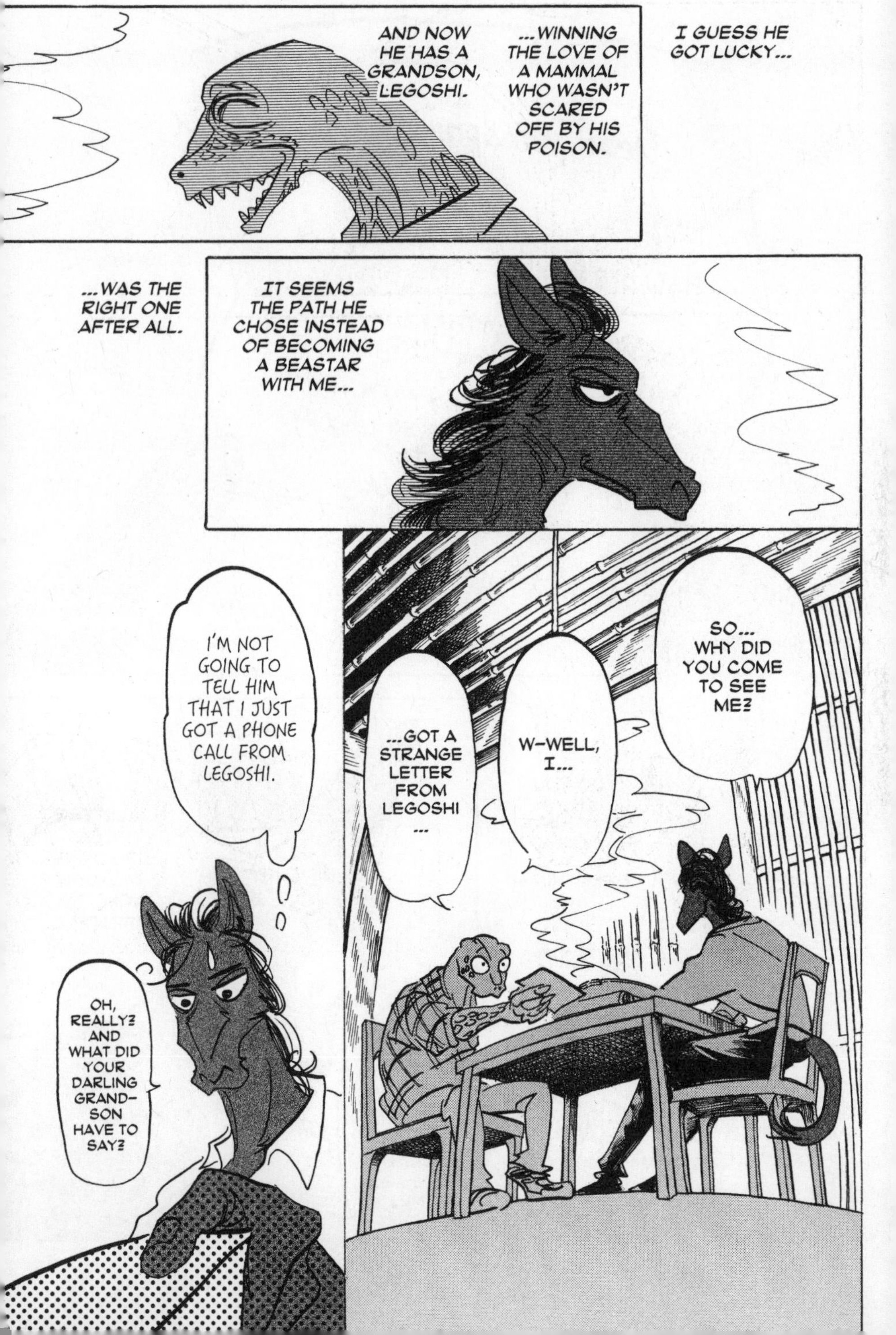
I GUESS HE GOT LUCKY...
...WINNING THE LOVE OF A MAMMAL WHO WASN'T SCARED OFF BY HIS POISON.
AND NOW HE HAS A GRANDSON, LEGOSHI.
IT SEEMS THE PATH HE CHOSE INSTEAD OF BECOMING A BEASTAR WITH ME...
...WAS THE RIGHT ONE AFTER ALL.
SO... WHY DID YOU COME TO SEE ME?
W-WELL, I...
...GOT A STRANGE LETTER FROM LEGOSHI...
I'M NOT GOING TO TELL HIM THAT I JUST GOT A PHONE CALL FROM LEGOSHI.
OH, REALLY? AND WHAT DID YOUR DARLING GRAND-SON HAVE TO SAY?

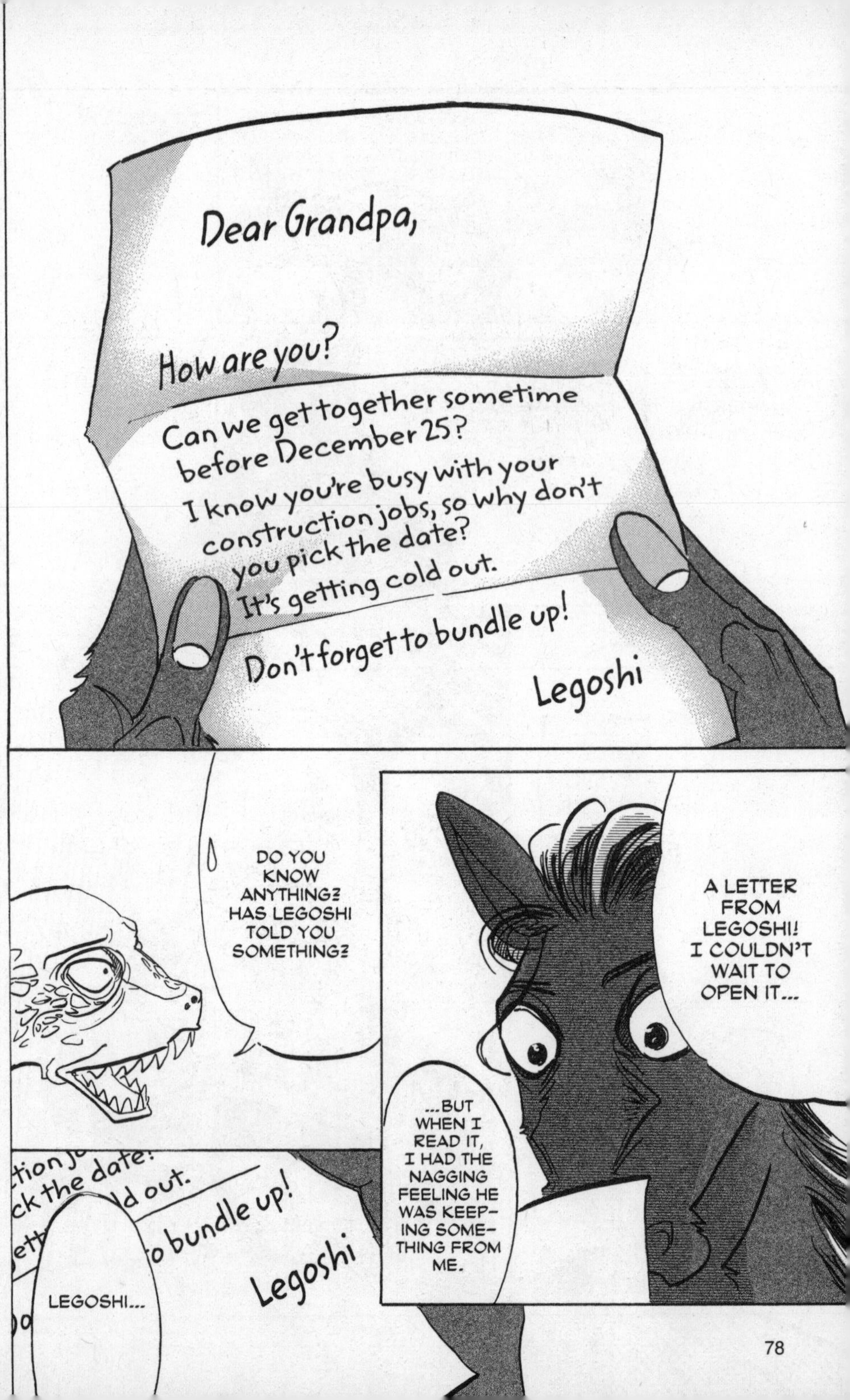
Dear Grandpa,
How are you?
Can we get together sometime before December 25?
I know you're busy with your construction jobs, so why don't you pick the date?
It's getting cold out.
Don't forget to bundle up!
Legoshi
A LETTER FROM LEGOSHI! I COULDN'T WAIT TO OPEN IT...
...BUT WHEN I READ IT, I HAD THE NAGGING FEELING HE WAS KEEPING SOMETHING FROM ME.
DO YOU KNOW ANYTHING? HAS LEGOSHI TOLD YOU SOMETHING?
Legoshi
LEGOSHI...

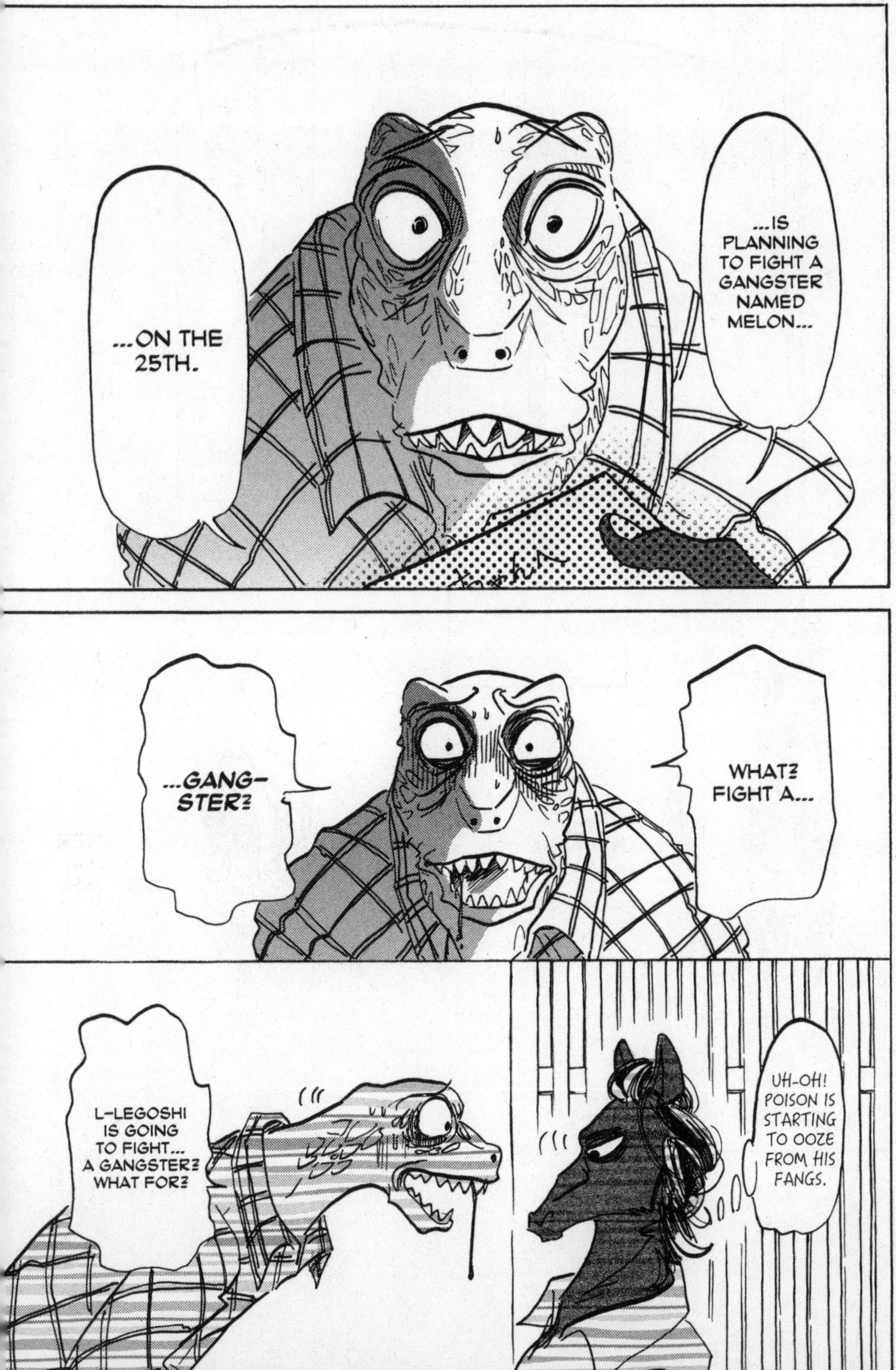
...IS PLANNING TO FIGHT A GANGSTER NAMED MELON...
...ON THE 25TH.
WHAT? FIGHT A...
...GANG-STER?
UH-OH! POISON IS STARTING TO OOZE FROM HIS FANGS.
L-LEGOSHI IS GOING TO FIGHT... A GANGSTER? WHAT FOR?

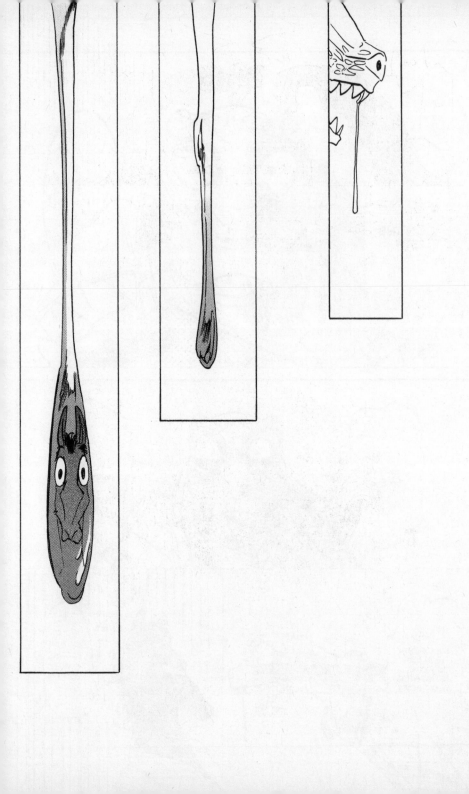

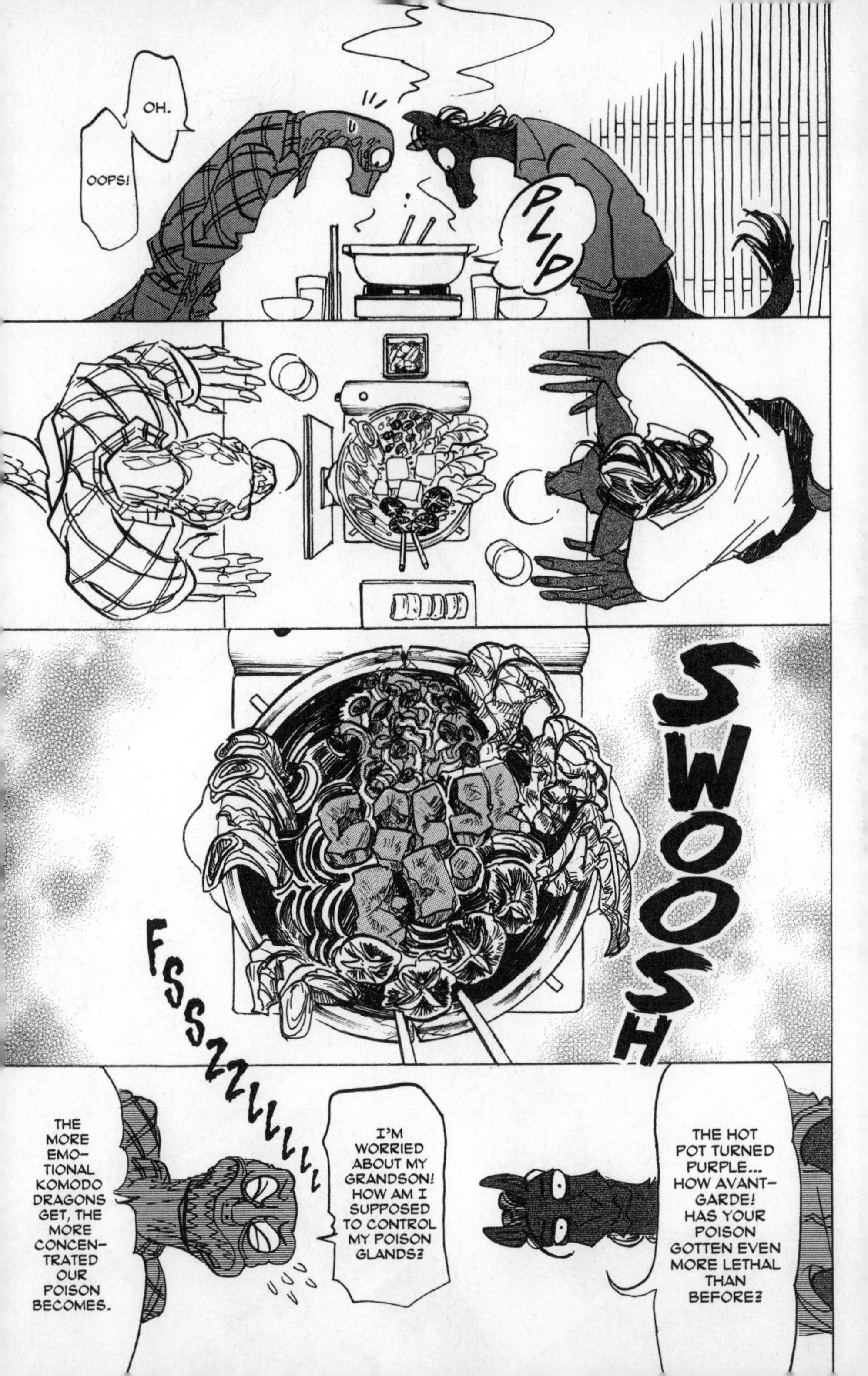
PLIP
OH.
OOPS!
SWOOSH
FSSZZLLLLLL
THE HOT POT TURNED PURPLE... HOW AVANT-GARDE! HAS YOUR POISON GOTTEN EVEN MORE LETHAL THAN BEFORE?
I'M WORRIED ABOUT MY GRANDSON! HOW AM I SUPPOSED TO CONTROL MY POISON GLANDS?
THE MORE EMOTIONAL KOMODO DRAGONS GET, THE MORE CONCENTRATED OUR POISON BECOMES.

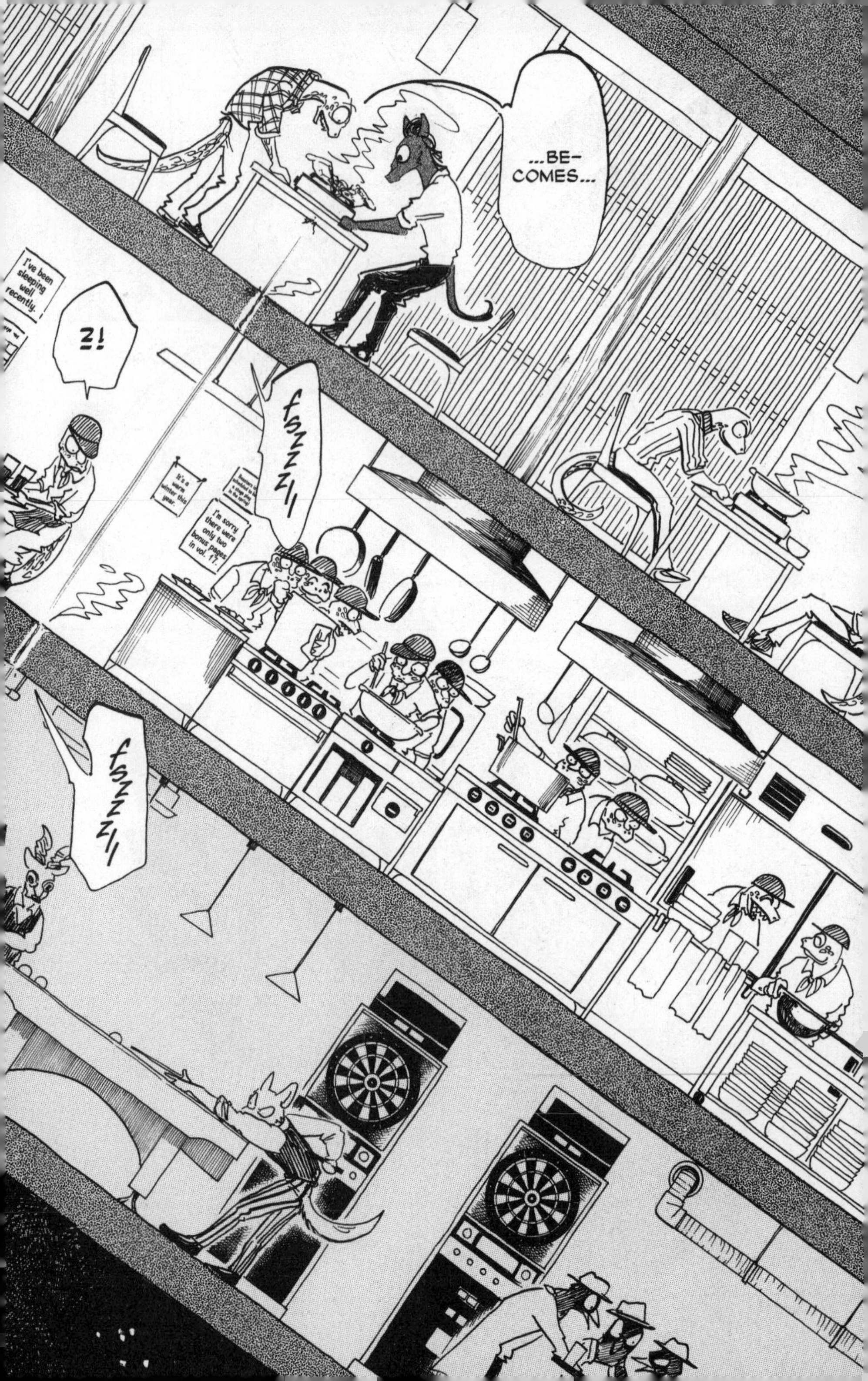
...BE-
COMES...
!?
fszzz!!
I've been sleeping well recently.
It's a warm winter this year.
I'm sorry there were only two bonus pages in vol. 17.
fszzz!!

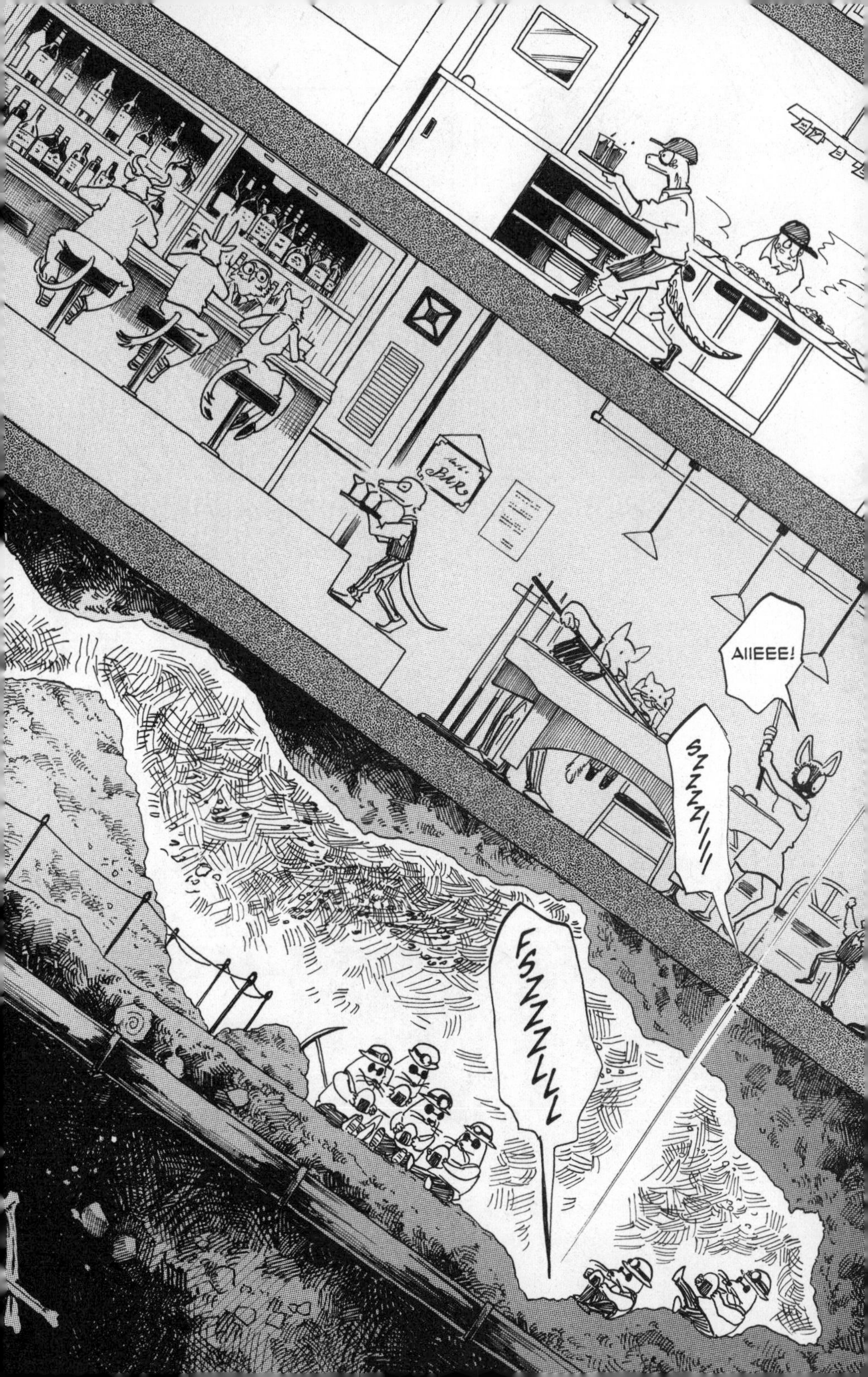
BAR
AIIEEE!
SZZZZ////
FSZZZZZVVV

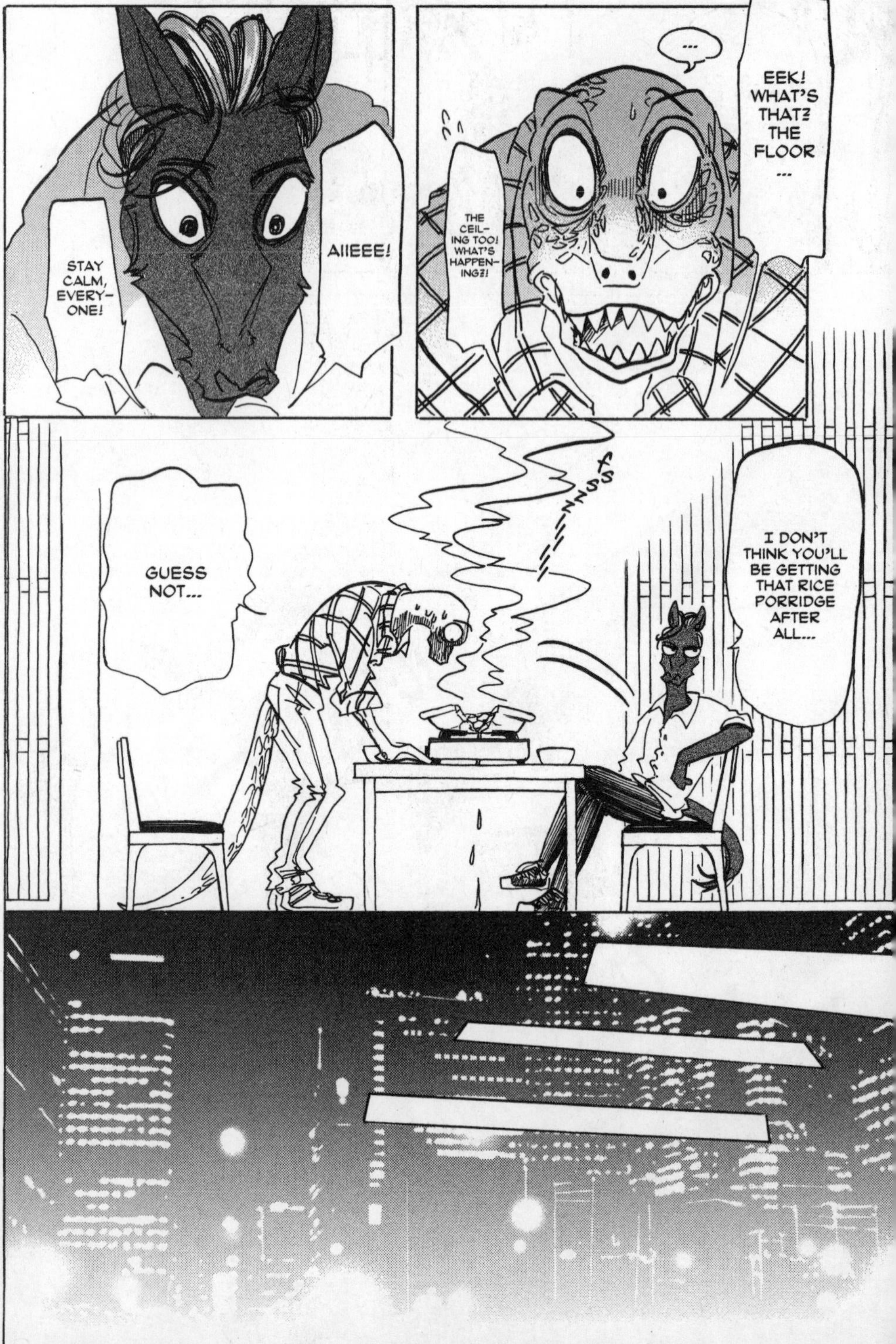
...
EEK! WHAT'S THAT? THE FLOOR ...
THE CEIL-ING TOO! WHAT'S HAPPEN-ING?!
AIIEEE!
STAY CALM, EVERY-ONE!
I DON'T THINK YOU'LL BE GETTING THAT RICE PORRIDGE AFTER ALL...
GUESS NOT...

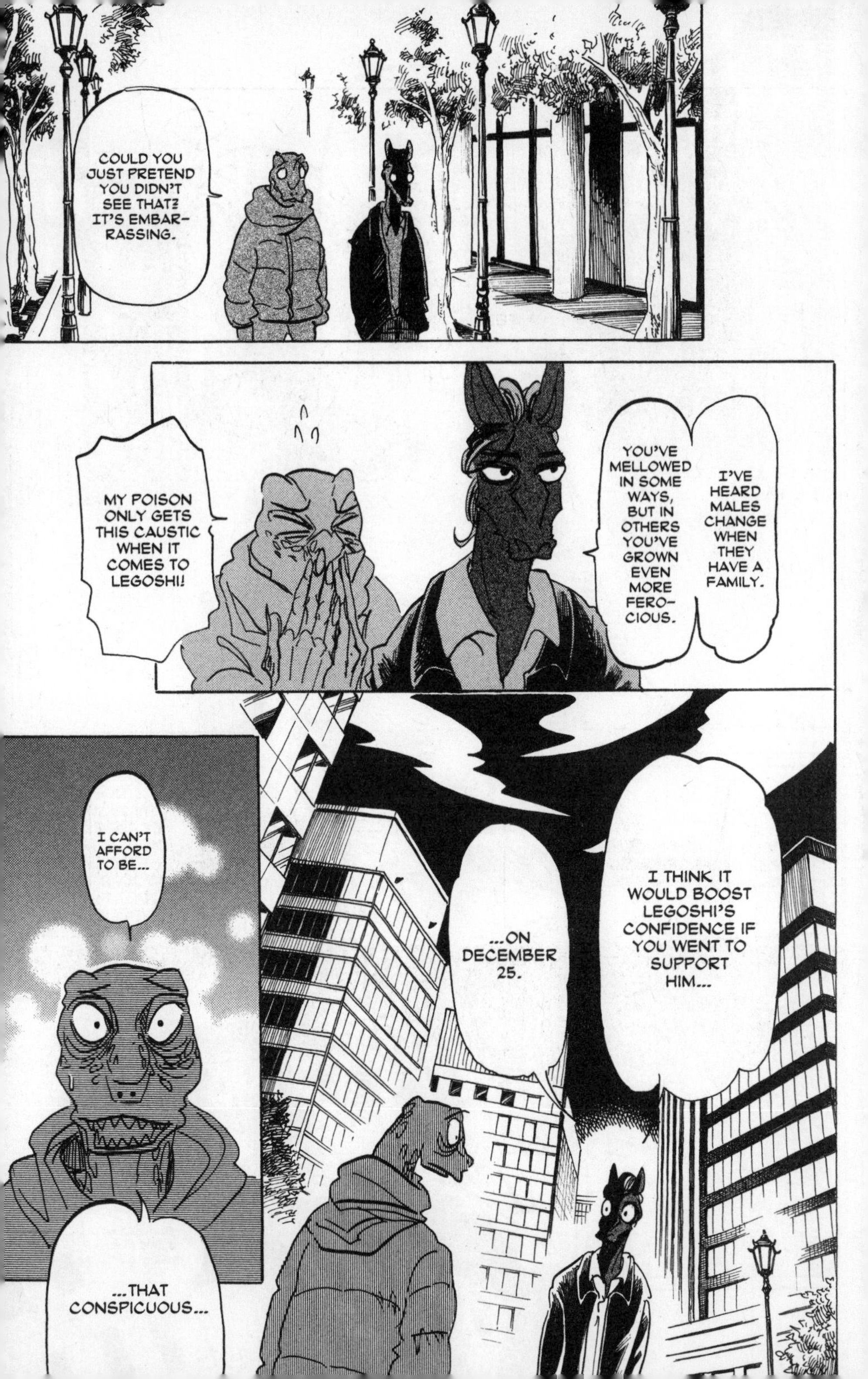
COULD YOU JUST PRETEND YOU DIDN'T SEE THAT? IT'S EMBARRASSING.
I'VE HEARD MALES CHANGE WHEN THEY HAVE A FAMILY.
YOU'VE MELLOWED IN SOME WAYS, BUT IN OTHERS YOU'VE GROWN EVEN MORE FEROCIOUS.
MY POISON ONLY GETS THIS CAUSTIC WHEN IT COMES TO LEGOSHI!
I THINK IT WOULD BOOST LEGOSHI'S CONFIDENCE IF YOU WENT TO SUPPORT HIM...
...ON DECEMBER 25.
I CAN'T AFFORD TO BE...
...THAT CONSPICUOUS...

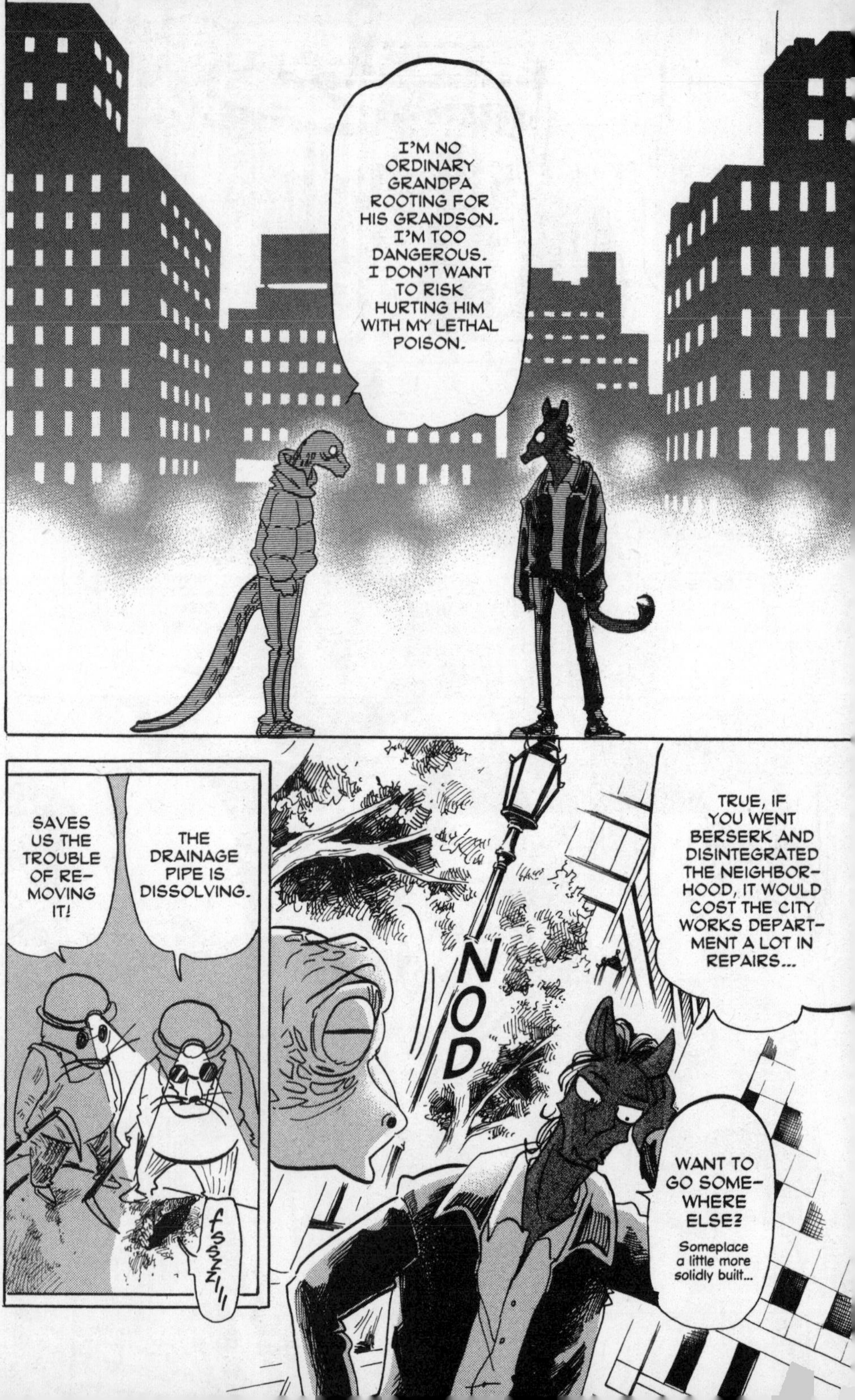
I'M NO ORDINARY GRANDPA ROOTING FOR HIS GRANDSON. I'M TOO DANGEROUS. I DON'T WANT TO RISK HURTING HIM WITH MY LETHAL POISON.
TRUE, IF YOU WENT BERSERK AND DISINTEGRATED THE NEIGHBOR-HOOD, IT WOULD COST THE CITY WORKS DEPART-MENT A LOT IN REPAIRS...
NOD
WANT TO GO SOME-WHERE ELSE?
Someplace a little more solidly built...
THE DRAINAGE PIPE IS DISSOLVING.
SAVES US THE TROUBLE OF RE-MOVING IT!
fsszz

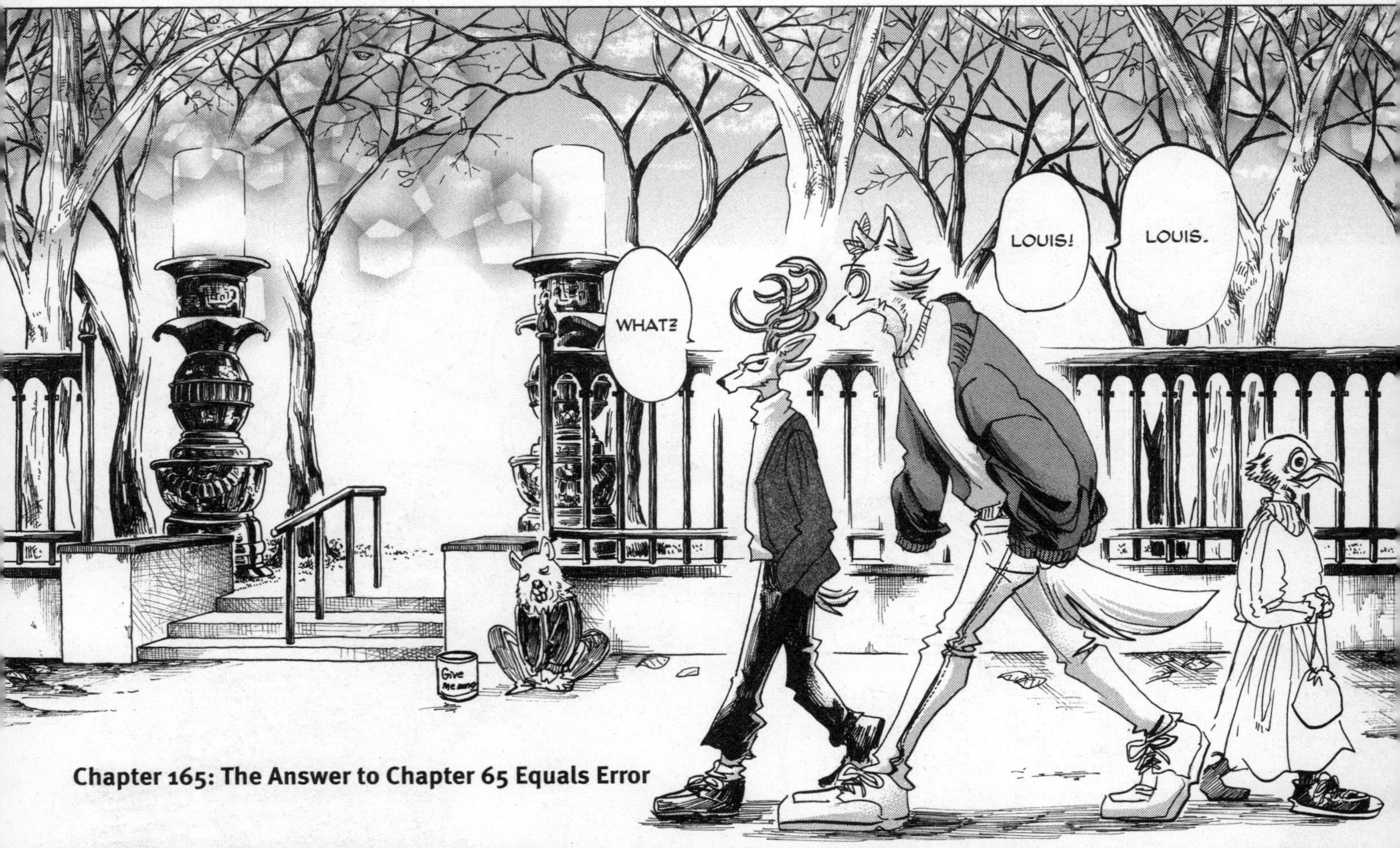
LOUIS.
LOUIS!
WHAT?
Give

Chapter 165: The Answer to Chapter 65 Equals Error

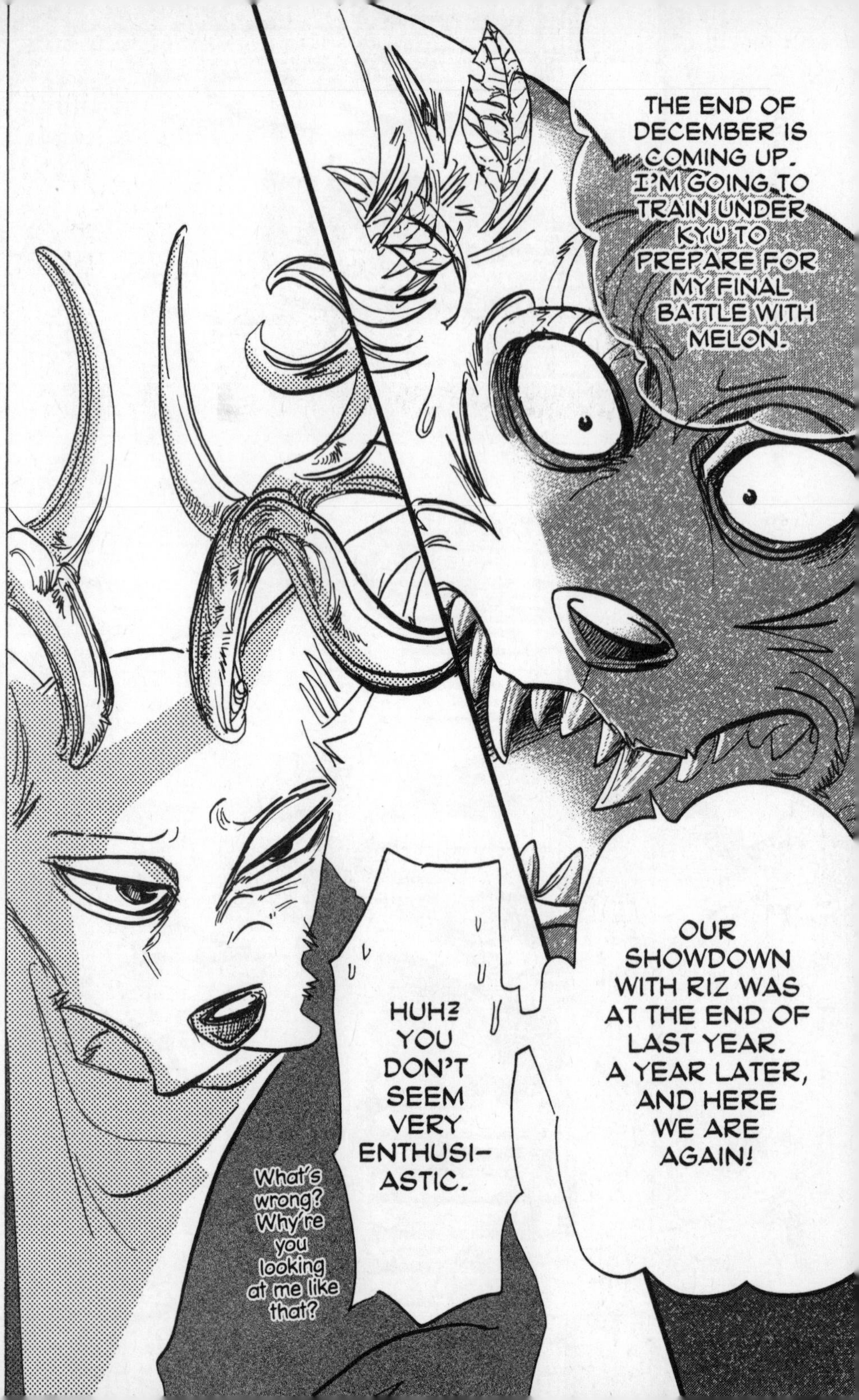
THE END OF DECEMBER IS COMING UP. I'M GOING TO TRAIN UNDER KYU TO PREPARE FOR MY FINAL BATTLE WITH MELON.
OUR SHOWDOWN WITH RIZ WAS AT THE END OF LAST YEAR. A YEAR LATER, AND HERE WE ARE AGAIN!
HUH? YOU DON'T SEEM VERY ENTHUSI-ASTIC.
What's wrong? Why're you looking at me like that?

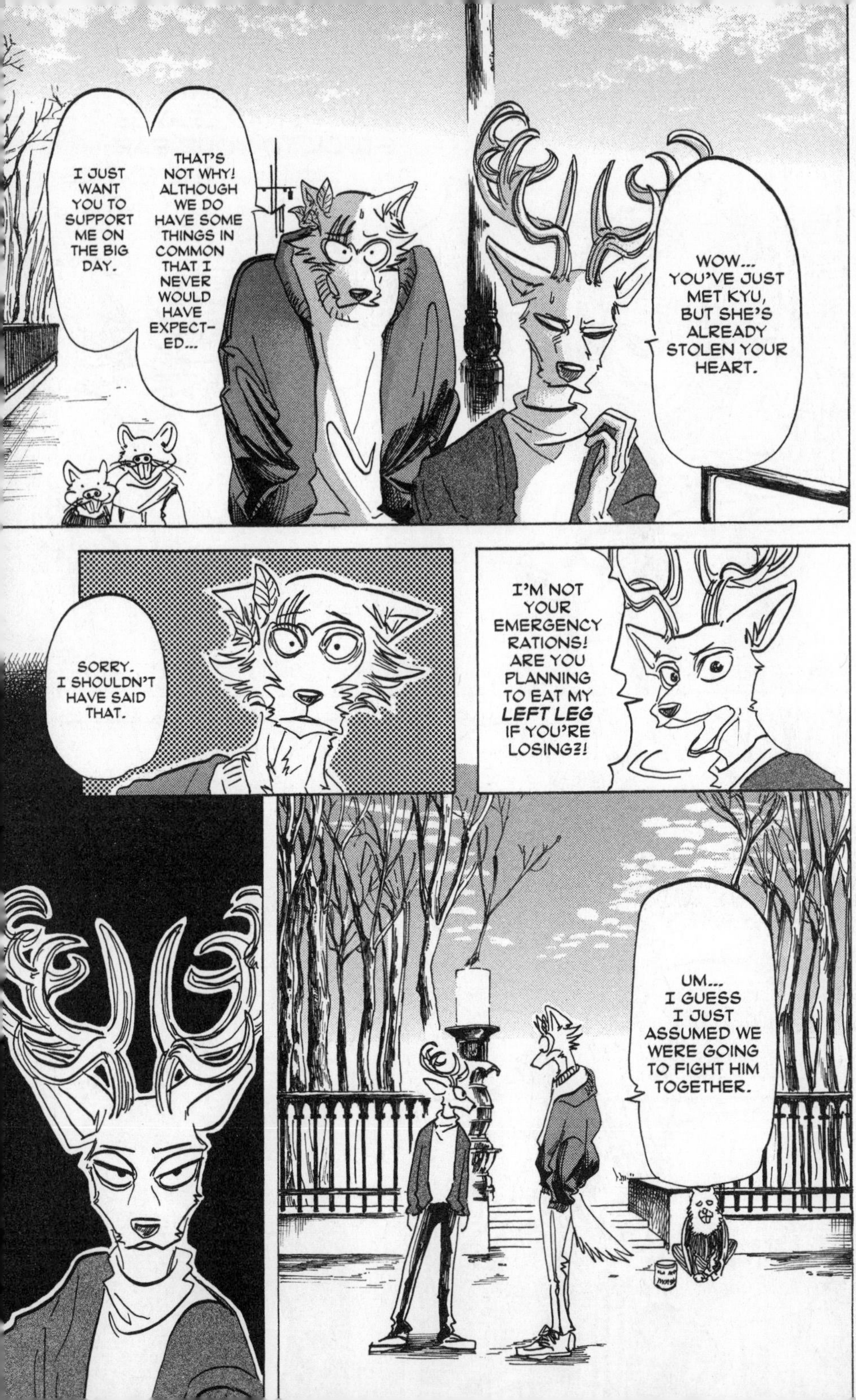
WOW... YOU'VE JUST MET KYU, BUT SHE'S ALREADY STOLEN YOUR HEART.
THAT'S NOT WHY! ALTHOUGH WE DO HAVE SOME THINGS IN COMMON THAT I NEVER WOULD HAVE EXPECT-ED...
I JUST WANT YOU TO SUPPORT ME ON THE BIG DAY.
I'M NOT YOUR EMERGENCY RATIONS! ARE YOU PLANNING TO EAT MY *LEFT LEG* IF YOU'RE LOSING?!
SORRY. I SHOULDN'T HAVE SAID THAT.
UM... I GUESS I JUST ASSUMED WE WERE GOING TO FIGHT HIM TOGETHER.

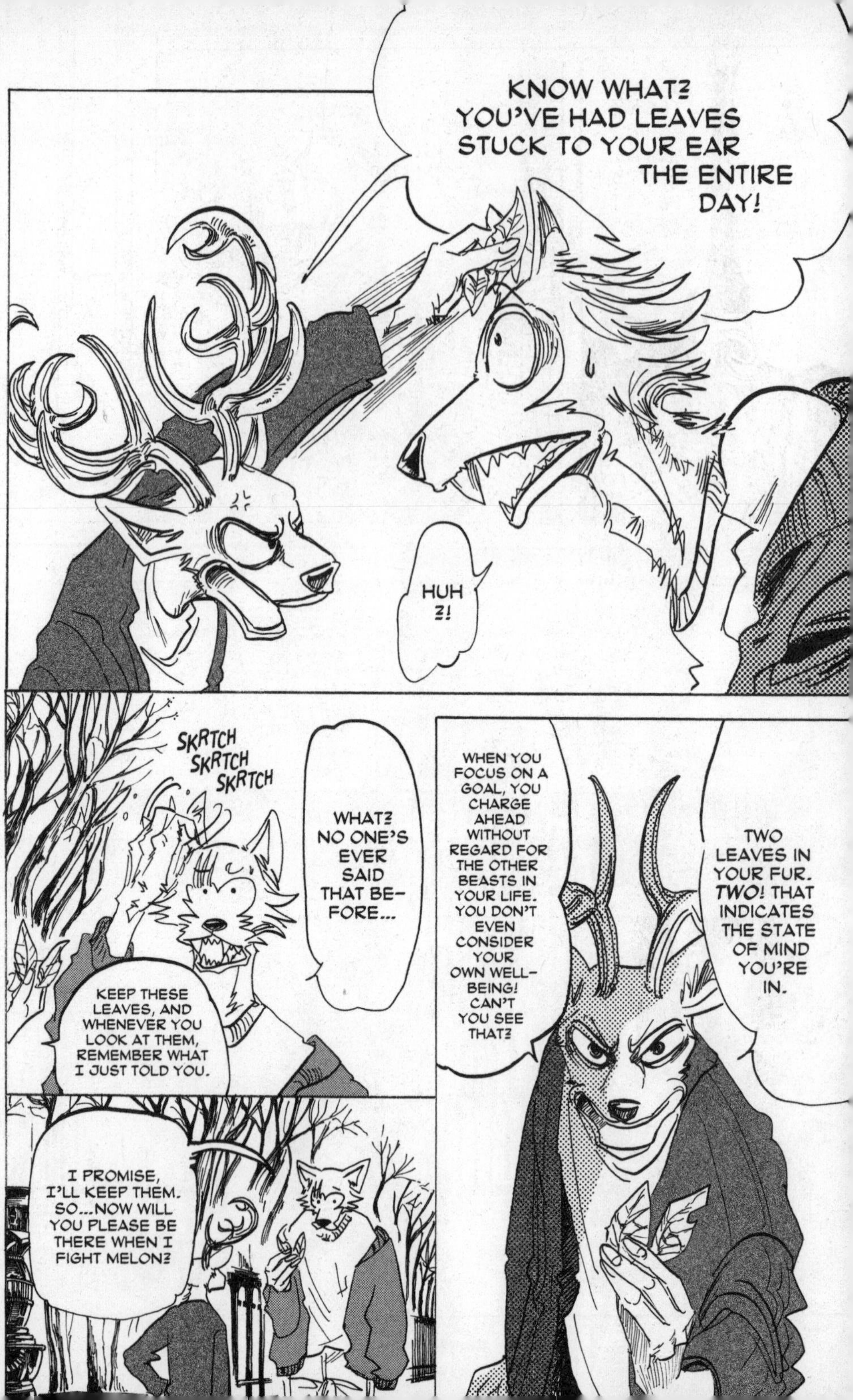
KNOW WHAT? YOU'VE HAD LEAVES STUCK TO YOUR EAR THE ENTIRE DAY!
HUH?!
TWO LEAVES IN YOUR FUR. *TWO*! THAT INDICATES THE STATE OF MIND YOU'RE IN.
WHEN YOU FOCUS ON A GOAL, YOU CHARGE AHEAD WITHOUT REGARD FOR THE OTHER BEASTS IN YOUR LIFE. YOU DON'T EVEN CONSIDER YOUR OWN WELL-BEING! CAN'T YOU SEE THAT?
WHAT? NO ONE'S EVER SAID THAT BE-FORE...
SKRTCH SKRTCH SKRTCH
KEEP THESE LEAVES, AND WHENEVER YOU LOOK AT THEM, REMEMBER WHAT I JUST TOLD YOU.
I PROMISE, I'LL KEEP THEM. SO...NOW WILL YOU PLEASE BE THERE WHEN I FIGHT MELON?

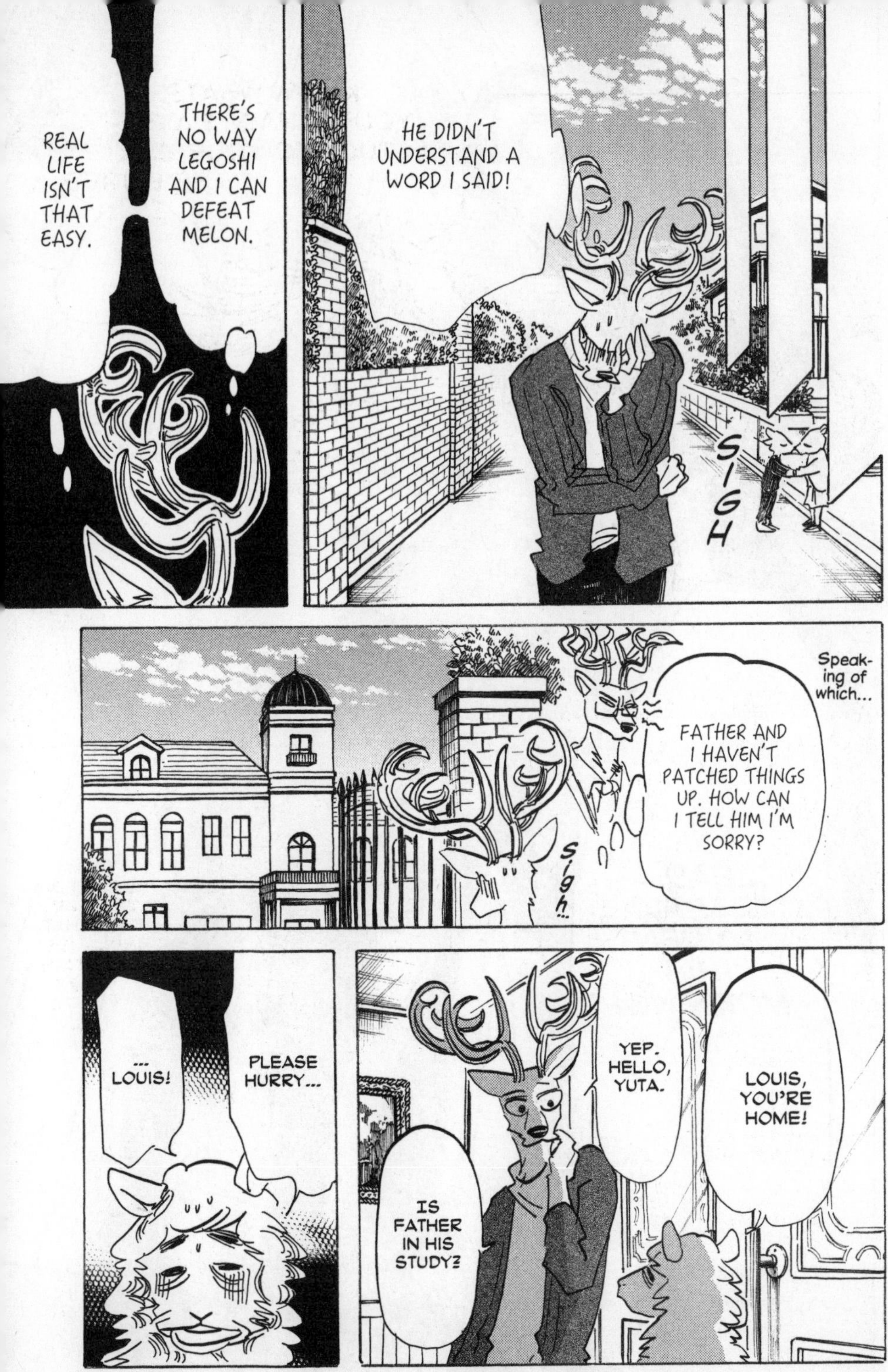
HE DIDN'T UNDERSTAND A WORD I SAID!
SIGH
THERE'S NO WAY LEGOSHI AND I CAN DEFEAT MELON.
REAL LIFE ISN'T THAT EASY.
Speak-ing of which...
FATHER AND I HAVEN'T PATCHED THINGS UP. HOW CAN I TELL HIM I'M SORRY?
Sigh...
LOUIS, YOU'RE HOME!
YEP. HELLO, YUTA.
IS FATHER IN HIS STUDY?
PLEASE HURRY...
...LOUIS!

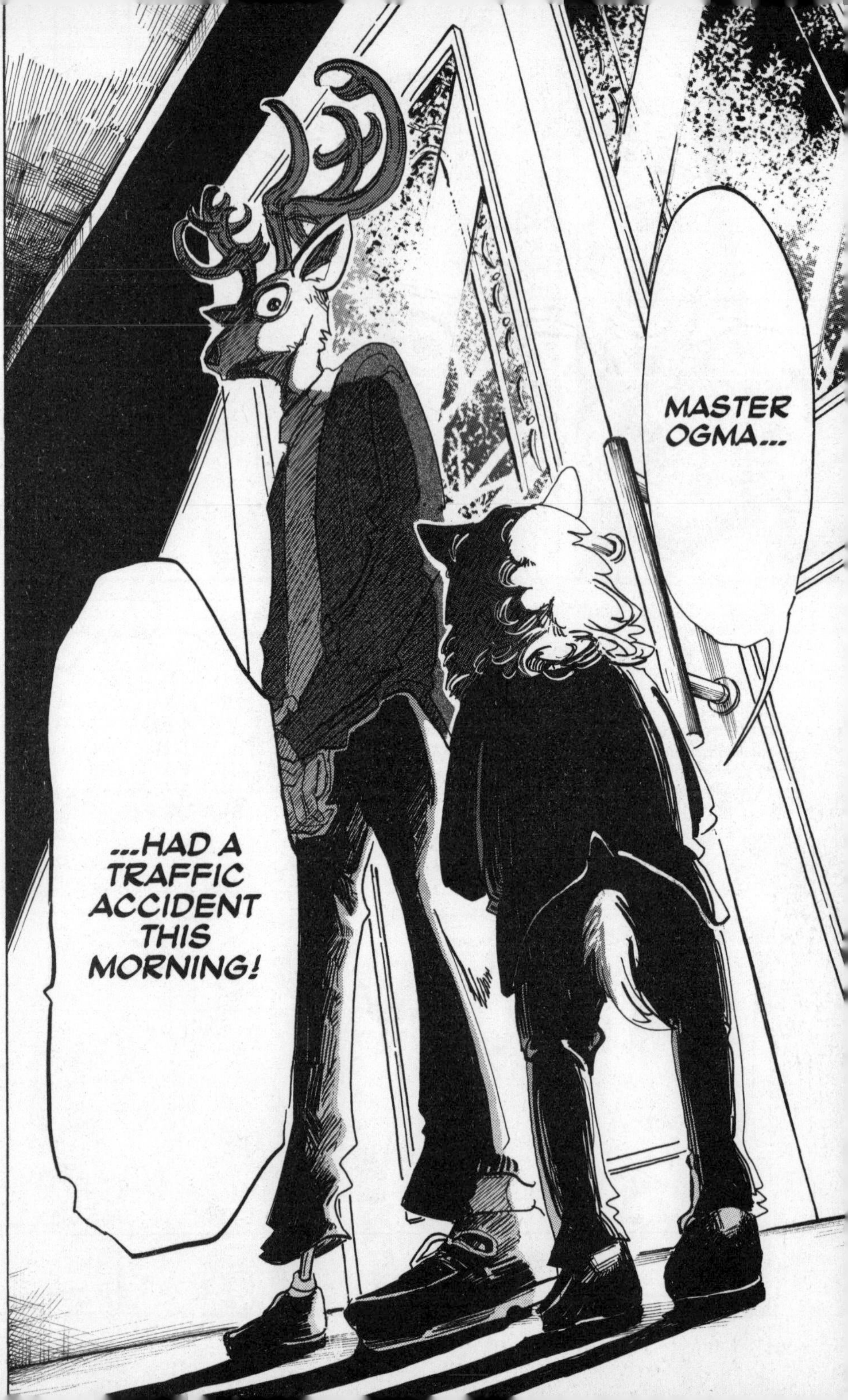
MASTER OGMA...
...HAD A TRAFFIC ACCIDENT THIS MORNING!

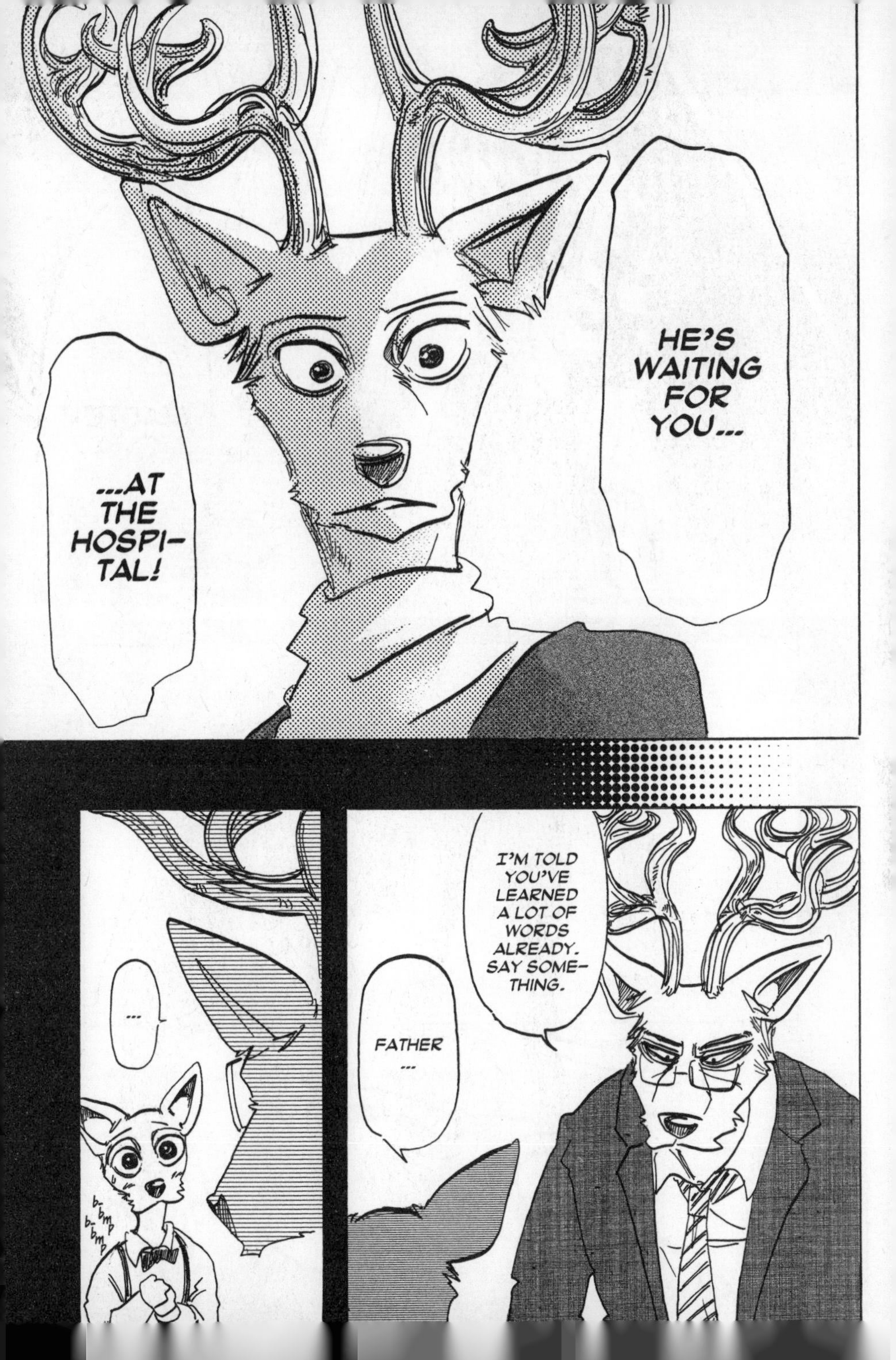
HE'S WAITING FOR YOU...
...AT THE HOSPITAL!
I'M TOLD YOU'VE LEARNED A LOT OF WORDS ALREADY. SAY SOMETHING.
FATHER ...
...
b-bmp b-bmp

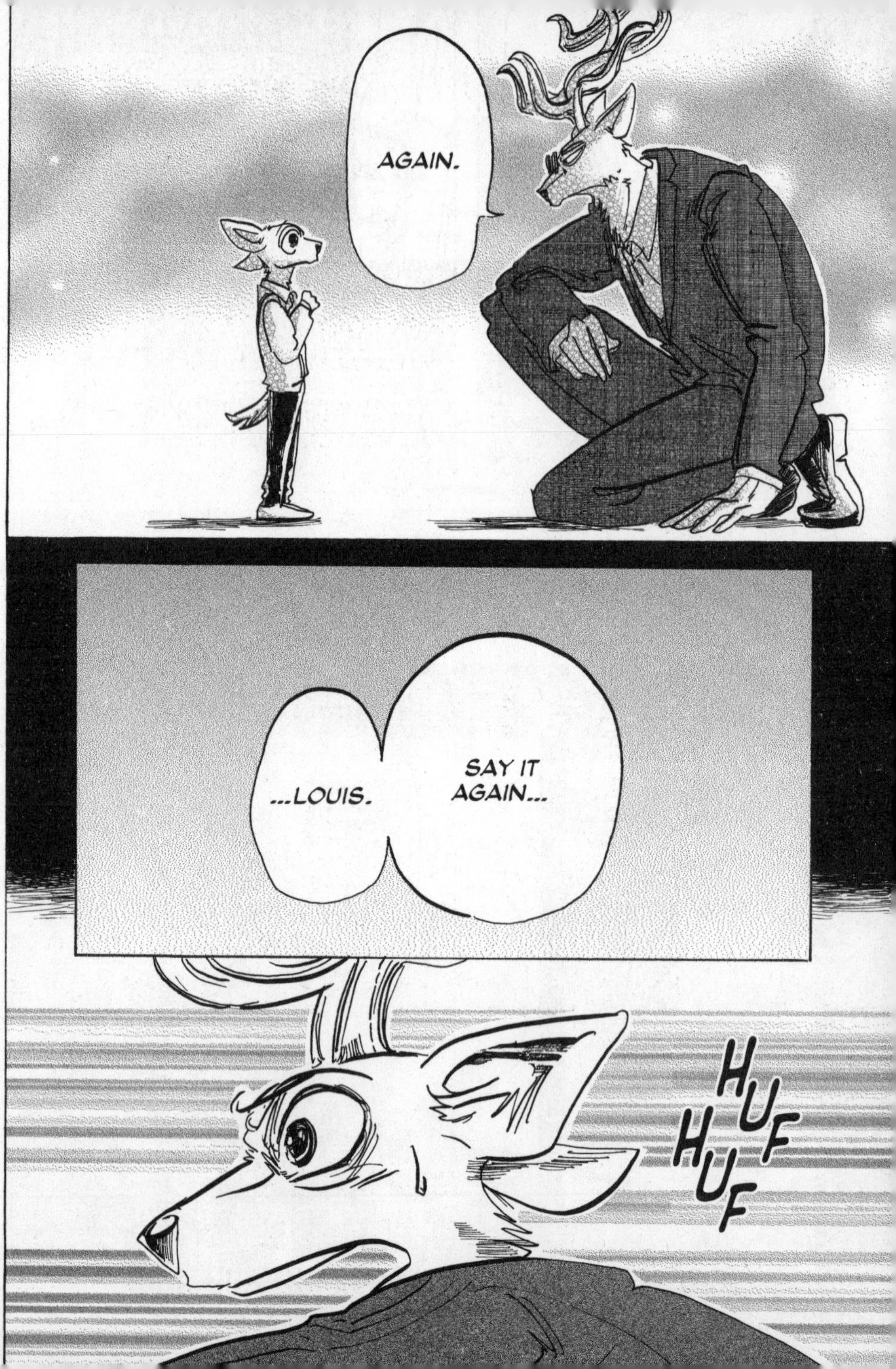
AGAIN.
SAY IT AGAIN...
...LOUIS.
HUF HUF

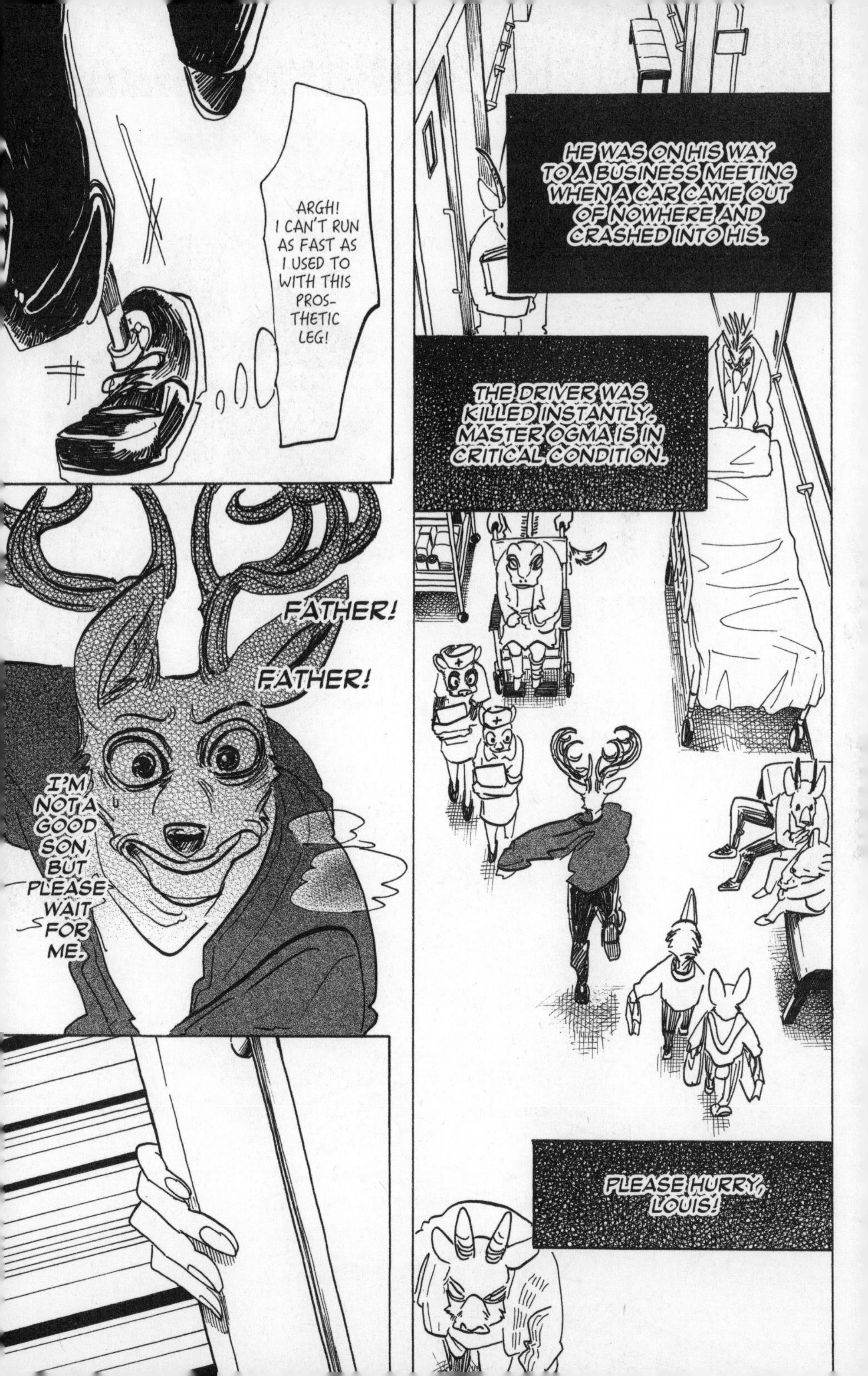
HE WAS ON HIS WAY TO A BUSINESS MEETING WHEN A CAR CAME OUT OF NOWHERE AND CRASHED INTO HIS.
THE DRIVER WAS KILLED INSTANTLY. MASTER OGMA IS IN CRITICAL CONDITION.
PLEASE HURRY, LOUIS!
ARGH! I CAN'T RUN AS FAST AS I USED TO WITH THIS PROS-THETIC LEG!
FATHER!
FATHER!
I'M NOT A GOOD SON, BUT PLEASE WAIT FOR ME.

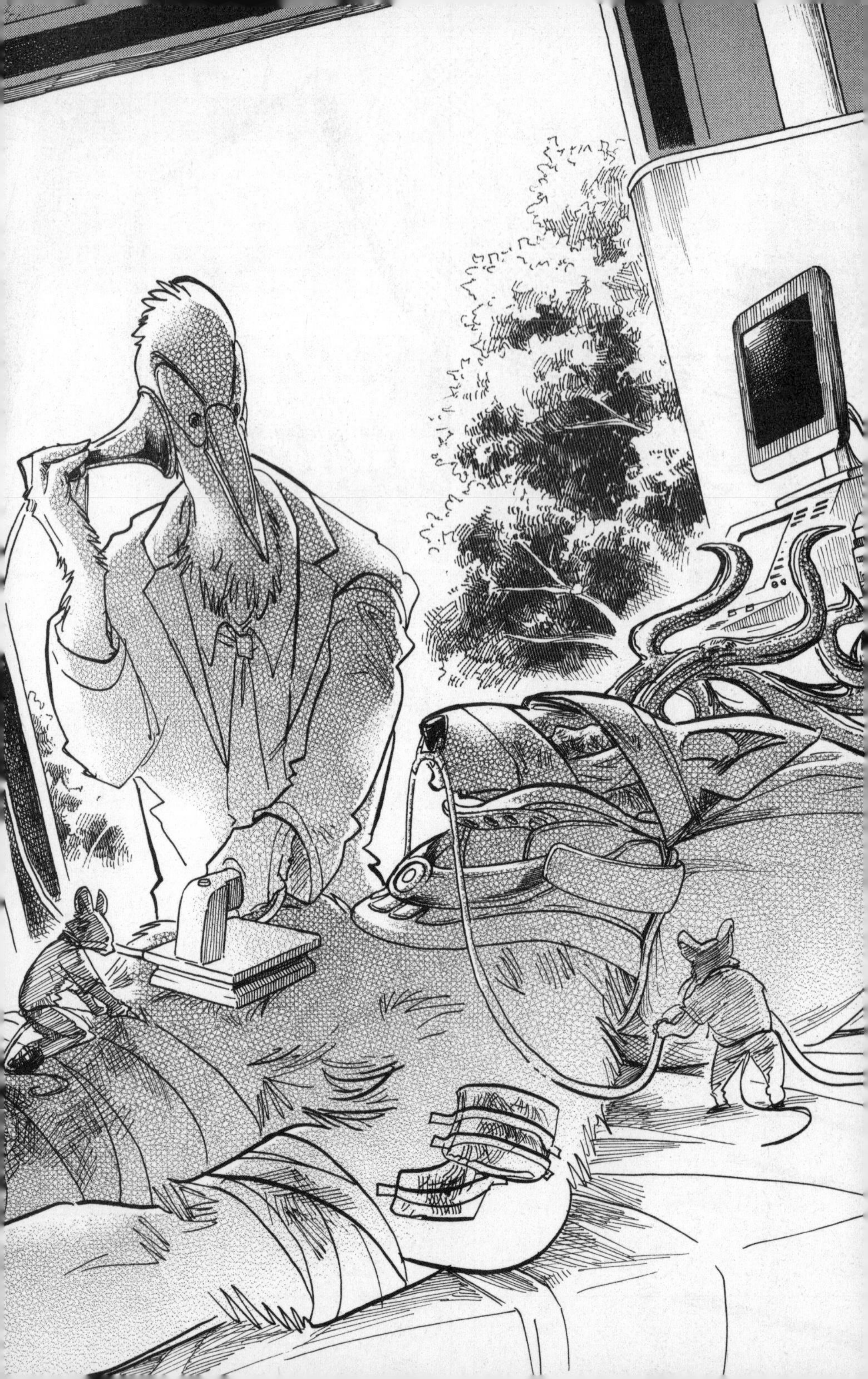

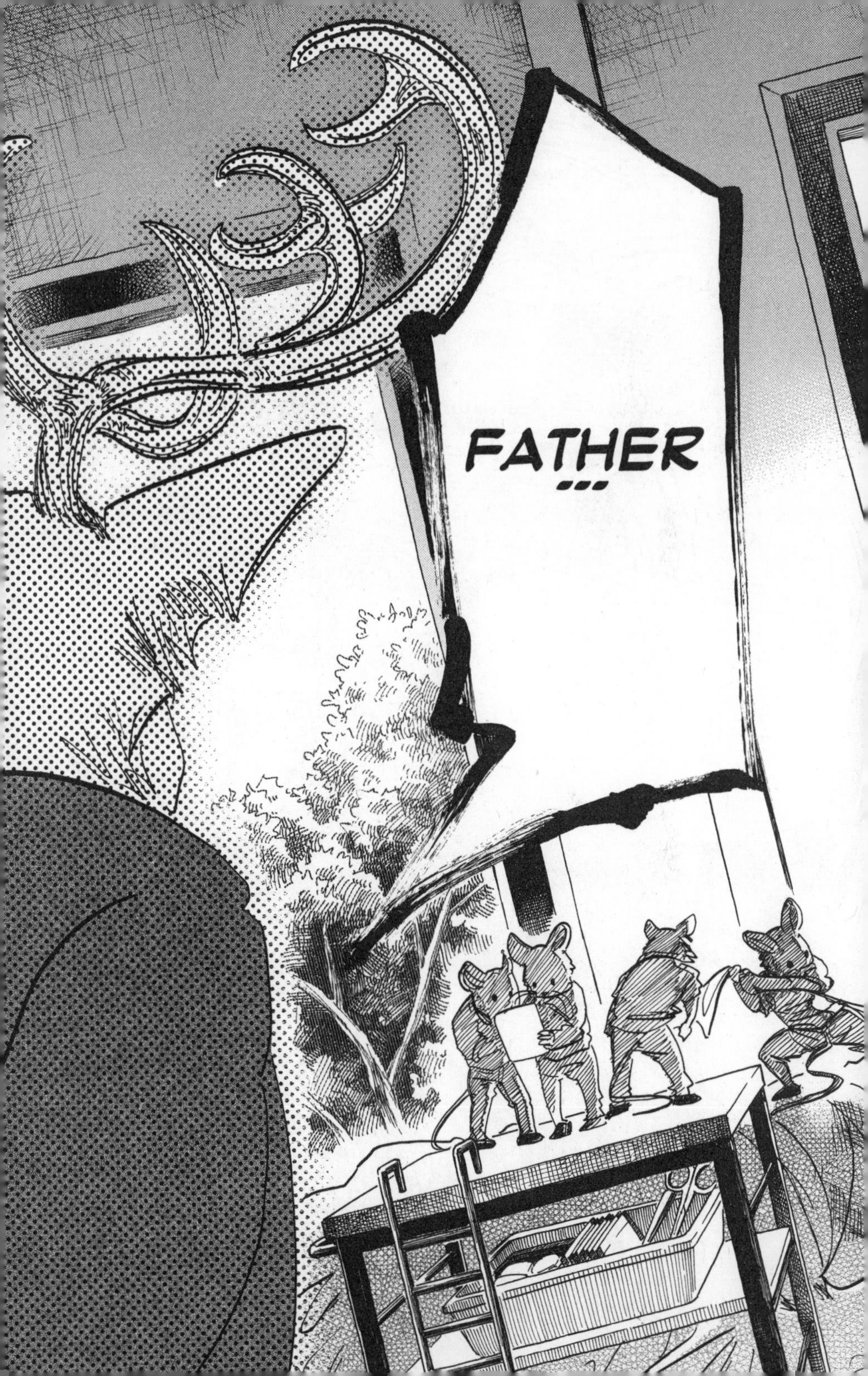
FATHER...

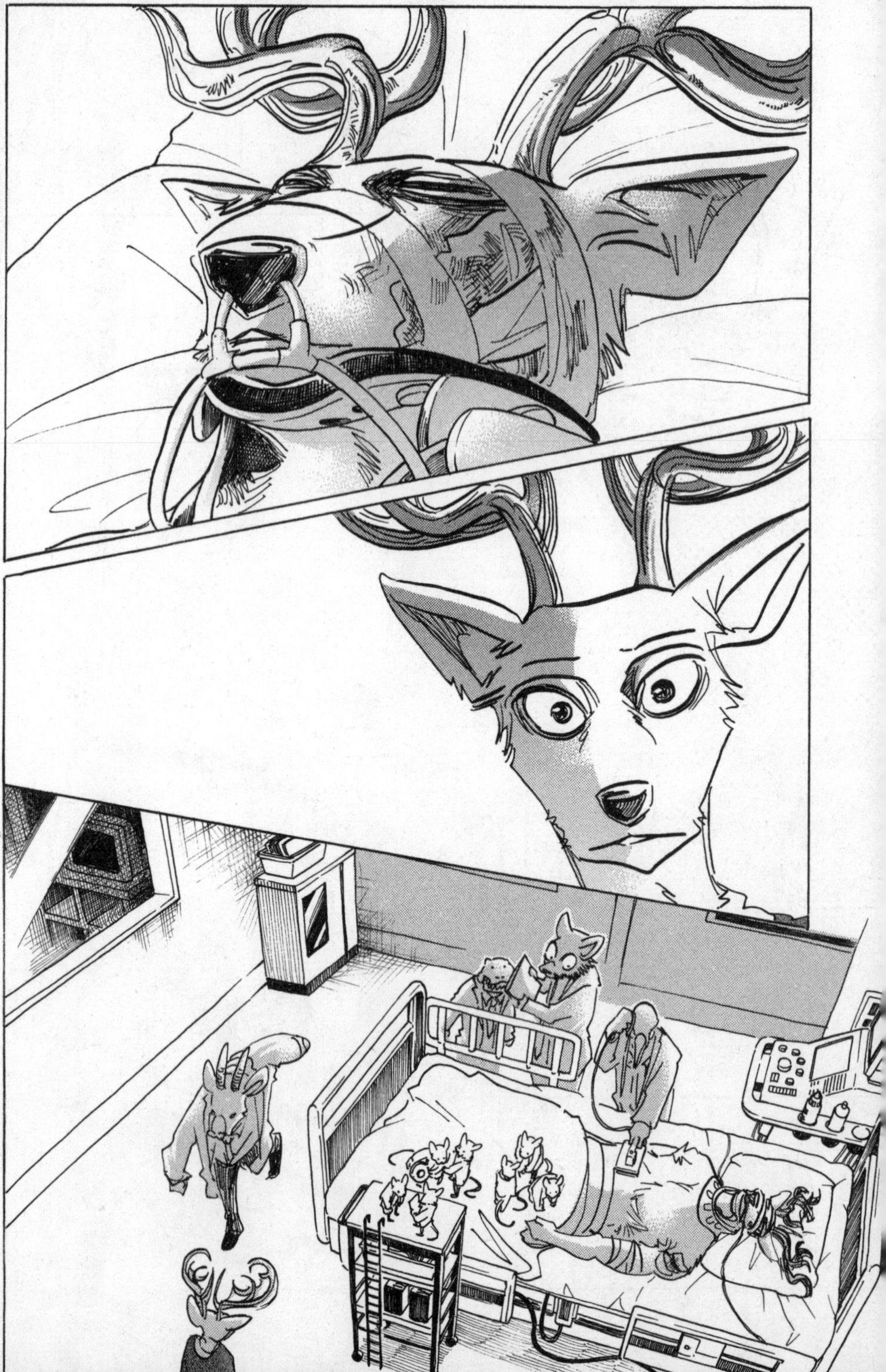

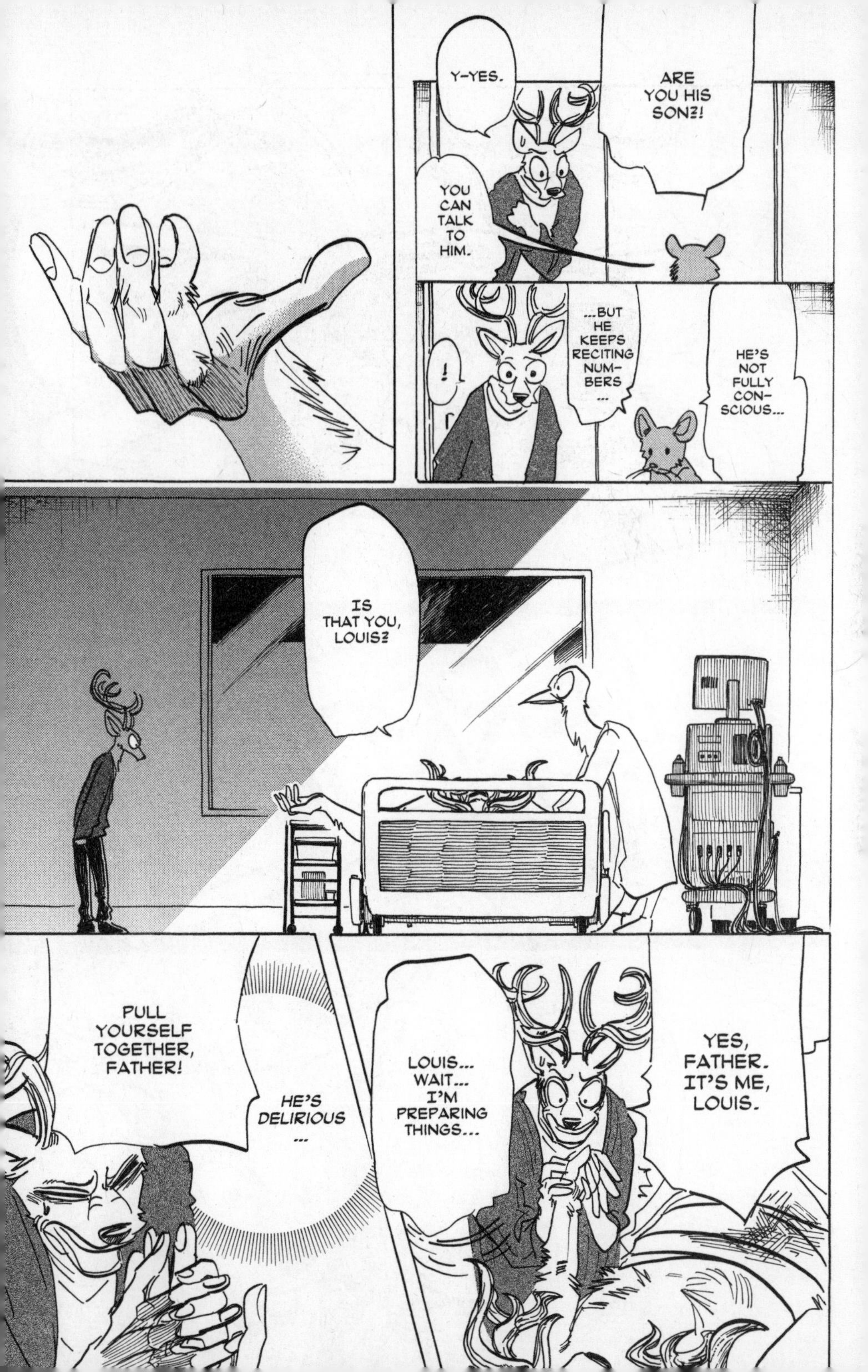
ARE YOU HIS SON?!
Y-YES.
YOU CAN TALK TO HIM.
HE'S NOT FULLY CON-SCIOUS...
...BUT HE KEEPS RECITING NUM-BERS...
!
IS THAT YOU, LOUIS?
YES, FATHER. IT'S ME, LOUIS.
LOUIS... WAIT... I'M PREPARING THINGS...
PULL YOURSELF TOGETHER, FATHER!
HE'S DELIRIOUS...

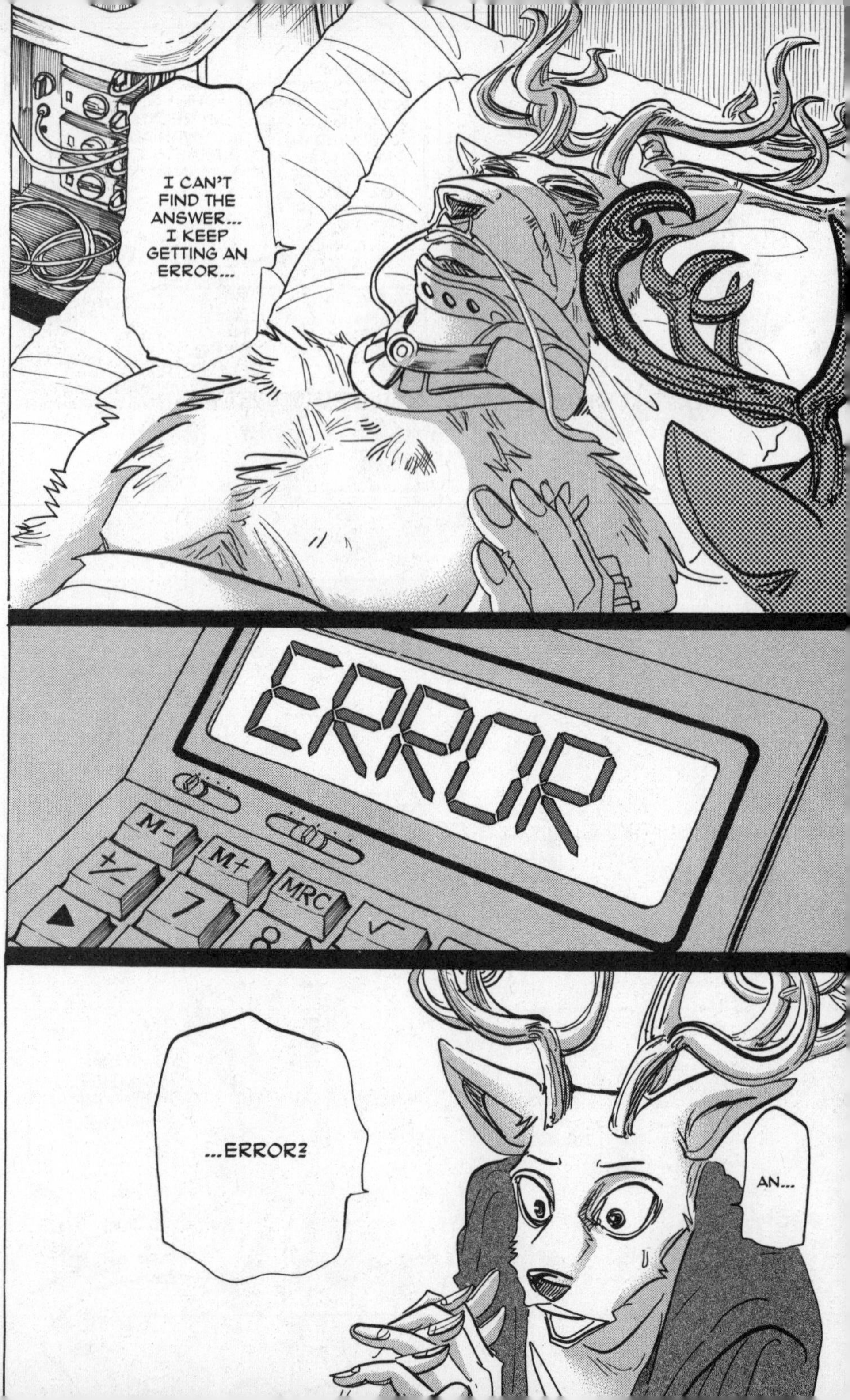
I CAN'T FIND THE ANSWER... I KEEP GETTING AN ERROR...
ERROR
M-
M+
MRC
AN...
...ERROR?

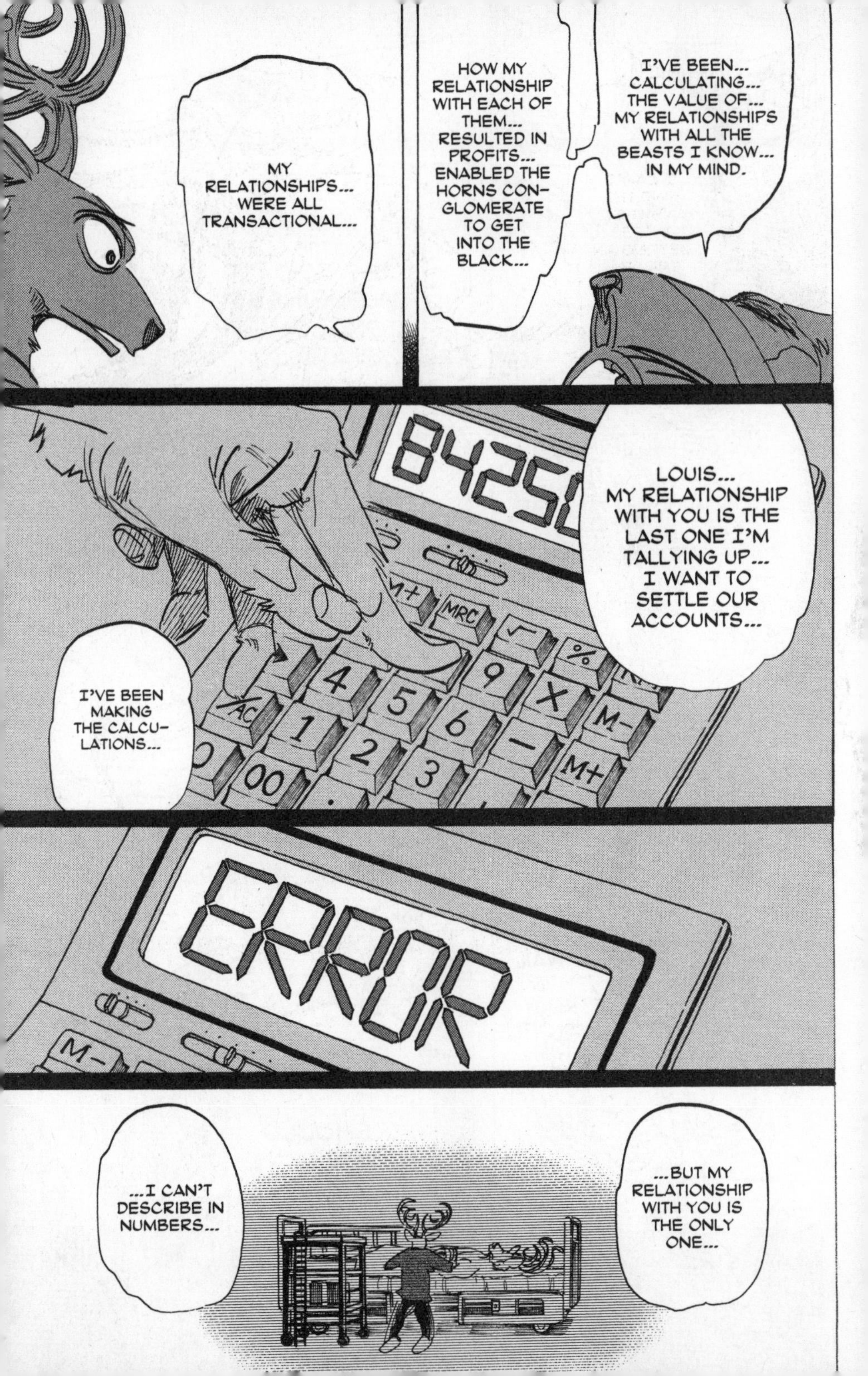
I'VE BEEN... CALCULATING... THE VALUE OF... MY RELATIONSHIPS WITH ALL THE BEASTS I KNOW... IN MY MIND.
HOW MY RELATIONSHIP WITH EACH OF THEM... RESULTED IN PROFITS... ENABLED THE HORNS CONGLOMERATE TO GET INTO THE BLACK...
MY RELATIONSHIPS... WERE ALL TRANSACTIONAL...
LOUIS... MY RELATIONSHIP WITH YOU IS THE LAST ONE I'M TALLYING UP... I WANT TO SETTLE OUR ACCOUNTS...
I'VE BEEN MAKING THE CALCULATIONS...
ERROR
...BUT MY RELATIONSHIP WITH YOU IS THE ONLY ONE...
...I CAN'T DESCRIBE IN NUMBERS...

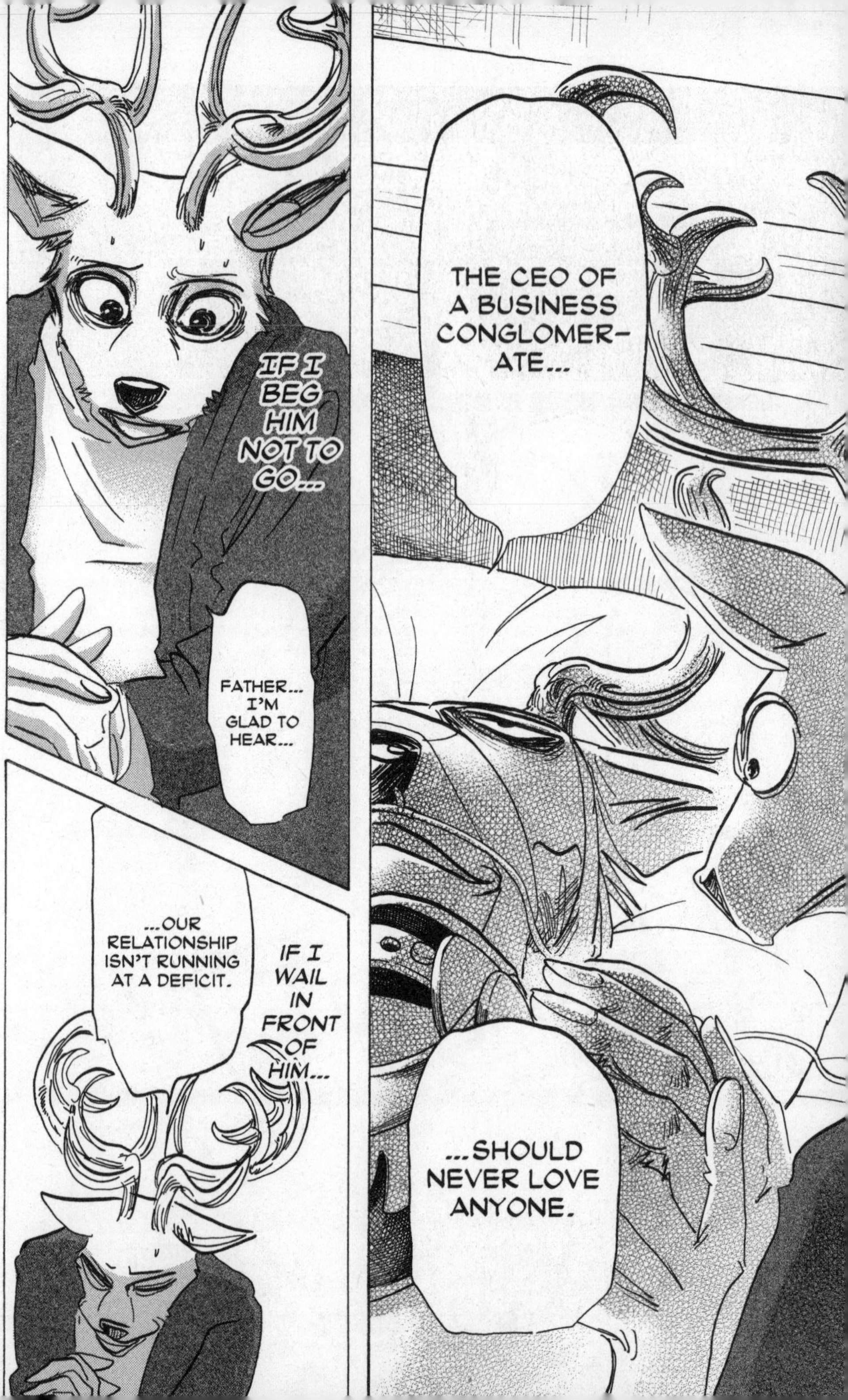
THE CEO OF A BUSINESS CONGLOMER-ATE...
...SHOULD NEVER LOVE ANYONE.
IF I BEG HIM NOT TO GO...
FATHER... I'M GLAD TO HEAR...
...OUR RELATIONSHIP ISN'T RUNNING AT A DEFICIT.
IF I WAIL IN FRONT OF HIM...

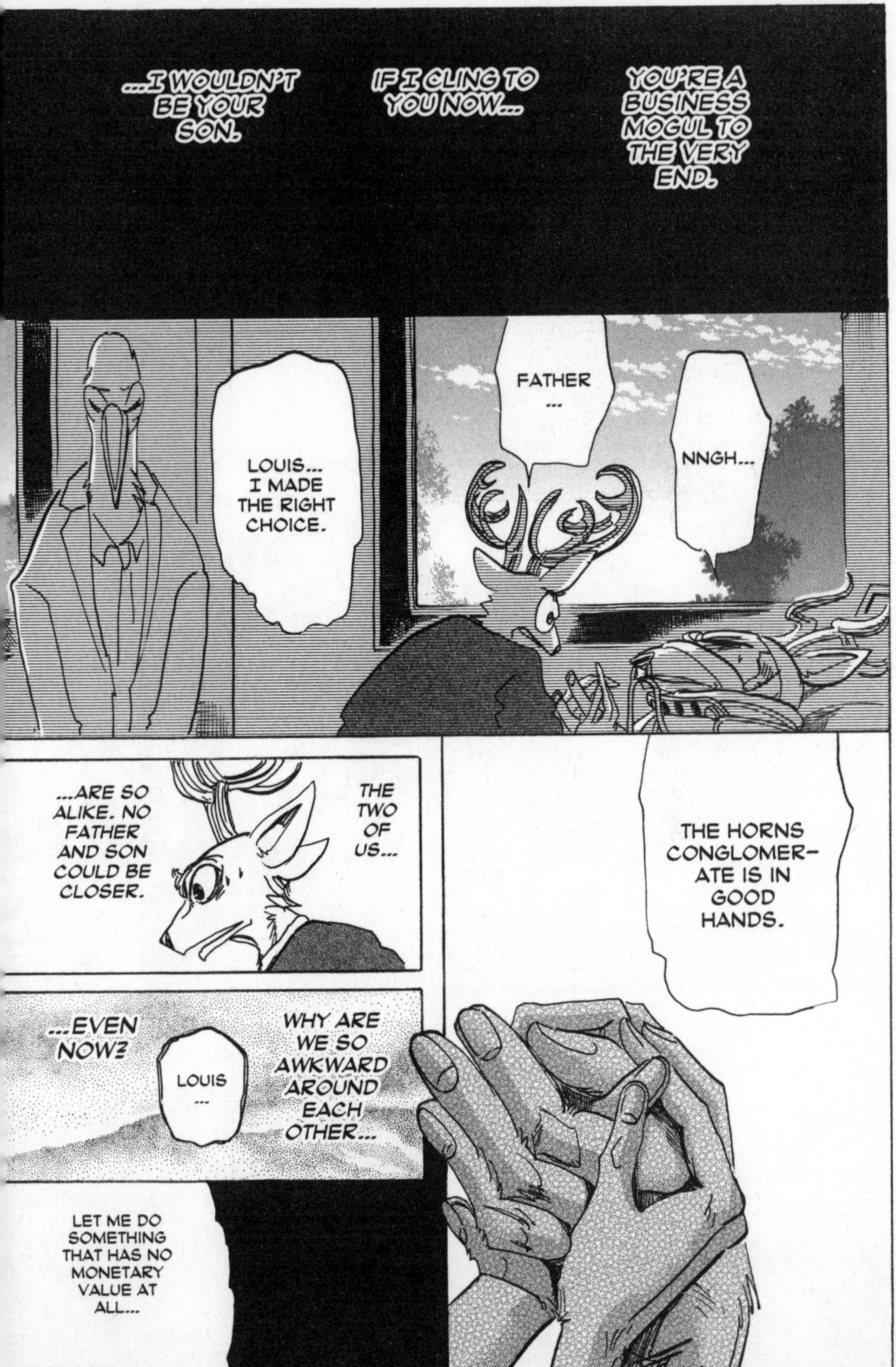
YOU'RE A BUSINESS MOGUL TO THE VERY END.
IF I CLING TO YOU NOW...
...I WOULDN'T BE YOUR SON.
NNGH...
FATHER ...
LOUIS... I MADE THE RIGHT CHOICE.
THE HORNS CONGLOMER-ATE IS IN GOOD HANDS.
THE TWO OF US...
...ARE SO ALIKE. NO FATHER AND SON COULD BE CLOSER.
WHY ARE WE SO AWKWARD AROUND EACH OTHER...
LOUIS ...
...EVEN NOW?
LET ME DO SOMETHING THAT HAS NO MONETARY VALUE AT ALL...

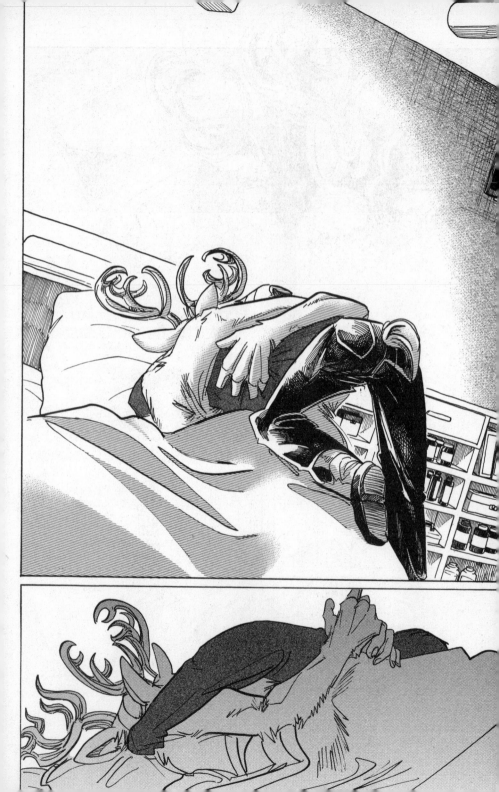

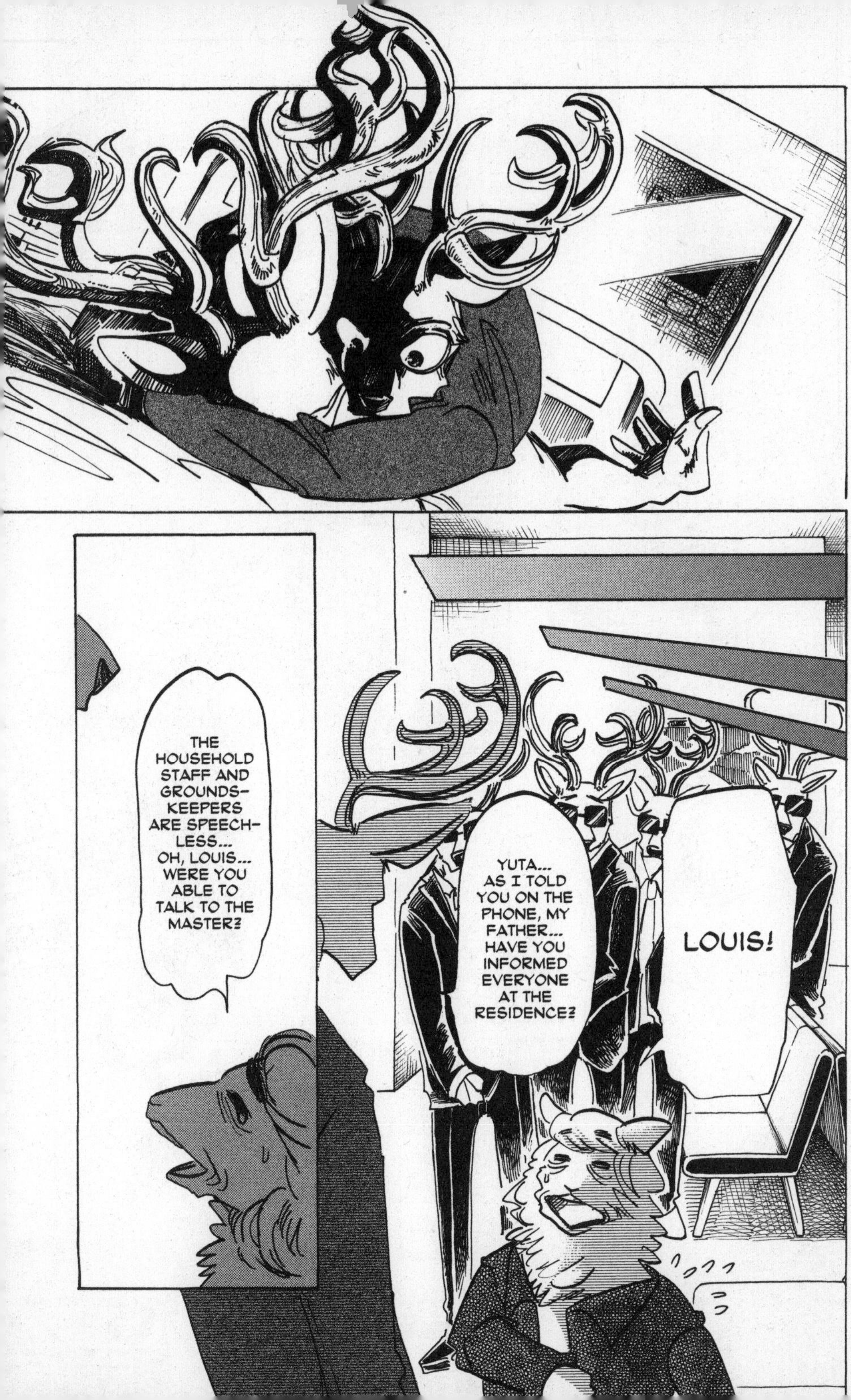
LOUIS!
YUTA... AS I TOLD YOU ON THE PHONE, MY FATHER... HAVE YOU INFORMED EVERYONE AT THE RESIDENCE?
THE HOUSEHOLD STAFF AND GROUNDS-KEEPERS ARE SPEECH-LESS... OH, LOUIS... WERE YOU ABLE TO TALK TO THE MASTER?

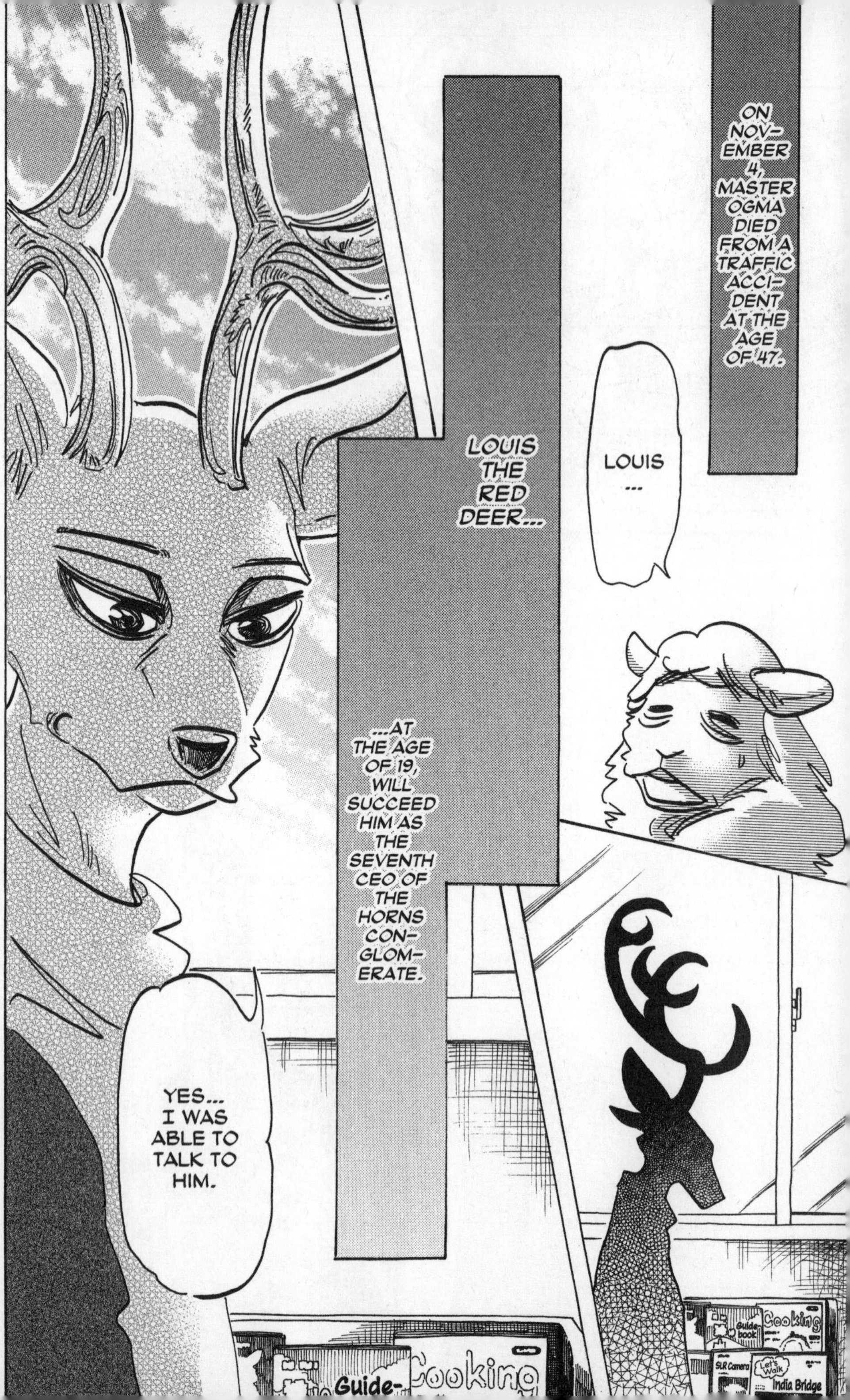
ON NOV-EMBER 4, MASTER OGMA DIED FROM A TRAFFIC ACCI-DENT AT THE AGE OF 47.
LOUIS ...
LOUIS THE RED DEER...
...AT THE AGE OF 19, WILL SUCCEED HIM AS THE SEVENTH CEO OF THE HORNS CON-GLOM-ERATE.
YES... I WAS ABLE TO TALK TO HIM.
Guide-book
Cooking
SLR Camera
Let's Walk
India Bridge
Guide-
Cooking

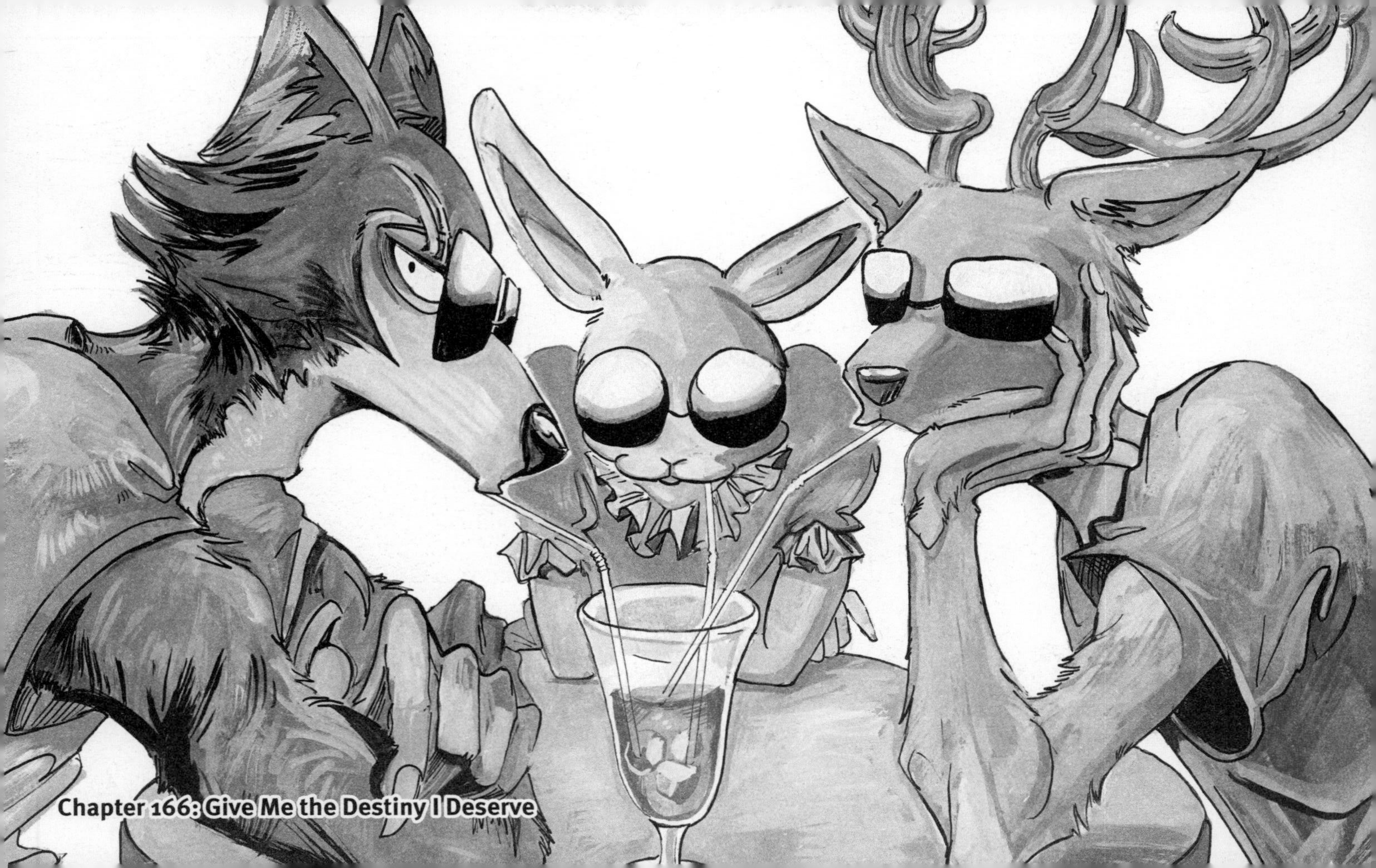
Chapter 166: Give Me the Destiny I Deserve

BEASTARS
Vol. 19

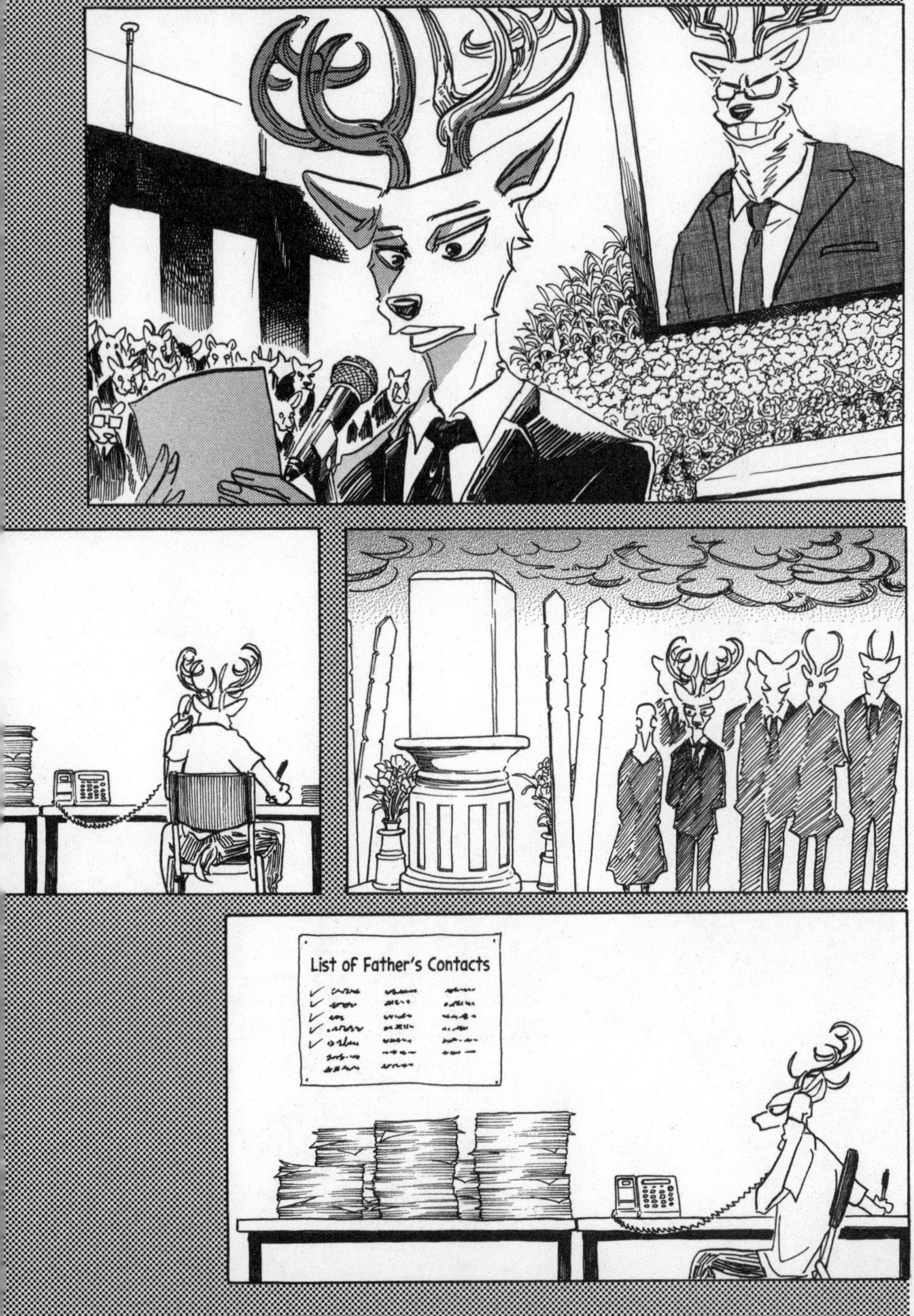
List of Father's Contacts

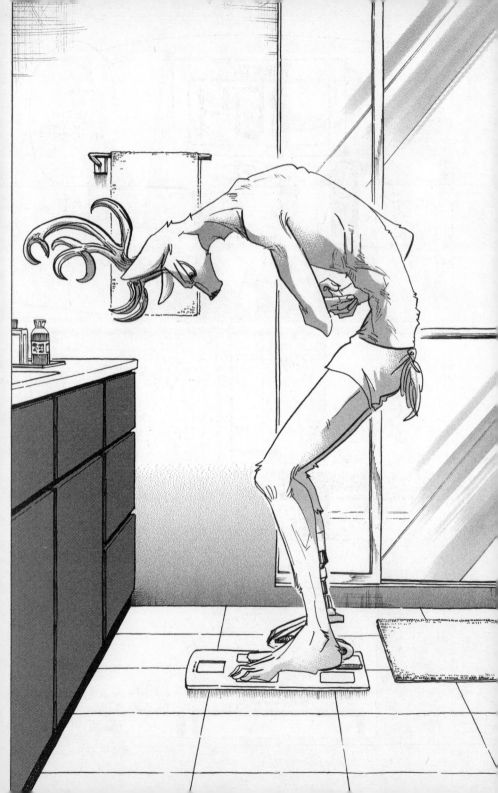

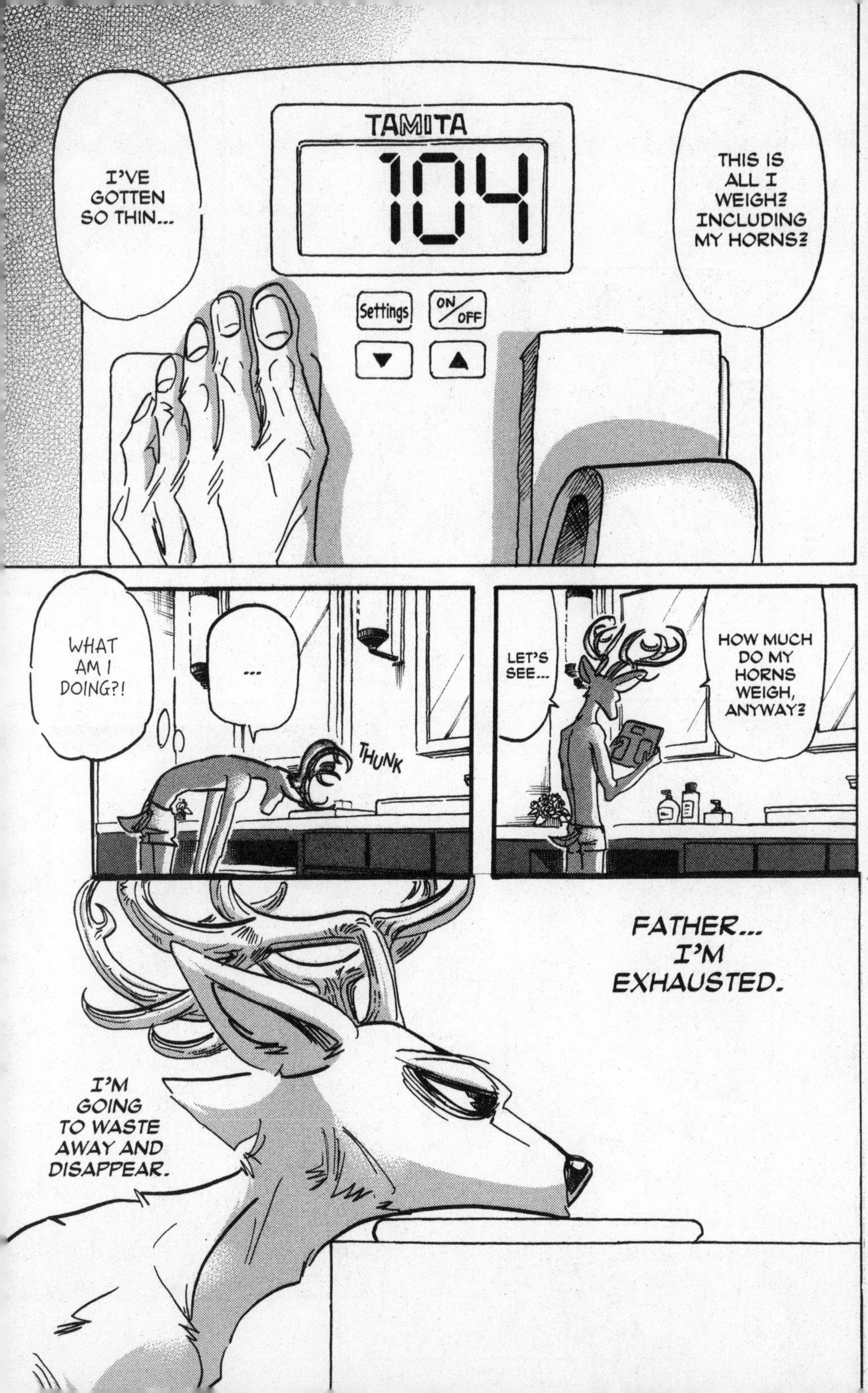
TAMITA
104
Settings
ON/OFF
THIS IS ALL I WEIGH? INCLUDING MY HORNS?
I'VE GOTTEN SO THIN...
HOW MUCH DO MY HORNS WEIGH, ANYWAY?
LET'S SEE...
...
THUNK
WHAT AM I DOING?!
FATHER... I'M EXHAUSTED.
I'M GOING TO WASTE AWAY AND DISAPPEAR.

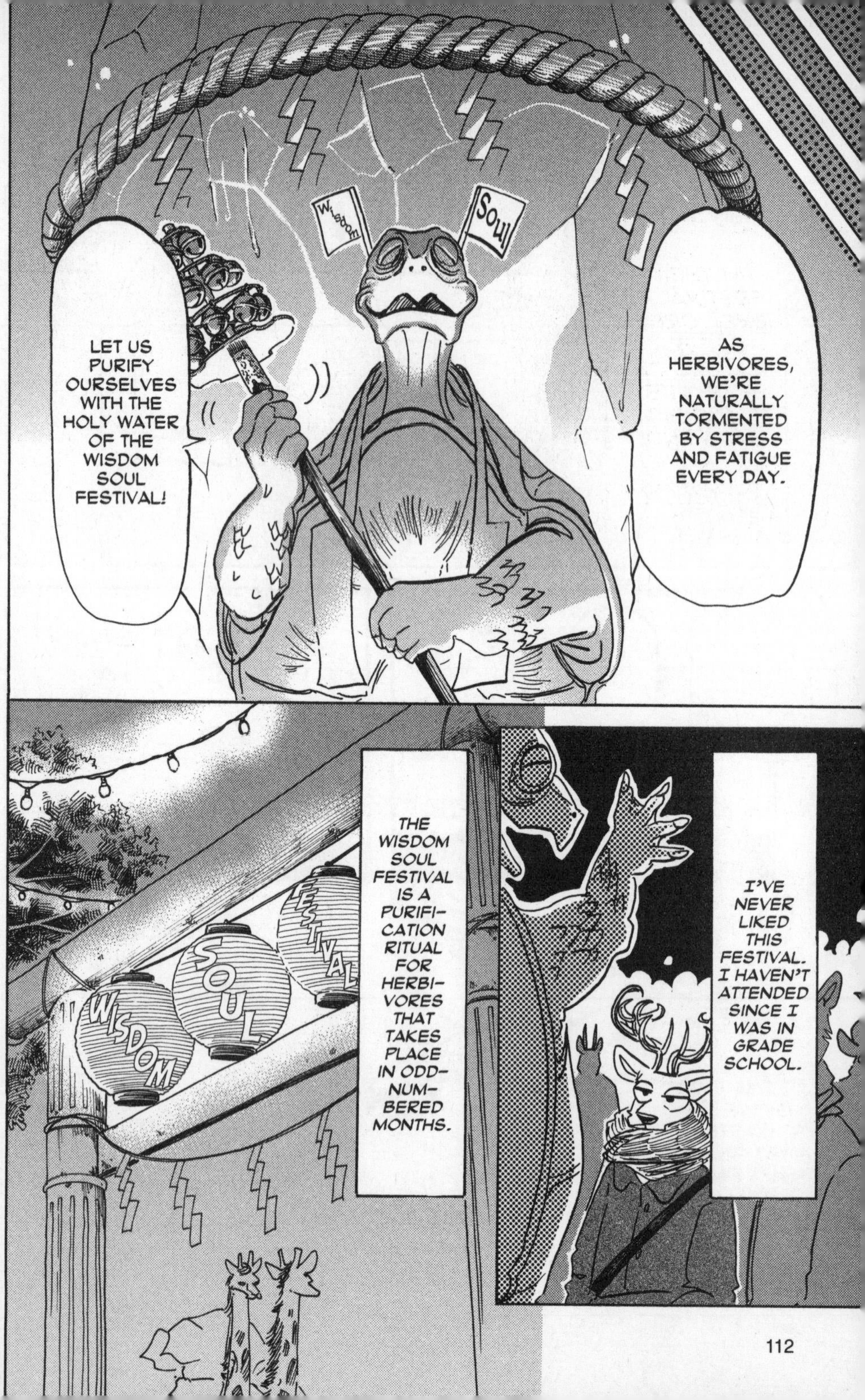
Soul
Wisdom
AS HERBIVORES, WE'RE NATURALLY TORMENTED BY STRESS AND FATIGUE EVERY DAY.
LET US PURIFY OURSELVES WITH THE HOLY WATER OF THE WISDOM SOUL FESTIVAL!
I'VE NEVER LIKED THIS FESTIVAL. I HAVEN'T ATTENDED SINCE I WAS IN GRADE SCHOOL.
THE WISDOM SOUL FESTIVAL IS A PURIFICATION RITUAL FOR HERBIVORES THAT TAKES PLACE IN ODD-NUMBERED MONTHS.
FESTIVAL
SOUL
WISDOM

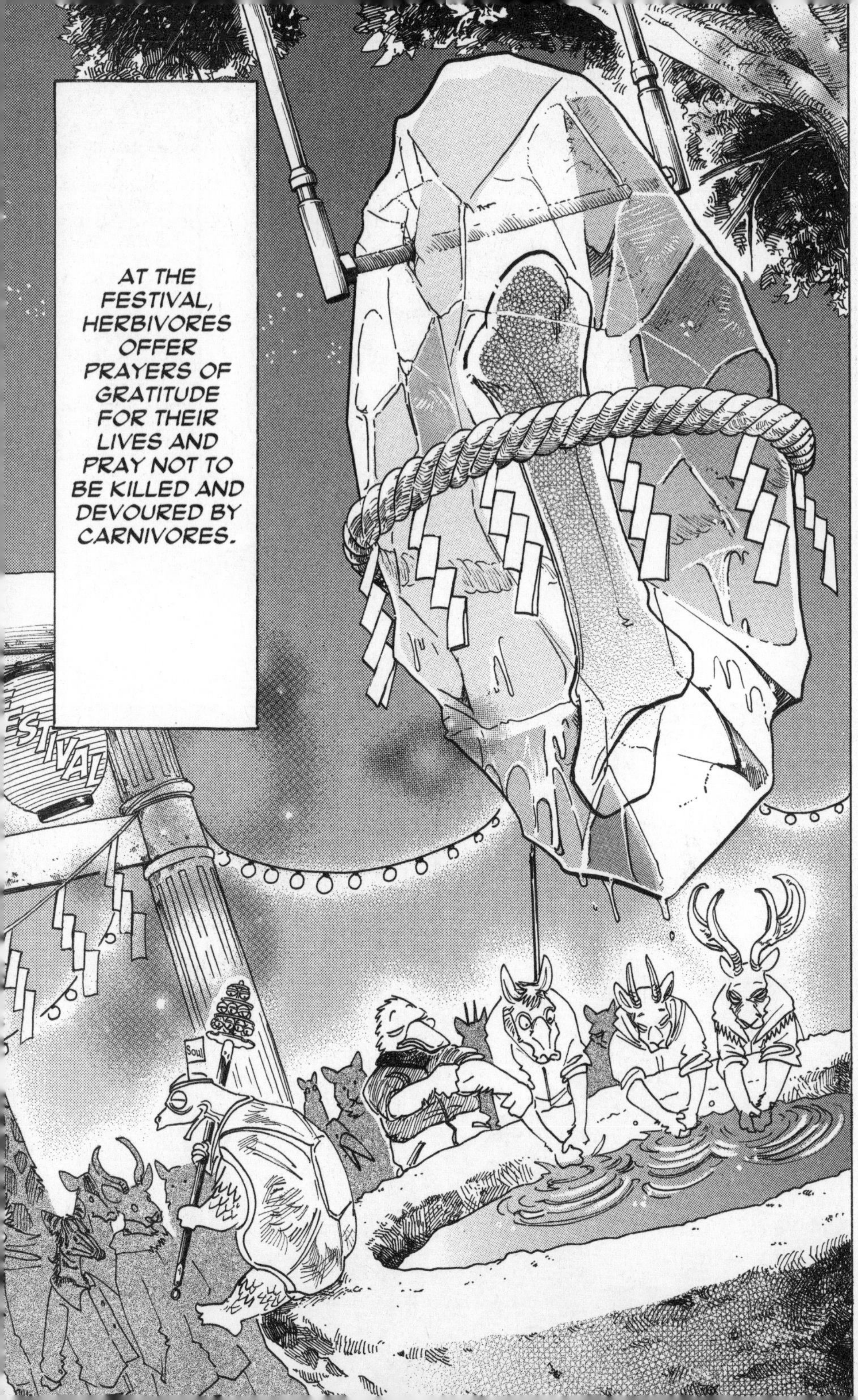
AT THE FESTIVAL, HERBIVORES OFFER PRAYERS OF GRATITUDE FOR THEIR LIVES AND PRAY NOT TO BE KILLED AND DEVOURED BY CARNIVORES.
Soul

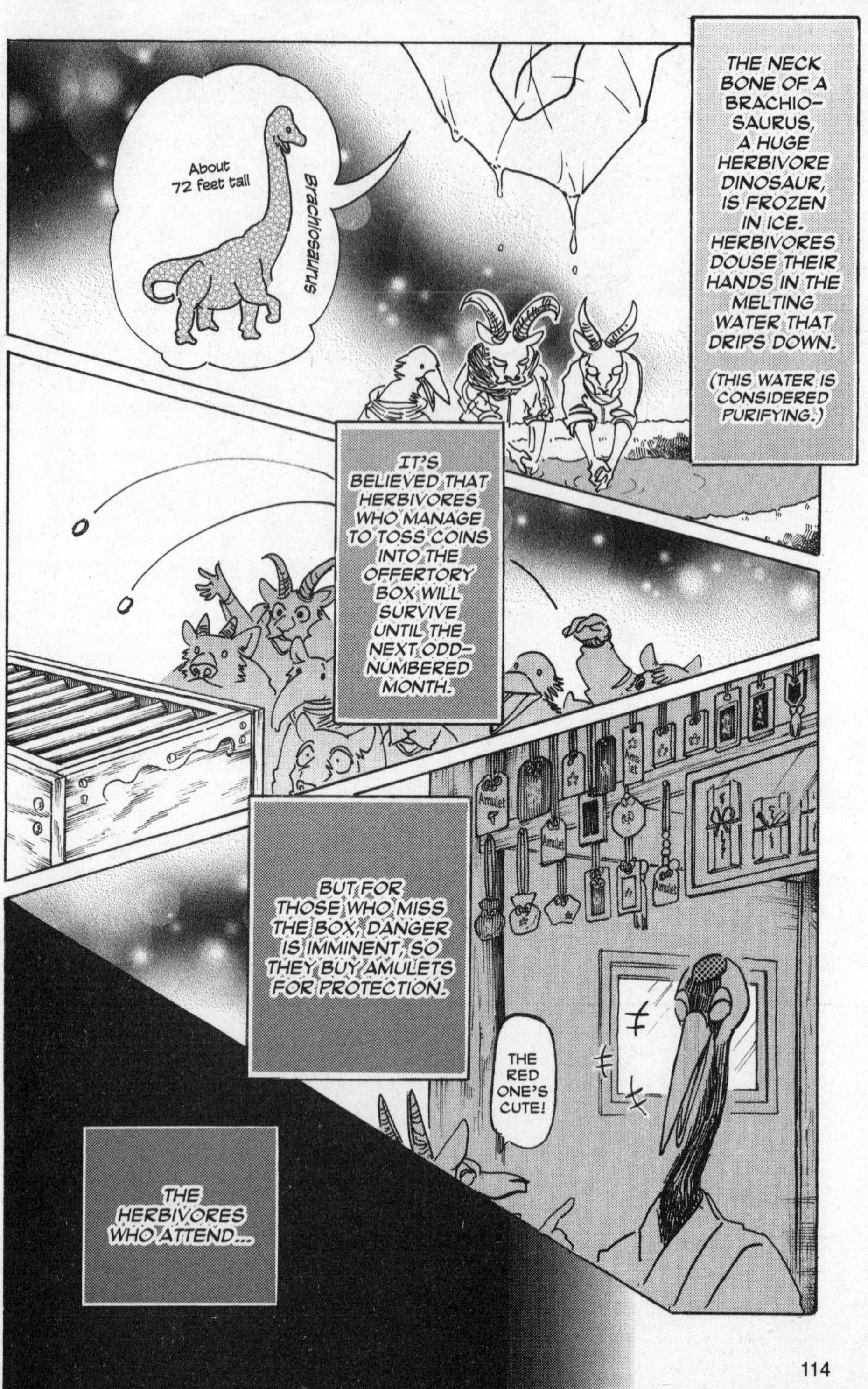
THE NECK BONE OF A BRACHIOSAURUS, A HUGE HERBIVORE DINOSAUR, IS FROZEN IN ICE. HERBIVORES DOUSE THEIR HANDS IN THE MELTING WATER THAT DRIPS DOWN.
(THIS WATER IS CONSIDERED PURIFYING.)
About 72 feet tall
Brachiosaurus
IT'S BELIEVED THAT HERBIVORES WHO MANAGE TO TOSS COINS INTO THE OFFERTORY BOX WILL SURVIVE UNTIL THE NEXT ODD-NUMBERED MONTH.
Amulet
Amulet
Amulet
Amulet
BUT FOR THOSE WHO MISS THE BOX, DANGER IS IMMINENT, SO THEY BUY AMULETS FOR PROTECTION.
THE RED ONE'S CUTE!
THE HERBIVORES WHO ATTEND...

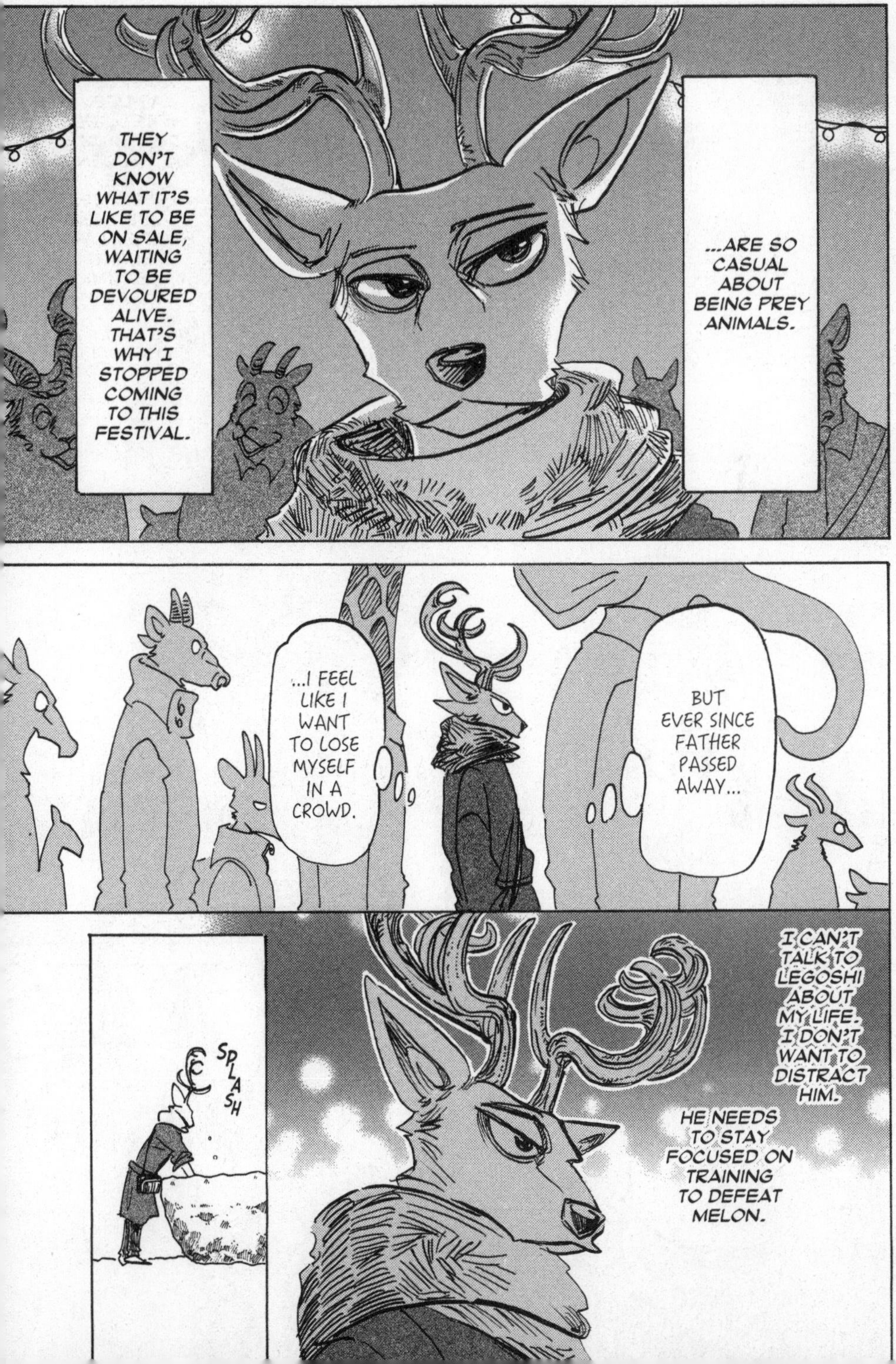
...ARE SO CASUAL ABOUT BEING PREY ANIMALS.
THEY DON'T KNOW WHAT IT'S LIKE TO BE ON SALE, WAITING TO BE DEVOURED ALIVE. THAT'S WHY I STOPPED COMING TO THIS FESTIVAL.
BUT EVER SINCE FATHER PASSED AWAY...
...I FEEL LIKE I WANT TO LOSE MYSELF IN A CROWD.
I CAN'T TALK TO LEGOSHI ABOUT MY LIFE. I DON'T WANT TO DISTRACT HIM.
HE NEEDS TO STAY FOCUSED ON TRAINING TO DEFEAT MELON.
SPLASH

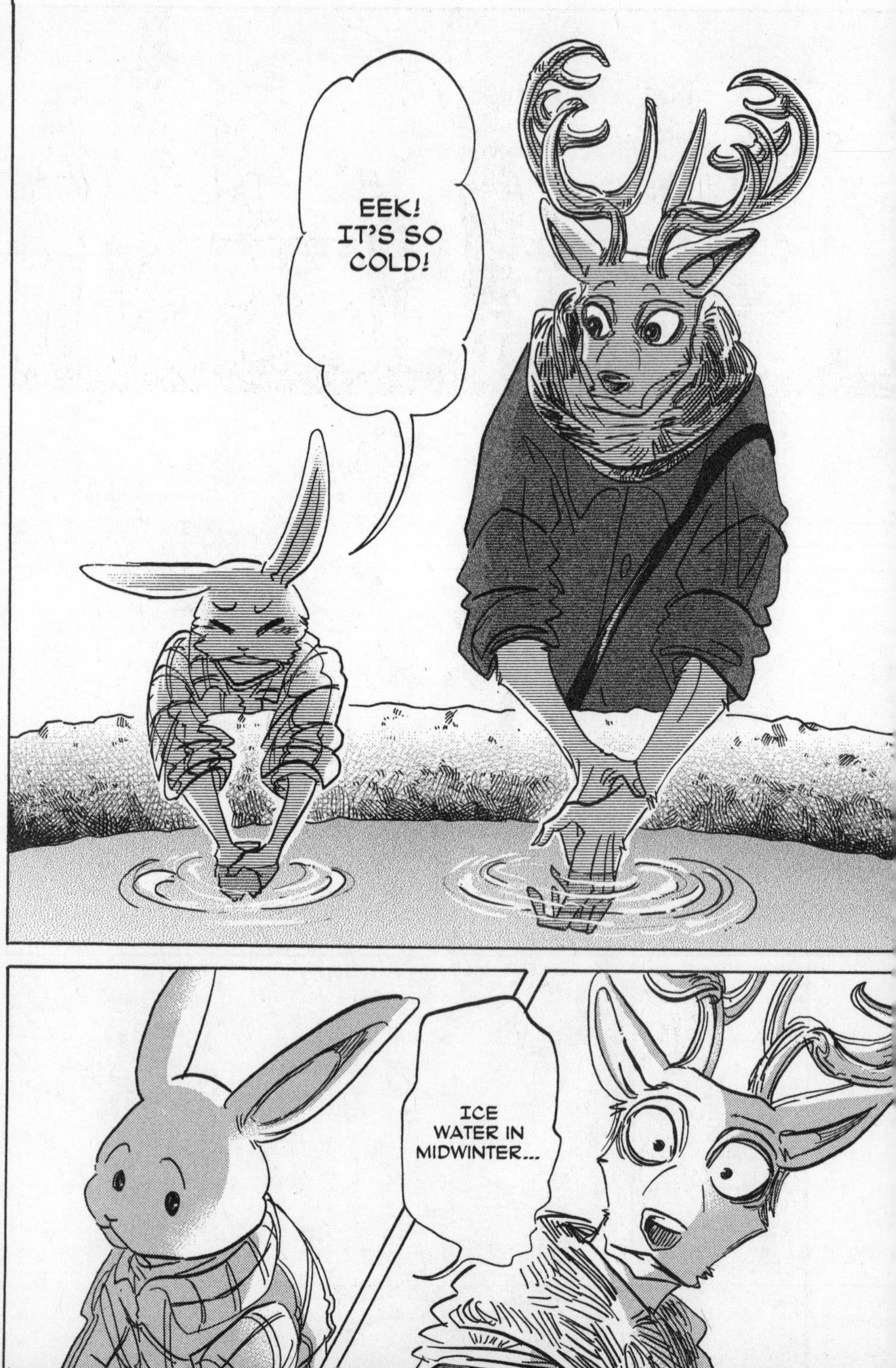
EEK! IT'S SO COLD!
ICE WATER IN MIDWINTER...

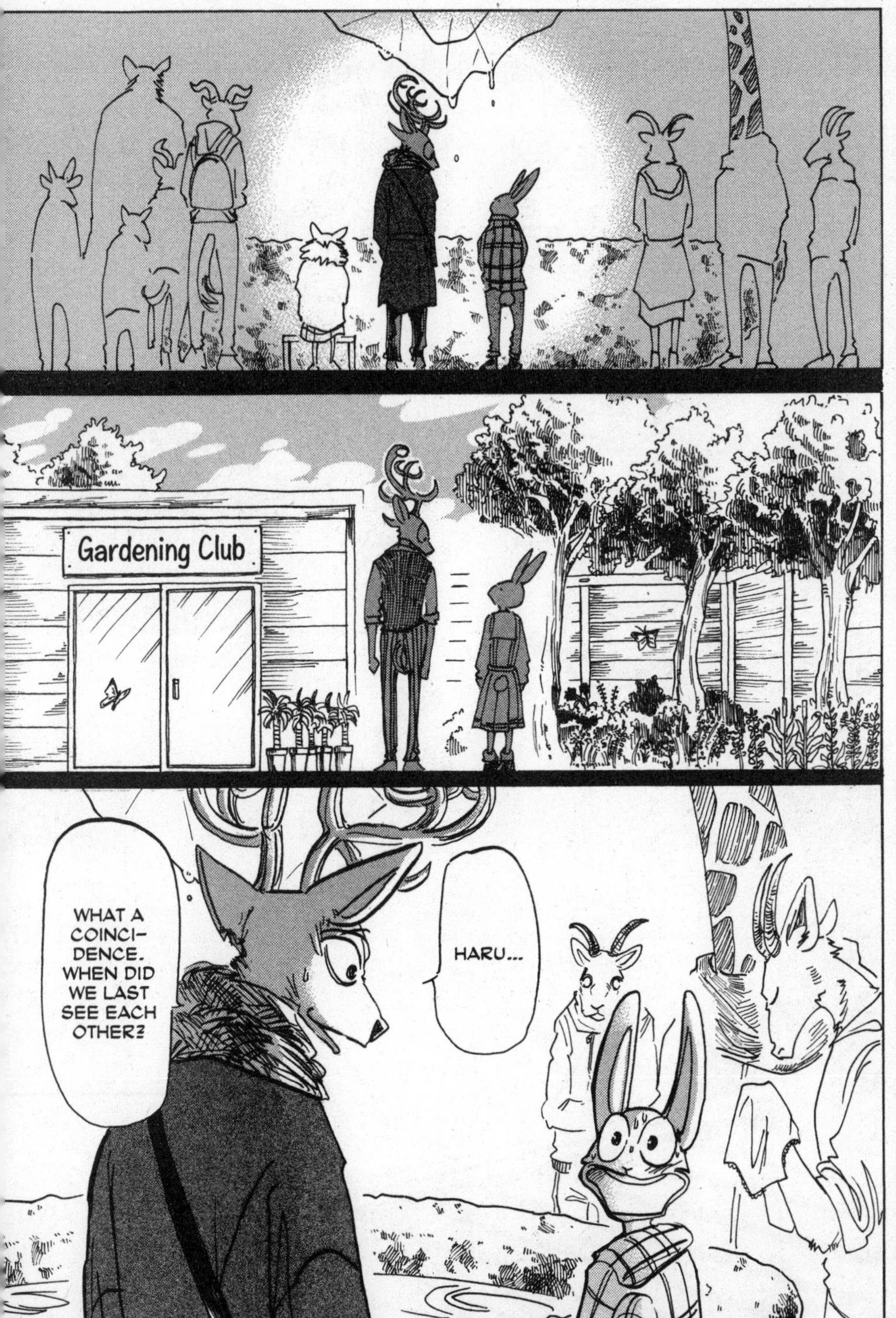
Gardening Club
HARU...
WHAT A COINCIDENCE. WHEN DID WE LAST SEE EACH OTHER?

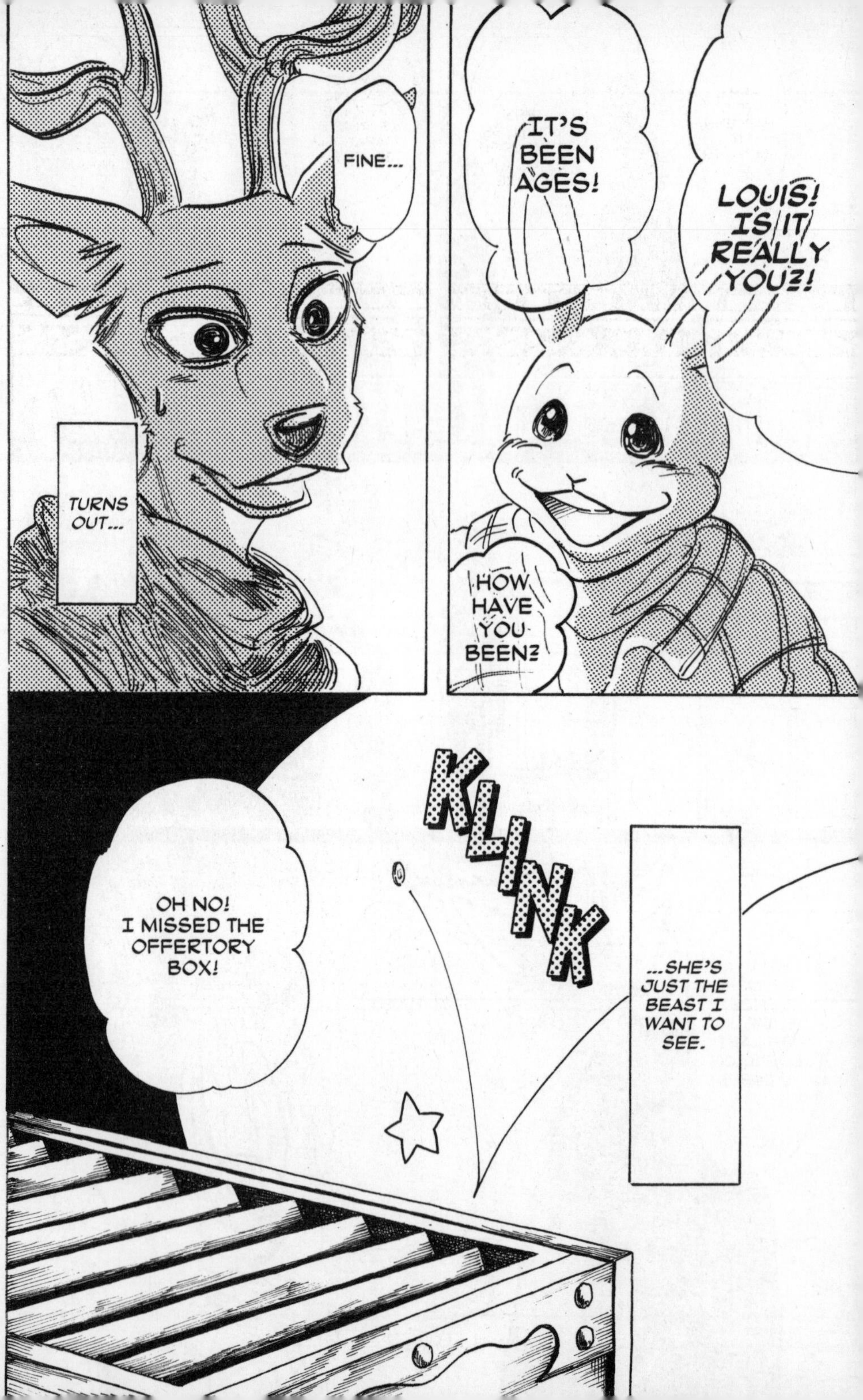
LOUIS! IS IT REALLY YOU?!
IT'S BEEN AGES!
HOW HAVE YOU BEEN?
FINE...
TURNS OUT...
...SHE'S JUST THE BEAST I WANT TO SEE.
KLINK
OH NO! I MISSED THE OFFERTORY BOX!

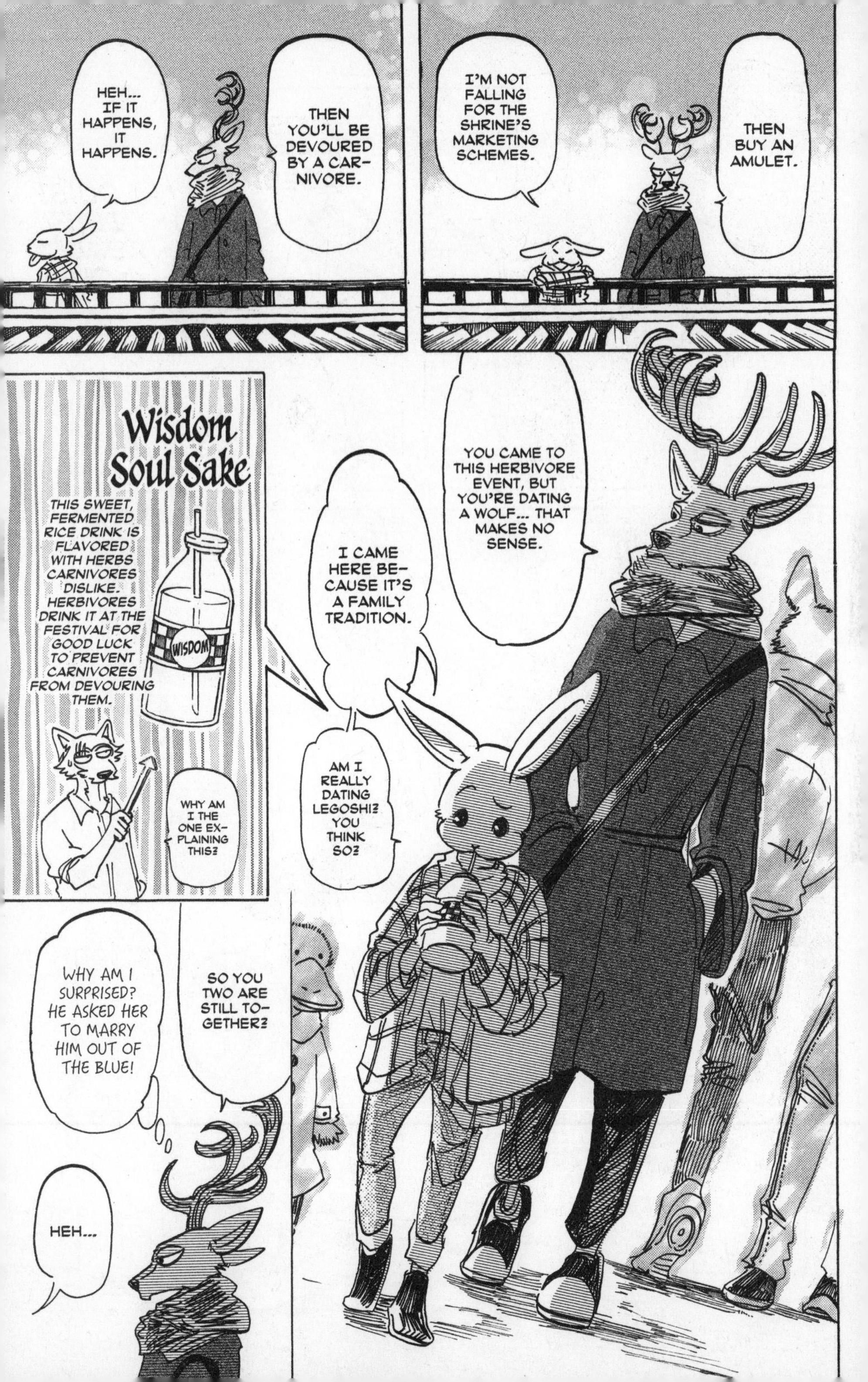
THEN BUY AN AMULET.
I'M NOT FALLING FOR THE SHRINE'S MARKETING SCHEMES.
THEN YOU'LL BE DEVOURED BY A CARNIVORE.
HEH... IF IT HAPPENS, IT HAPPENS.
YOU CAME TO THIS HERBIVORE EVENT, BUT YOU'RE DATING A WOLF... THAT MAKES NO SENSE.
I CAME HERE BECAUSE IT'S A FAMILY TRADITION.
AM I REALLY DATING LEGOSHI? YOU THINK SO?
Wisdom Soul Sake
THIS SWEET, FERMENTED RICE DRINK IS FLAVORED WITH HERBS CARNIVORES DISLIKE. HERBIVORES DRINK IT AT THE FESTIVAL FOR GOOD LUCK TO PREVENT CARNIVORES FROM DEVOURING THEM.
WISDOM
WHY AM I THE ONE EXPLAINING THIS?
SO YOU TWO ARE STILL TOGETHER?
WHY AM I SURPRISED? HE ASKED HER TO MARRY HIM OUT OF THE BLUE!
HEH...

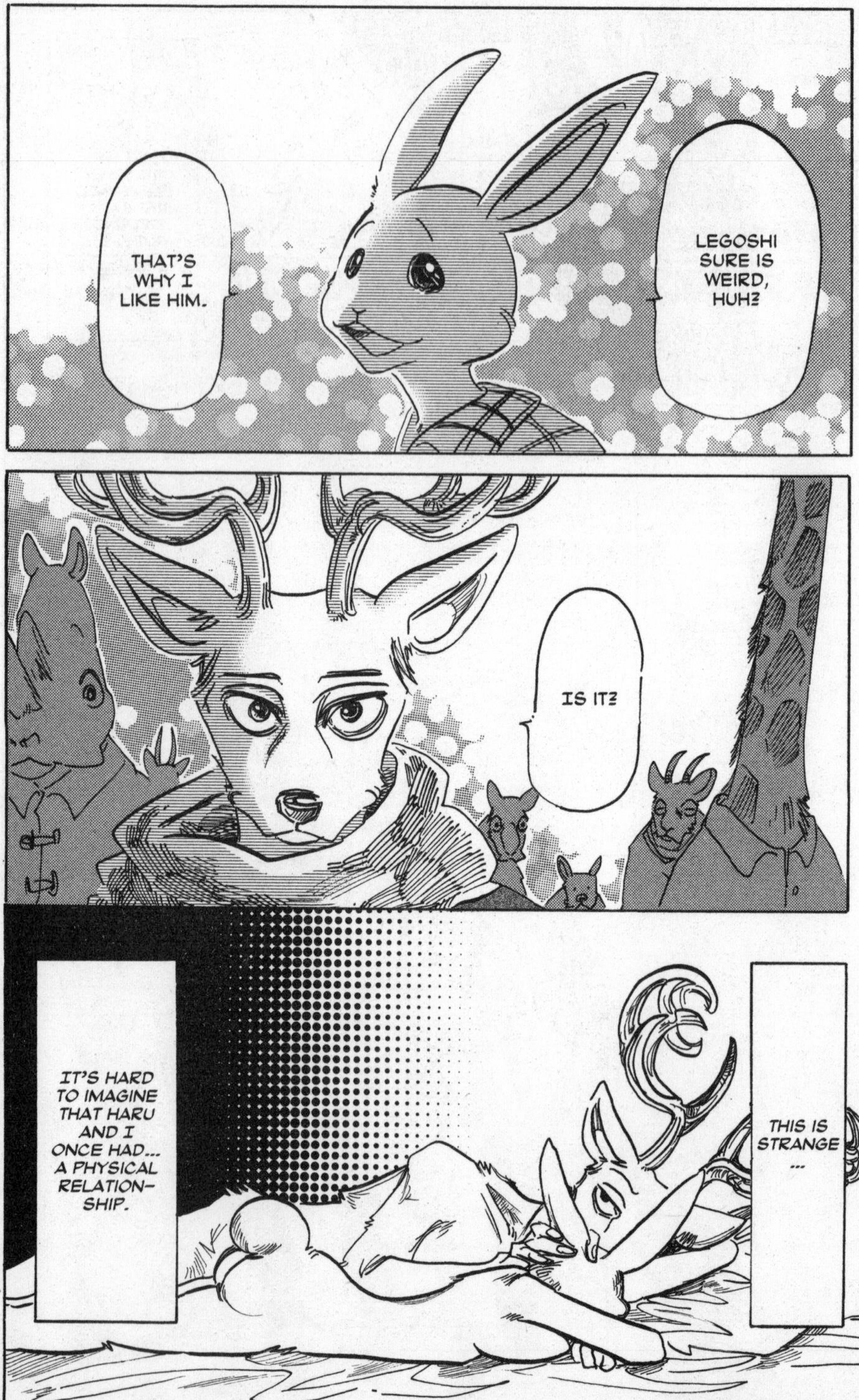
LEGOSHI SURE IS WEIRD, HUH?
THAT'S WHY I LIKE HIM.
IS IT?
THIS IS STRANGE...
IT'S HARD TO IMAGINE THAT HARU AND I ONCE HAD... A PHYSICAL RELATION-SHIP.

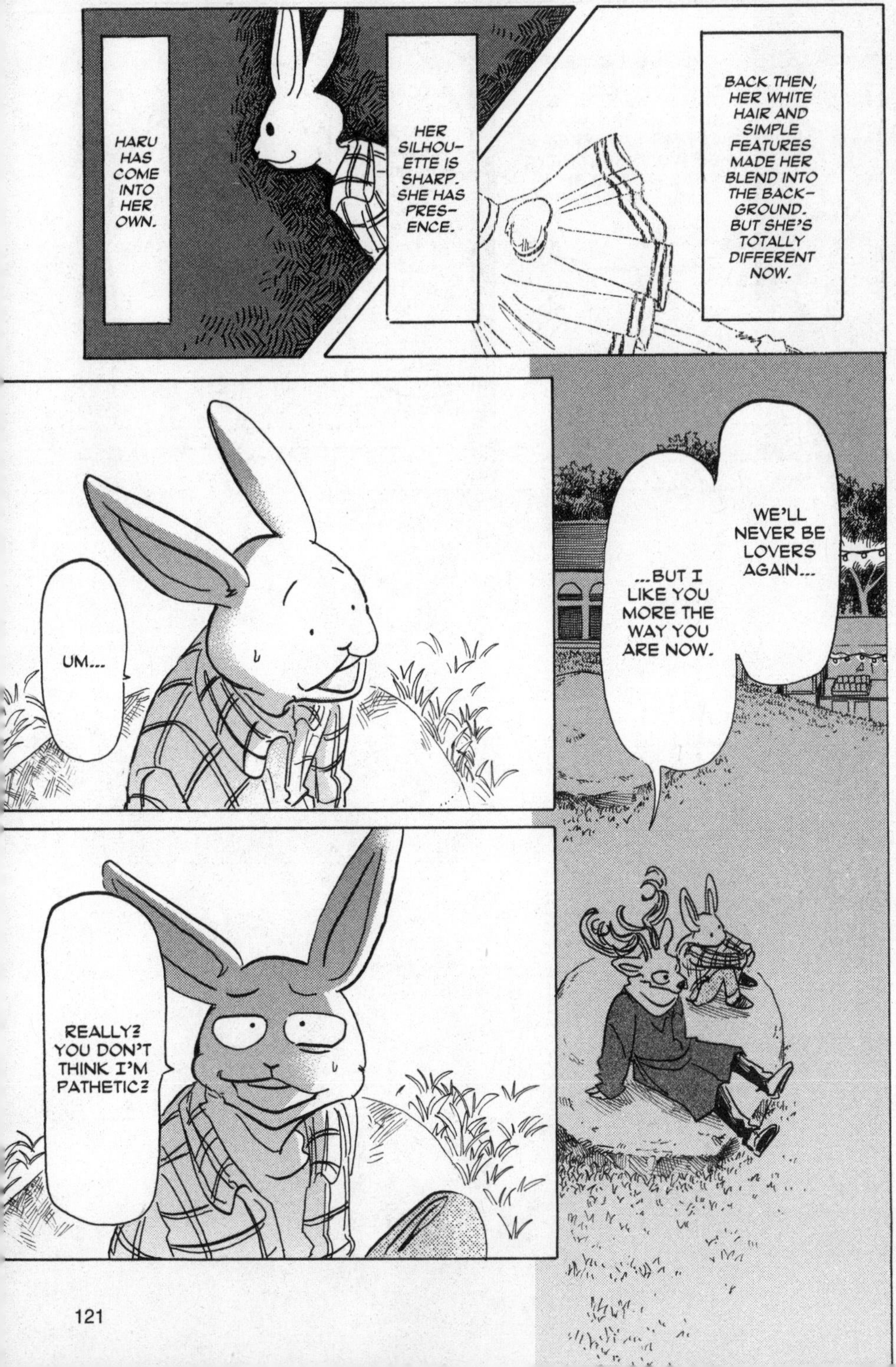
BACK THEN, HER WHITE HAIR AND SIMPLE FEATURES MADE HER BLEND INTO THE BACK-GROUND. BUT SHE'S TOTALLY DIFFERENT NOW.
HER SILHOU-ETTE IS SHARP. SHE HAS PRES-ENCE.
HARU HAS COME INTO HER OWN.
WE'LL NEVER BE LOVERS AGAIN...
...BUT I LIKE YOU MORE THE WAY YOU ARE NOW.
UM...
REALLY? YOU DON'T THINK I'M PATHETIC?

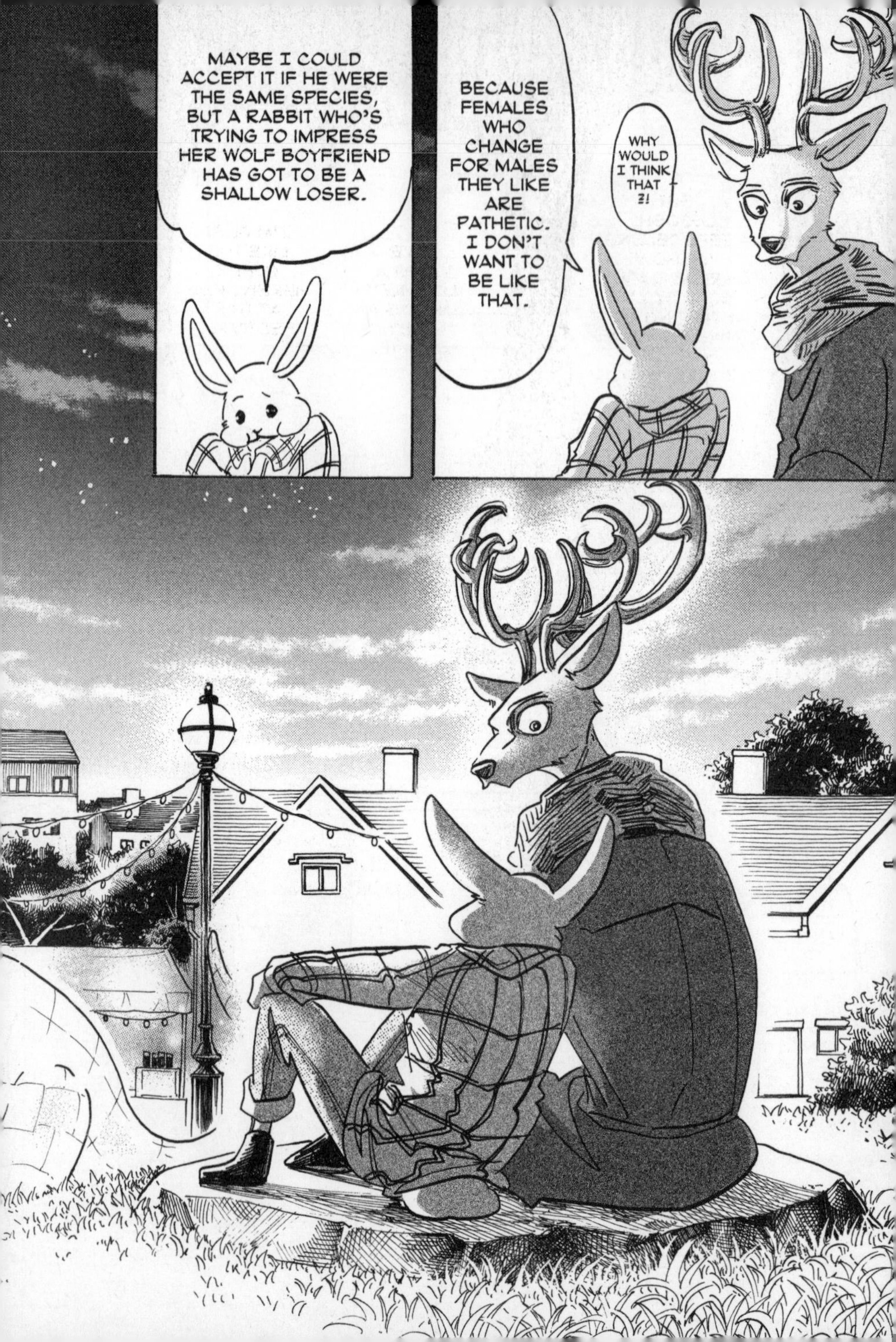
MAYBE I COULD ACCEPT IT IF HE WERE THE SAME SPECIES, BUT A RABBIT WHO'S TRYING TO IMPRESS HER WOLF BOYFRIEND HAS GOT TO BE A SHALLOW LOSER.
BECAUSE FEMALES WHO CHANGE FOR MALES THEY LIKE ARE PATHETIC. I DON'T WANT TO BE LIKE THAT.
WHY WOULD I THINK THAT ?!

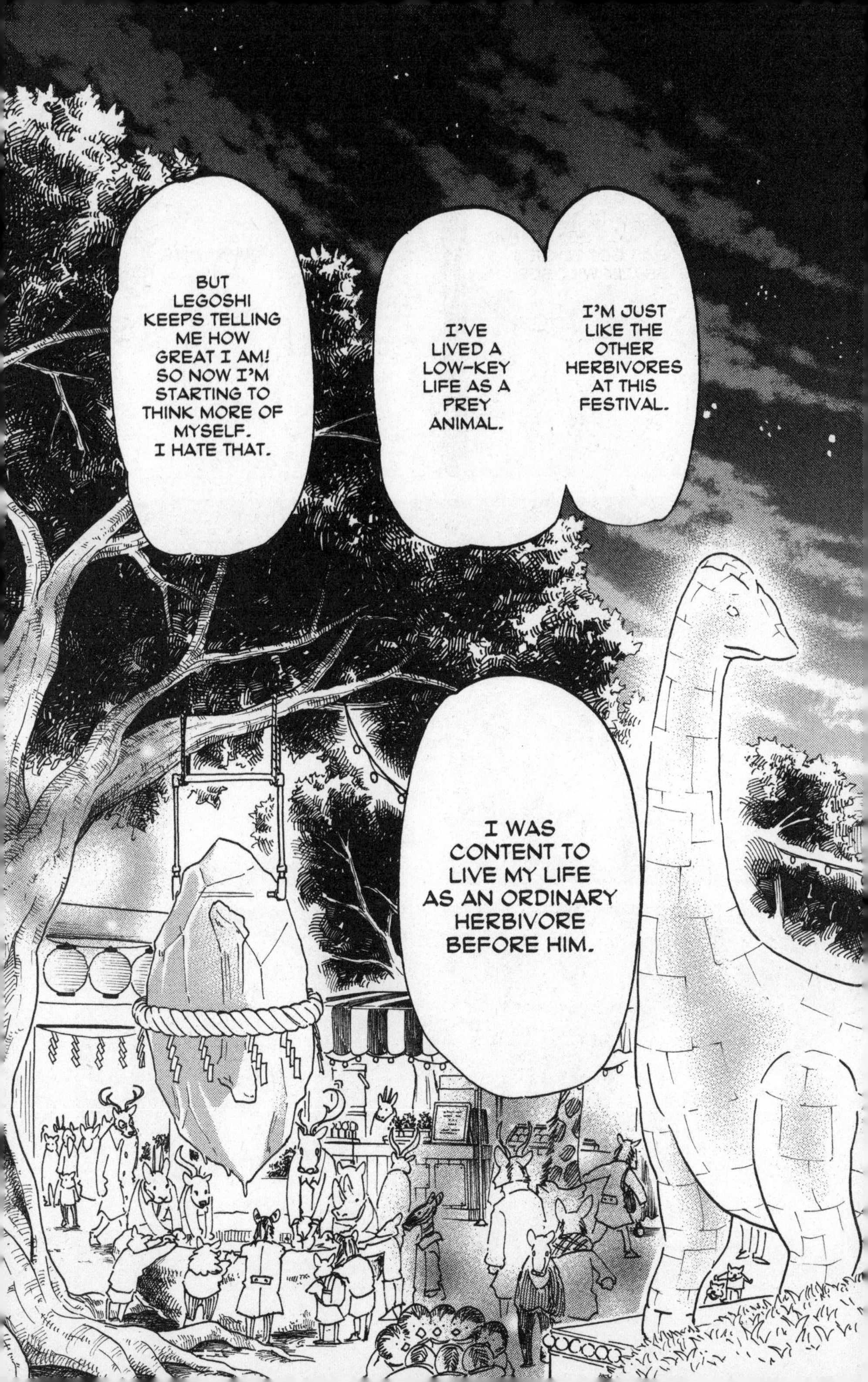
I'M JUST LIKE THE OTHER HERBIVORES AT THIS FESTIVAL.
I'VE LIVED A LOW-KEY LIFE AS A PREY ANIMAL.
BUT LEGOSHI KEEPS TELLING ME HOW GREAT I AM! SO NOW I'M STARTING TO THINK MORE OF MYSELF. I HATE THAT.
I WAS CONTENT TO LIVE MY LIFE AS AN ORDINARY HERBIVORE BEFORE HIM.

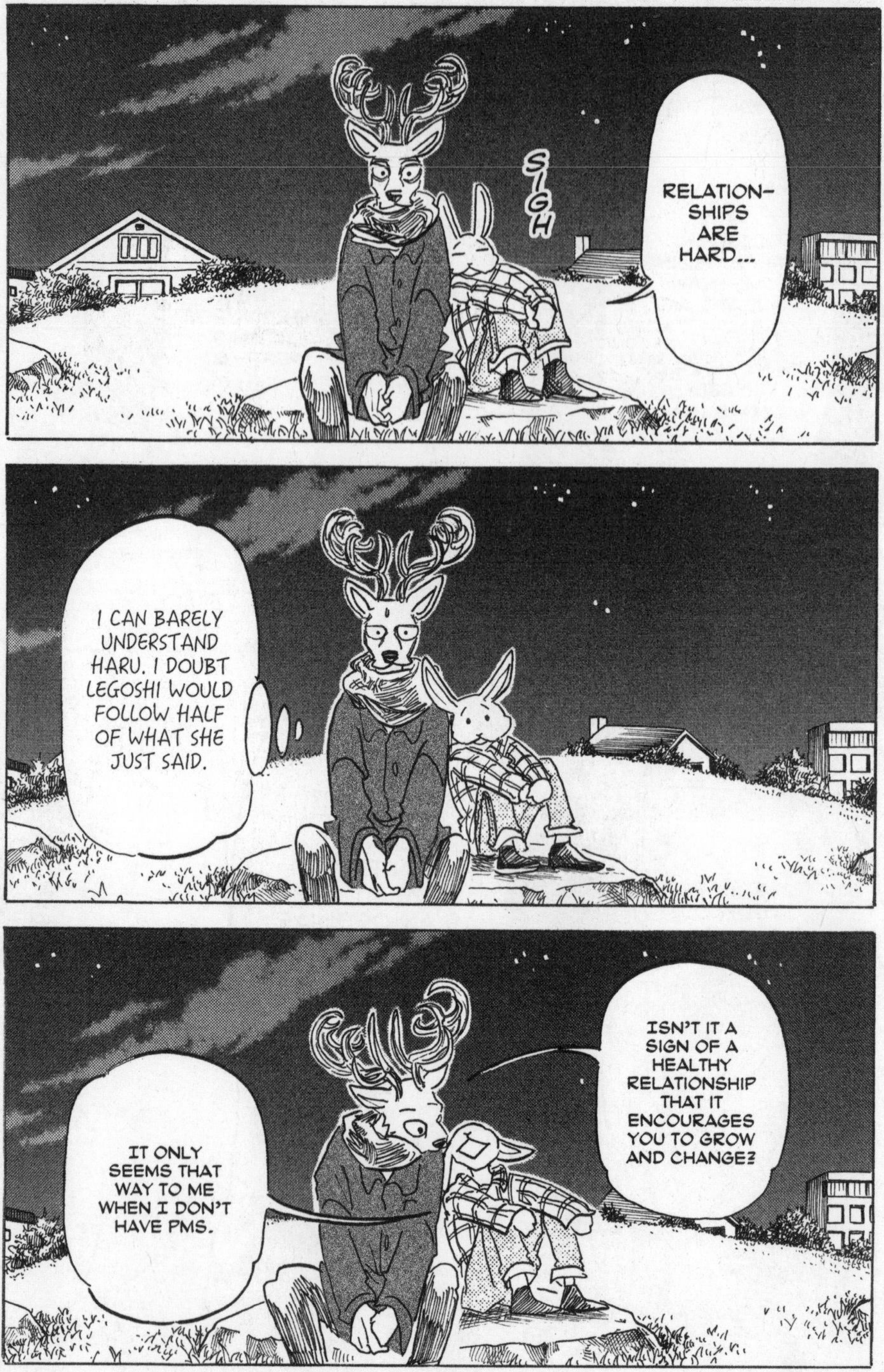
RELATION-SHIPS ARE HARD...
SIGH
I CAN BARELY UNDERSTAND HARU. I DOUBT LEGOSHI WOULD FOLLOW HALF OF WHAT SHE JUST SAID.
ISN'T IT A SIGN OF A HEALTHY RELATIONSHIP THAT IT ENCOURAGES YOU TO GROW AND CHANGE?
IT ONLY SEEMS THAT WAY TO ME WHEN I DON'T HAVE PMS.

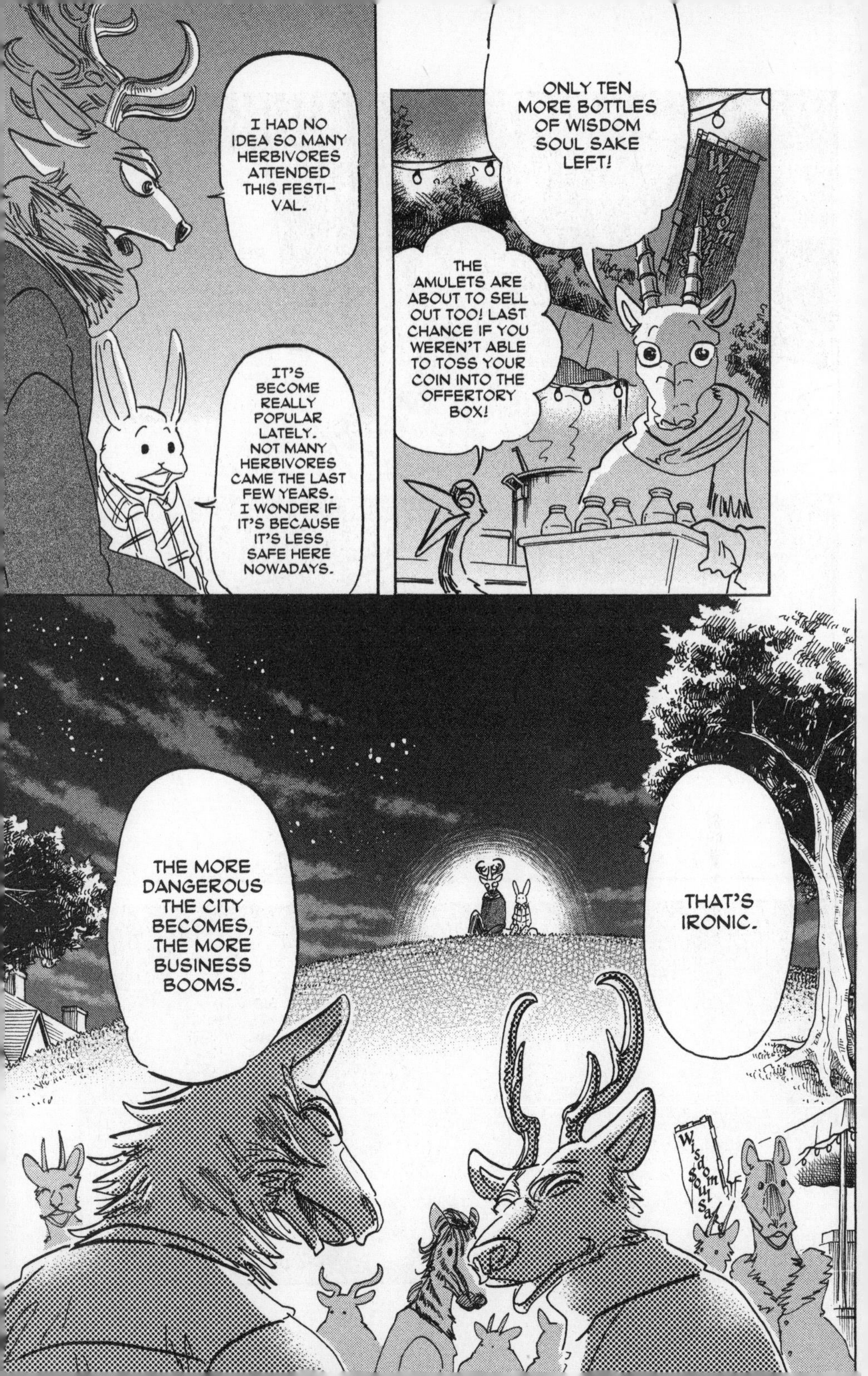
ONLY TEN MORE BOTTLES OF WISDOM SOUL SAKE LEFT!
THE AMULETS ARE ABOUT TO SELL OUT TOO! LAST CHANCE IF YOU WEREN'T ABLE TO TOSS YOUR COIN INTO THE OFFERTORY BOX!
I HAD NO IDEA SO MANY HERBIVORES ATTENDED THIS FESTIVAL.
IT'S BECOME REALLY POPULAR LATELY. NOT MANY HERBIVORES CAME THE LAST FEW YEARS. I WONDER IF IT'S BECAUSE IT'S LESS SAFE HERE NOWADAYS.
THAT'S IRONIC.
THE MORE DANGEROUS THE CITY BECOMES, THE MORE BUSINESS BOOMS.

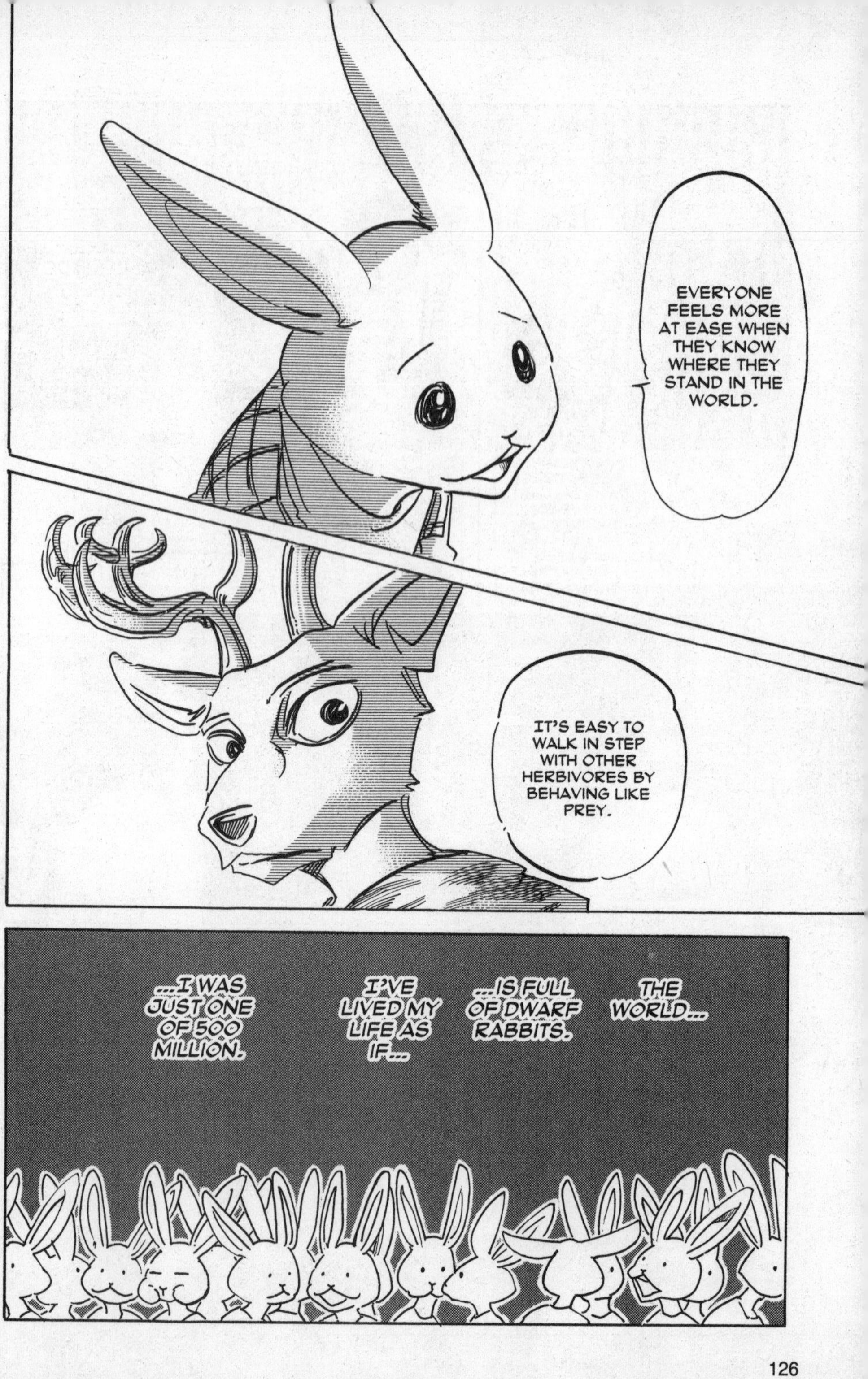
EVERYONE FEELS MORE AT EASE WHEN THEY KNOW WHERE THEY STAND IN THE WORLD.
IT'S EASY TO WALK IN STEP WITH OTHER HERBIVORES BY BEHAVING LIKE PREY.
THE WORLD...
...IS FULL OF DWARF RABBITS.
I'VE LIVED MY LIFE AS IF...
...I WAS JUST ONE OF 500 MILLION.

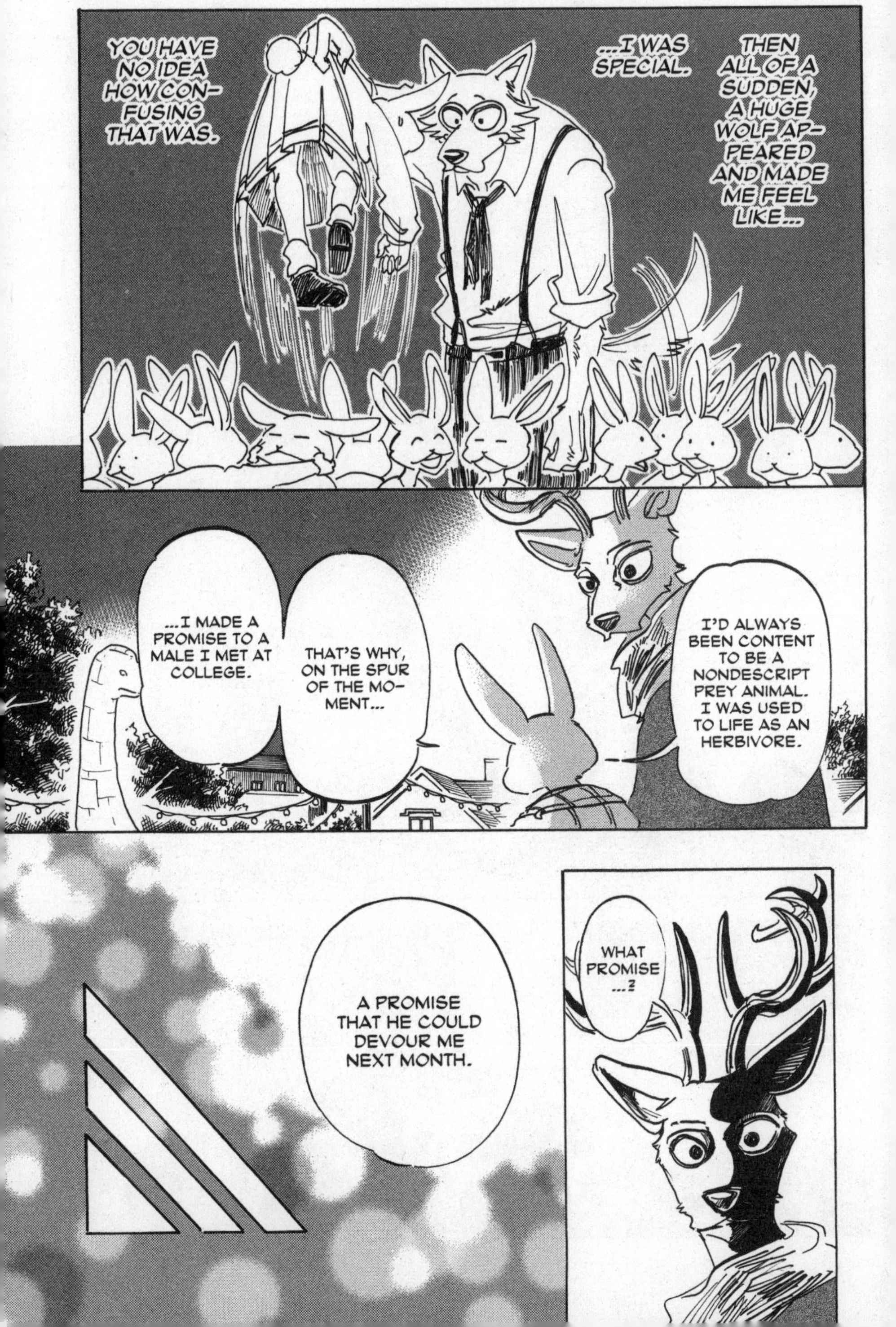
THEN ALL OF A SUDDEN, A HUGE WOLF AP-PEARED AND MADE ME FEEL LIKE...
...I WAS SPECIAL.
YOU HAVE NO IDEA HOW CON-FUSING THAT WAS.
I'D ALWAYS BEEN CONTENT TO BE A NONDESCRIPT PREY ANIMAL. I WAS USED TO LIFE AS AN HERBIVORE.
THAT'S WHY, ON THE SPUR OF THE MO-MENT...
...I MADE A PROMISE TO A MALE I MET AT COLLEGE.
WHAT PROMISE...?
A PROMISE THAT HE COULD DEVOUR ME NEXT MONTH.

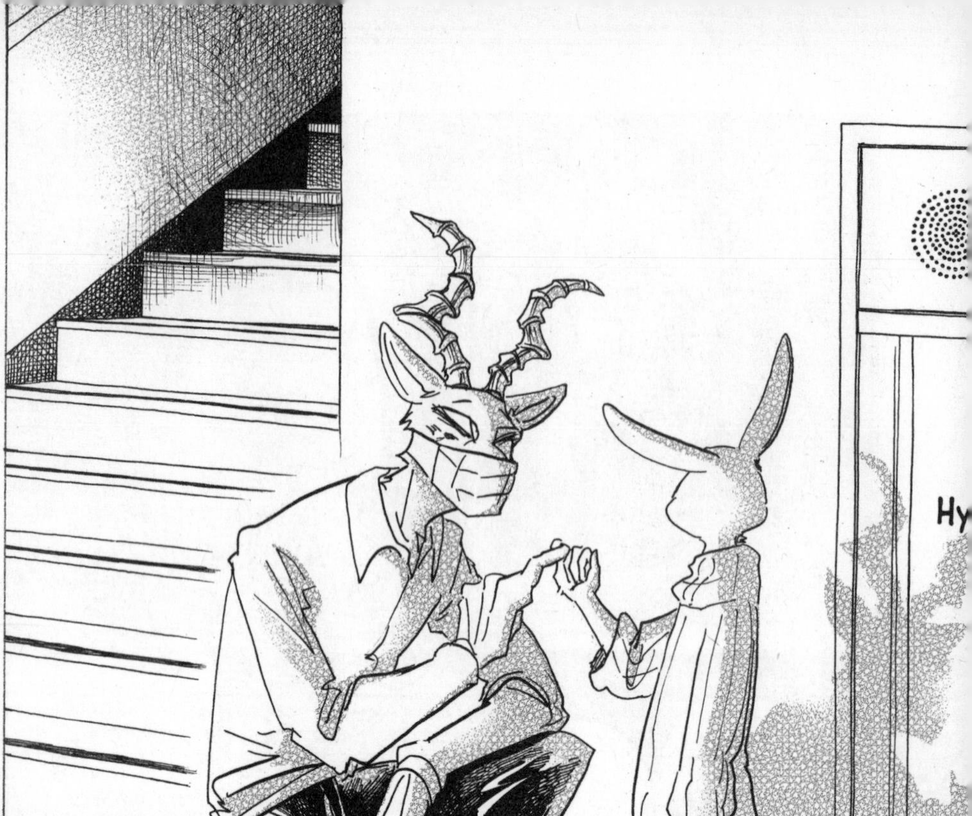
Hy

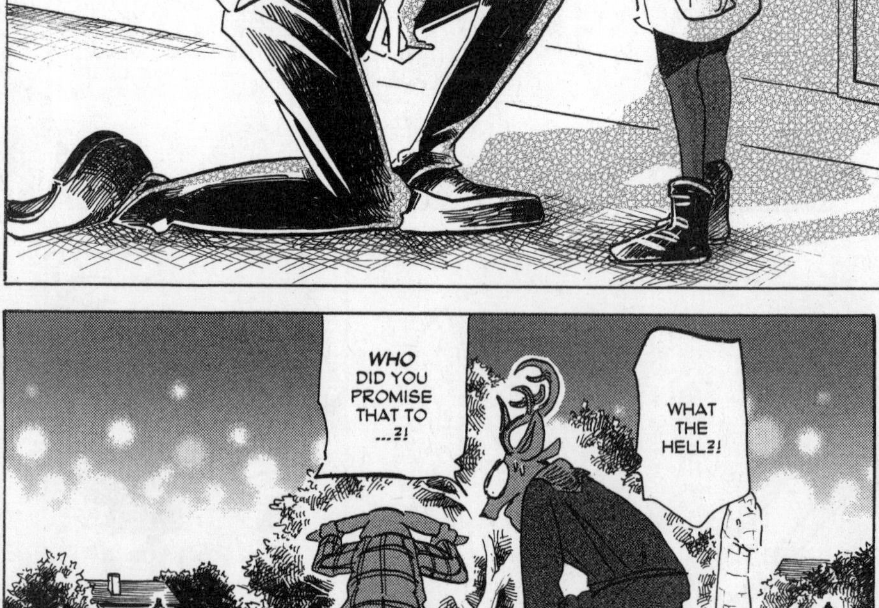
WHAT THE HELL?!
WHO DID YOU PROMISE THAT TO...?!

BEASTARS
Vol. 19

Chapter 167: Crazy Party Quiz Show

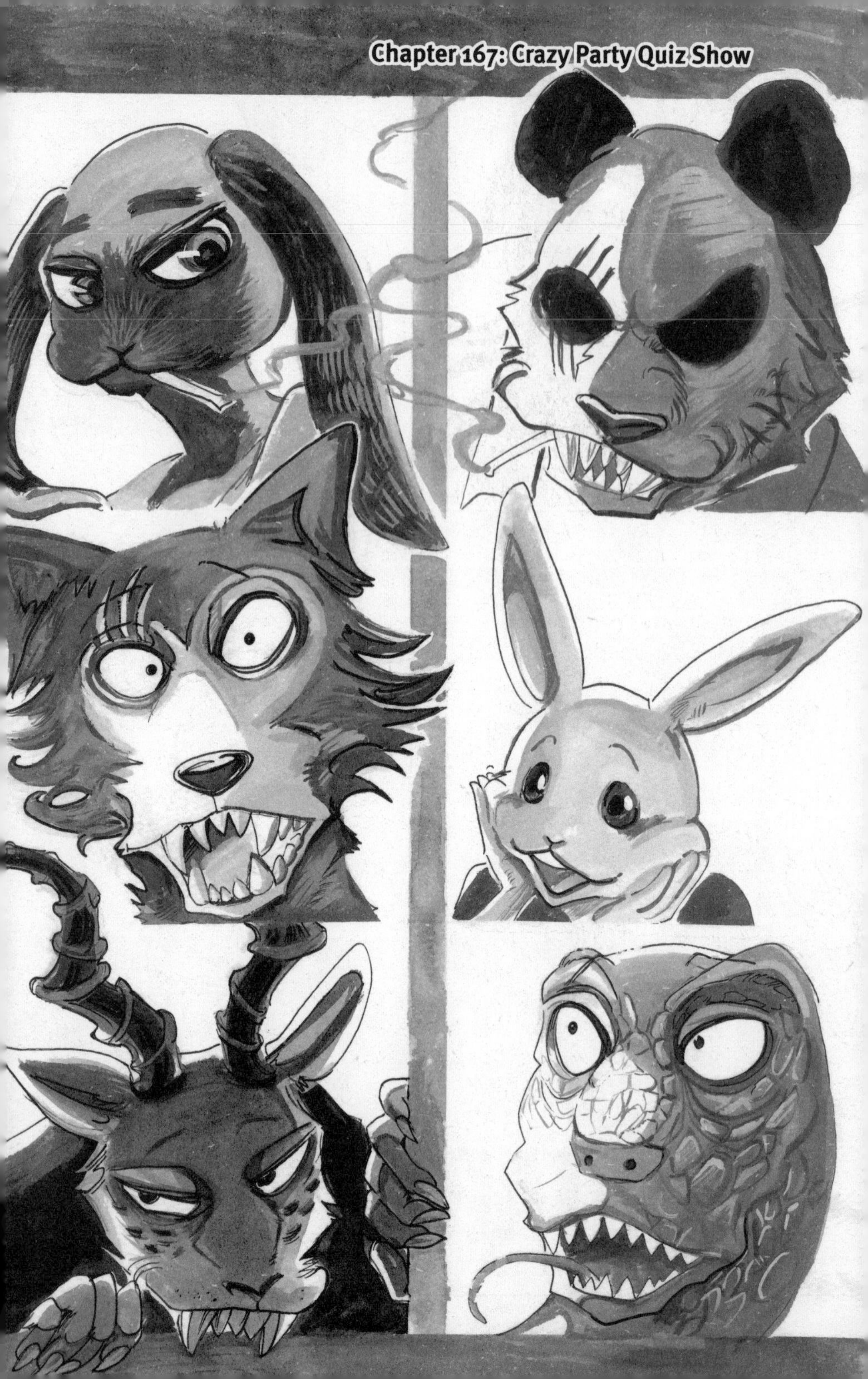

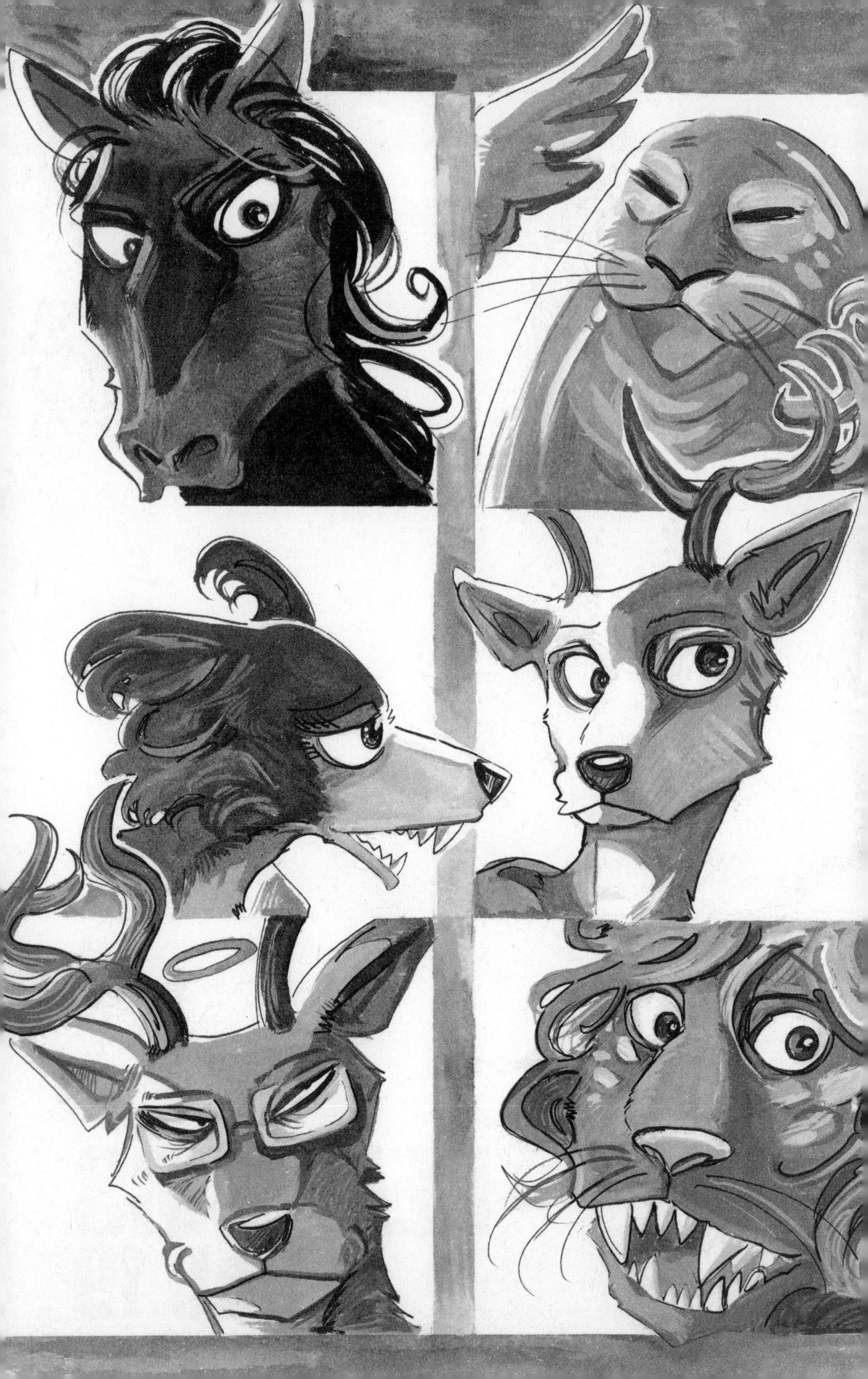

BEASTARS
Vol. 19

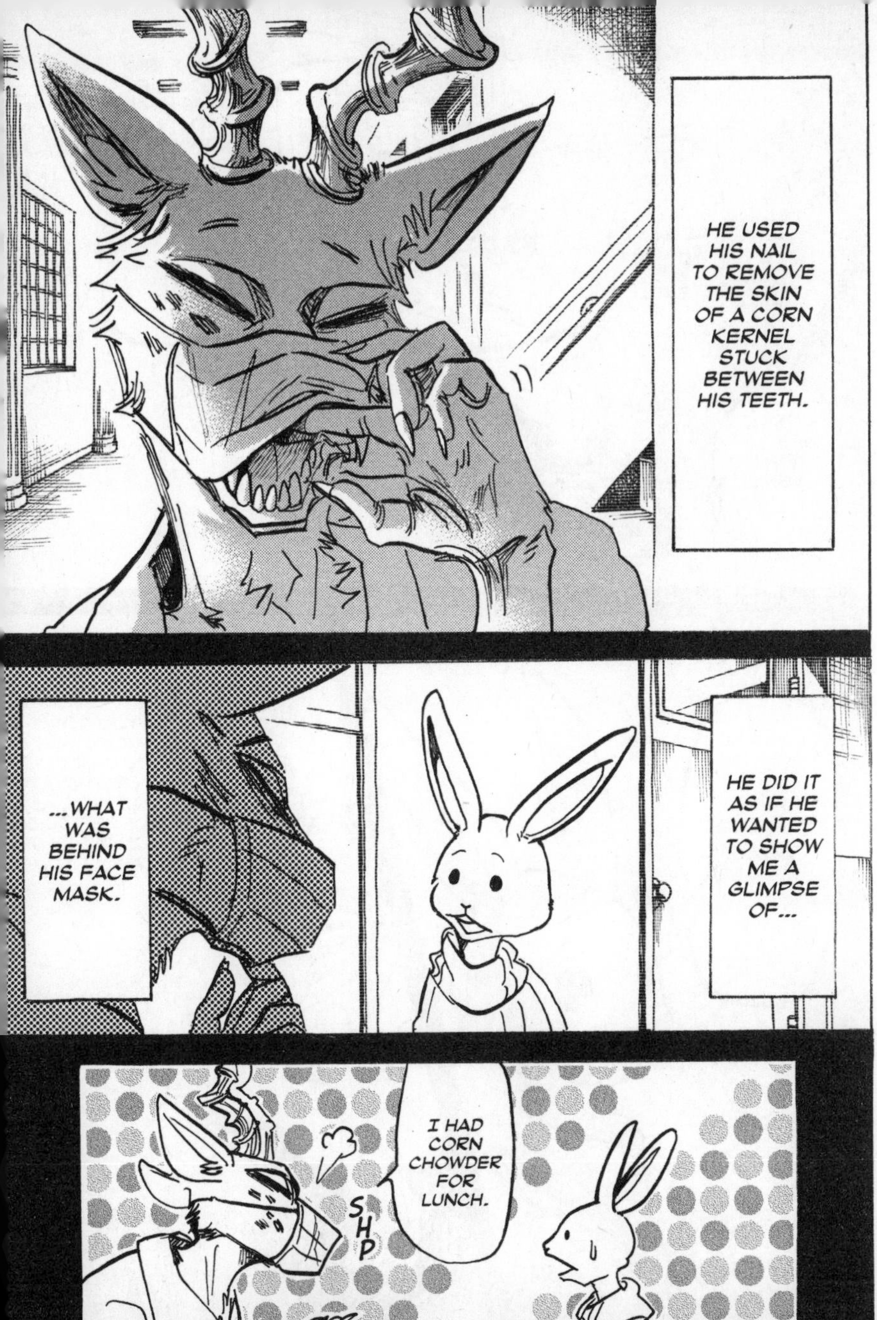
HE USED HIS NAIL TO REMOVE THE SKIN OF A CORN KERNEL STUCK BETWEEN HIS TEETH.
HE DID IT AS IF HE WANTED TO SHOW ME A GLIMPSE OF...
...WHAT WAS BEHIND HIS FACE MASK.
I HAD CORN CHOWDER FOR LUNCH.
SHP

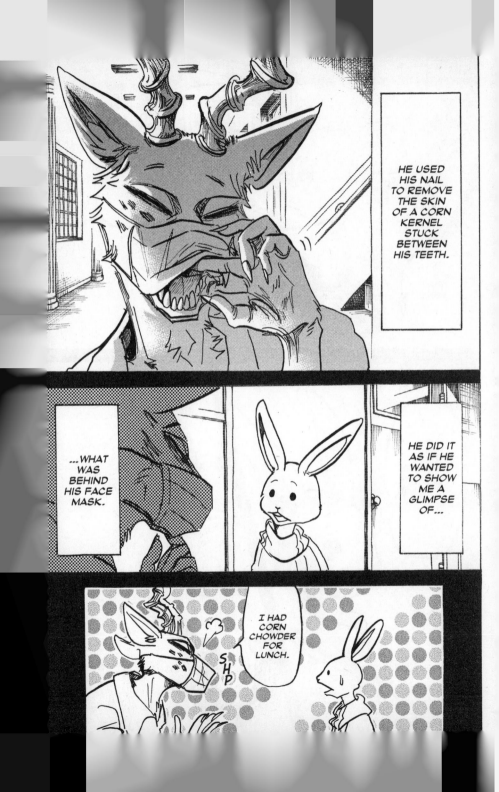

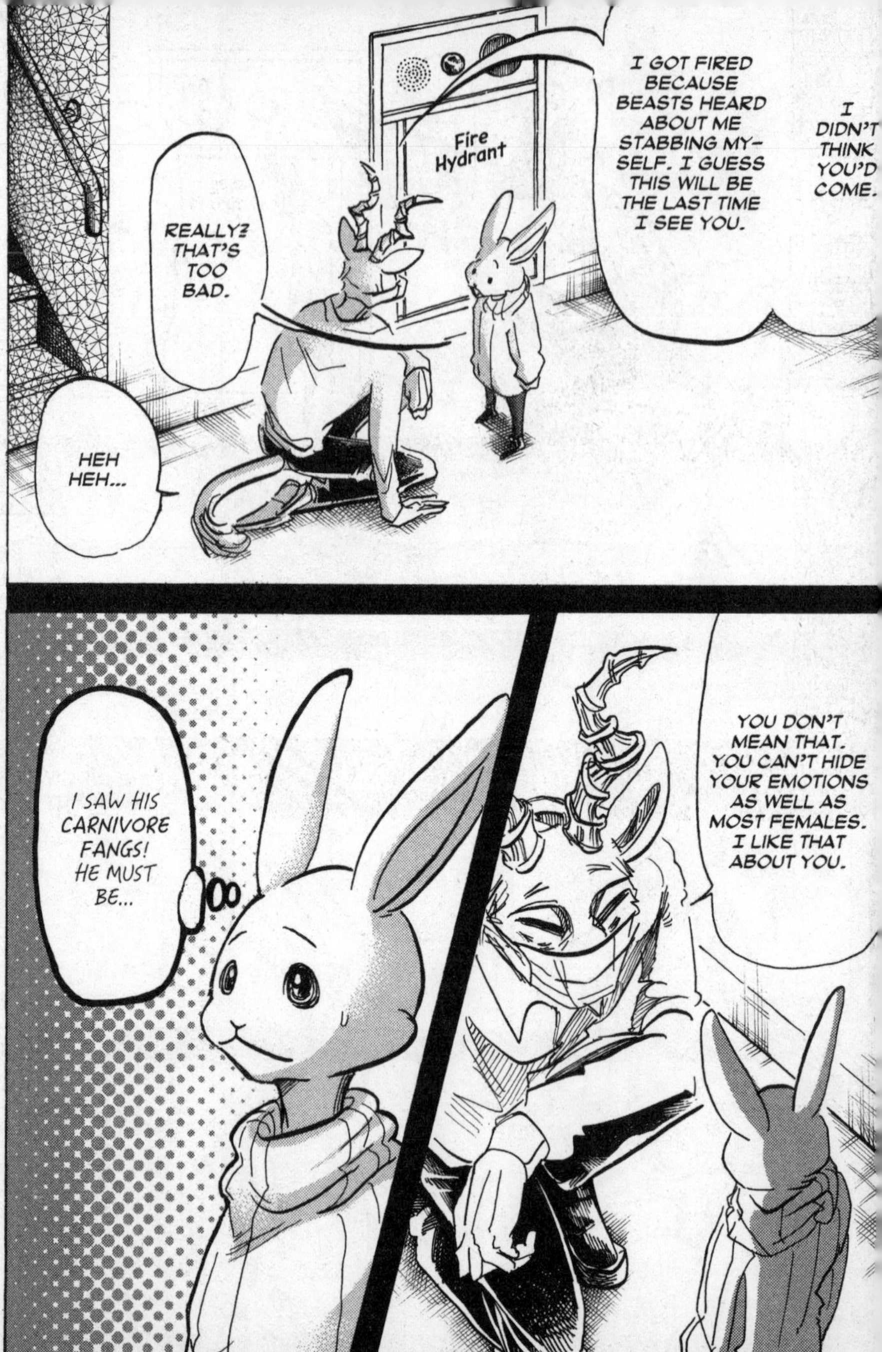

I DIDN'T THINK YOU'D COME.
I GOT FIRED BECAUSE BEASTS HEARD ABOUT ME STABBING MY-SELF. I GUESS THIS WILL BE THE LAST TIME I SEE YOU.
Fire Hydrant
REALLY? THAT'S TOO BAD.
HEH HEH...
YOU DON'T MEAN THAT. YOU CAN'T HIDE YOUR EMOTIONS AS WELL AS MOST FEMALES. I LIKE THAT ABOUT YOU.
I SAW HIS CARNIVORE FANGS! HE MUST BE...

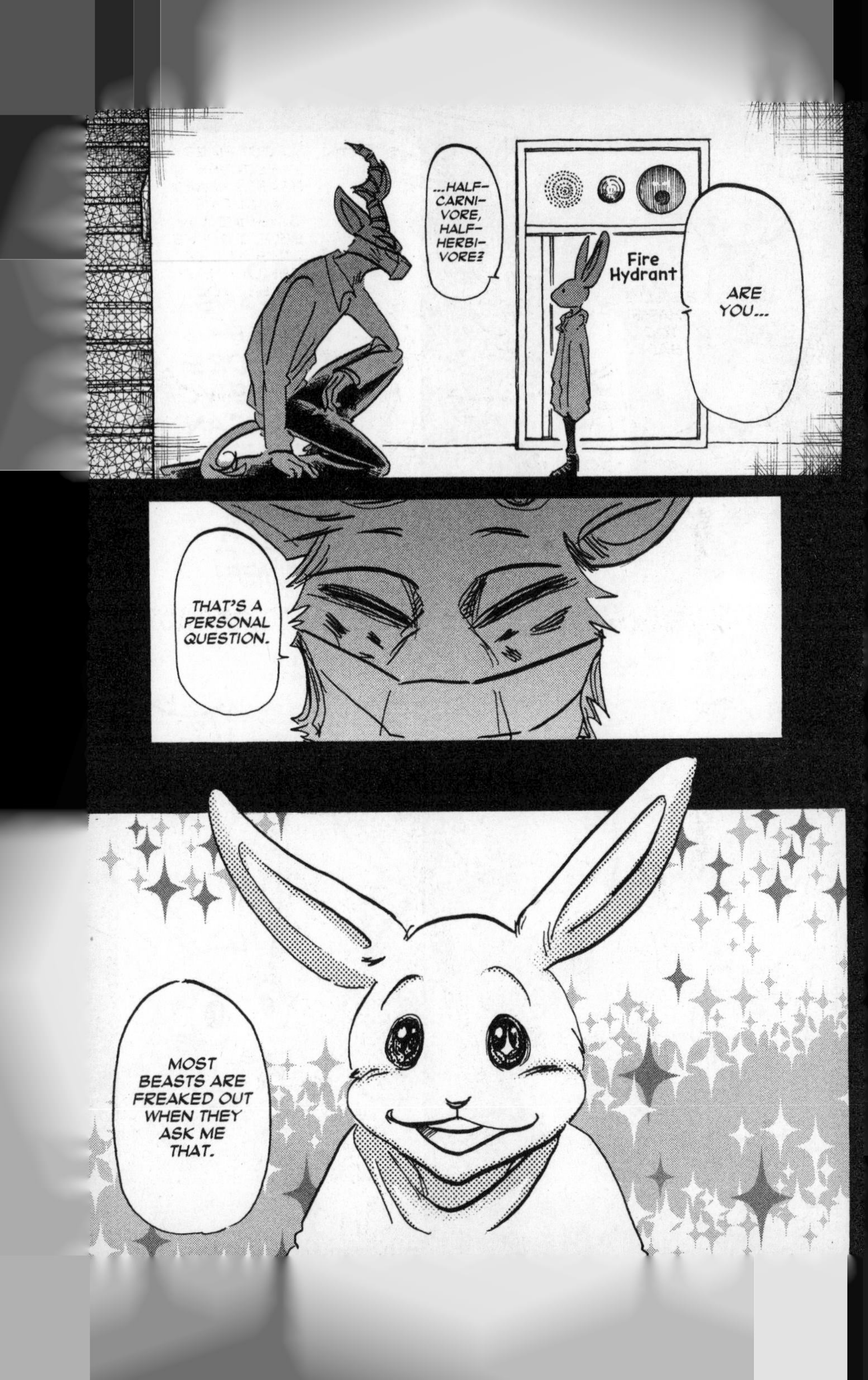
ARE YOU...
...HALF-CARNIVORE, HALF-HERBIVORE?
Fire Hydrant
THAT'S A PERSONAL QUESTION.
MOST BEASTS ARE FREAKED OUT WHEN THEY ASK ME THAT.

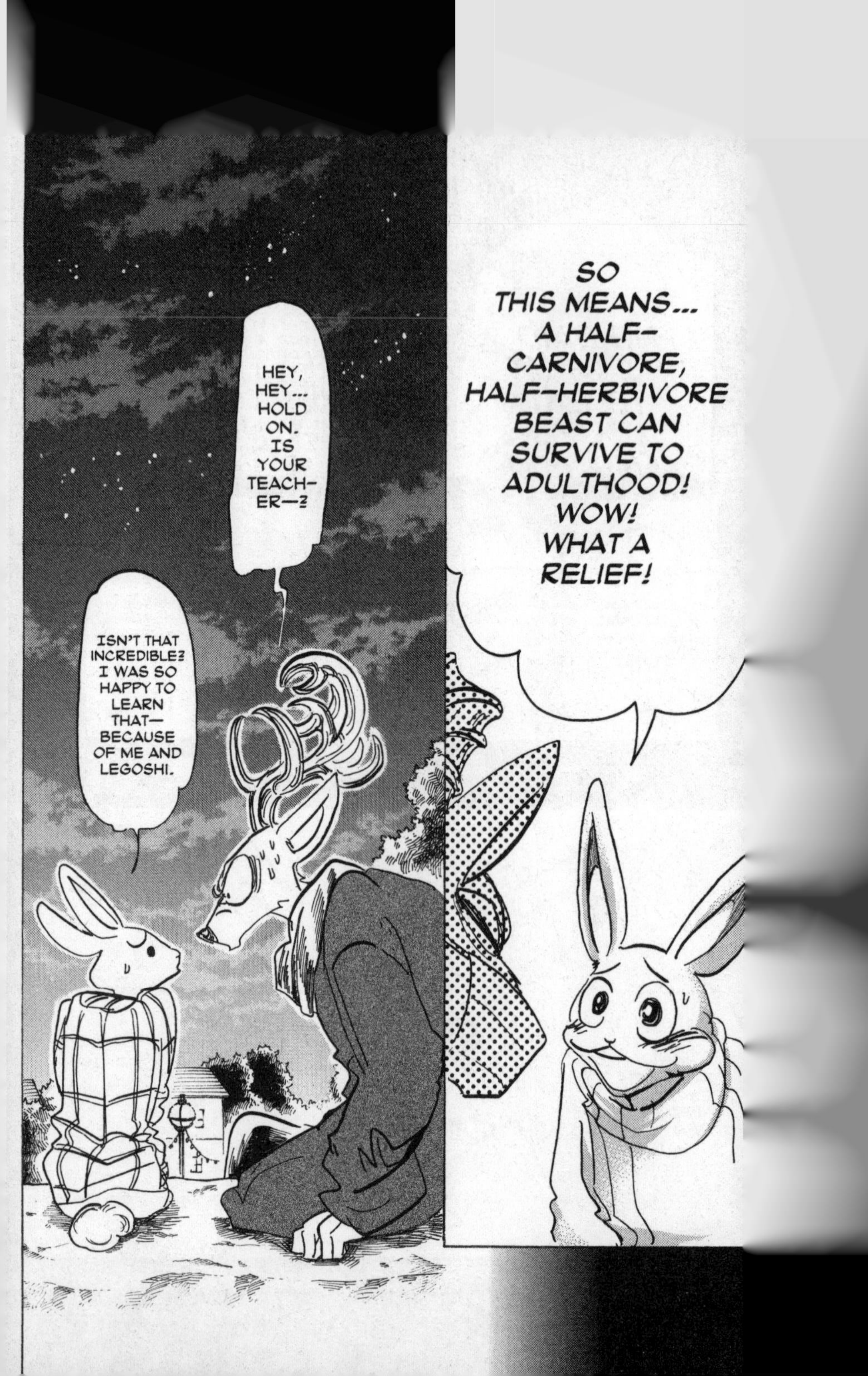
SO THIS MEANS... A HALF-CARNIVORE, HALF-HERBIVORE BEAST CAN SURVIVE TO ADULTHOOD! WOW! WHAT A RELIEF!
HEY, HEY... HOLD ON. IS YOUR TEACHER—?
ISN'T THAT INCREDIBLE? I WAS SO HAPPY TO LEARN THAT—BECAUSE OF ME AND LEGOSHI.

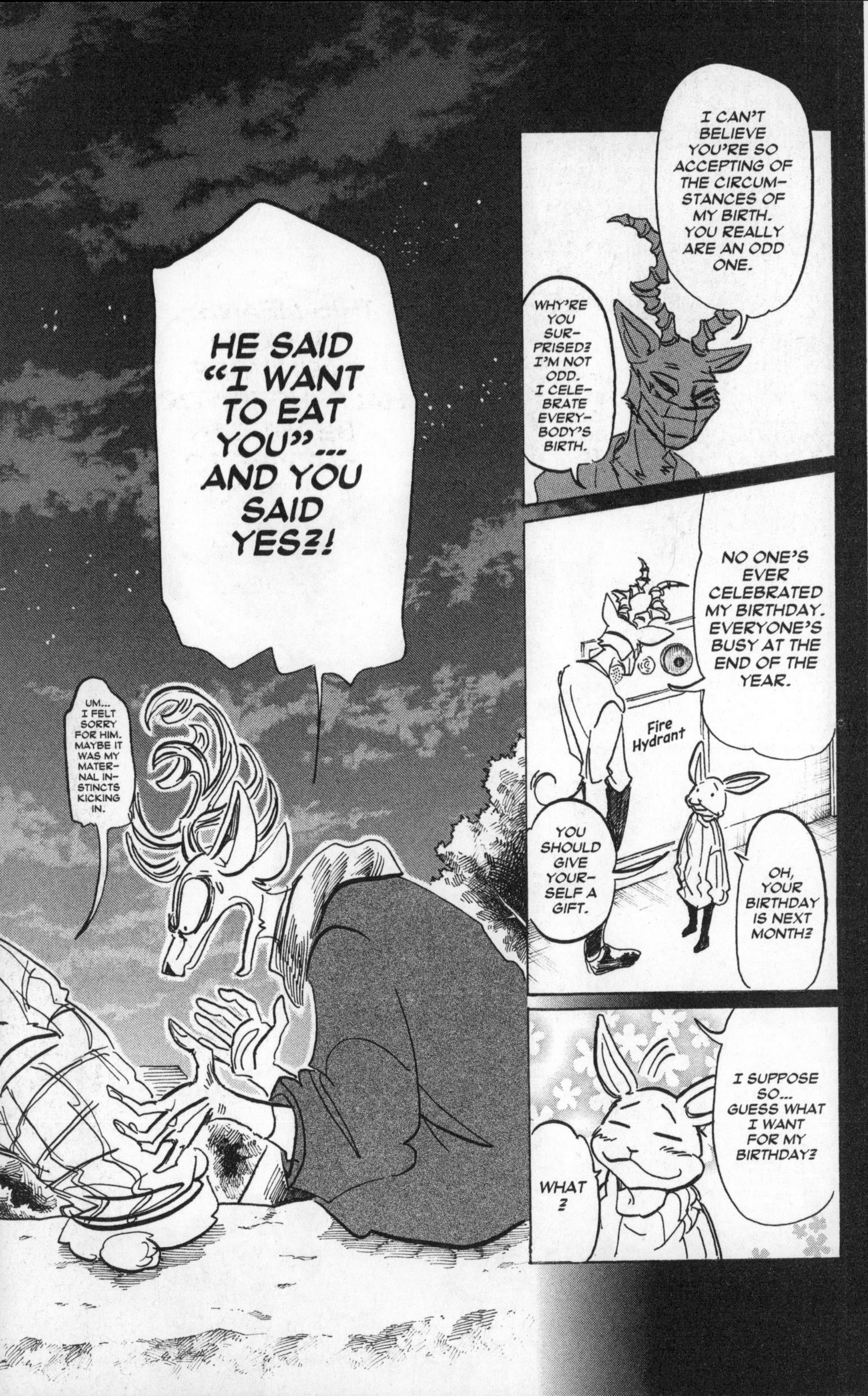
I CAN'T BELIEVE YOU'RE SO ACCEPTING OF THE CIRCUM-STANCES OF MY BIRTH. YOU REALLY ARE AN ODD ONE.
WHY'RE YOU SUR-PRISED? I'M NOT ODD. I CELE-BRATE EVERY-BODY'S BIRTH.
NO ONE'S EVER CELEBRATED MY BIRTHDAY. EVERYONE'S BUSY AT THE END OF THE YEAR.
Fire Hydrant
OH, YOUR BIRTHDAY IS NEXT MONTH?
YOU SHOULD GIVE YOUR-SELF A GIFT.
I SUPPOSE SO... GUESS WHAT I WANT FOR MY BIRTHDAY?
WHAT ?
HE SAID "I WANT TO EAT YOU"... AND YOU SAID YES?!
UM... I FELT SORRY FOR HIM. MAYBE IT WAS MY MATER-NAL IN-STINCTS KICKING IN.

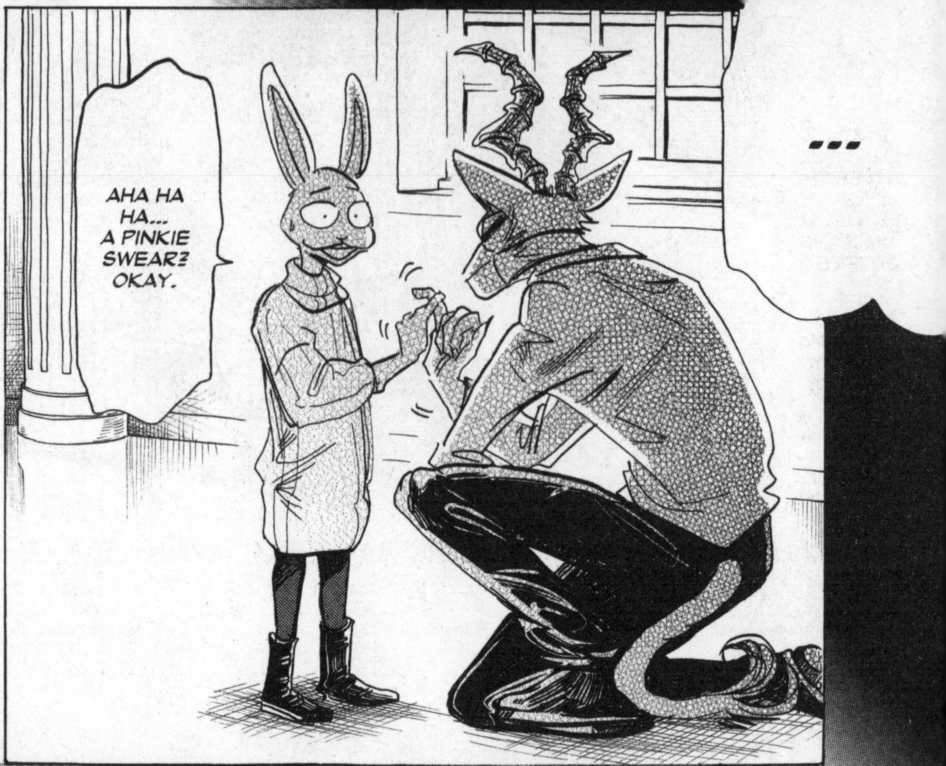
...
AHA HA HA... A PINKIE SWEAR? OKAY.
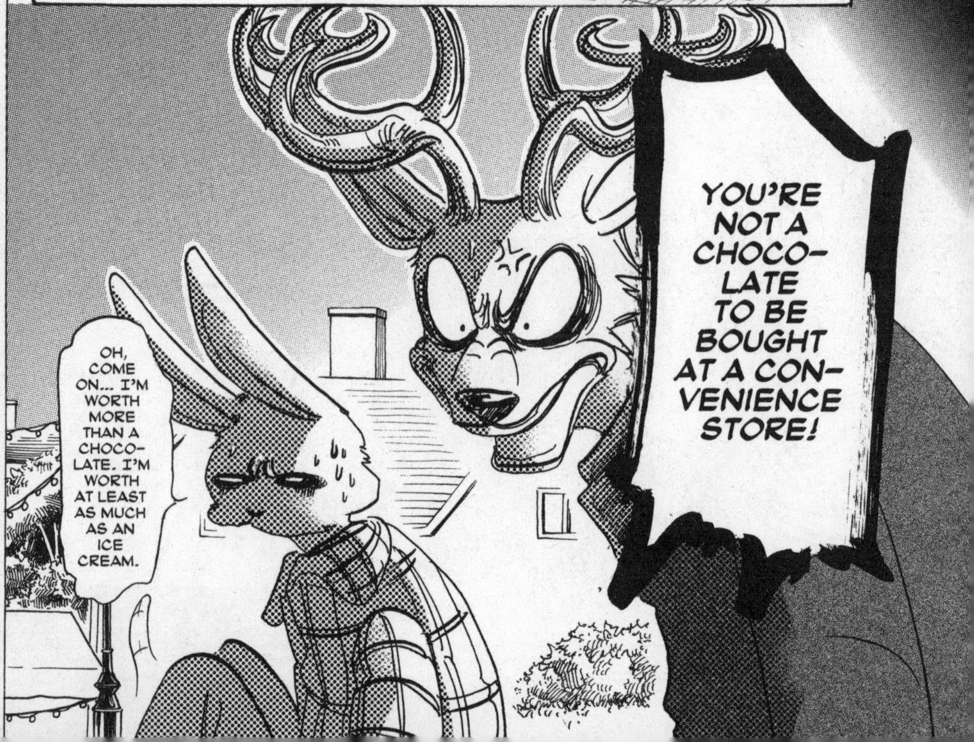
YOU'RE NOT A CHOCO-LATE TO BE BOUGHT AT A CON-VENIENCE STORE!
OH, COME ON... I'M WORTH MORE THAN A CHOCO-LATE. I'M WORTH AT LEAST AS MUCH AS AN ICE CREAM.

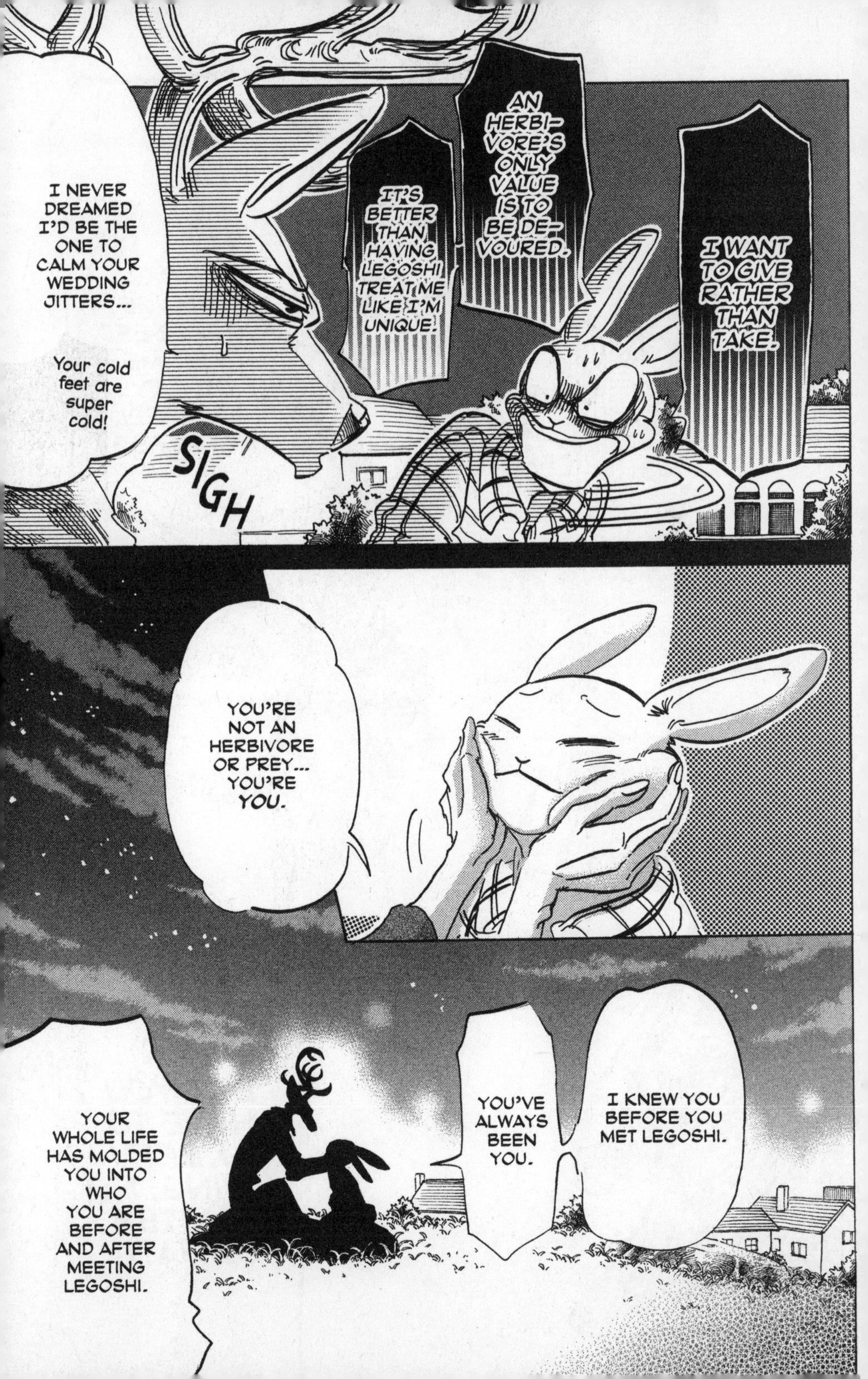
I WANT TO GIVE RATHER THAN TAKE.
AN HERBIVORE'S ONLY VALUE IS TO BE DEVOURED.
IT'S BETTER THAN HAVING LEGOSHI TREAT ME LIKE I'M UNIQUE.
I NEVER DREAMED I'D BE THE ONE TO CALM YOUR WEDDING JITTERS...
Your cold feet are super cold!
SIGH
YOU'RE NOT AN HERBIVORE OR PREY... YOU'RE YOU.
I KNEW YOU BEFORE YOU MET LEGOSHI.
YOU'VE ALWAYS BEEN YOU.
YOUR WHOLE LIFE HAS MOLDED YOU INTO WHO YOU ARE BEFORE AND AFTER MEETING LEGOSHI.

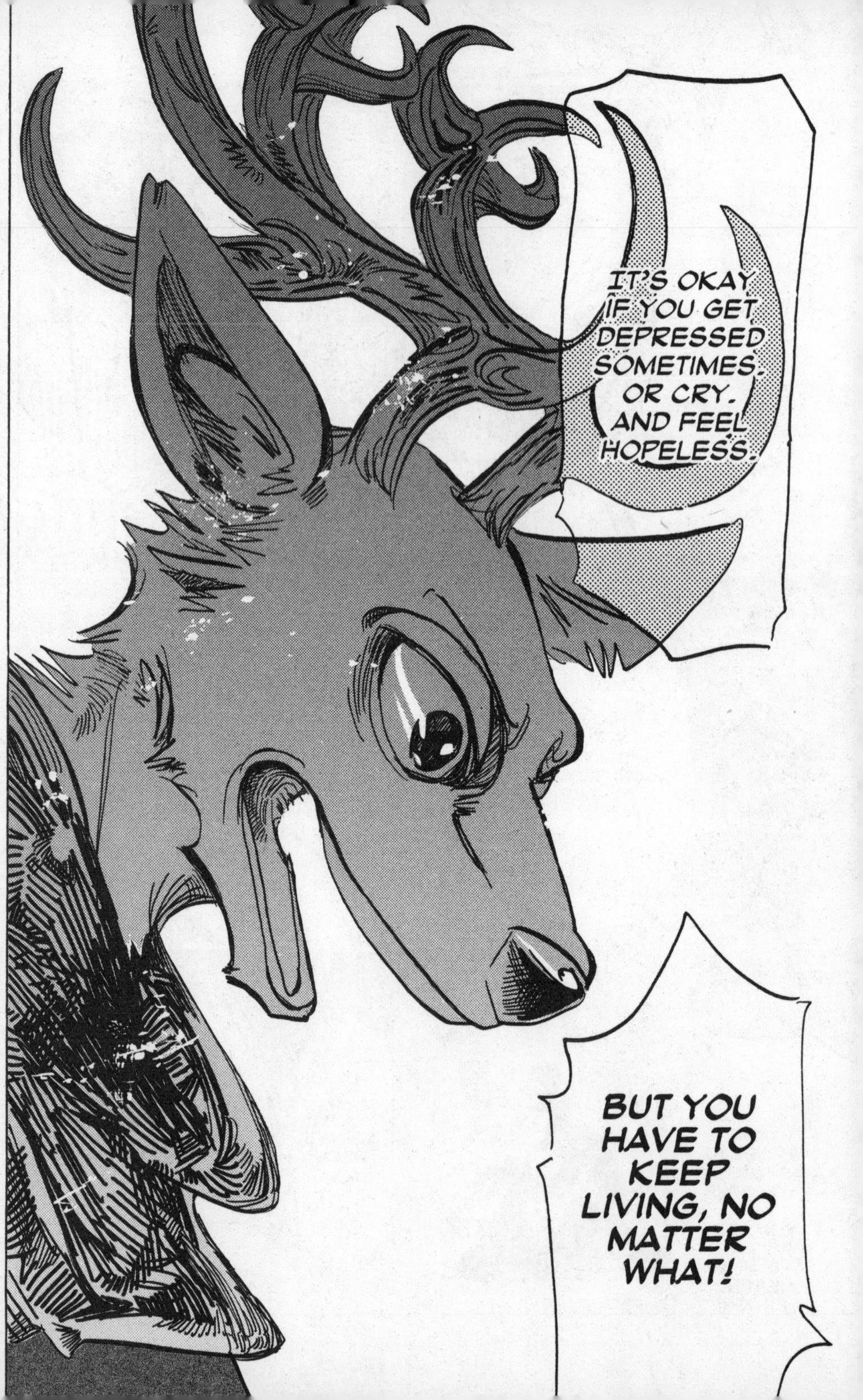
IT'S OKAY IF YOU GET DEPRESSED SOMETIMES. OR CRY. AND FEEL HOPELESS.
BUT YOU HAVE TO KEEP LIVING, NO MATTER WHAT!

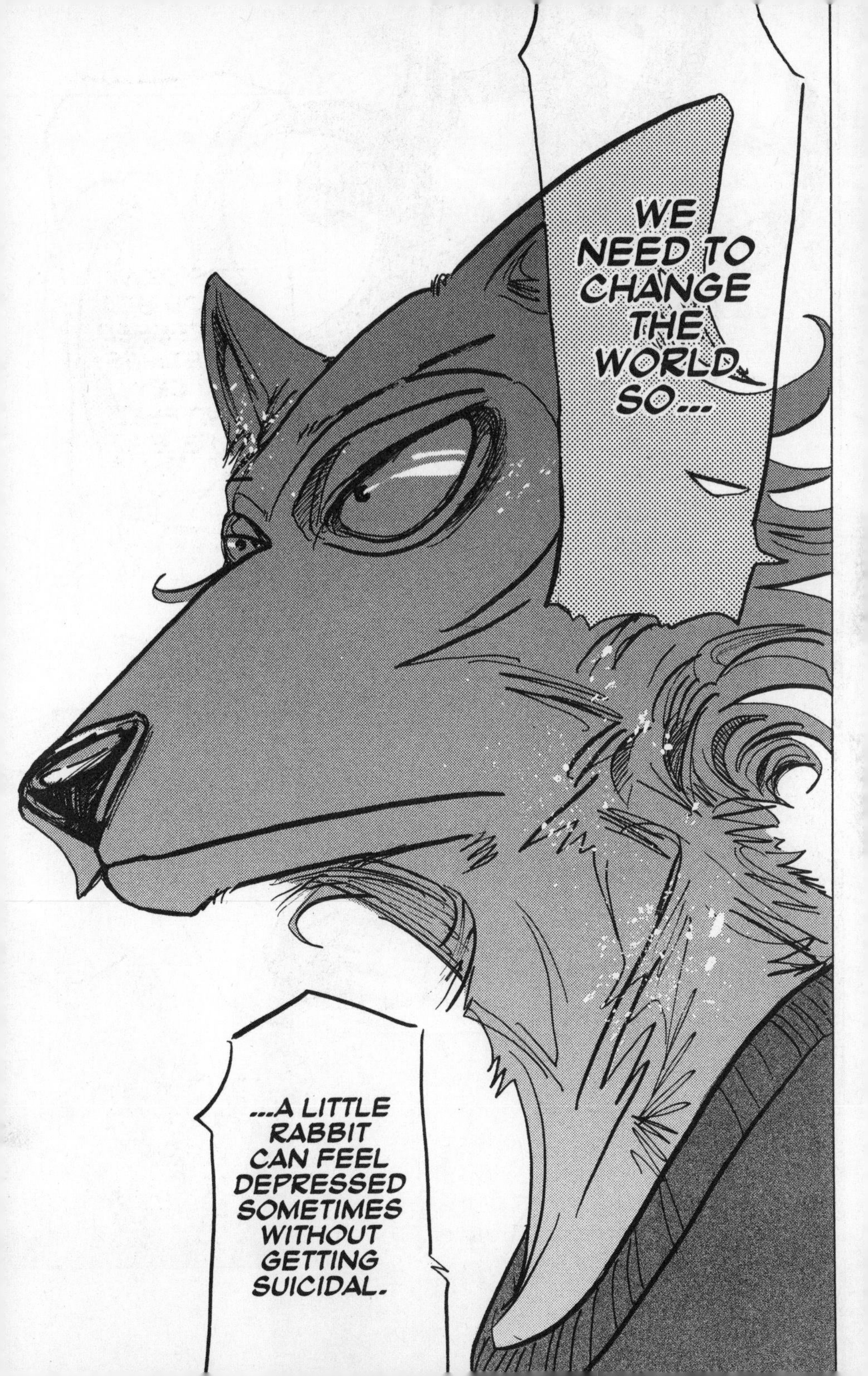
WE NEED TO CHANGE THE WORLD SO...
...A LITTLE RABBIT CAN FEEL DEPRESSED SOMETIMES WITHOUT GETTING SUICIDAL.

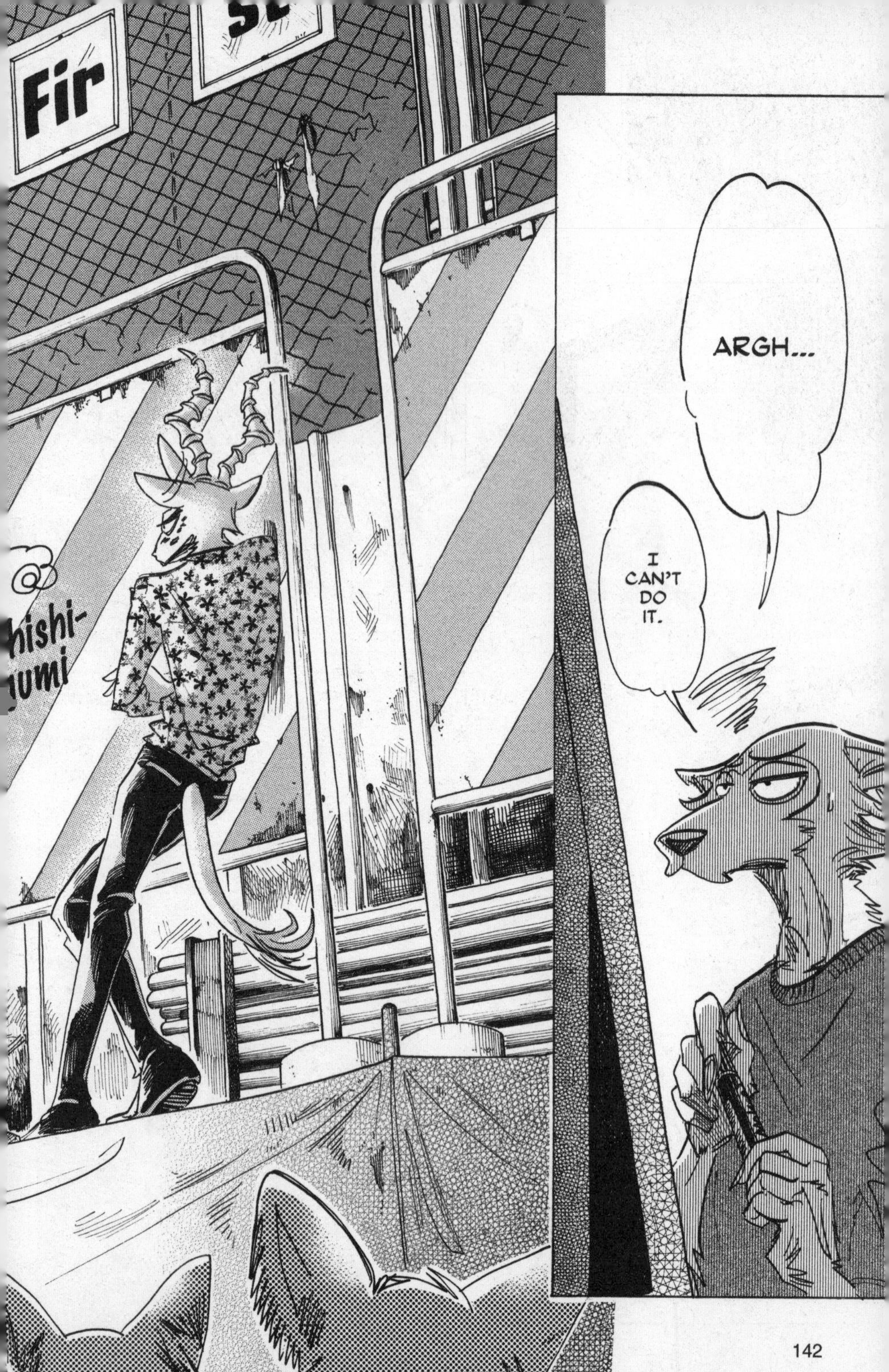
ARGH...
I CAN'T DO IT.

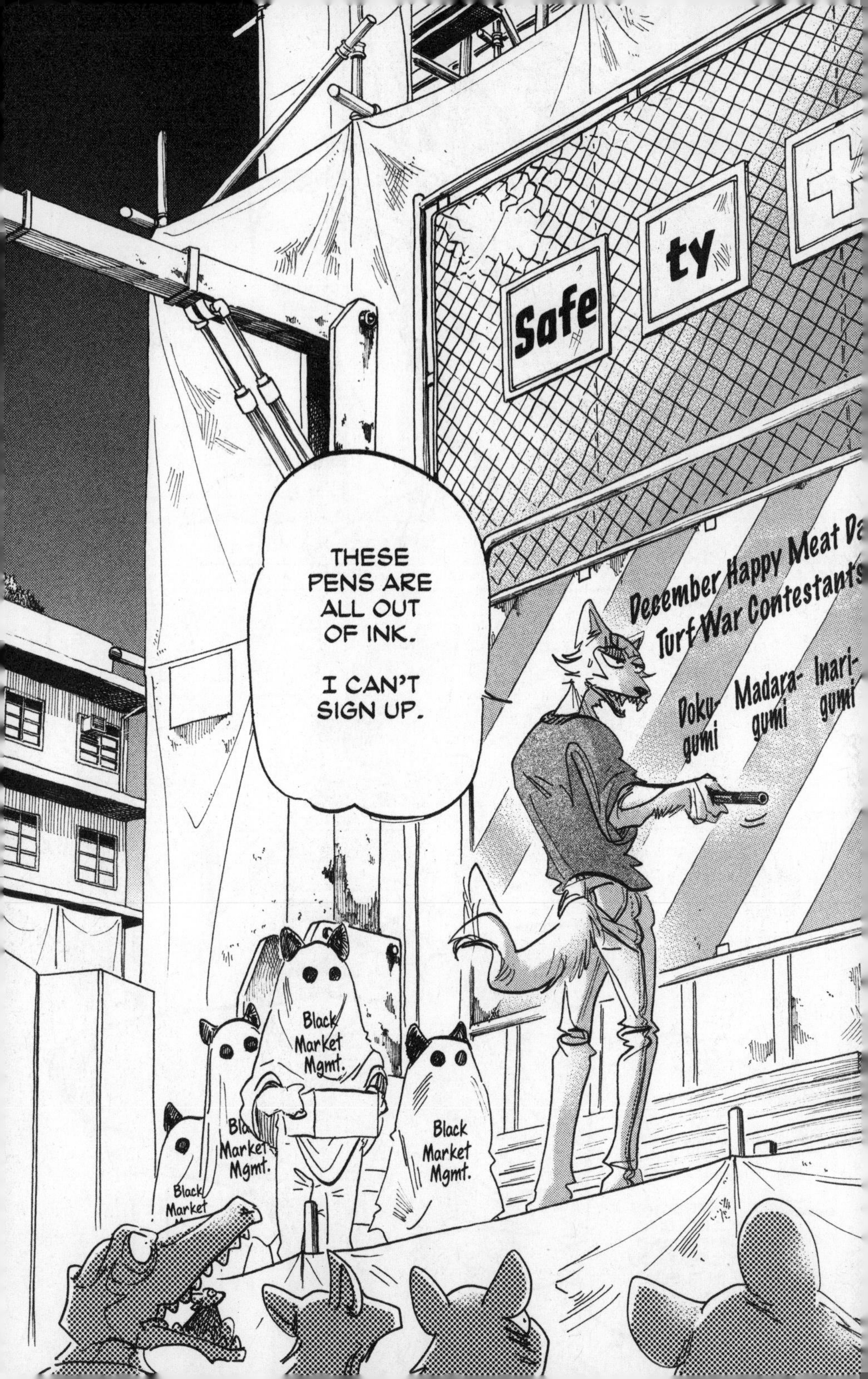
Safe
ty
December Happy Meat Da
Turf War Contestants
Doku-gumi
Madara-gumi
Inari-gumi
THESE PENS ARE ALL OUT OF INK.
I CAN'T SIGN UP.
Black Market Mgmt.
Black Market Mgmt.
Bla Market Mgmt.
Black Market

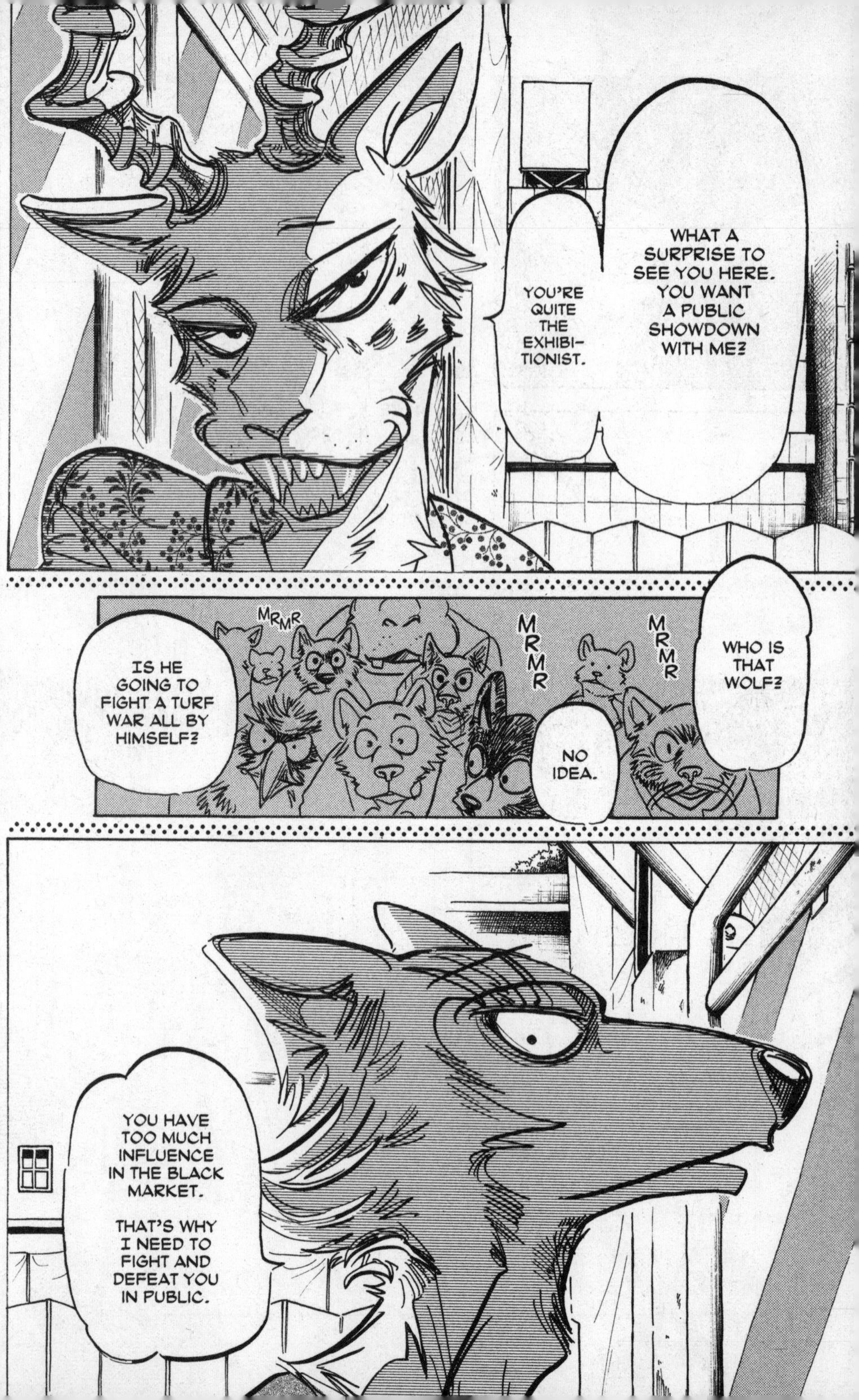
WHAT A SURPRISE TO SEE YOU HERE. YOU WANT A PUBLIC SHOWDOWN WITH ME?
YOU'RE QUITE THE EXHIBITIONIST.
WHO IS THAT WOLF?
MRMR
NO IDEA.
MRMR
MRMR
IS HE GOING TO FIGHT A TURF WAR ALL BY HIMSELF?
YOU HAVE TOO MUCH INFLUENCE IN THE BLACK MARKET.
THAT'S WHY I NEED TO FIGHT AND DEFEAT YOU IN PUBLIC.

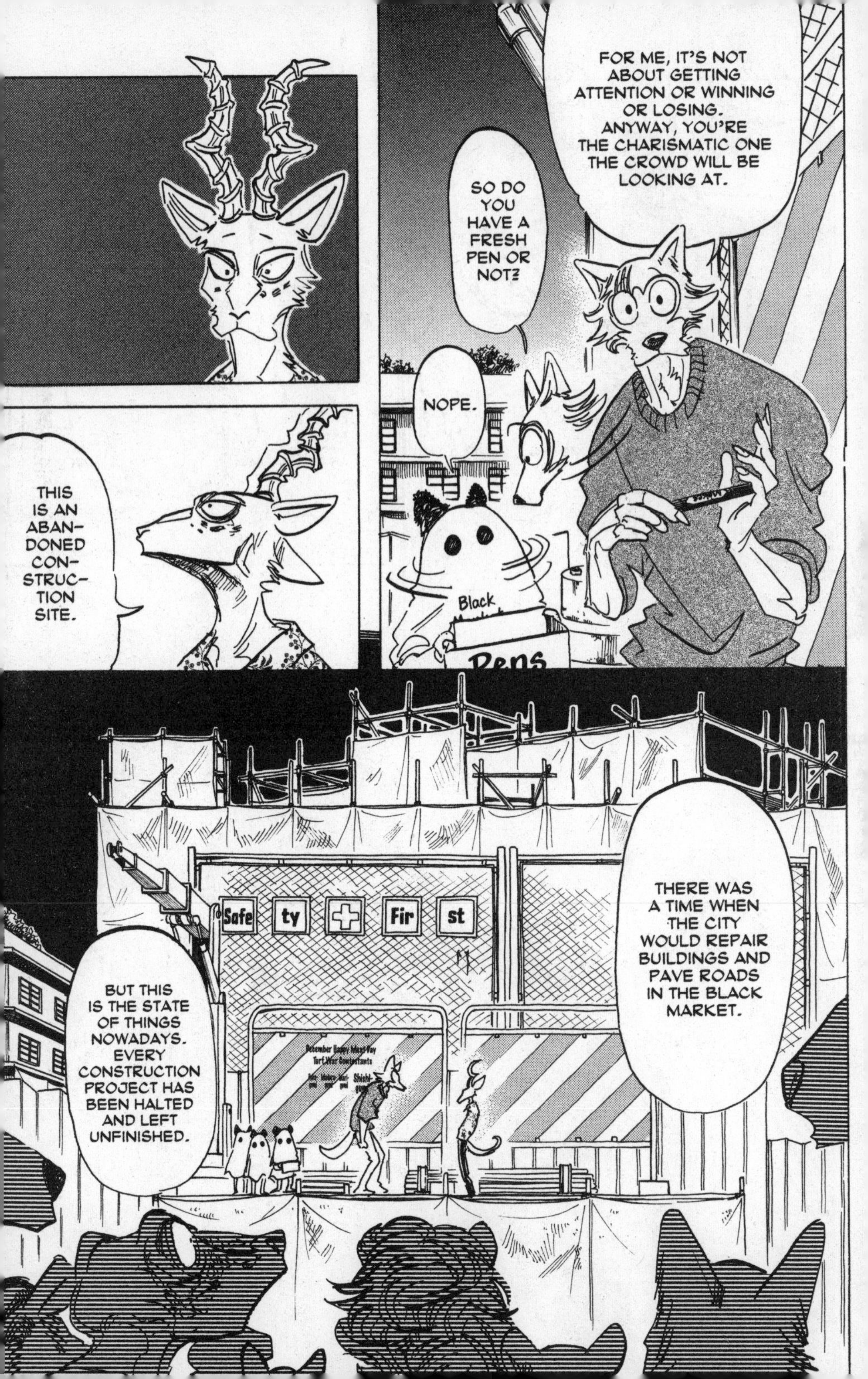
FOR ME, IT'S NOT ABOUT GETTING ATTENTION OR WINNING OR LOSING. ANYWAY, YOU'RE THE CHARISMATIC ONE THE CROWD WILL BE LOOKING AT.
SO DO YOU HAVE A FRESH PEN OR NOT?
NOPE.
Black
Pens
THIS IS AN ABANDONED CONSTRUCTION SITE.
THERE WAS A TIME WHEN THE CITY WOULD REPAIR BUILDINGS AND PAVE ROADS IN THE BLACK MARKET.
Safe ty Fir st
BUT THIS IS THE STATE OF THINGS NOWADAYS. EVERY CONSTRUCTION PROJECT HAS BEEN HALTED AND LEFT UNFINISHED.

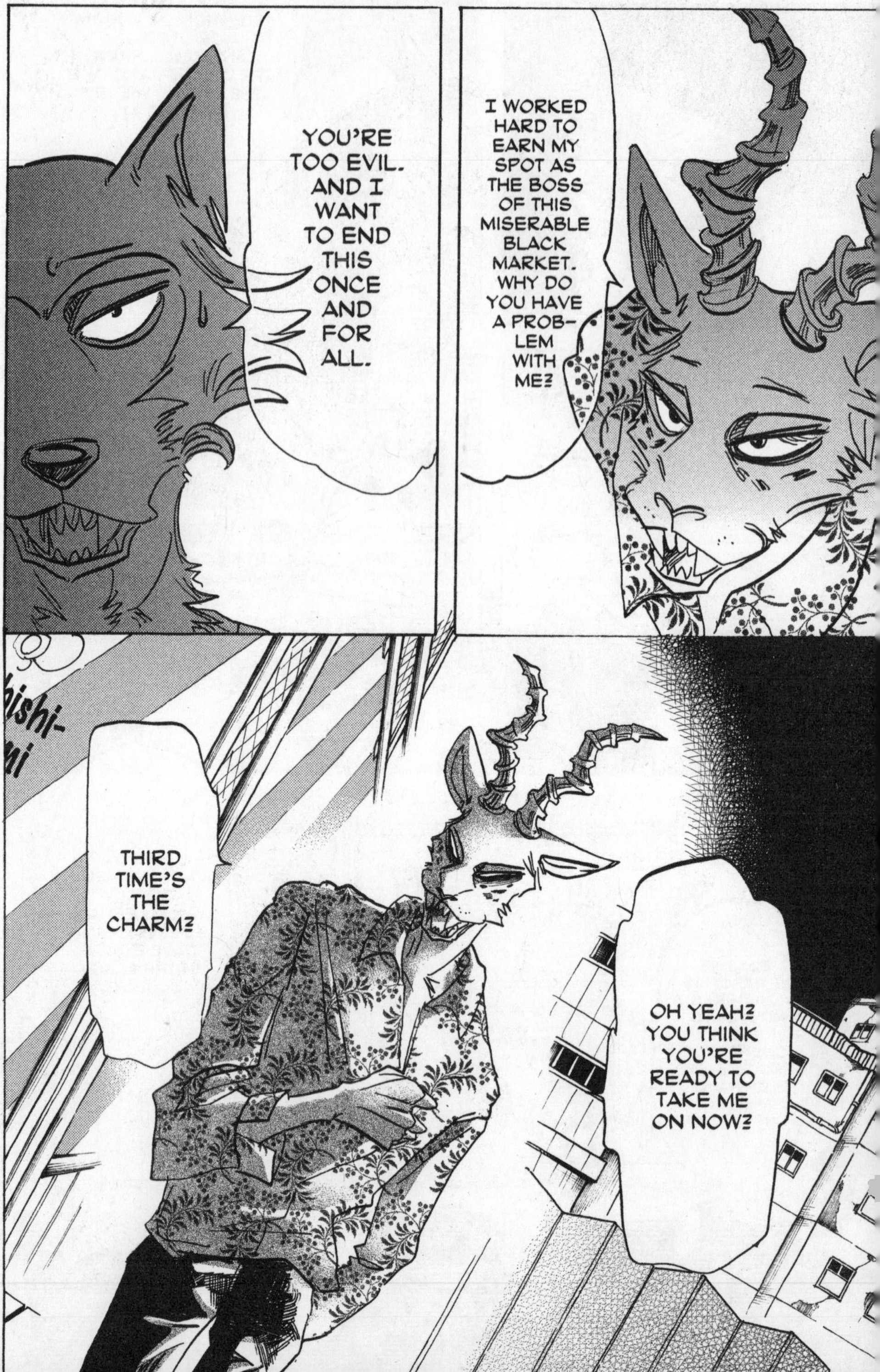
I WORKED HARD TO EARN MY SPOT AS THE BOSS OF THIS MISERABLE BLACK MARKET. WHY DO YOU HAVE A PROB-LEM WITH ME?
YOU'RE TOO EVIL. AND I WANT TO END THIS ONCE AND FOR ALL.
THIRD TIME'S THE CHARM?
OH YEAH? YOU THINK YOU'RE READY TO TAKE ME ON NOW?

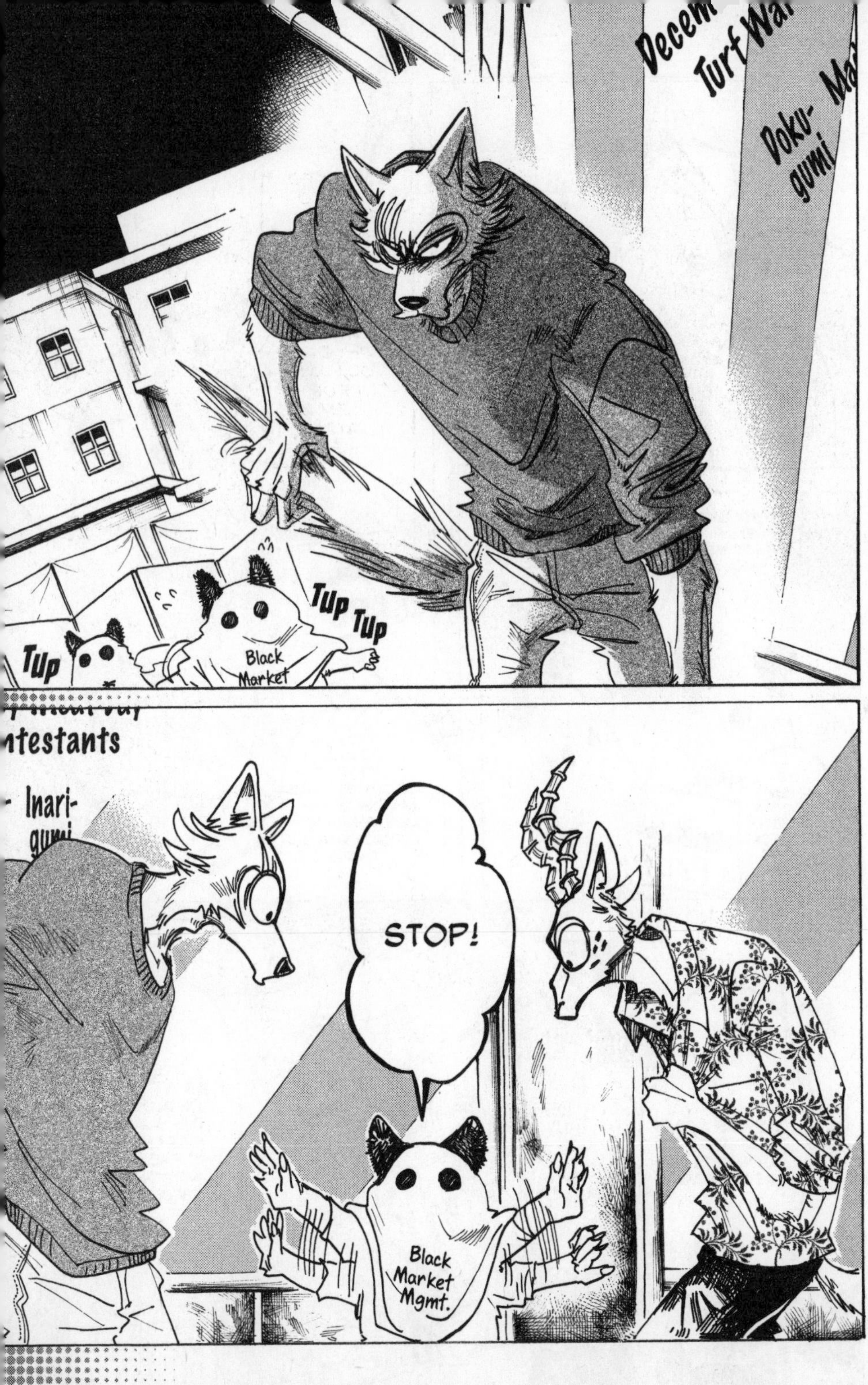
Decem
Turf Wa
Doku-gumi
Ma
TUP TUP
Black Market
TUP
ntestants
Inari-
STOP!
Black Market Mgmt.

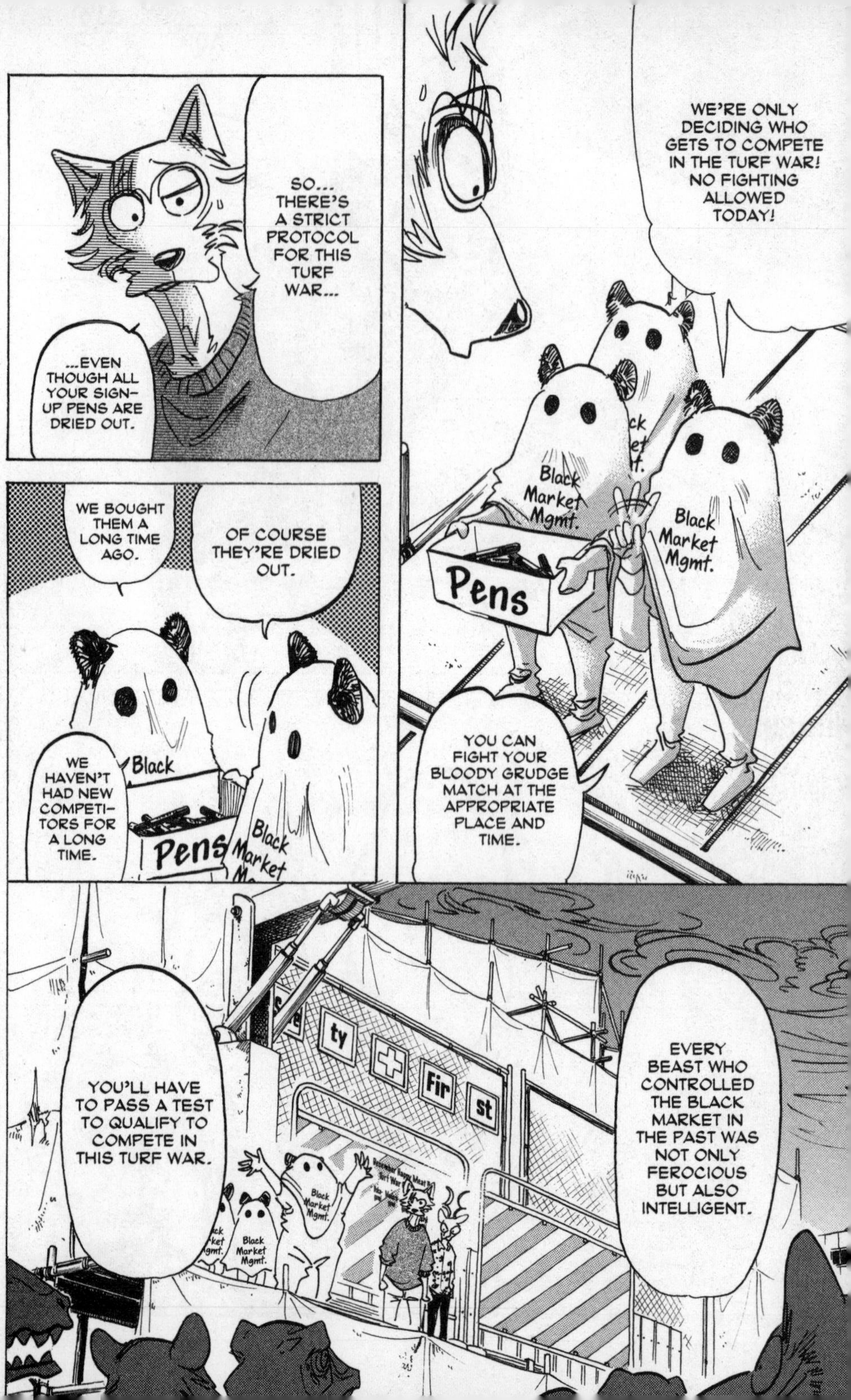
WE'RE ONLY DECIDING WHO GETS TO COMPETE IN THE TURF WAR! NO FIGHTING ALLOWED TODAY!
Black Market Mgmt.
Black Market Mgmt.
Pens
YOU CAN FIGHT YOUR BLOODY GRUDGE MATCH AT THE APPROPRIATE PLACE AND TIME.
SO... THERE'S A STRICT PROTOCOL FOR THIS TURF WAR...
...EVEN THOUGH ALL YOUR SIGN-UP PENS ARE DRIED OUT.
OF COURSE THEY'RE DRIED OUT.
WE BOUGHT THEM A LONG TIME AGO.
WE HAVEN'T HAD NEW COMPETITORS FOR A LONG TIME.
Black
Pens
Black Market
ty
Fir
st
EVERY BEAST WHO CONTROLLED THE BLACK MARKET IN THE PAST WAS NOT ONLY FEROCIOUS BUT ALSO INTELLIGENT.
Black Market Mgmt.
Black Market Mgmt.
YOU'LL HAVE TO PASS A TEST TO QUALIFY TO COMPETE IN THIS TURF WAR.

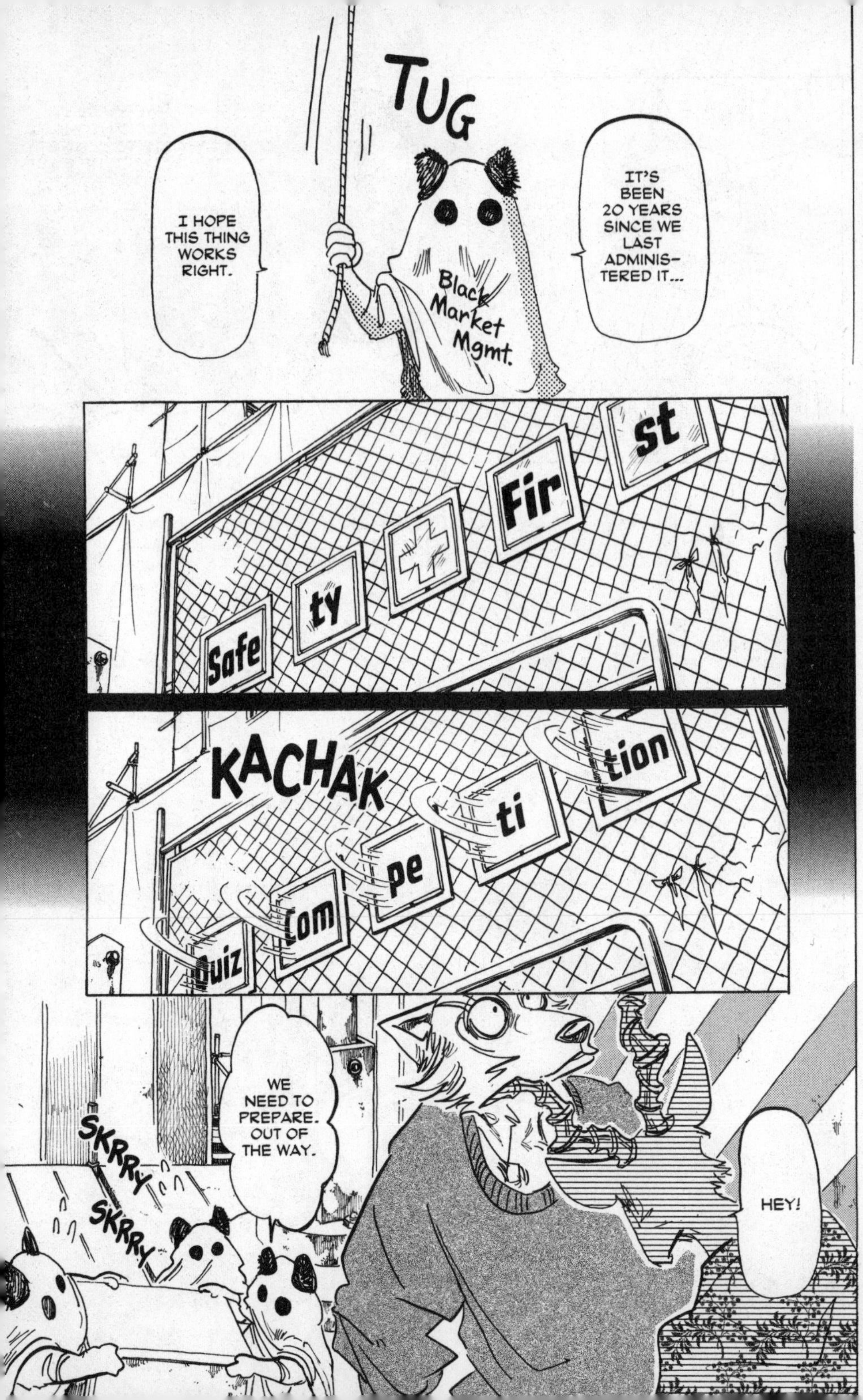
TUG
IT'S BEEN 20 YEARS SINCE WE LAST ADMINIS-TERED IT...
Black Market Mgmt.
I HOPE THIS THING WORKS RIGHT.
Safety First
KACHAK
Quiz Competition
HEY!
WE NEED TO PREPARE. OUT OF THE WAY.
SKRRY
SKRRY

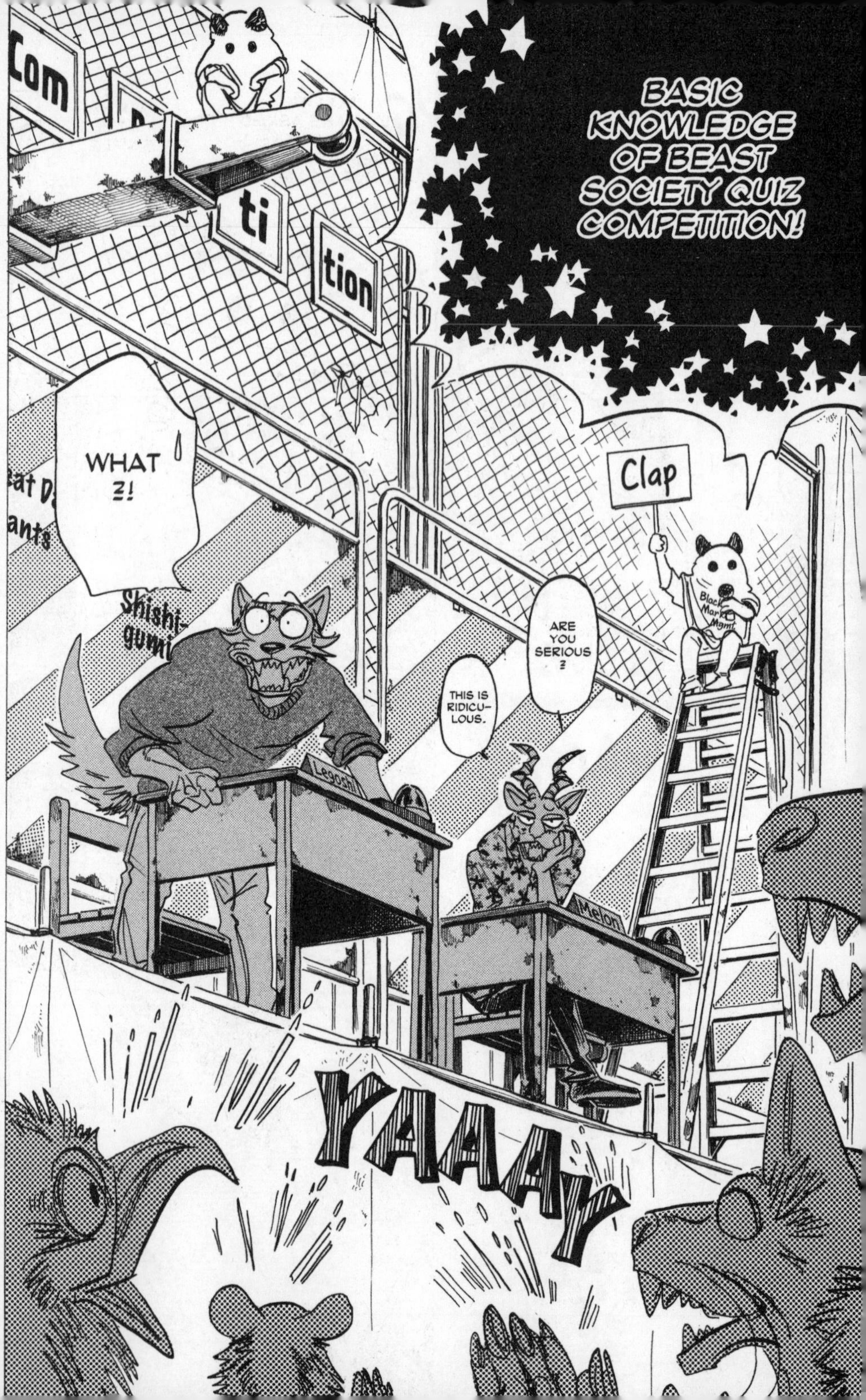
BASIC KNOWLEDGE OF BEAST SOCIETY QUIZ COMPETITION!
Clap
ARE YOU SERIOUS?
THIS IS RIDICULOUS.
WHAT?!
Shishi-gumi
Legoshi
Melon
YAAAY

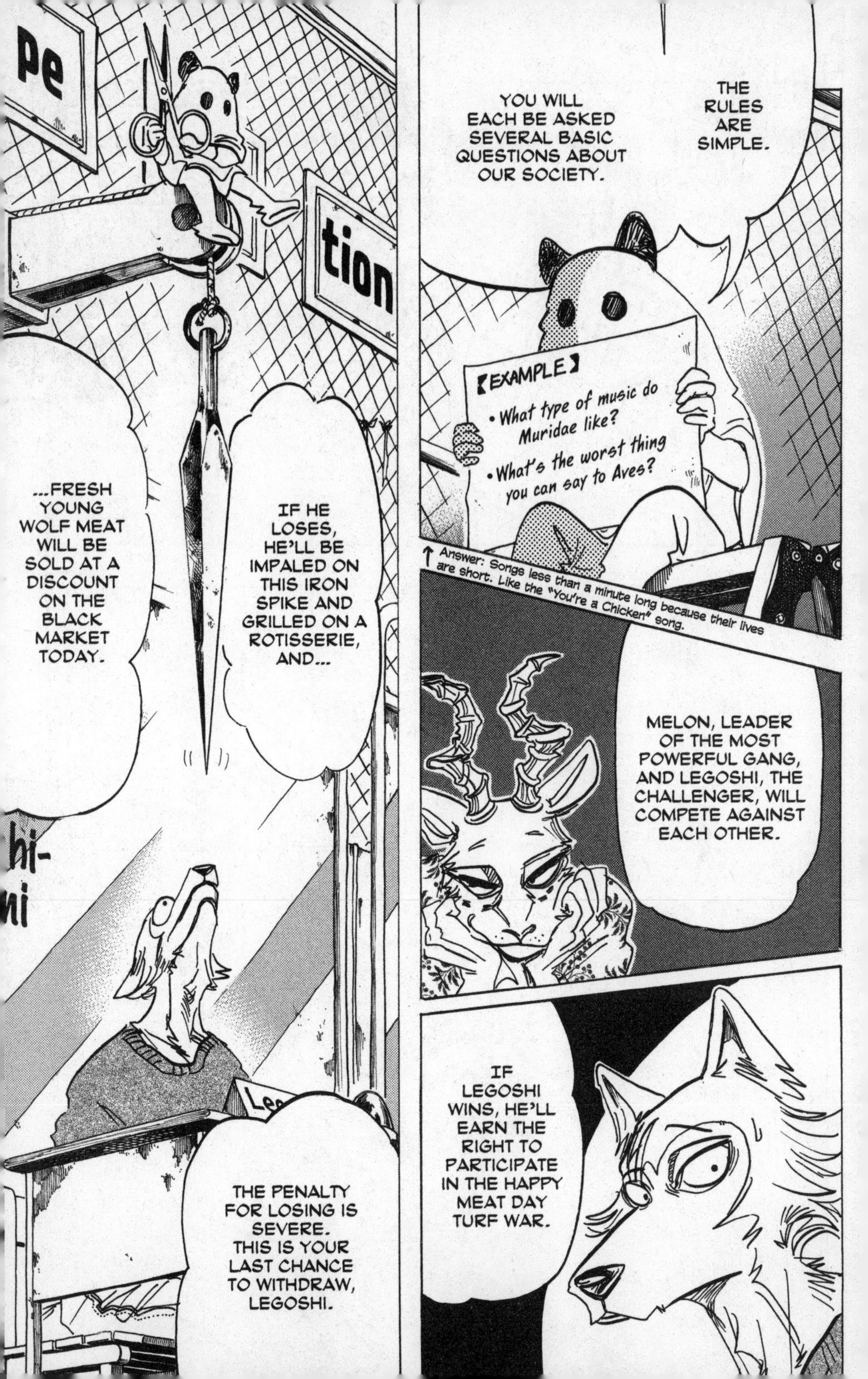
THE RULES ARE SIMPLE.
YOU WILL EACH BE ASKED SEVERAL BASIC QUESTIONS ABOUT OUR SOCIETY.
【EXAMPLE】
• What type of music do Muridae like?
• What's the worst thing you can say to Aves?
↑ Answer: Songs less than a minute long because their lives are short. Like the "You're a Chicken" song.
MELON, LEADER OF THE MOST POWERFUL GANG, AND LEGOSHI, THE CHALLENGER, WILL COMPETE AGAINST EACH OTHER.
IF LEGOSHI WINS, HE'LL EARN THE RIGHT TO PARTICIPATE IN THE HAPPY MEAT DAY TURF WAR.
pe
tion
IF HE LOSES, HE'LL BE IMPALED ON THIS IRON SPIKE AND GRILLED ON A ROTISSERIE, AND...
...FRESH YOUNG WOLF MEAT WILL BE SOLD AT A DISCOUNT ON THE BLACK MARKET TODAY.
THE PENALTY FOR LOSING IS SEVERE. THIS IS YOUR LAST CHANCE TO WITHDRAW, LEGOSHI.

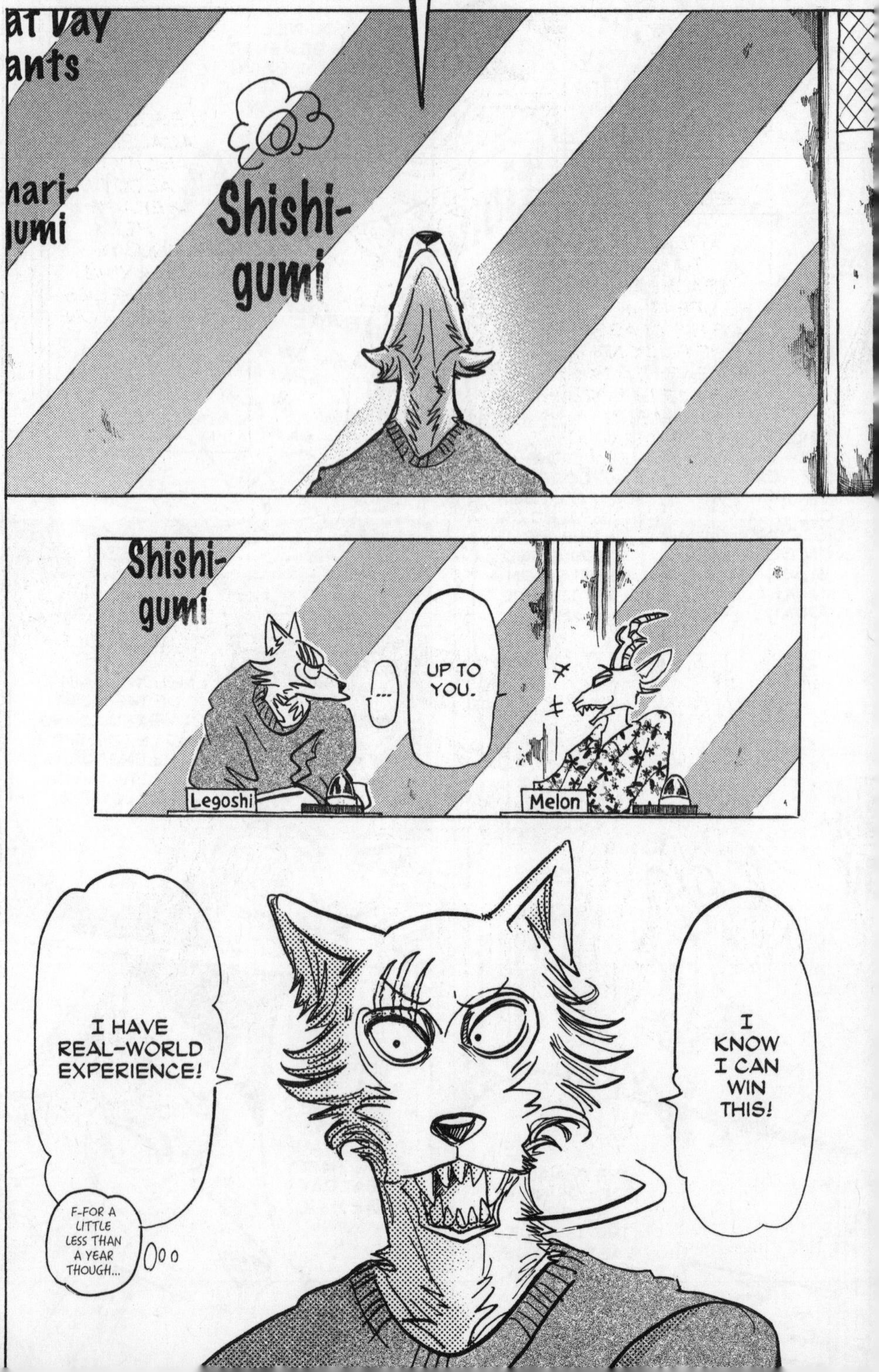
at Day
ants
mari-
gumi
Shishi-gumi
Shishi-gumi
UP TO YOU.
...
Legoshi
Melon
I KNOW I CAN WIN THIS!
I HAVE REAL-WORLD EXPERIENCE!
F-FOR A LITTLE LESS THAN A YEAR THOUGH...

Chapter 168: Both of Their Final Answers

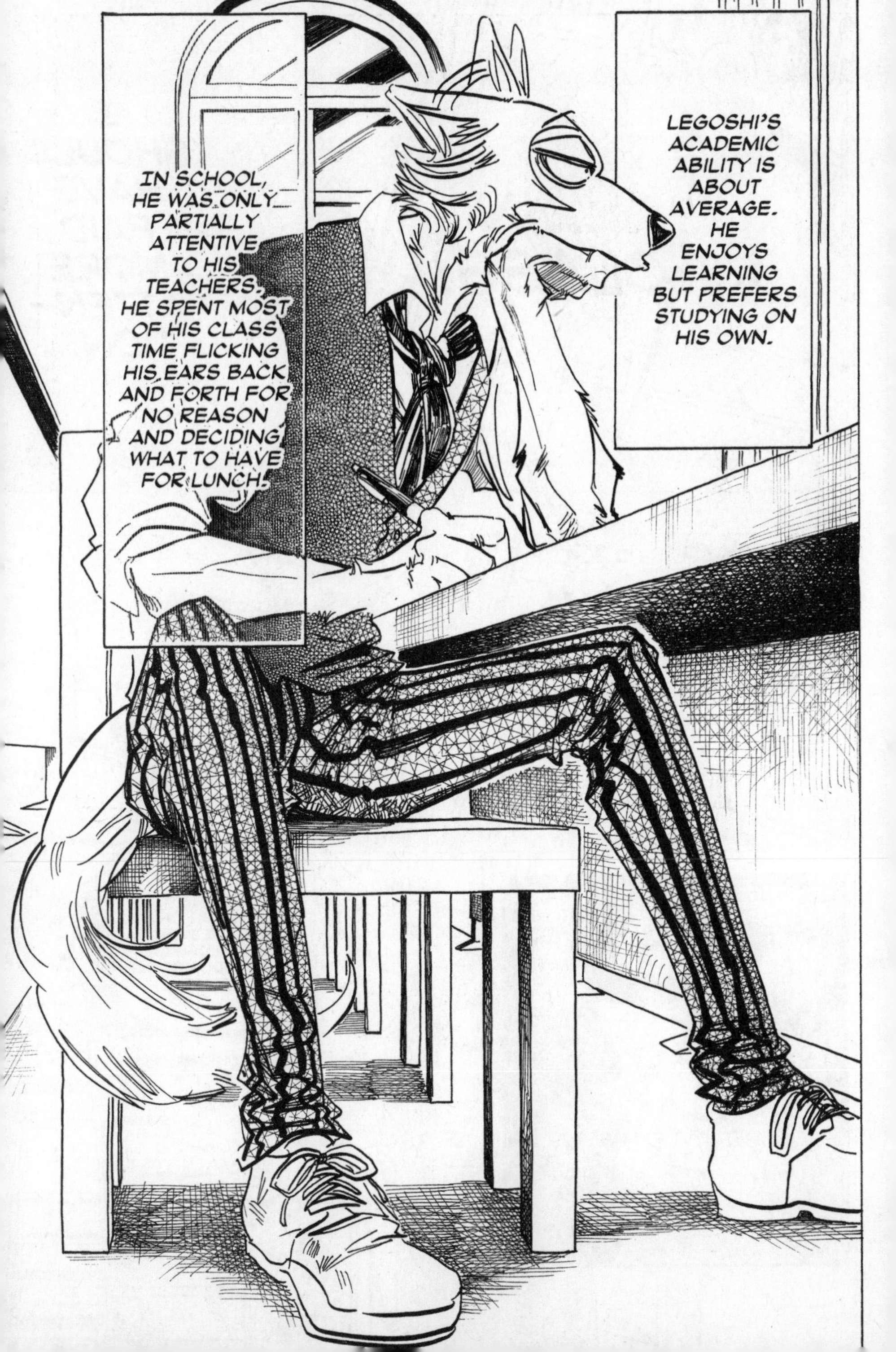
LEGOSHI'S ACADEMIC ABILITY IS ABOUT AVERAGE. HE ENJOYS LEARNING BUT PREFERS STUDYING ON HIS OWN.
IN SCHOOL, HE WAS ONLY PARTIALLY ATTENTIVE TO HIS TEACHERS. HE SPENT MOST OF HIS CLASS TIME FLICKING HIS EARS BACK AND FORTH FOR NO REASON AND DECIDING WHAT TO HAVE FOR LUNCH.

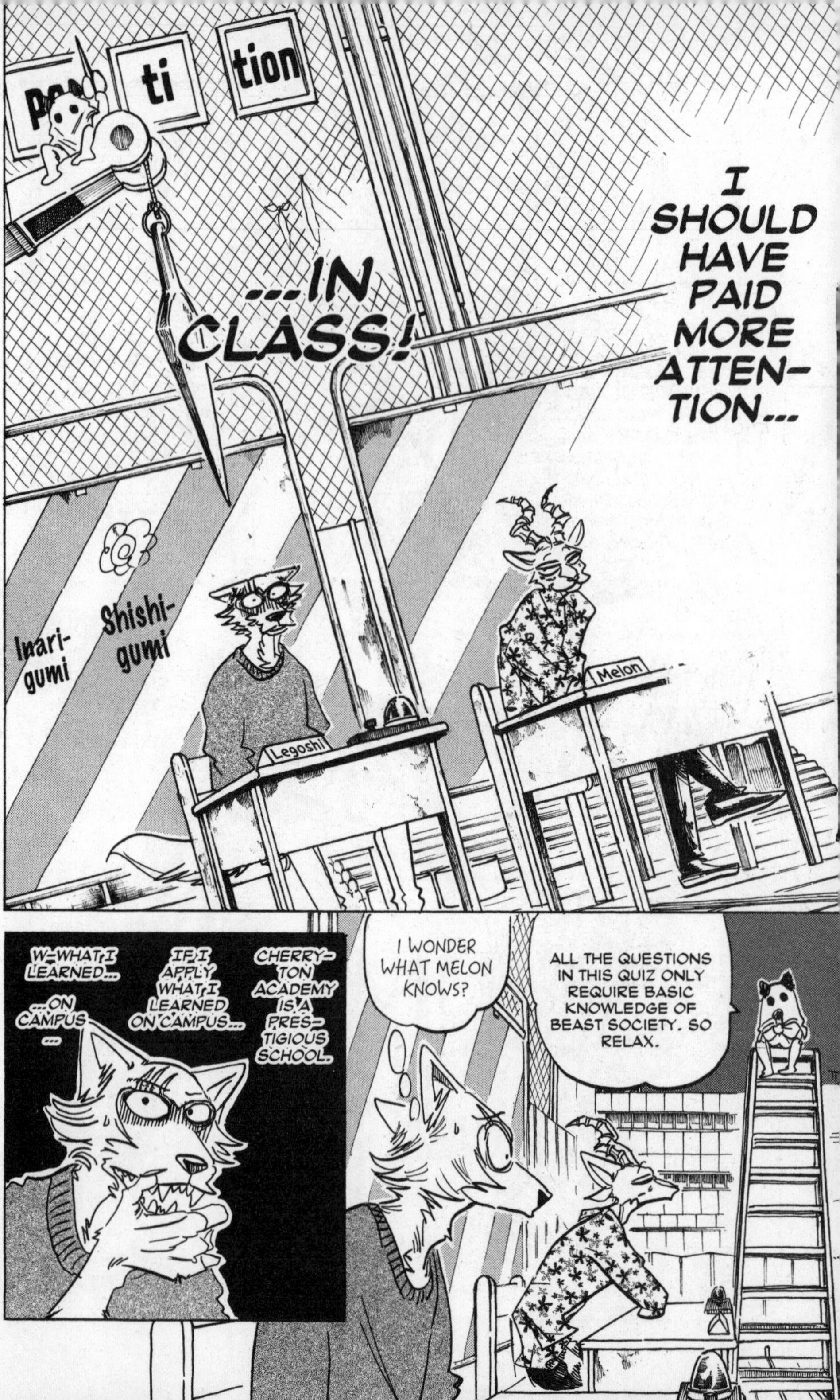
I SHOULD HAVE PAID MORE ATTEN-TION...
...IN CLASS!
ti
tion
Shishi-gumi
Inari-gumi
Melon
Legoshi
ALL THE QUESTIONS IN THIS QUIZ ONLY REQUIRE BASIC KNOWLEDGE OF BEAST SOCIETY. SO RELAX.
I WONDER WHAT MELON KNOWS?
CHERRY-TON ACADEMY IS A PRES-TIGIOUS SCHOOL.
IF I APPLY WHAT I LEARNED ON CAMPUS...
W-WHAT I LEARNED...
...ON CAMPUS...

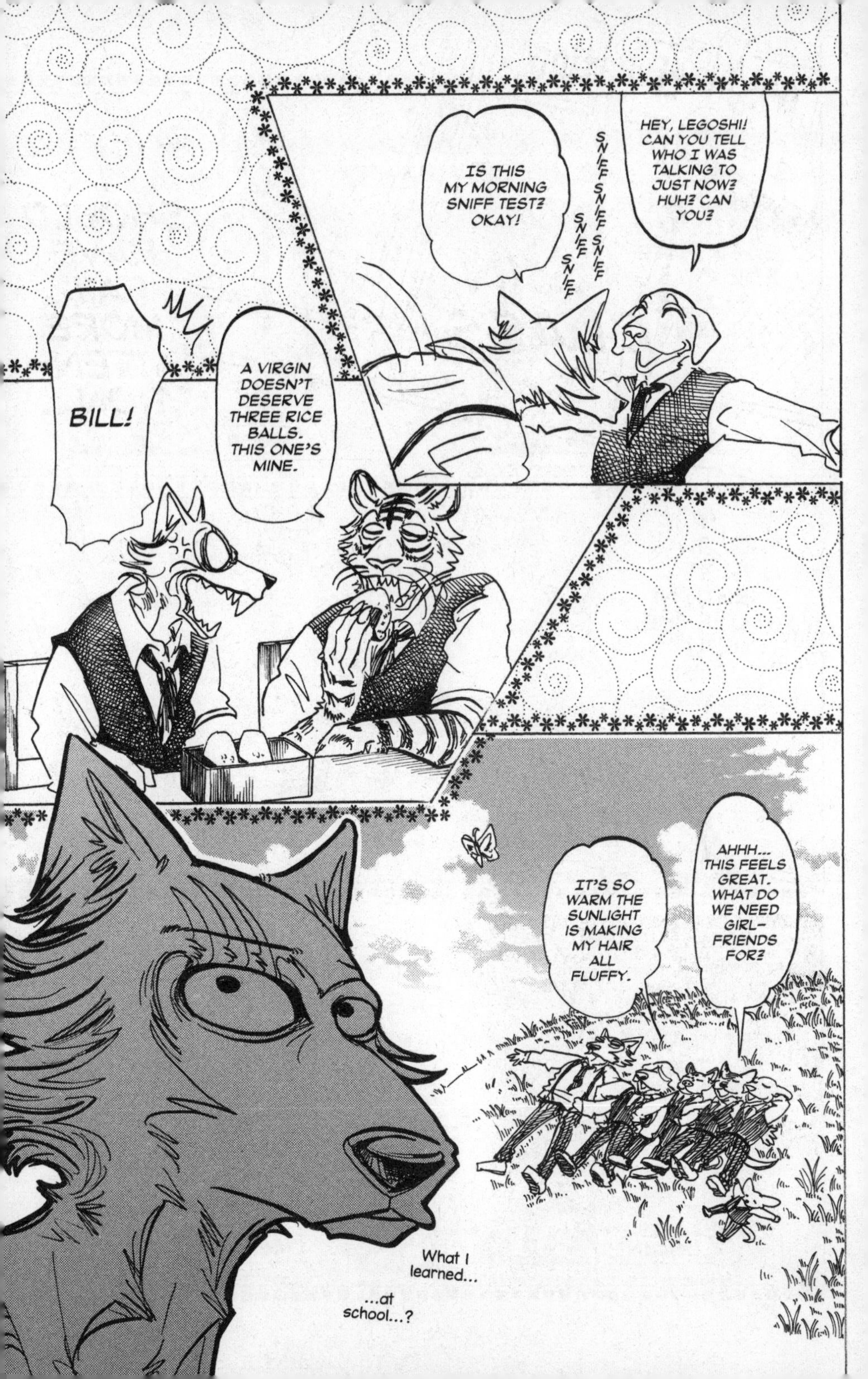
HEY, LEGOSHI! CAN YOU TELL WHO I WAS TALKING TO JUST NOW? HUH? CAN YOU?
SNIFF SNIFF SNIFF
SNIFF SNIFF
IS THIS MY MORNING SNIFF TEST? OKAY!
A VIRGIN DOESN'T DESERVE THREE RICE BALLS. THIS ONE'S MINE.
BILL!
AHHH... THIS FEELS GREAT. WHAT DO WE NEED GIRL-FRIENDS FOR?
IT'S SO WARM THE SUNLIGHT IS MAKING MY HAIR ALL FLUFFY.
What I learned...
...at school...?

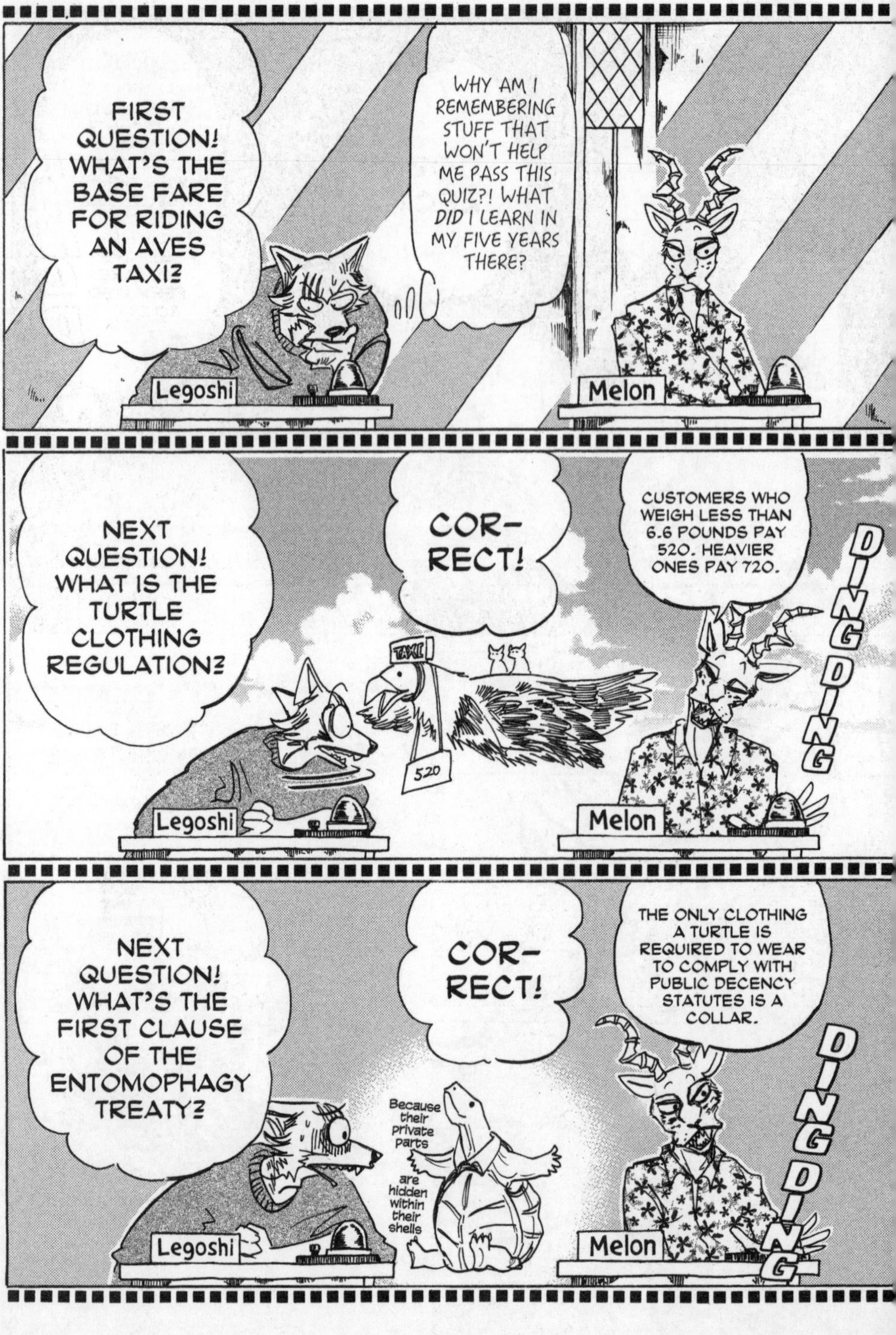
WHY AM I REMEMBERING STUFF THAT WON'T HELP ME PASS THIS QUIZ?! WHAT *DID* I LEARN IN MY FIVE YEARS THERE?
FIRST QUESTION! WHAT'S THE BASE FARE FOR RIDING AN AVES TAXI?
Melon
Legoshi
CUSTOMERS WHO WEIGH LESS THAN 6.6 POUNDS PAY 520. HEAVIER ONES PAY 720.
DING DING
CORRECT!
NEXT QUESTION! WHAT IS THE TURTLE CLOTHING REGULATION?
TAXI
520
Melon
Legoshi
THE ONLY CLOTHING A TURTLE IS REQUIRED TO WEAR TO COMPLY WITH PUBLIC DECENCY STATUTES IS A COLLAR.
DING DING
CORRECT!
NEXT QUESTION! WHAT'S THE FIRST CLAUSE OF THE ENTOMOPHAGY TREATY?
Because their private parts are hidden within their shells
Melon
Legoshi

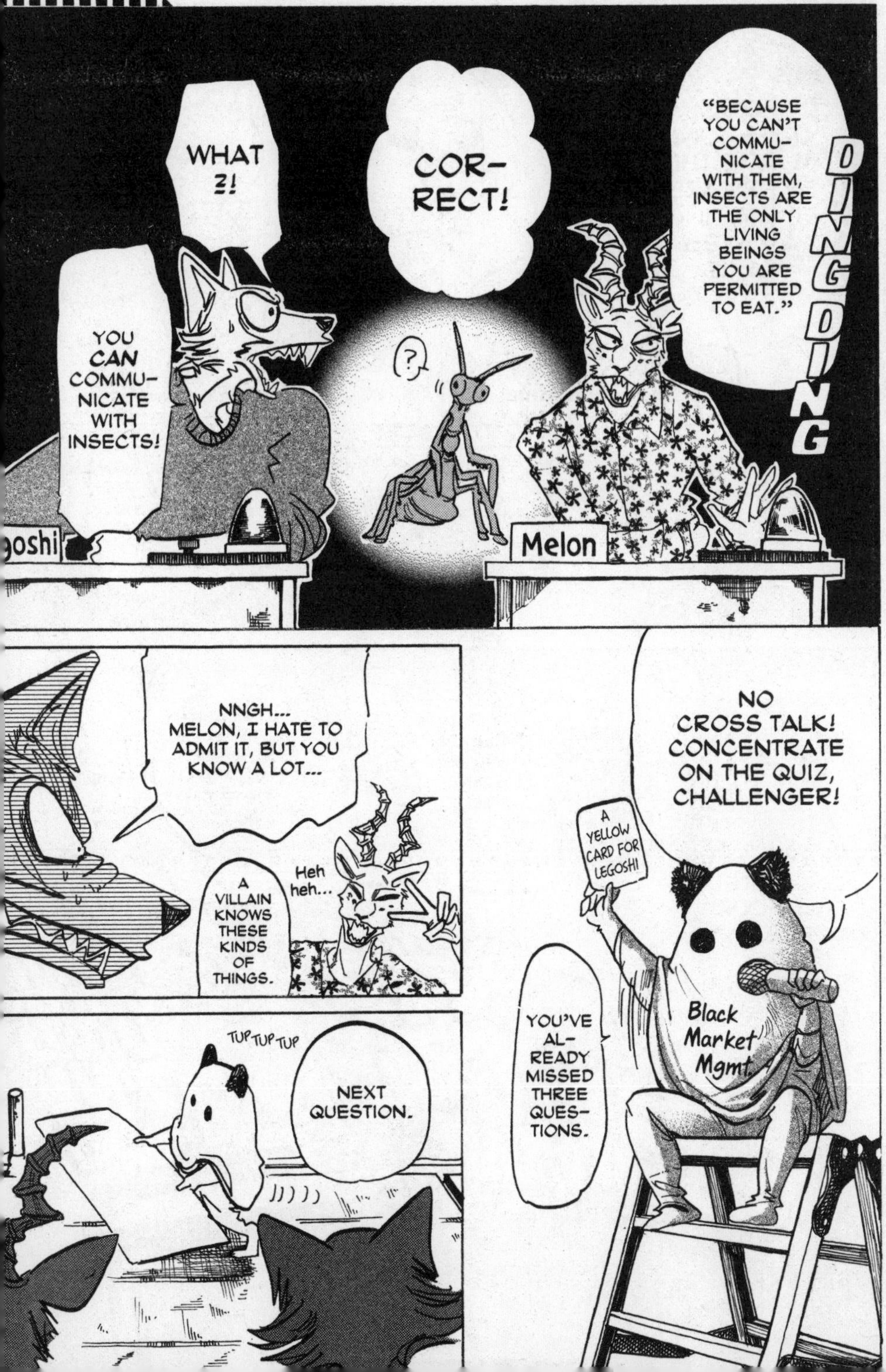
"BECAUSE YOU CAN'T COMMU- NICATE WITH THEM, INSECTS ARE THE ONLY LIVING BEINGS YOU ARE PERMITTED TO EAT."
DING DING
COR- RECT!
?
Melon
WHAT ?!
YOU CAN COMMU- NICATE WITH INSECTS!
goshi
NO CROSS TALK! CONCENTRATE ON THE QUIZ, CHALLENGER!
A YELLOW CARD FOR LEGOSHI!
Black Market Mgmt.
YOU'VE AL- READY MISSED THREE QUES- TIONS.
NNGH... MELON, I HATE TO ADMIT IT, BUT YOU KNOW A LOT...
Heh heh...
A VILLAIN KNOWS THESE KINDS OF THINGS.
TUP TUP TUP
NEXT QUESTION.

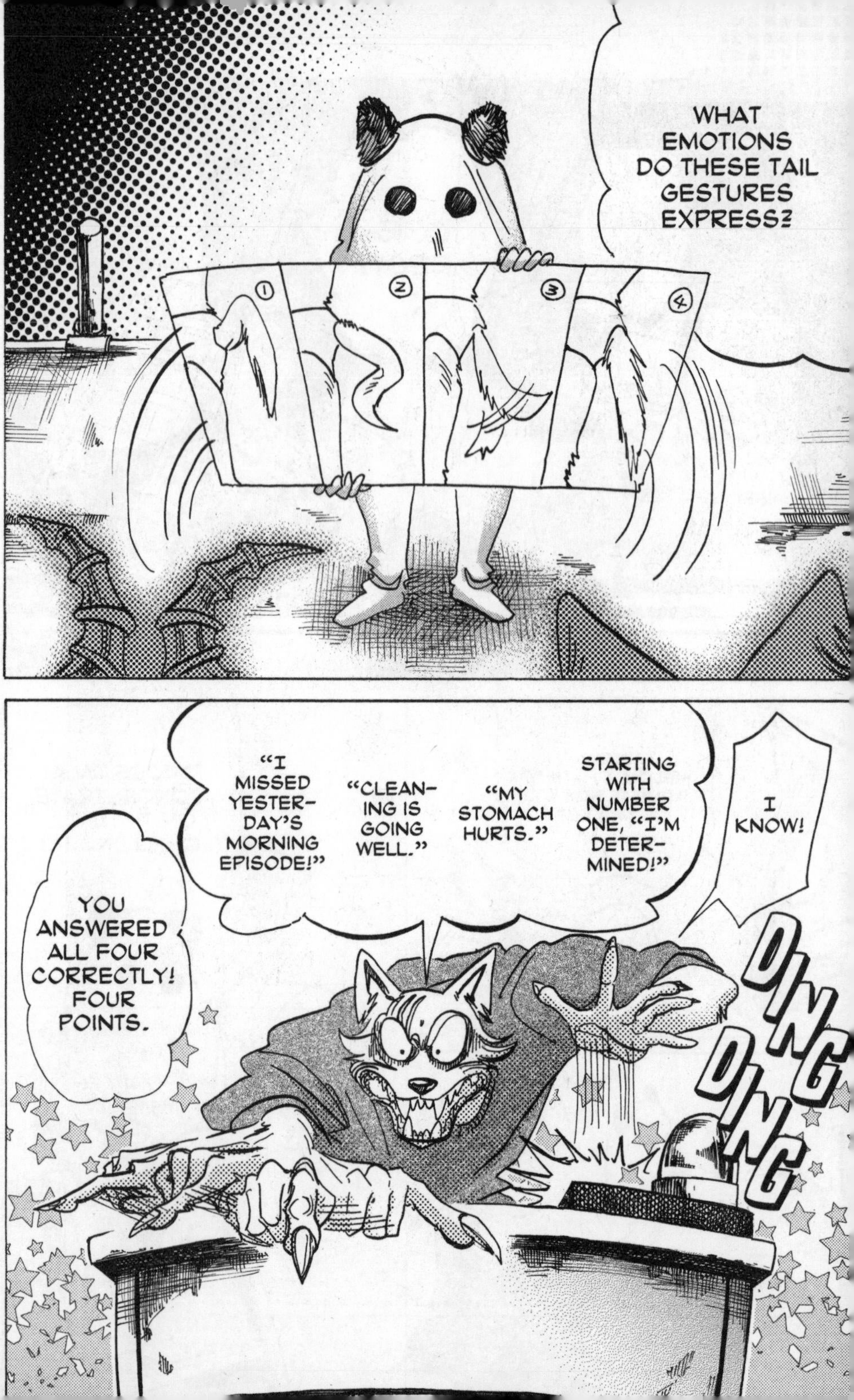
WHAT EMOTIONS DO THESE TAIL GESTURES EXPRESS?
I KNOW!
STARTING WITH NUMBER ONE, "I'M DETERMINED!"
"MY STOMACH HURTS."
"CLEANING IS GOING WELL."
"I MISSED YESTERDAY'S MORNING EPISODE!"
DING DING
YOU ANSWERED ALL FOUR CORRECTLY! FOUR POINTS.

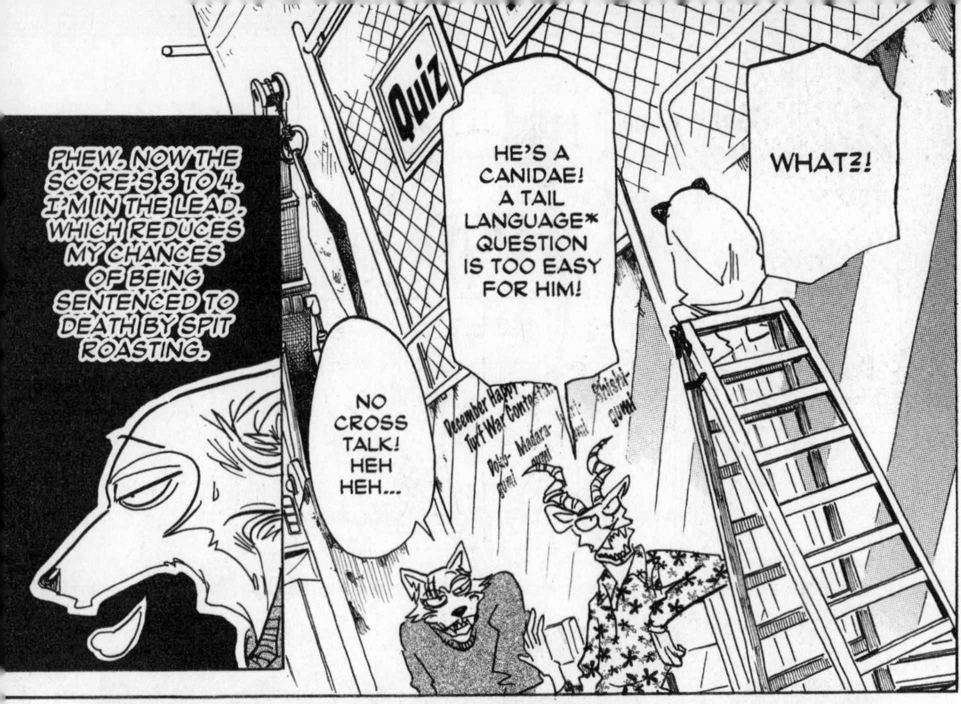
WHAT?!
Quiz
HE'S A CANIDAE! A TAIL LANGUAGE* QUESTION IS TOO EASY FOR HIM!
December Happy Turf War Contest
Shishi-gumi
Madara-gumi
NO CROSS TALK! HEH HEH...
PHEW. NOW THE SCORE'S 3 TO 4. I'M IN THE LEAD, WHICH REDUCES MY CHANCES OF BEING SENTENCED TO DEATH BY SPIT ROASTING.

*Tail language: Communicating emotions with your tail

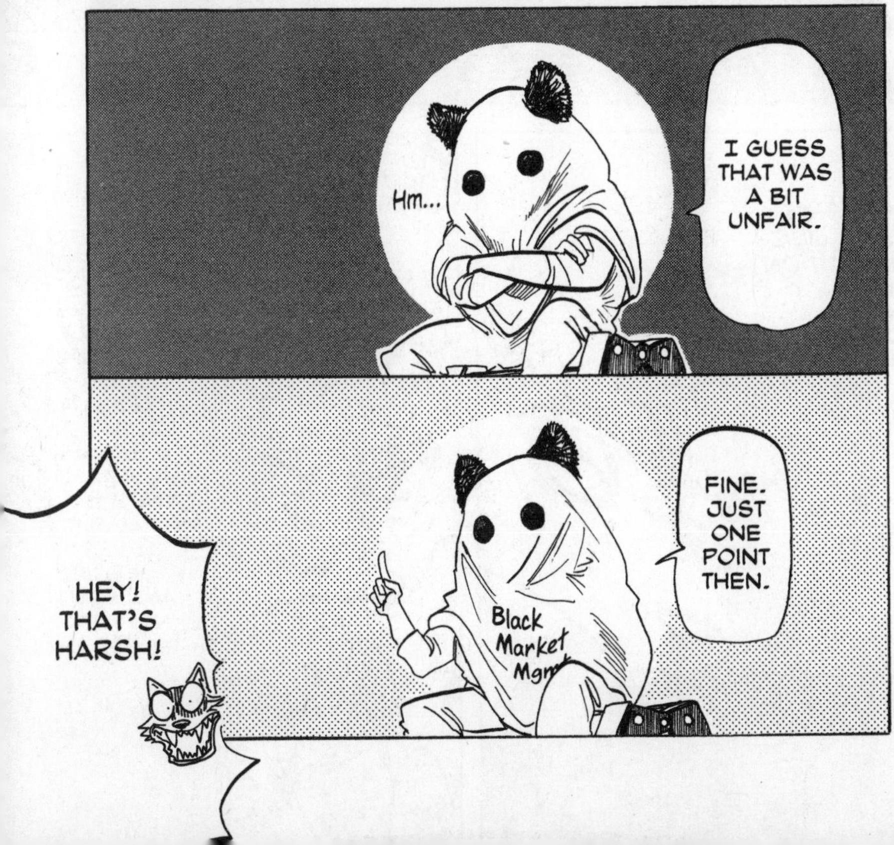
I GUESS THAT WAS A BIT UNFAIR.
Hm...
FINE. JUST ONE POINT THEN.
Black Market Mgm
HEY! THAT'S HARSH!

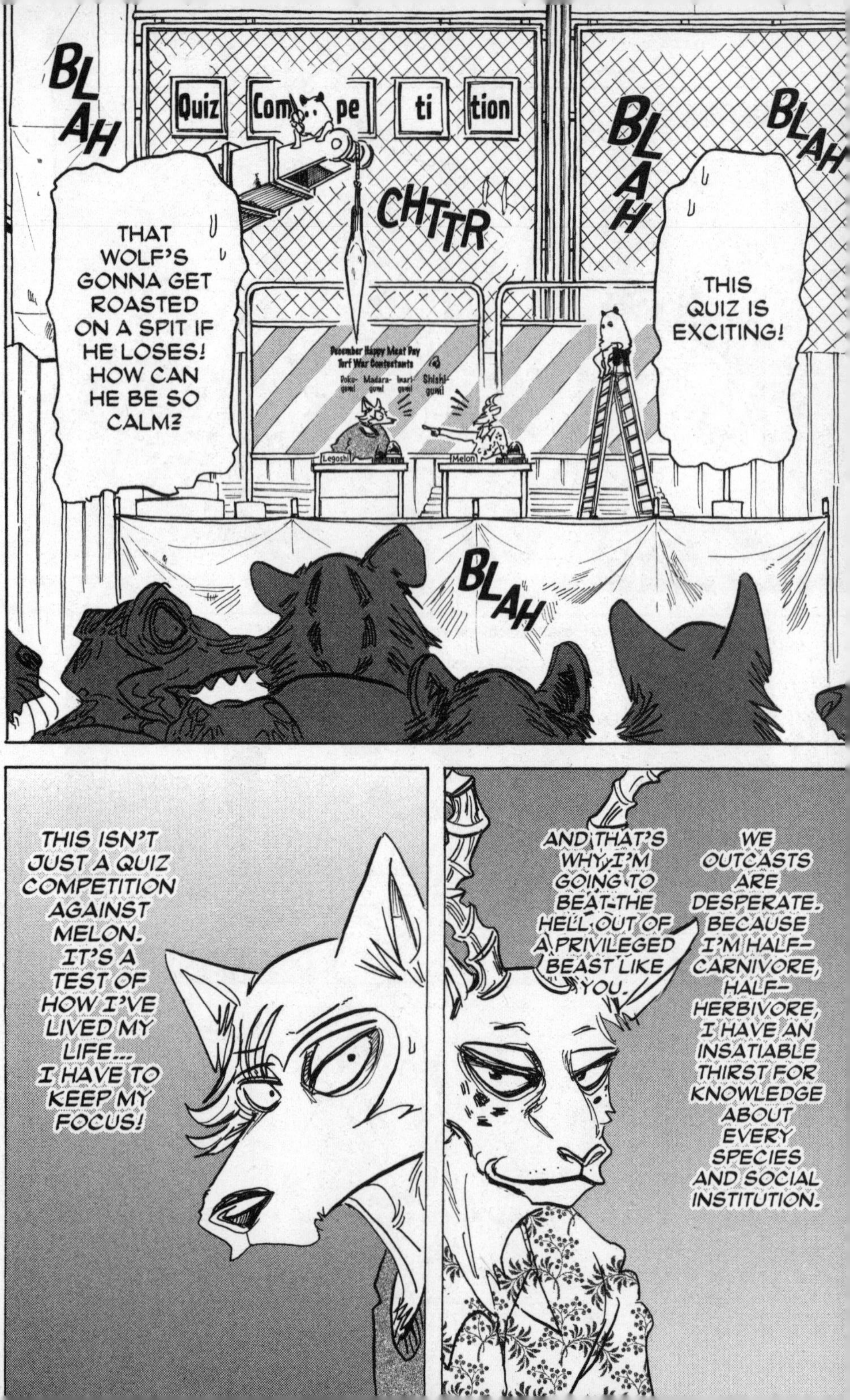
BLAH
BLAH
THIS QUIZ IS EXCITING!
Quiz Com pe ti tion
CHTTR
BLAH
THAT WOLF'S GONNA GET ROASTED ON A SPIT IF HE LOSES! HOW CAN HE BE SO CALM?
December Happy Meat Day Turf War Contestants
Doku-gumi Madara-gumi Inari-gumi Shishi-gumi
Melon
Legoshi
BLAH
WE OUTCASTS ARE DESPERATE. BECAUSE I'M HALF-CARNIVORE, HALF-HERBIVORE, I HAVE AN INSATIABLE THIRST FOR KNOWLEDGE ABOUT EVERY SPECIES AND SOCIAL INSTITUTION.
AND THAT'S WHY I'M GOING TO BEAT THE HELL OUT OF A PRIVILEGED BEAST LIKE YOU.
THIS ISN'T JUST A QUIZ COMPETITION AGAINST MELON. IT'S A TEST OF HOW I'VE LIVED MY LIFE... I HAVE TO KEEP MY FOCUS!

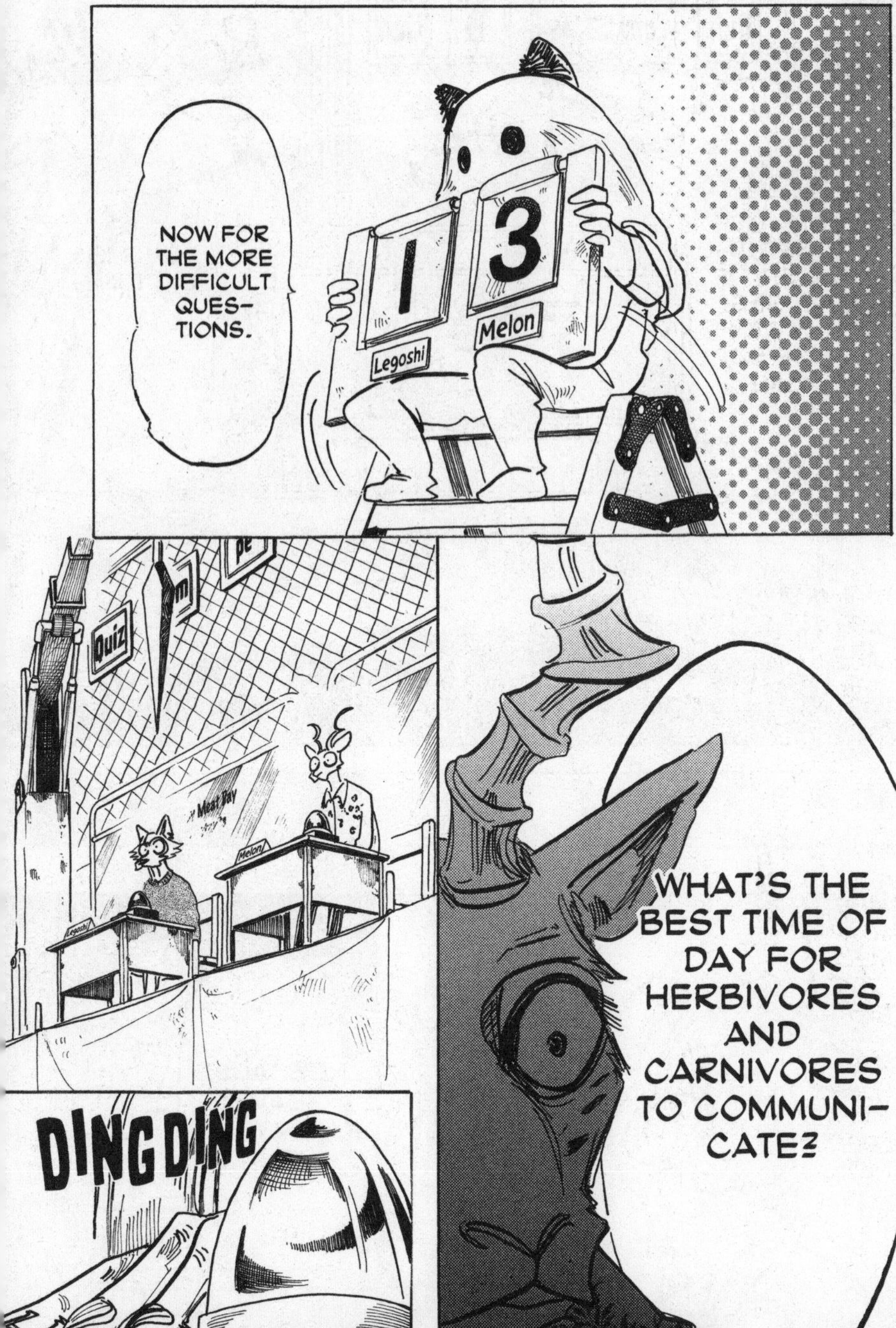
NOW FOR THE MORE DIFFICULT QUES-TIONS.
1 3
Legoshi
Melon
WHAT'S THE BEST TIME OF DAY FOR HERBIVORES AND CARNIVORES TO COMMUNI-CATE?
Quiz
Meat Day
Melon
Legoshi
DING DING

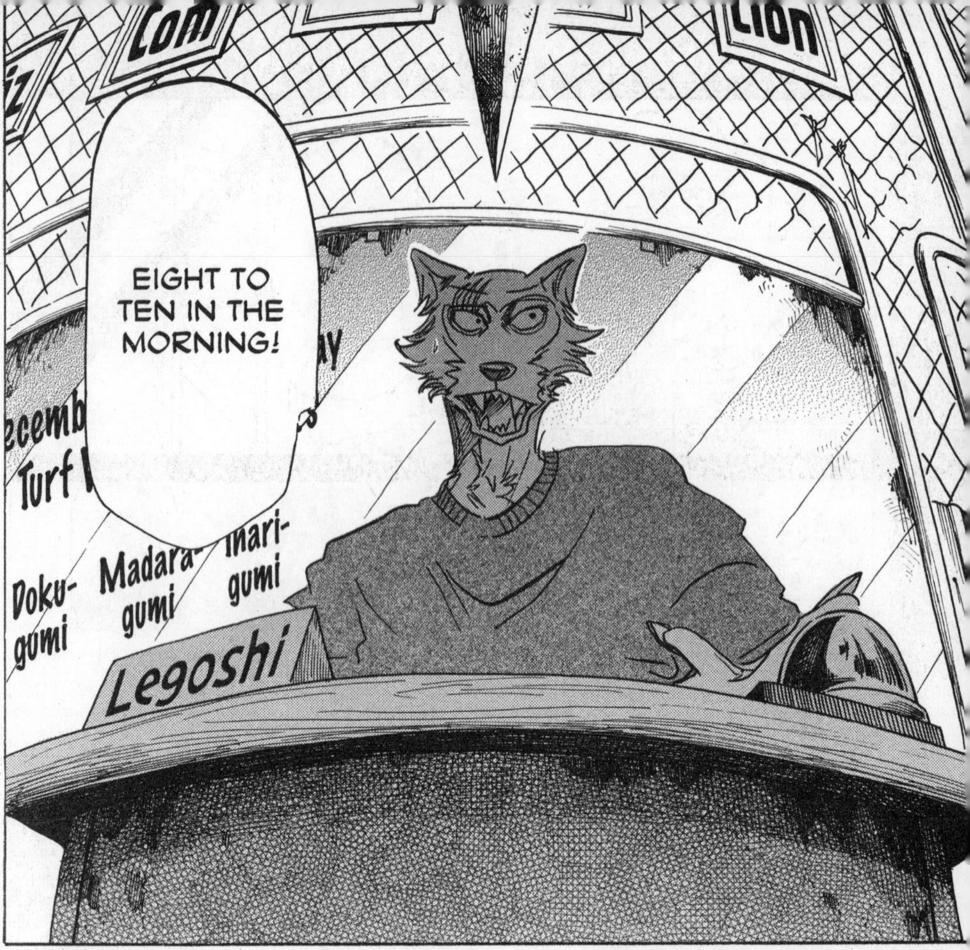
EIGHT TO TEN IN THE MORNING!
Inari-gumi
Madara-gumi
Doku-gumi
Legoshi
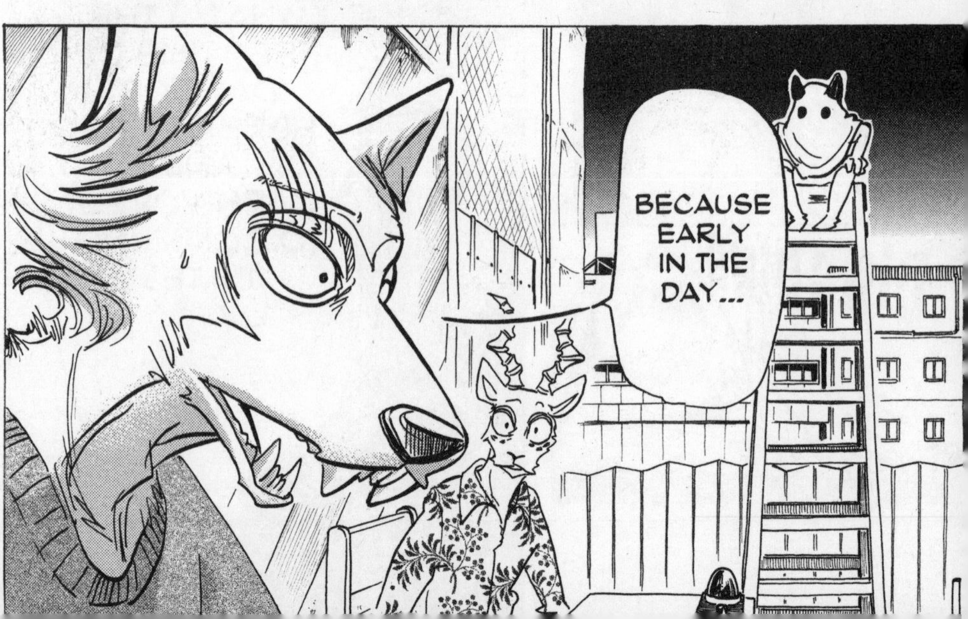
BECAUSE EARLY IN THE DAY...

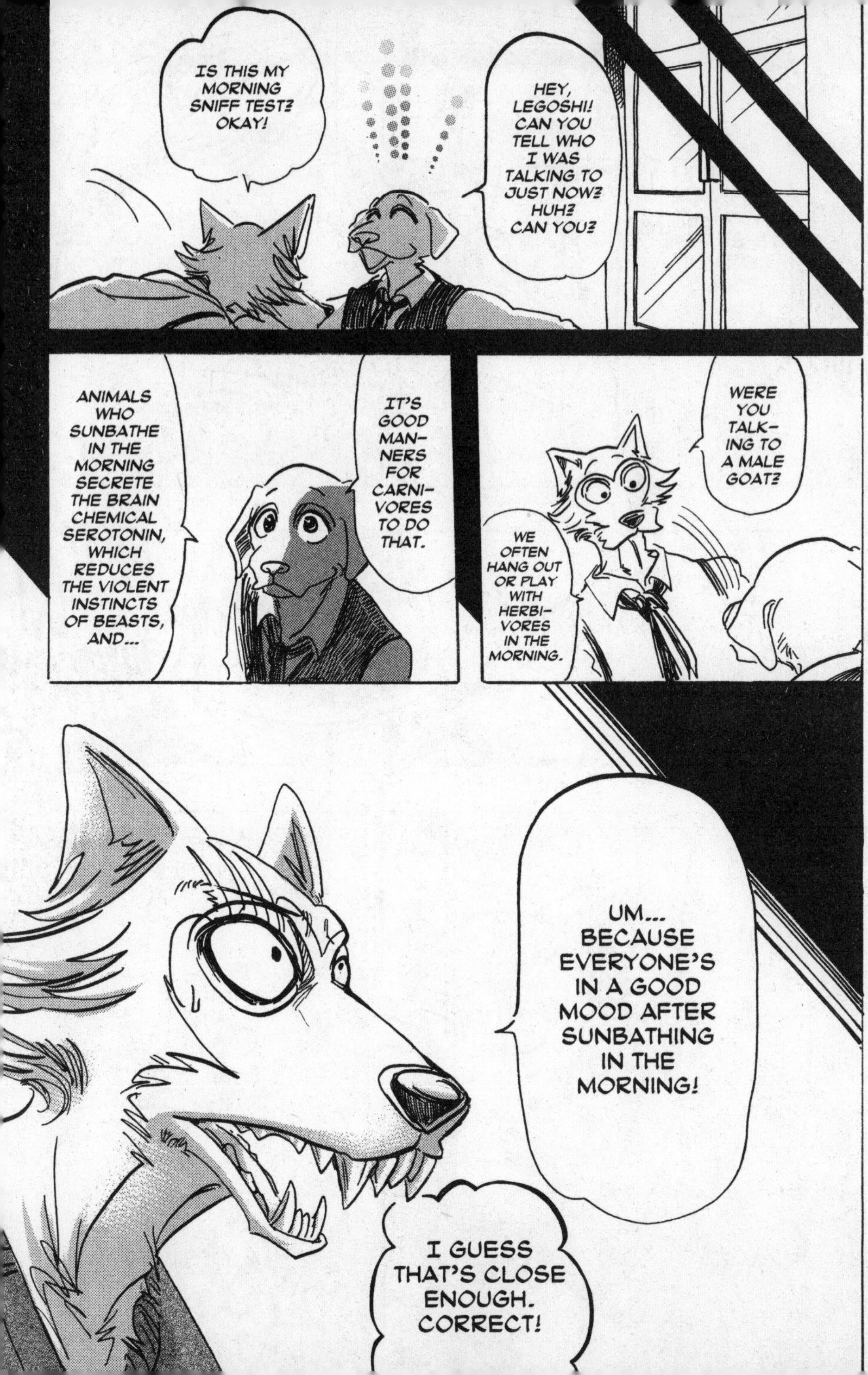
HEY, LEGOSHI! CAN YOU TELL WHO I WAS TALKING TO JUST NOW? HUH? CAN YOU?
IS THIS MY MORNING SNIFF TEST? OKAY!
WERE YOU TALK-ING TO A MALE GOAT?
WE OFTEN HANG OUT OR PLAY WITH HERBI-VORES IN THE MORNING.
IT'S GOOD MAN-NERS FOR CARNI-VORES TO DO THAT.
ANIMALS WHO SUNBATHE IN THE MORNING SECRETE THE BRAIN CHEMICAL SEROTONIN, WHICH REDUCES THE VIOLENT INSTINCTS OF BEASTS, AND...
UM... BECAUSE EVERYONE'S IN A GOOD MOOD AFTER SUNBATHING IN THE MORNING!
I GUESS THAT'S CLOSE ENOUGH. CORRECT!

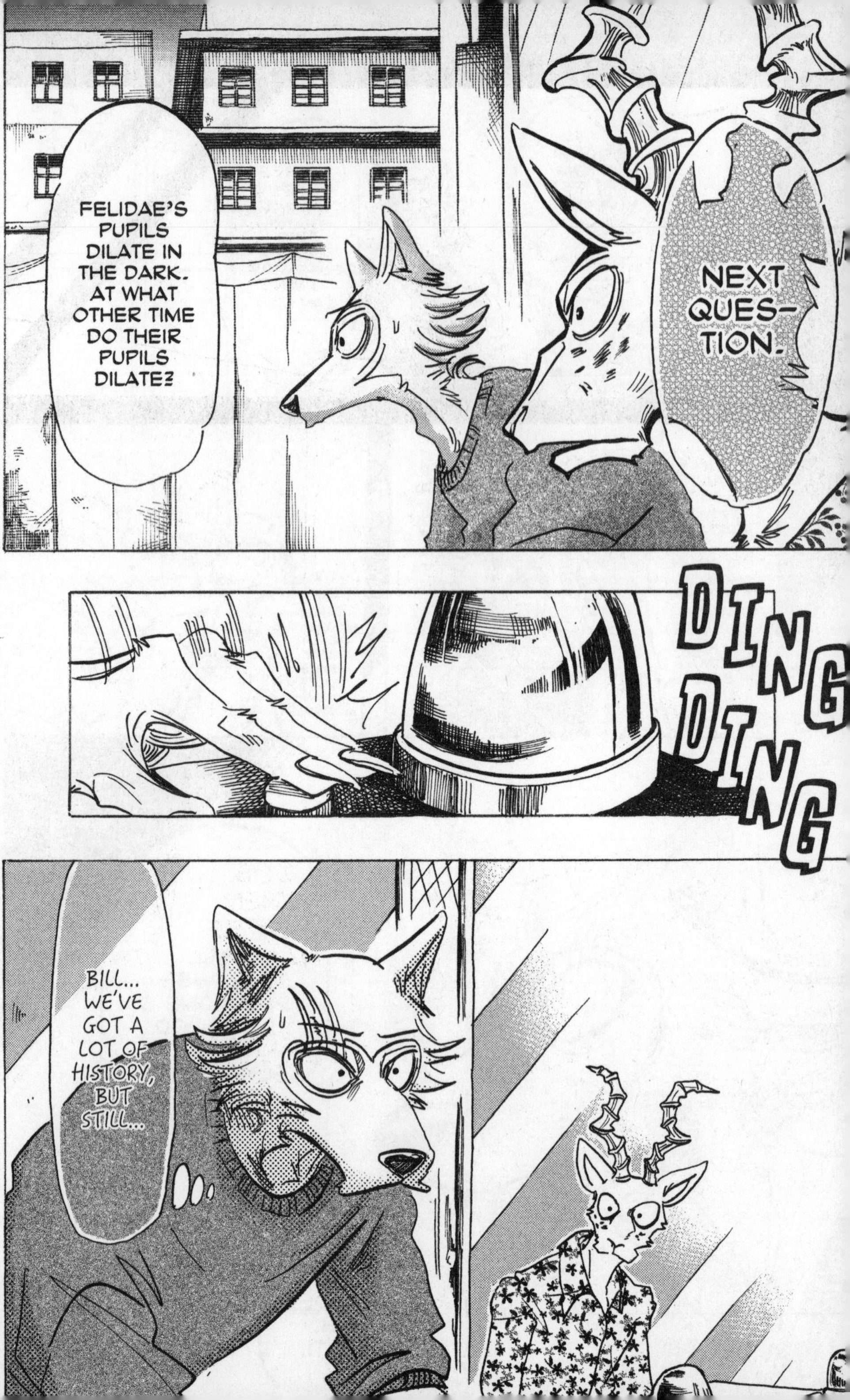
NEXT QUESTION.
FELIDAE'S PUPILS DILATE IN THE DARK. AT WHAT OTHER TIME DO THEIR PUPILS DILATE?
DING DING
BILL... WE'VE GOT A LOT OF HISTORY, BUT STILL...

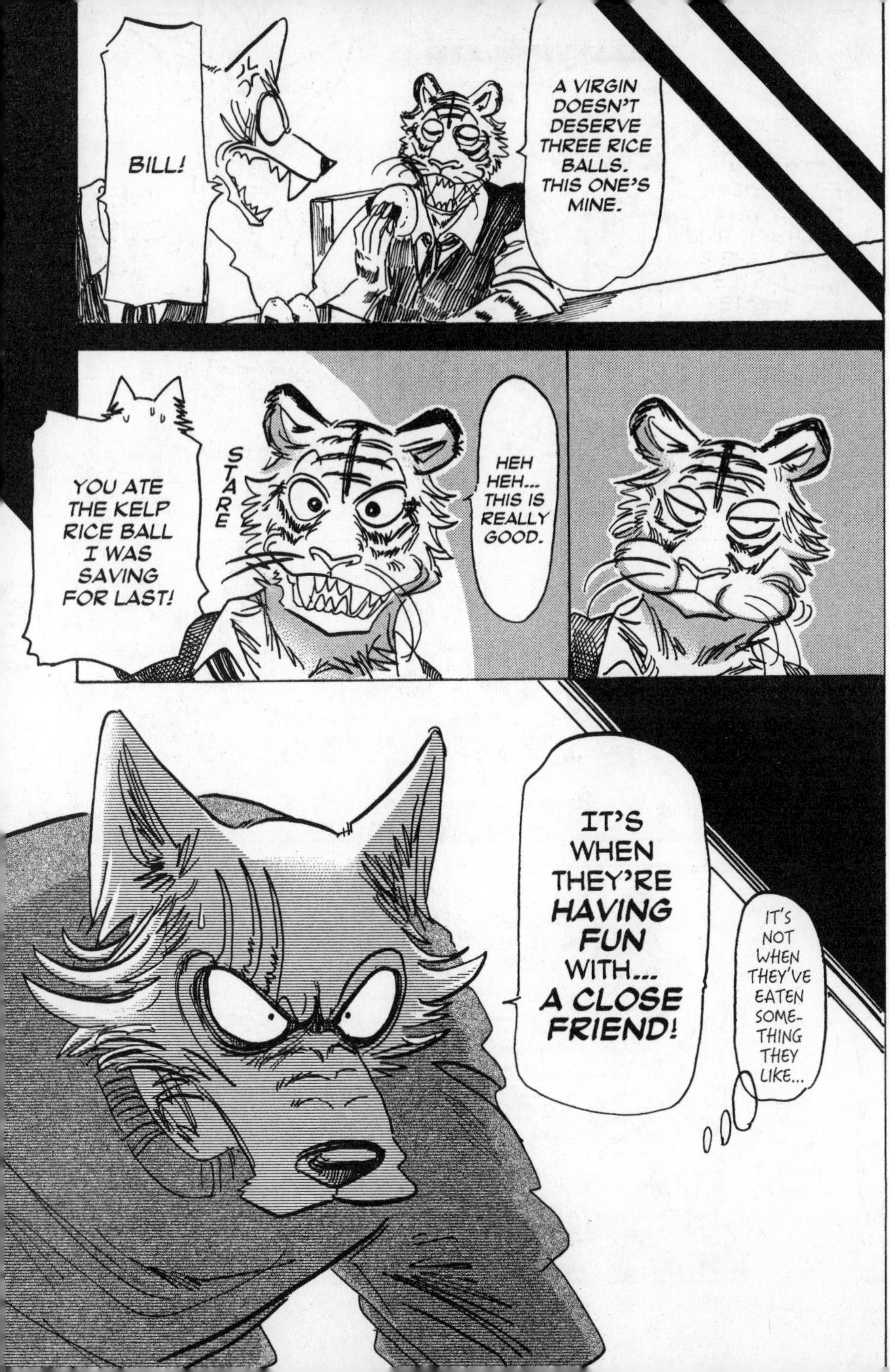
A VIRGIN DOESN'T DESERVE THREE RICE BALLS. THIS ONE'S MINE.
BILL!
HEH HEH... THIS IS REALLY GOOD.
STARE
YOU ATE THE KELP RICE BALL I WAS SAVING FOR LAST!
IT'S NOT WHEN THEY'VE EATEN SOME-THING THEY LIKE...
IT'S WHEN THEY'RE HAVING FUN WITH... A CLOSE FRIEND!

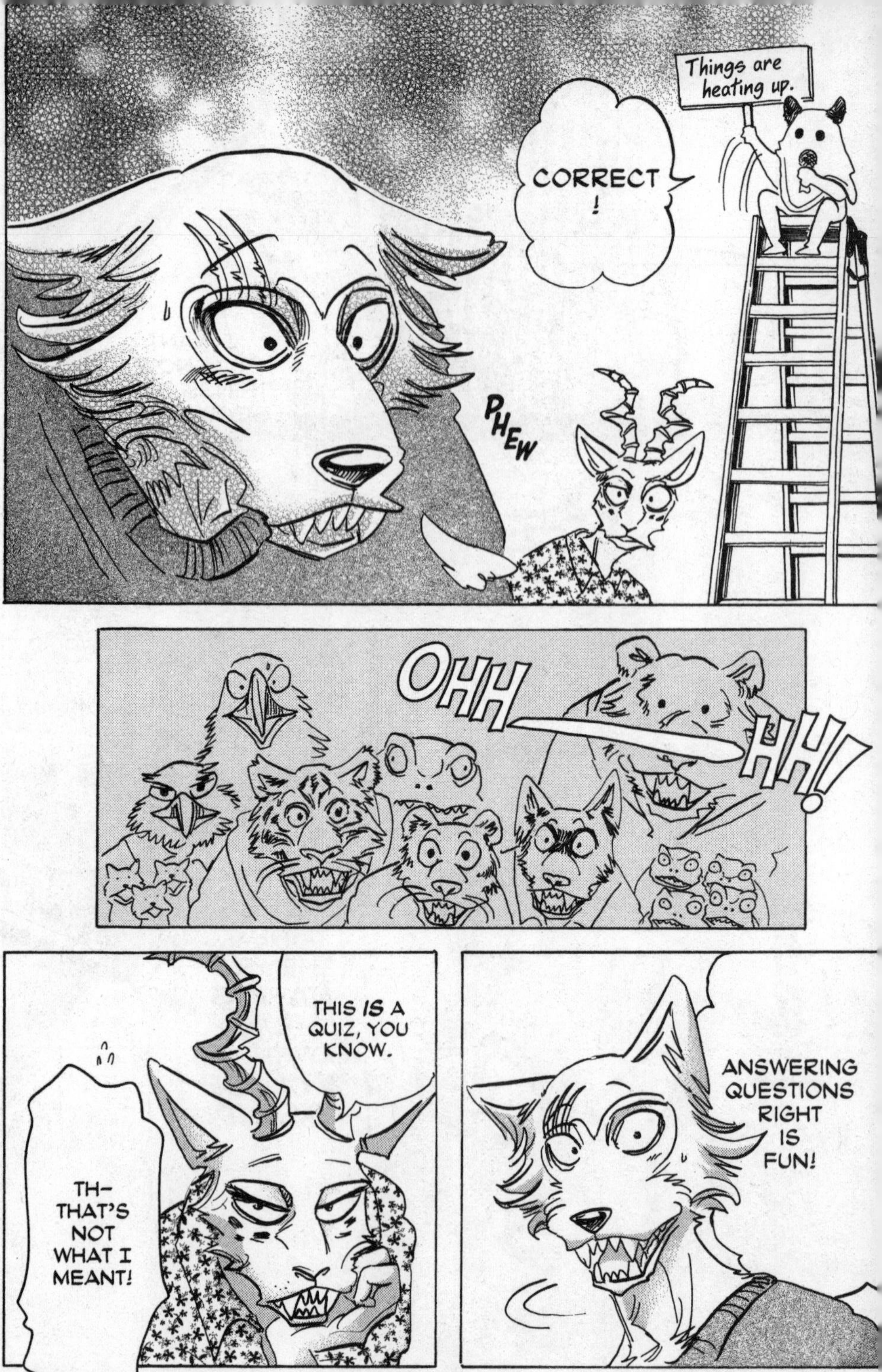
Things are heating up.
CORRECT!
PHEW
OHHHH!
ANSWERING QUESTIONS RIGHT IS FUN!
THIS *IS* A QUIZ, YOU KNOW.
TH-THAT'S NOT WHAT I MEANT!

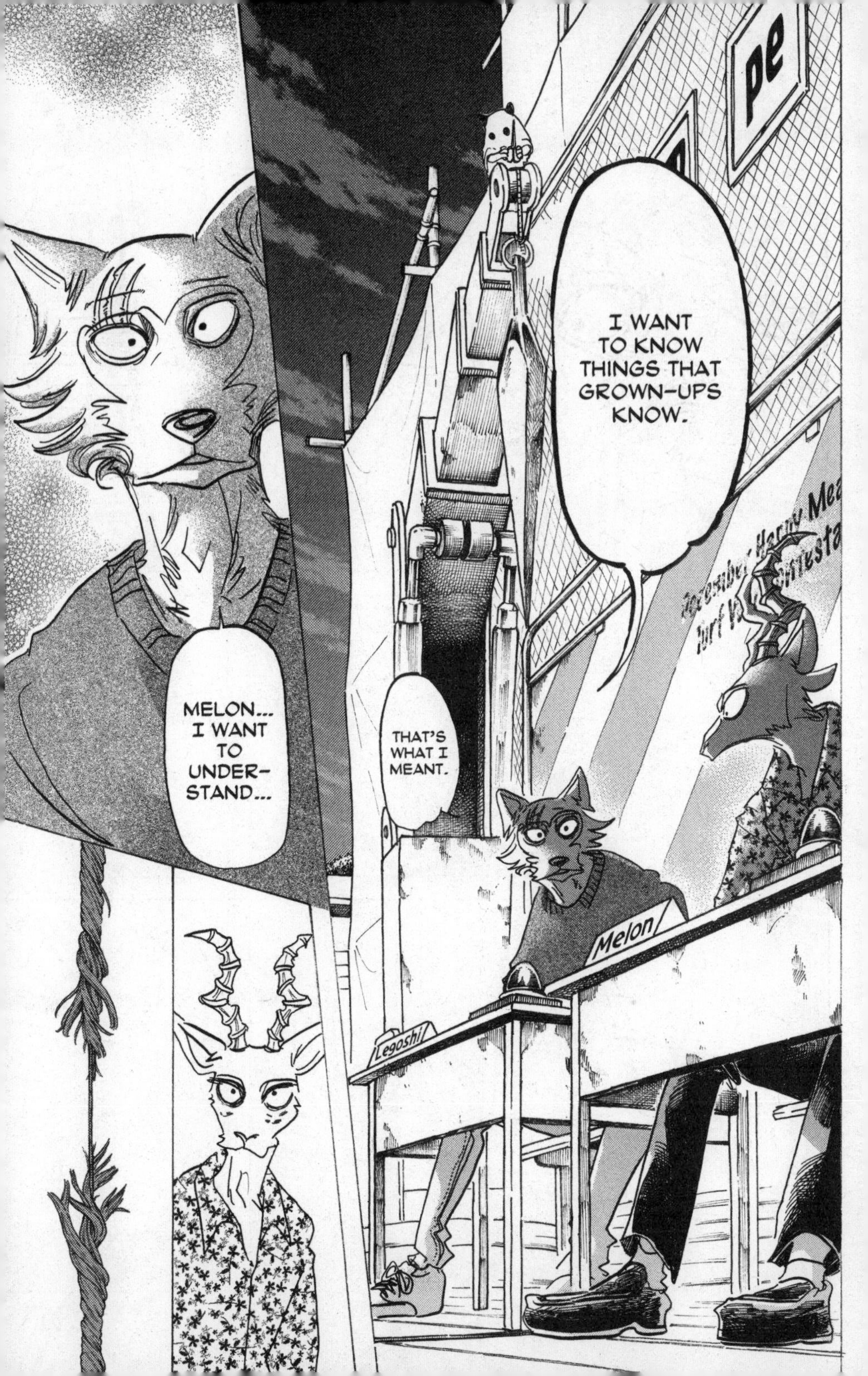
I WANT TO KNOW THINGS THAT GROWN-UPS KNOW.
THAT'S WHAT I MEANT.
Melon
Legoshi
MELON... I WANT TO UNDER-STAND...

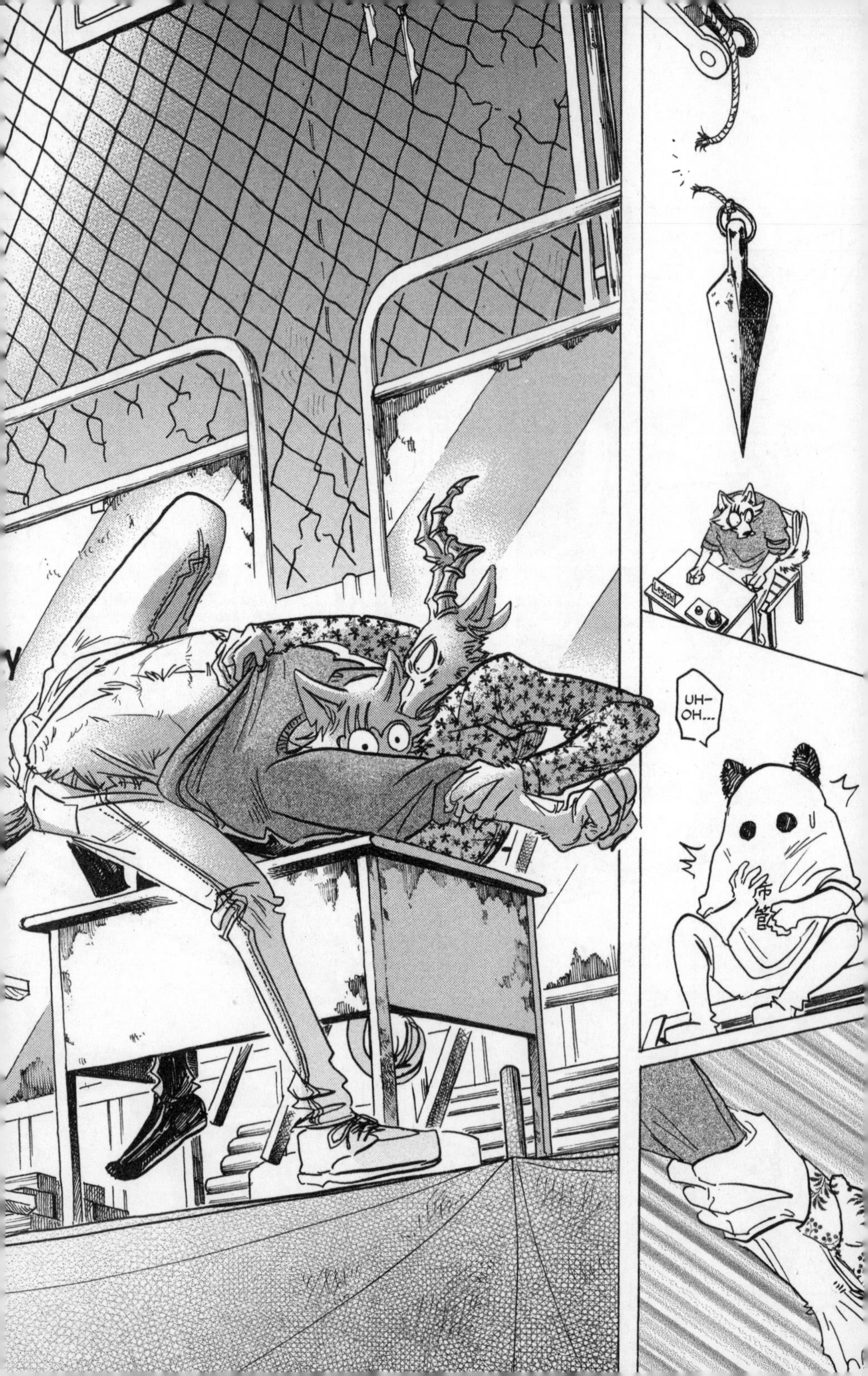
Legoshi
UH-OH...

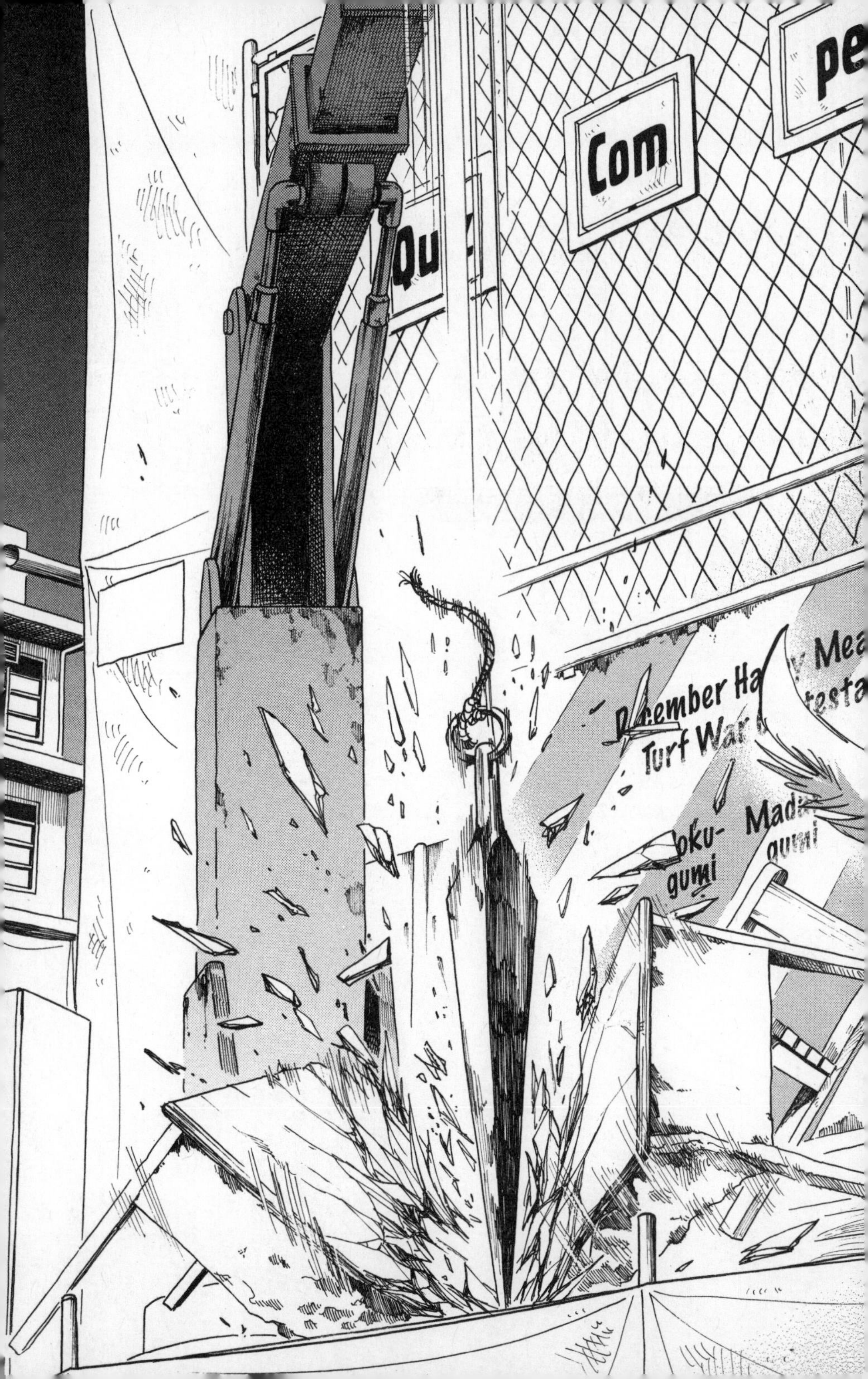
pe
Com
Qu
D cember Ha y Mea
Turf War testa
Madi
gumi
oku-
gumi

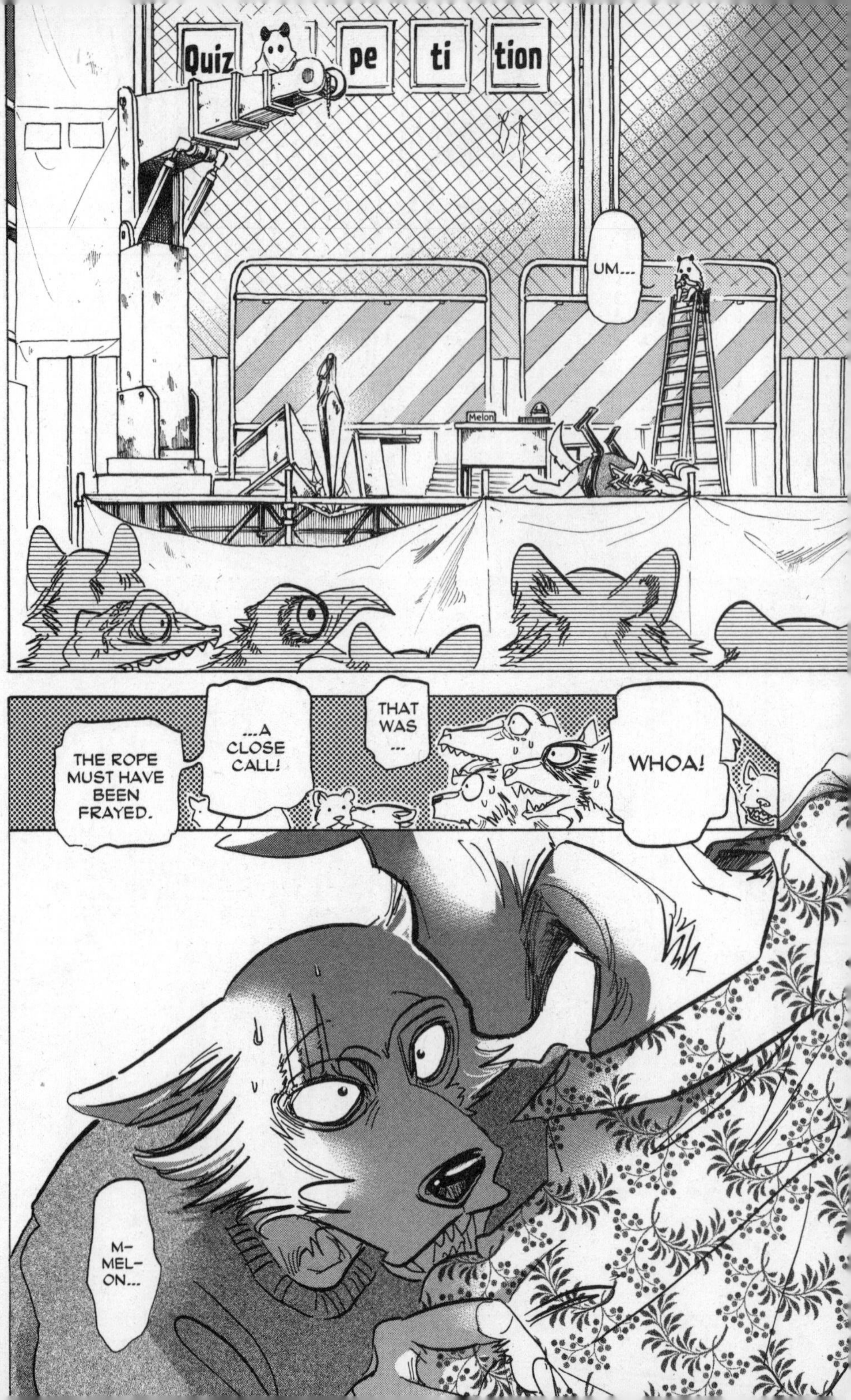
Quiz pe ti tion
UM...
Melon
WHOA!
THAT WAS ...
...A CLOSE CALL!
THE ROPE MUST HAVE BEEN FRAYED.
M-MEL-ON...

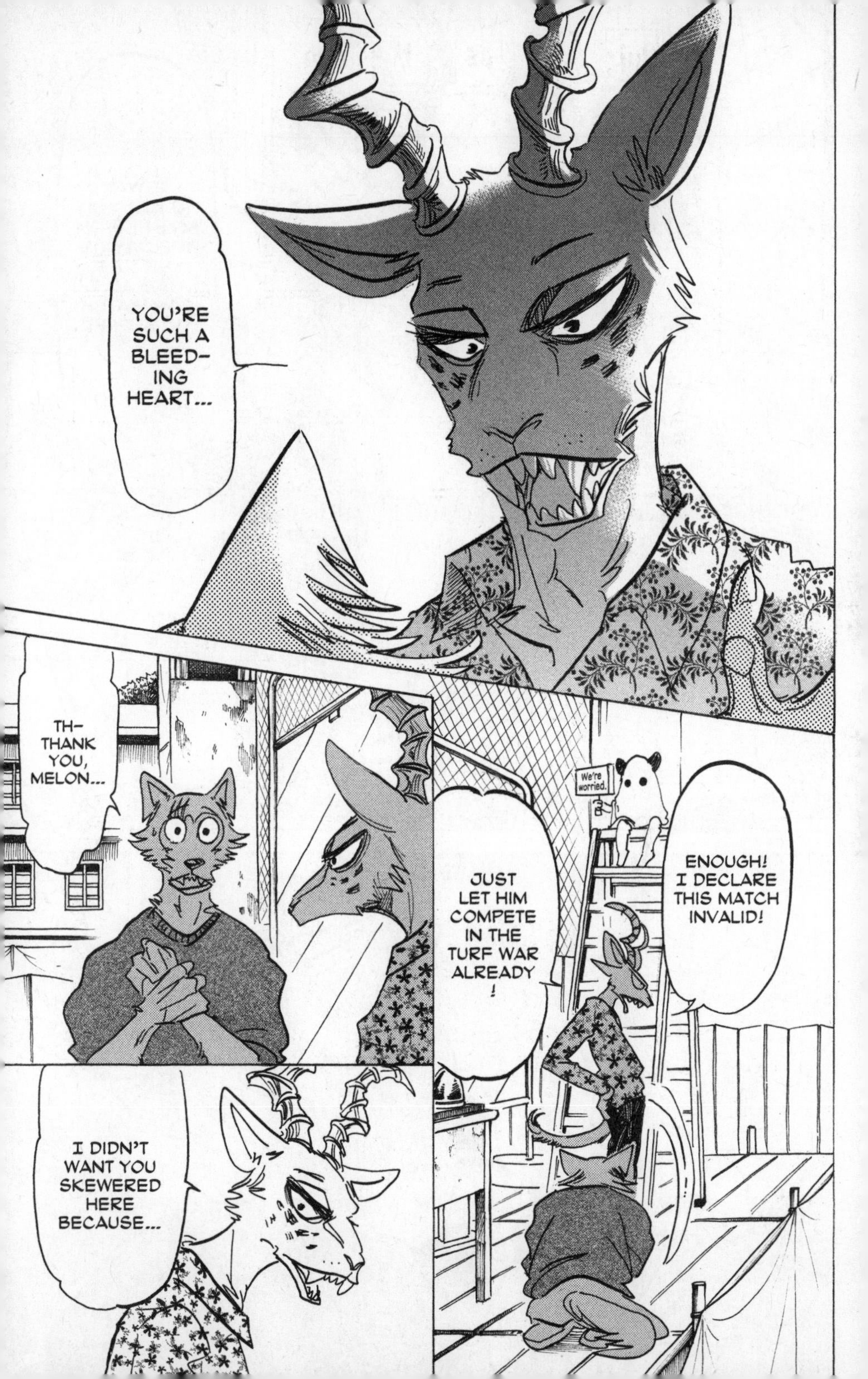
YOU'RE SUCH A BLEEDING HEART...
ENOUGH! I DECLARE THIS MATCH INVALID!
We're worried.
JUST LET HIM COMPETE IN THE TURF WAR ALREADY!
TH-THANK YOU, MELON...
I DIDN'T WANT YOU SKEWERED HERE BECAUSE...

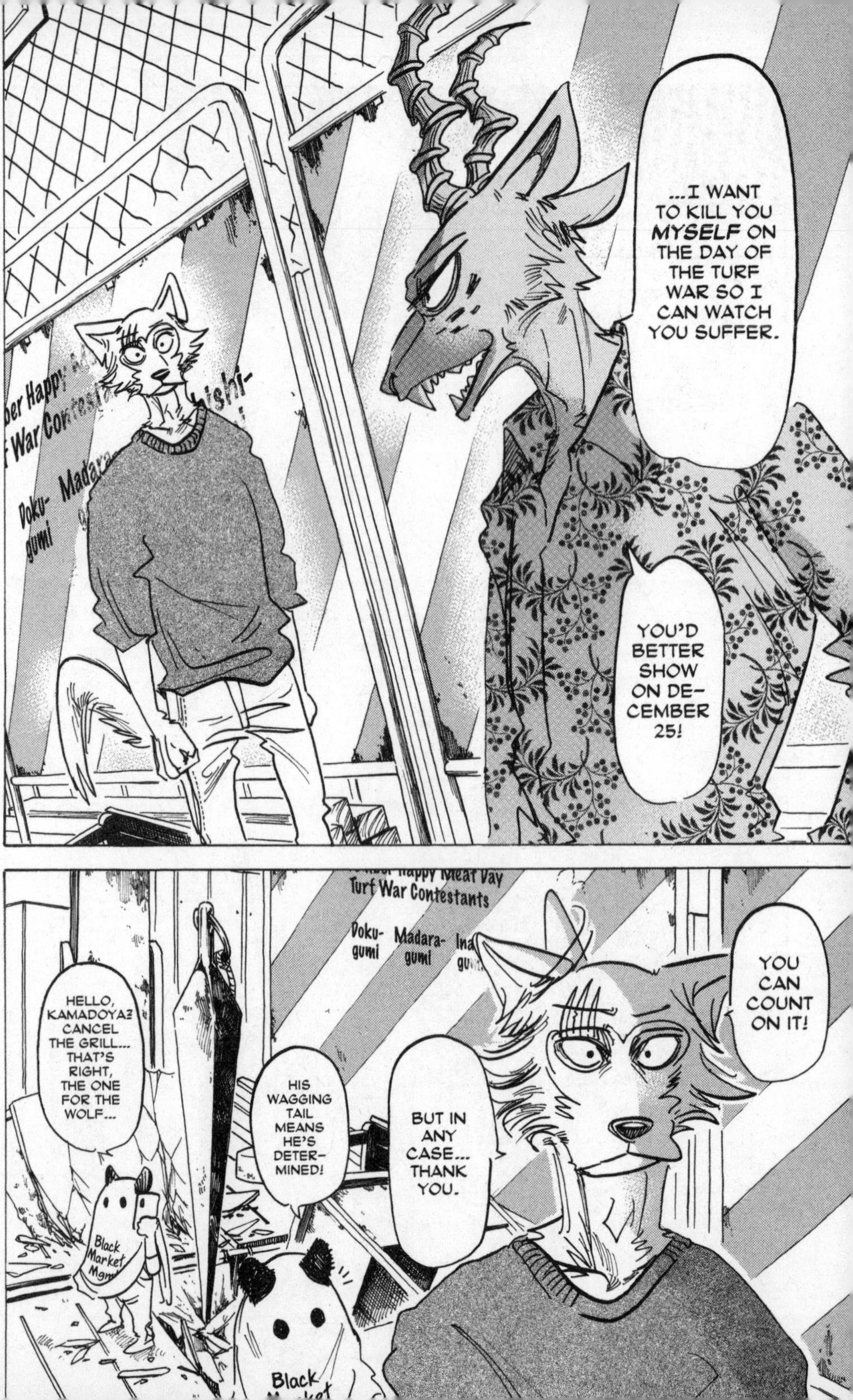
...I WANT TO KILL YOU *MYSELF* ON THE DAY OF THE TURF WAR SO I CAN WATCH YOU SUFFER.
YOU'D BETTER SHOW ON DE-CEMBER 25!
Turf War Contestants
Doku-gumi
Madara-gumi
YOU CAN COUNT ON IT!
BUT IN ANY CASE... THANK YOU.
HIS WAGGING TAIL MEANS HE'S DETER-MINED!
HELLO, KAMADOYA? CANCEL THE GRILL... THAT'S RIGHT, THE ONE FOR THE WOLF...
Black Market Mgmt

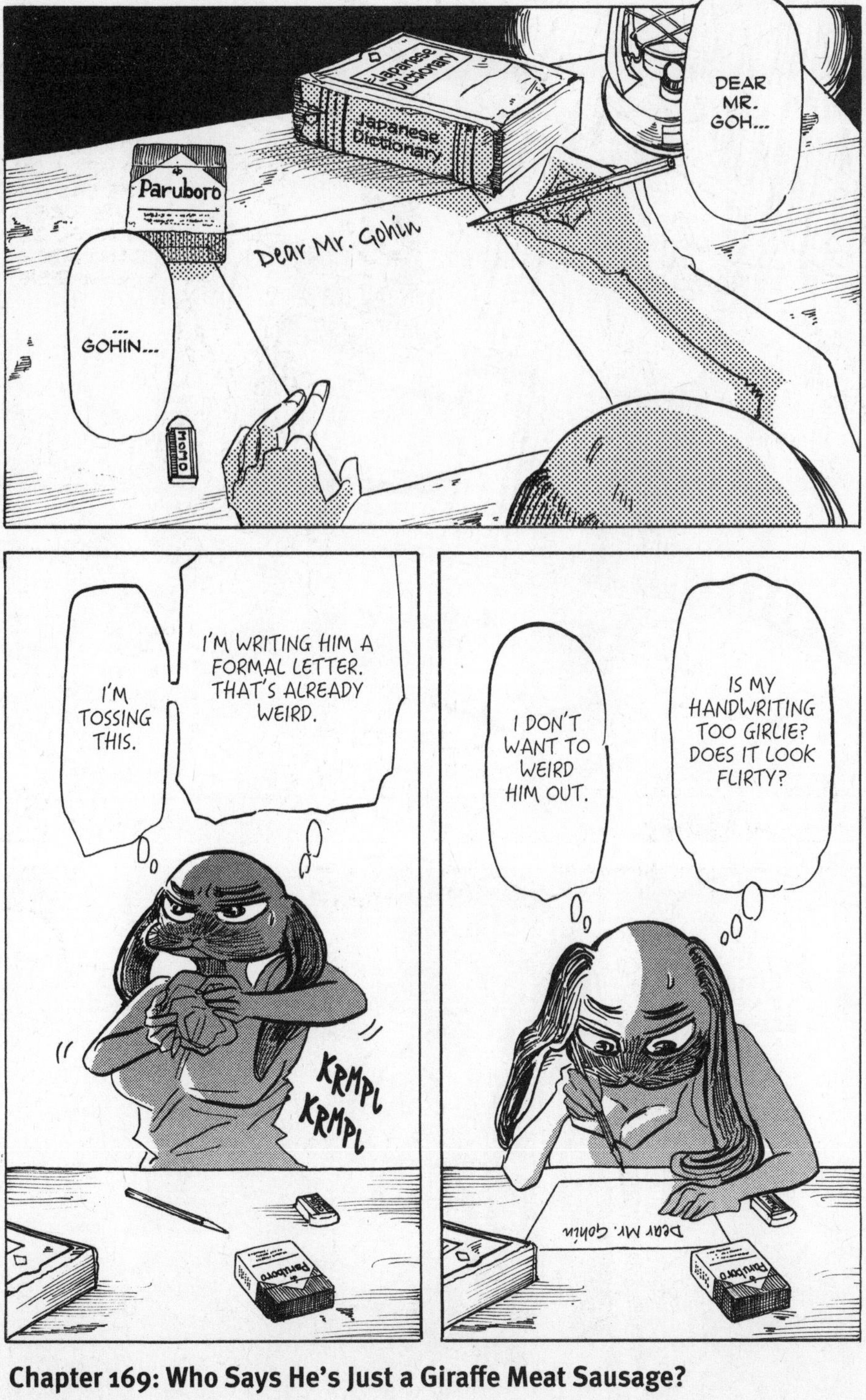
Japanese Dictionary
Japanese Dictionary
Paruboro
DEAR MR. GOH...
Dear Mr. Gohin
...GOHIN...
IS MY HANDWRITING TOO GIRLIE? DOES IT LOOK FLIRTY?
I DON'T WANT TO WEIRD HIM OUT.
Dear Mr. Gohin
I'M WRITING HIM A FORMAL LETTER. THAT'S ALREADY WEIRD.
I'M TOSSING THIS.
KRMPL KRMPL

Chapter 169: Who Says He's Just a Giraffe Meat Sausage?

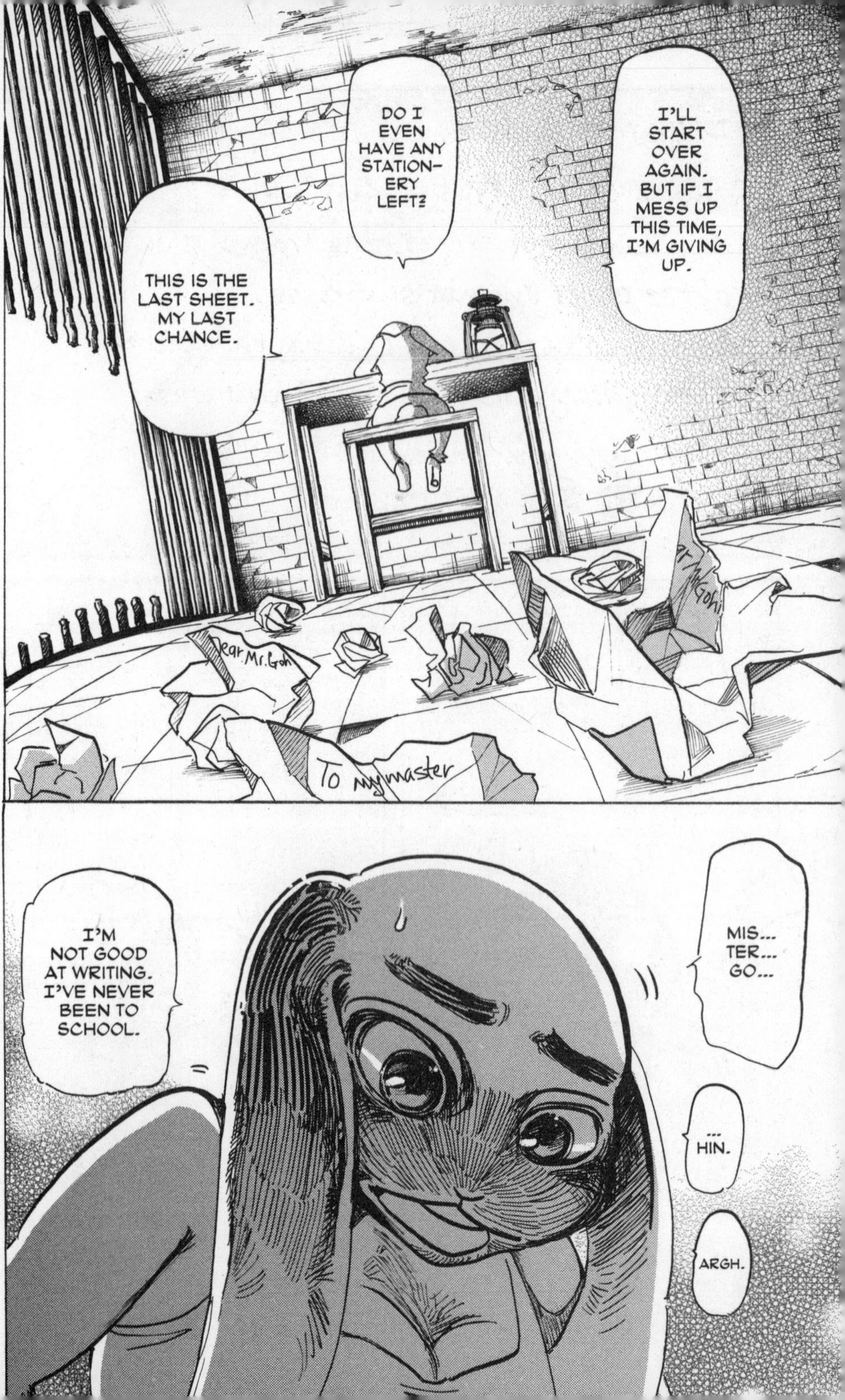
I'LL START OVER AGAIN. BUT IF I MESS UP THIS TIME, I'M GIVING UP.
DO I EVEN HAVE ANY STATION-ERY LEFT?
THIS IS THE LAST SHEET. MY LAST CHANCE.
Dear Mr. Goh
To my master
MIS... TER... GO...
... HIN.
ARGH.
I'M NOT GOOD AT WRITING. I'VE NEVER BEEN TO SCHOOL.

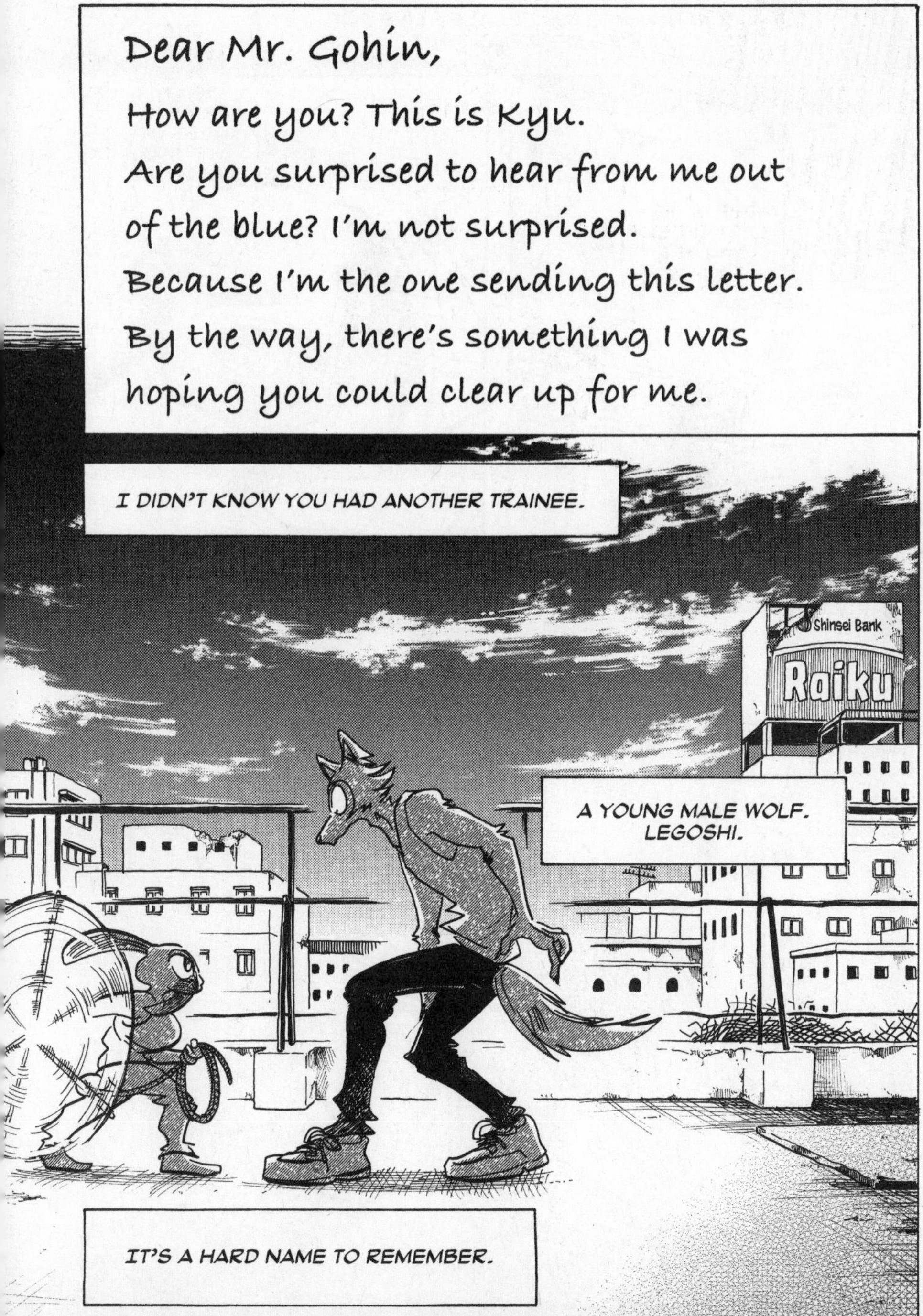
Dear Mr. Gohin,
How are you? This is Kyu.
Are you surprised to hear from me out of the blue? I'm not surprised.
Because I'm the one sending this letter.
By the way, there's something I was hoping you could clear up for me.
I DIDN'T KNOW YOU HAD ANOTHER TRAINEE.
A YOUNG MALE WOLF. LEGOSHI.
IT'S A HARD NAME TO REMEMBER.
Shinsei Bank
Raiku

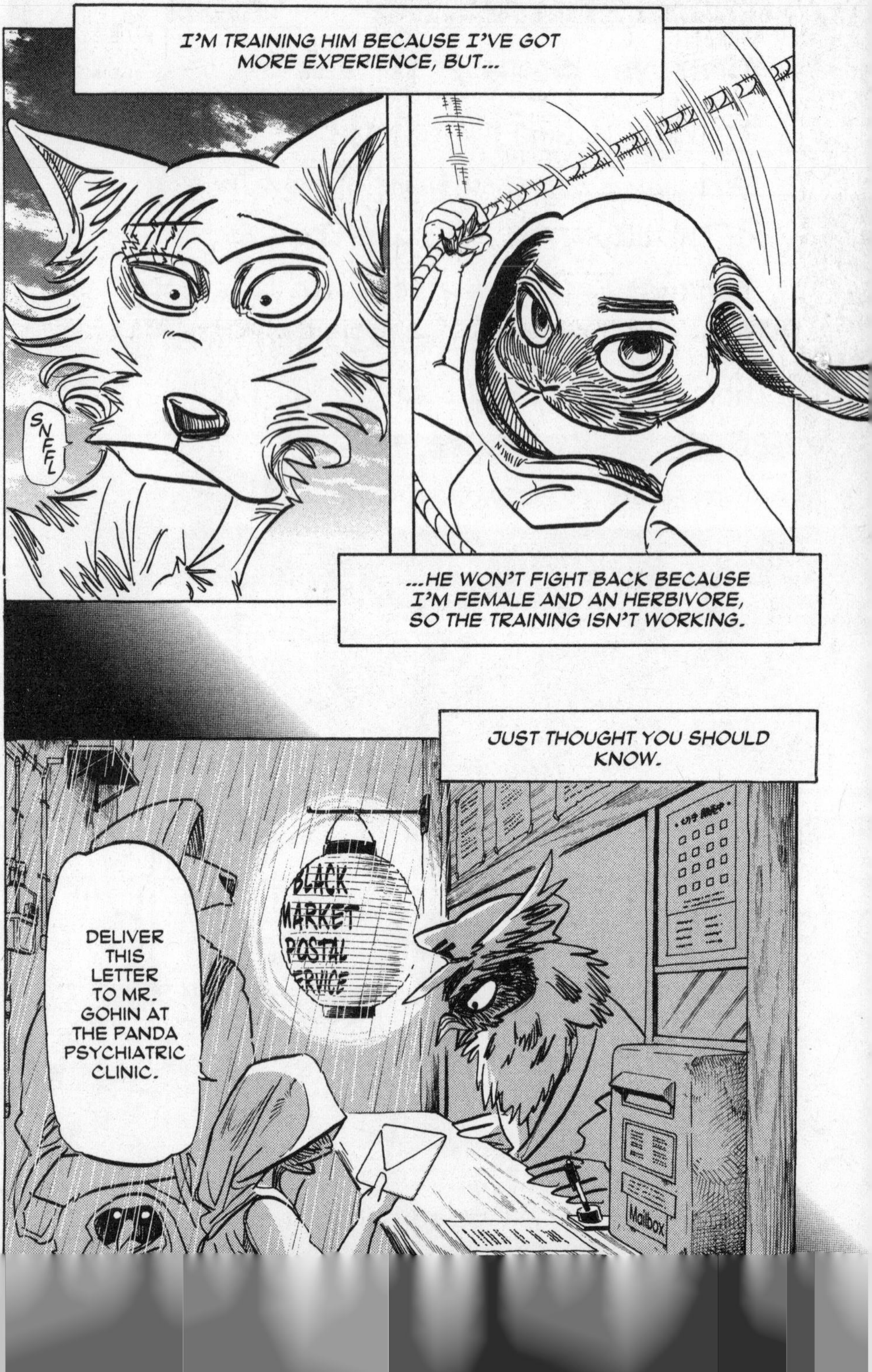
I'M TRAINING HIM BECAUSE I'VE GOT MORE EXPERIENCE, BUT...
SNFFL
...HE WON'T FIGHT BACK BECAUSE I'M FEMALE AND AN HERBIVORE, SO THE TRAINING ISN'T WORKING.
JUST THOUGHT YOU SHOULD KNOW.
BLACK MARKET POSTAL ERVICE
DELIVER THIS LETTER TO MR. GOHIN AT THE PANDA PSYCHIATRIC CLINIC.
Mailbox

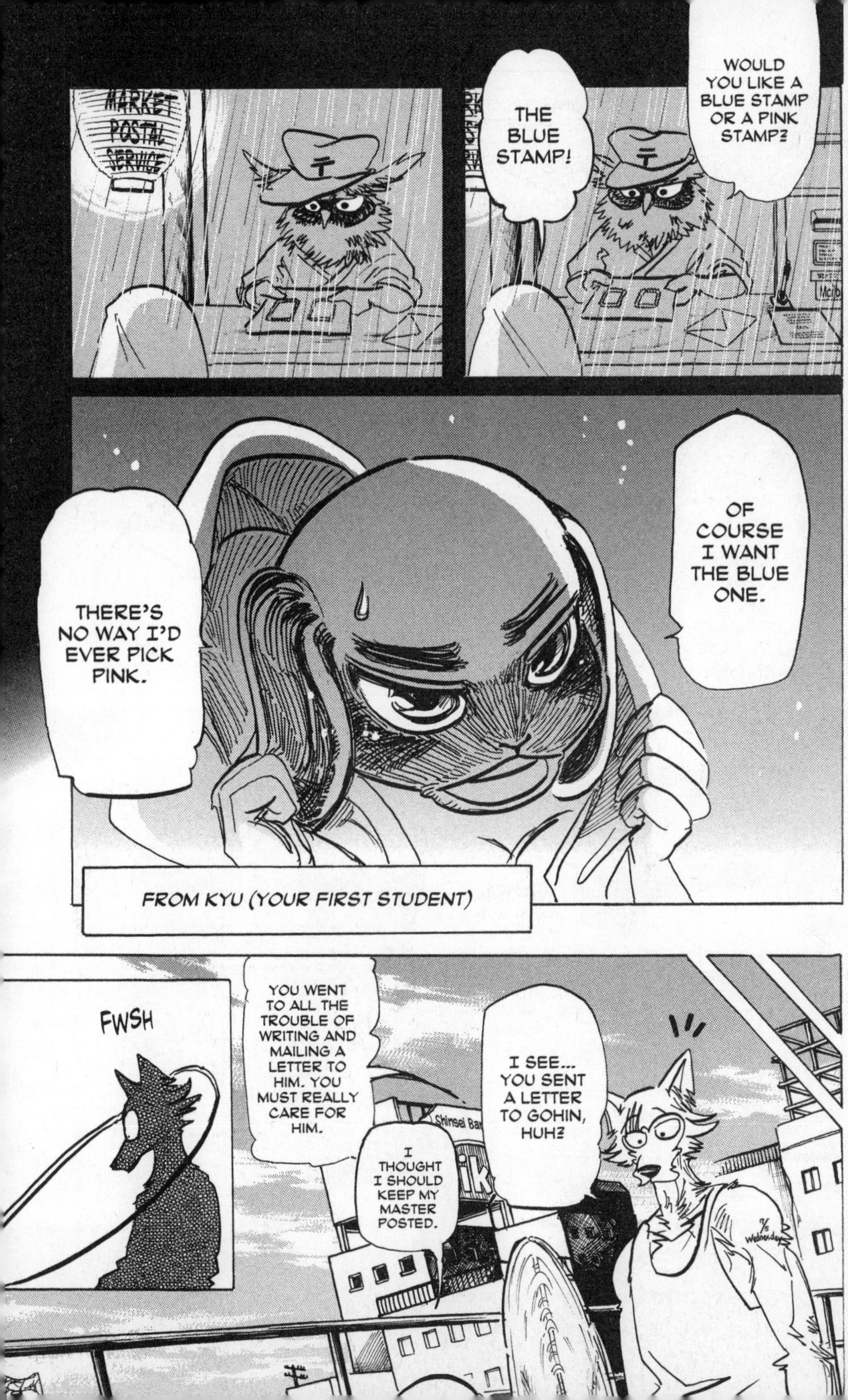
WOULD YOU LIKE A BLUE STAMP OR A PINK STAMP?
THE BLUE STAMP!
MARKET POSTAL SERVICE
OF COURSE I WANT THE BLUE ONE.
THERE'S NO WAY I'D EVER PICK PINK.
FROM KYU (YOUR FIRST STUDENT)
I SEE... YOU SENT A LETTER TO GOHIN, HUH?
YOU WENT TO ALL THE TROUBLE OF WRITING AND MAILING A LETTER TO HIM. YOU MUST REALLY CARE FOR HIM.
I THOUGHT I SHOULD KEEP MY MASTER POSTED.
7/5 Wednesday
FWSH

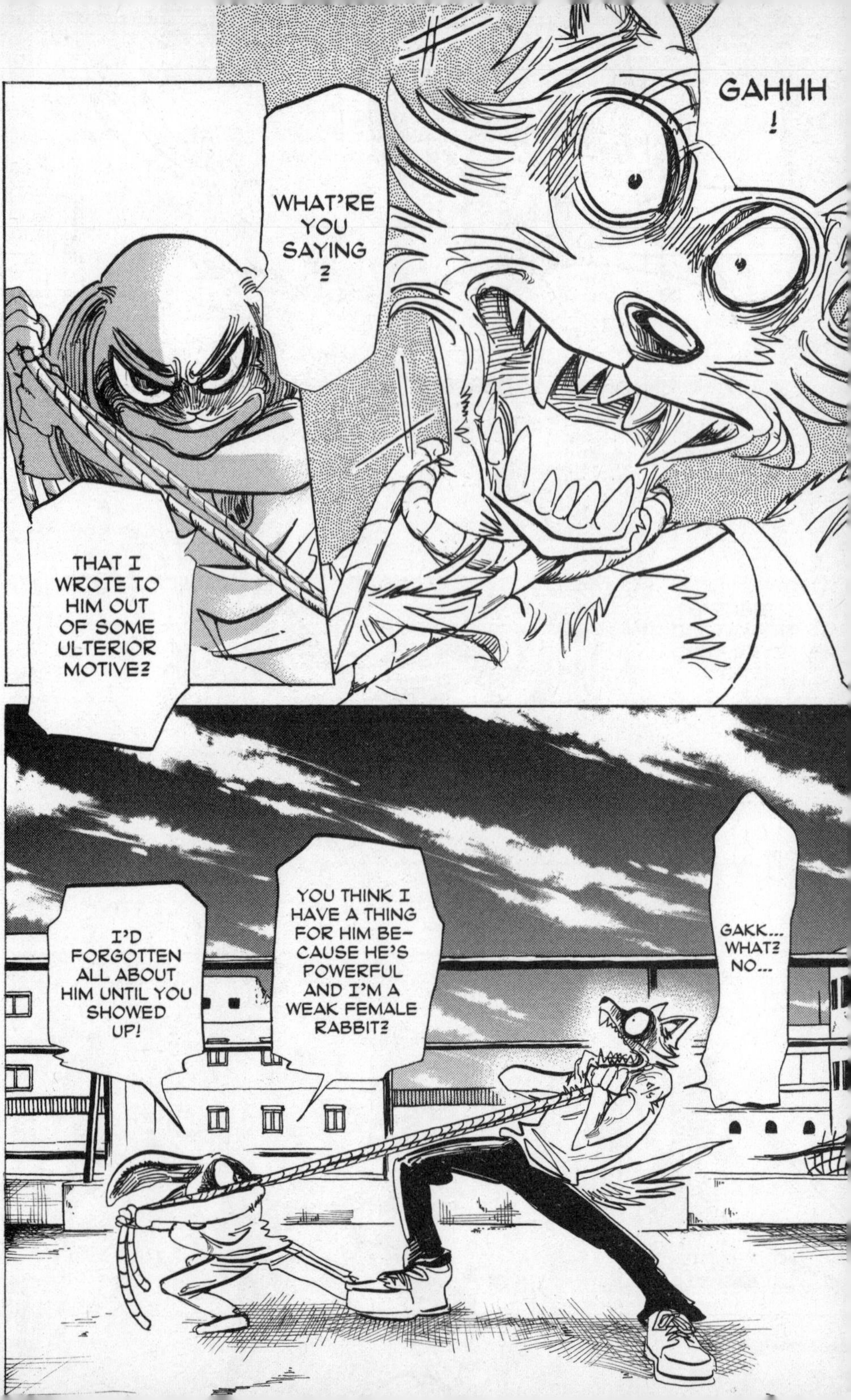
GAHHH!
WHAT'RE YOU SAYING?
THAT I WROTE TO HIM OUT OF SOME ULTERIOR MOTIVE?
GAKK... WHAT? NO...
YOU THINK I HAVE A THING FOR HIM BE-CAUSE HE'S POWERFUL AND I'M A WEAK FEMALE RABBIT?
I'D FORGOTTEN ALL ABOUT HIM UNTIL YOU SHOWED UP!

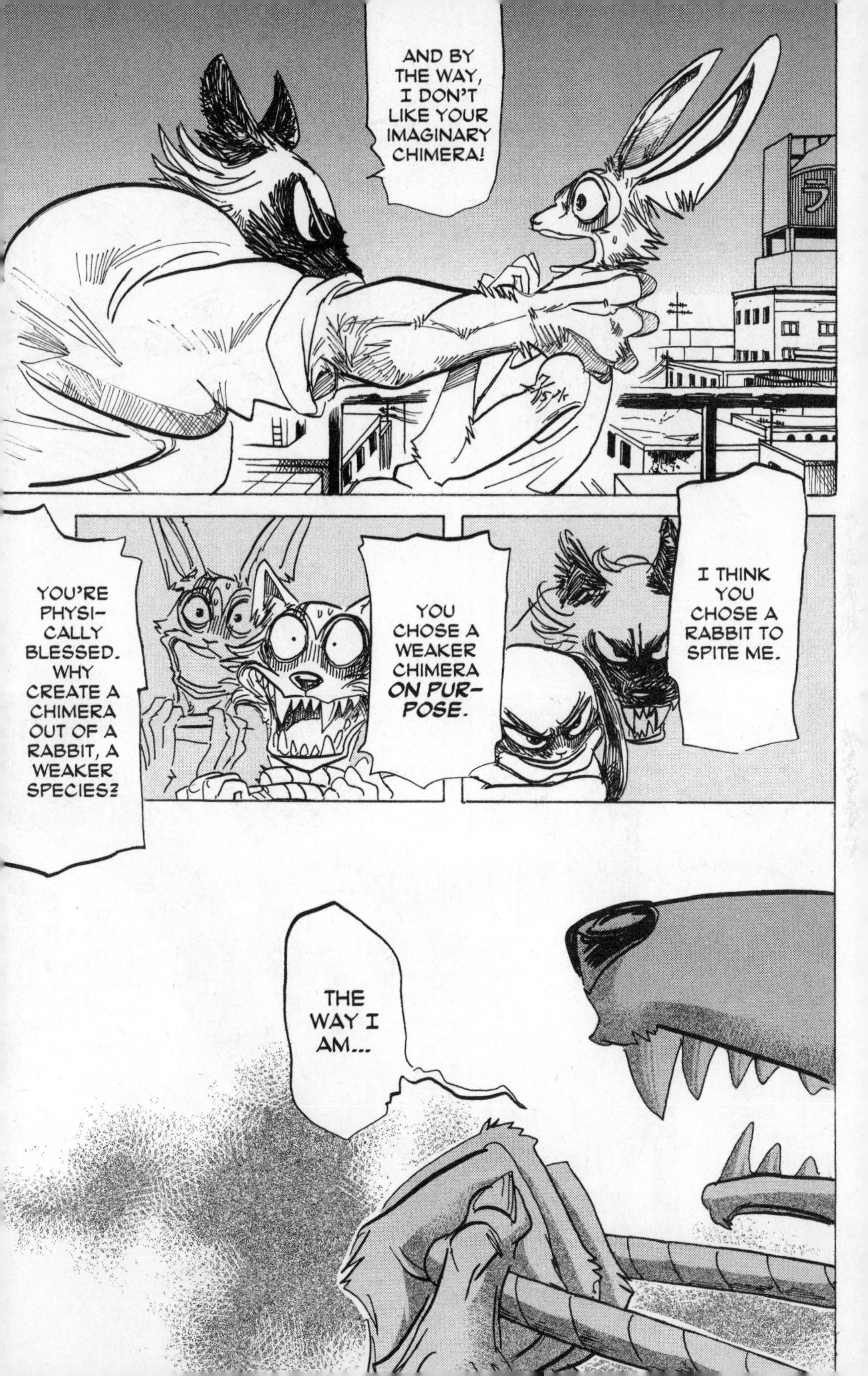
AND BY THE WAY, I DON'T LIKE YOUR IMAGINARY CHIMERA!
I THINK YOU CHOSE A RABBIT TO SPITE ME.
YOU CHOSE A WEAKER CHIMERA ON PURPOSE.
YOU'RE PHYSICALLY BLESSED. WHY CREATE A CHIMERA OUT OF A RABBIT, A WEAKER SPECIES?
THE WAY I AM...

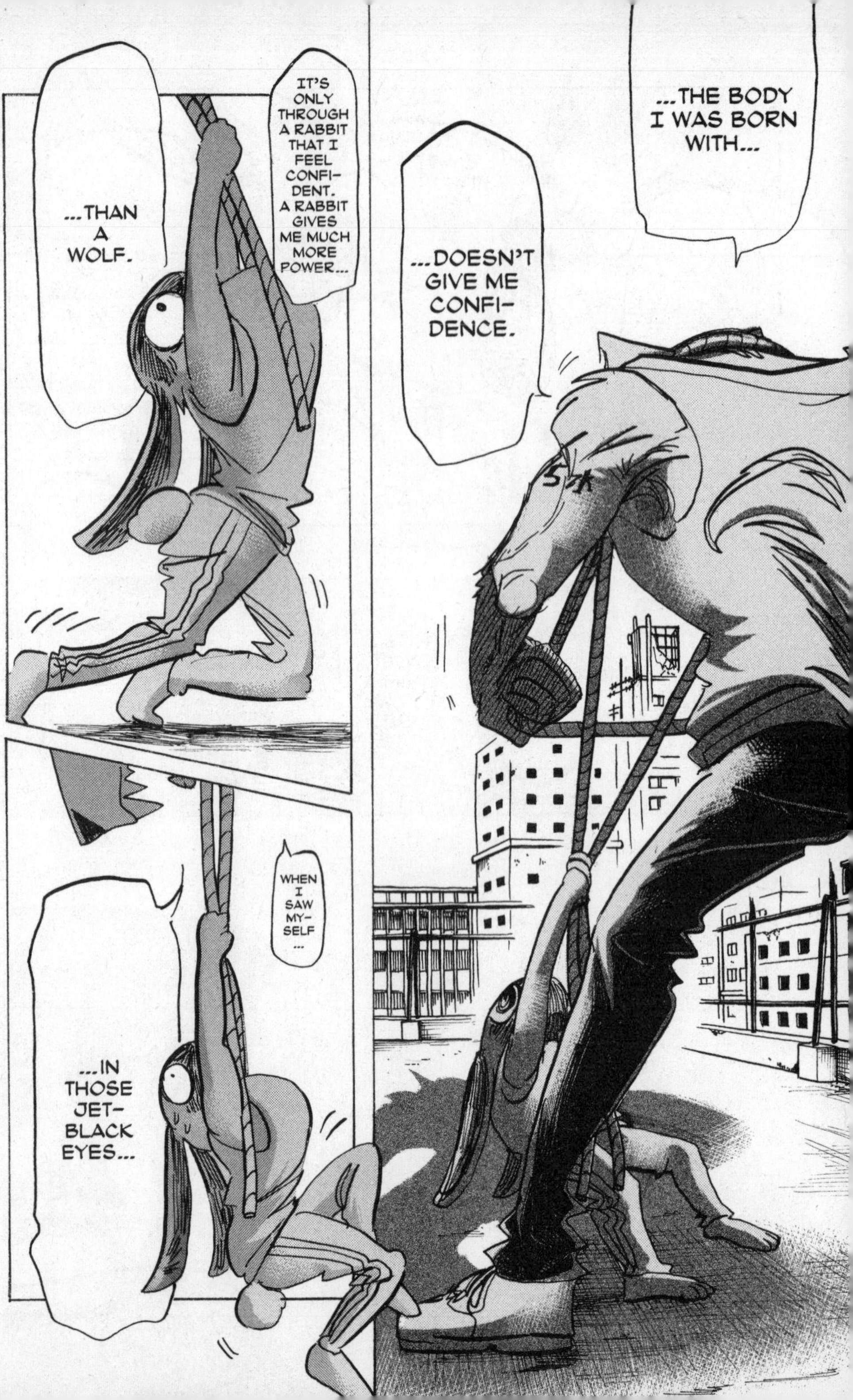
...THE BODY I WAS BORN WITH...
...DOESN'T GIVE ME CONFIDENCE.
IT'S ONLY THROUGH A RABBIT THAT I FEEL CONFIDENT. A RABBIT GIVES ME MUCH MORE POWER...
...THAN A WOLF.
WHEN I SAW MYSELF...
...IN THOSE JET-BLACK EYES...

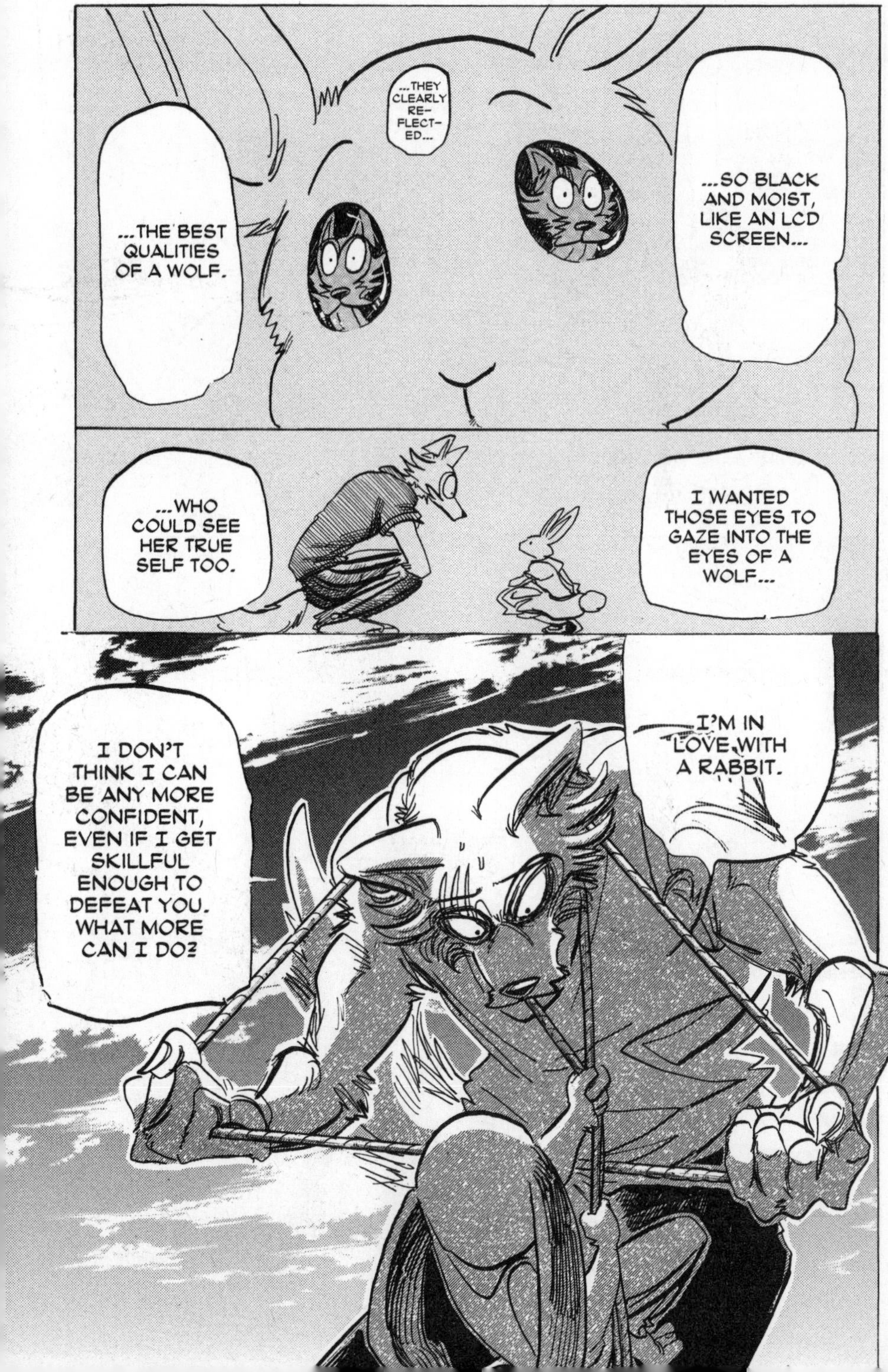
...SO BLACK AND MOIST, LIKE AN LCD SCREEN...
...THEY CLEARLY RE-FLECTED...
...THE BEST QUALITIES OF A WOLF.
I WANTED THOSE EYES TO GAZE INTO THE EYES OF A WOLF...
...WHO COULD SEE HER TRUE SELF TOO.
I'M IN LOVE WITH A RABBIT.
I DON'T THINK I CAN BE ANY MORE CONFIDENT, EVEN IF I GET SKILLFUL ENOUGH TO DEFEAT YOU. WHAT MORE CAN I DO?

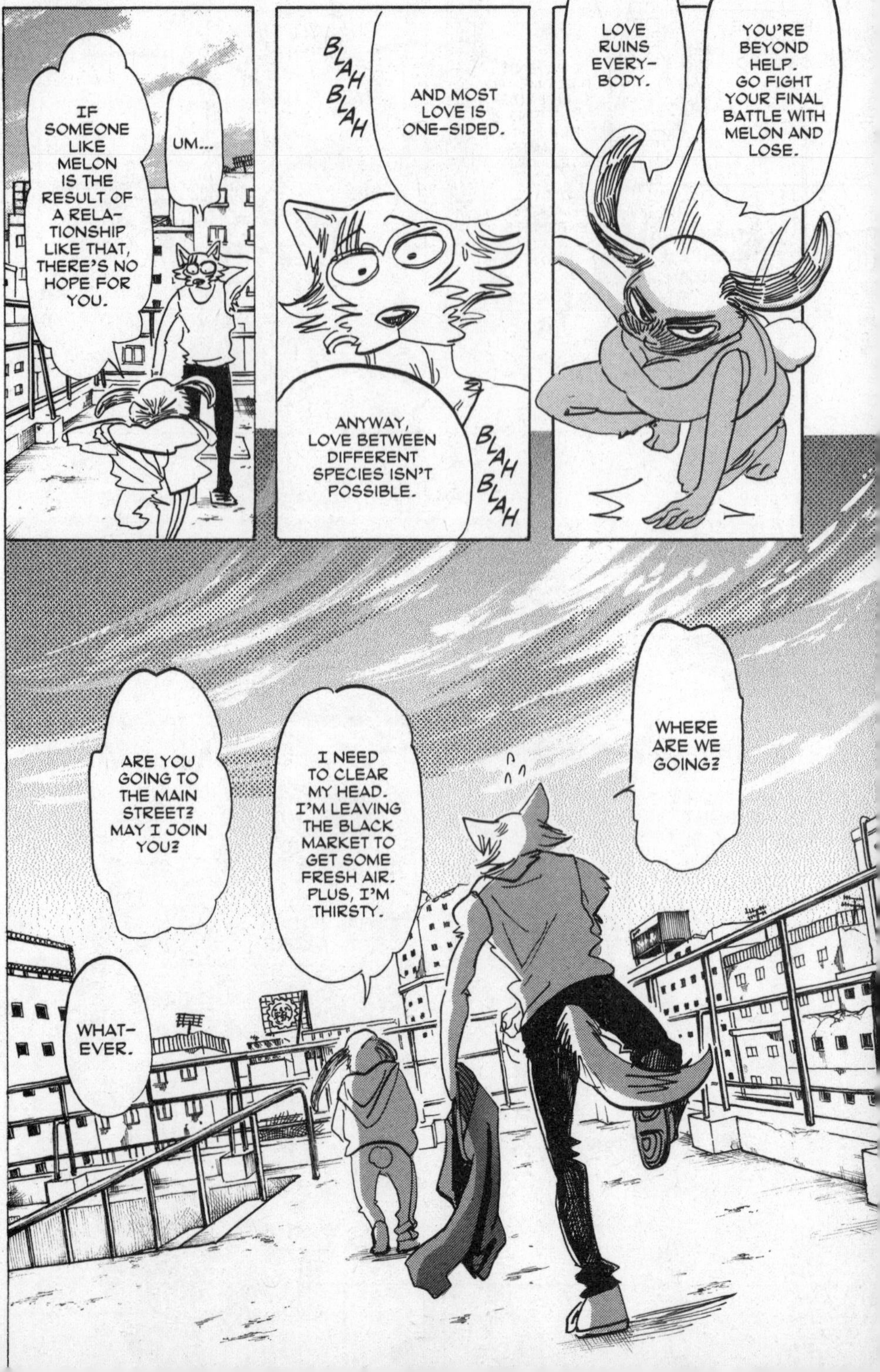
YOU'RE BEYOND HELP. GO FIGHT YOUR FINAL BATTLE WITH MELON AND LOSE.
LOVE RUINS EVERY-BODY.
AND MOST LOVE IS ONE-SIDED.
BLAH BLAH
ANYWAY, LOVE BETWEEN DIFFERENT SPECIES ISN'T POSSIBLE.
BLAH BLAH
UM...
IF SOMEONE LIKE MELON IS THE RESULT OF A RELA-TIONSHIP LIKE THAT, THERE'S NO HOPE FOR YOU.
WHERE ARE WE GOING?
I NEED TO CLEAR MY HEAD. I'M LEAVING THE BLACK MARKET TO GET SOME FRESH AIR. PLUS, I'M THIRSTY.
ARE YOU GOING TO THE MAIN STREET? MAY I JOIN YOU?
WHAT-EVER.

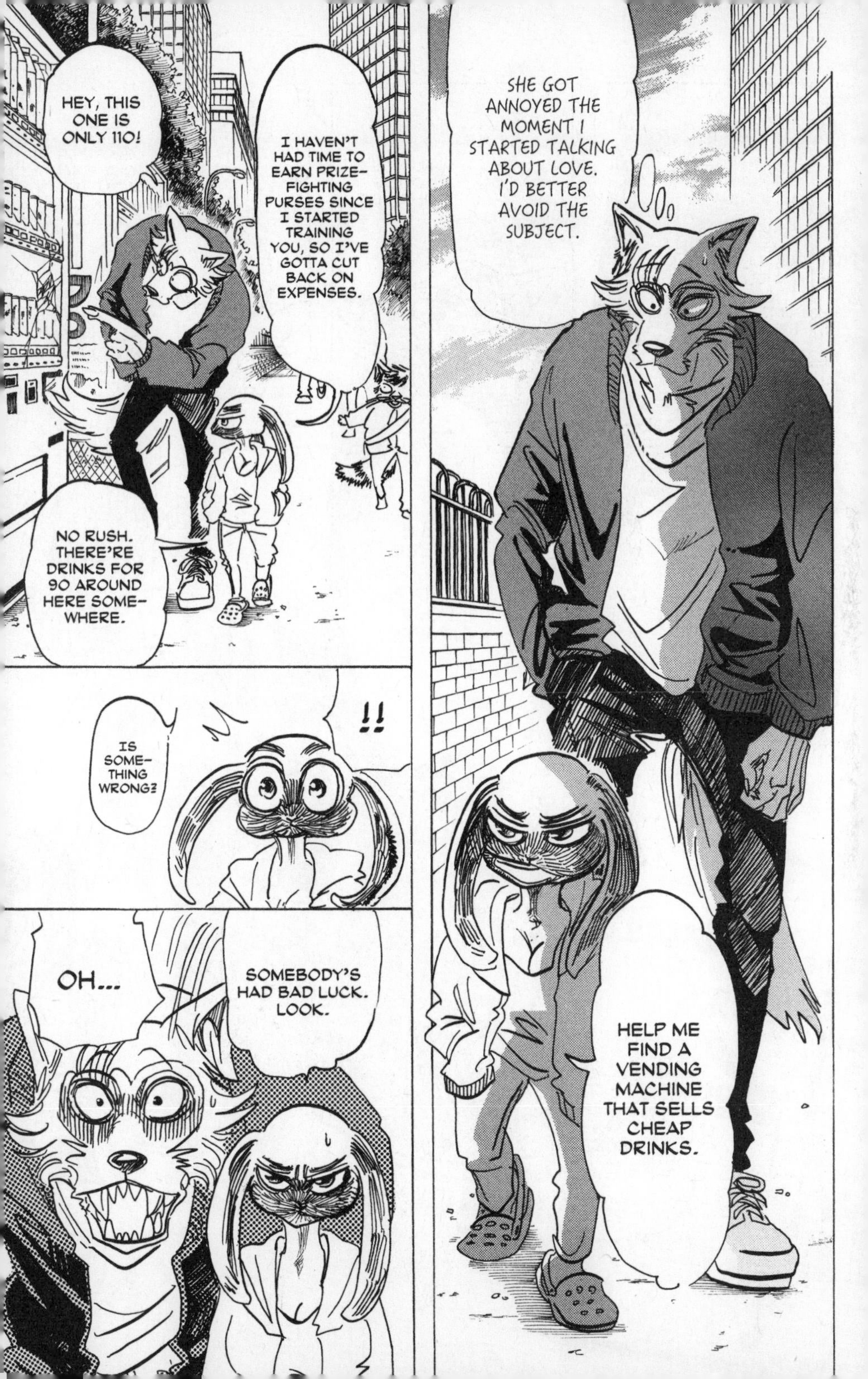
SHE GOT ANNOYED THE MOMENT I STARTED TALKING ABOUT LOVE. I'D BETTER AVOID THE SUBJECT.
HELP ME FIND A VENDING MACHINE THAT SELLS CHEAP DRINKS.
I HAVEN'T HAD TIME TO EARN PRIZE-FIGHTING PURSES SINCE I STARTED TRAINING YOU, SO I'VE GOTTA CUT BACK ON EXPENSES.
HEY, THIS ONE IS ONLY 110!
NO RUSH. THERE'RE DRINKS FOR 90 AROUND HERE SOME-WHERE.
!!
IS SOME-THING WRONG?
SOMEBODY'S HAD BAD LUCK. LOOK.
OH...

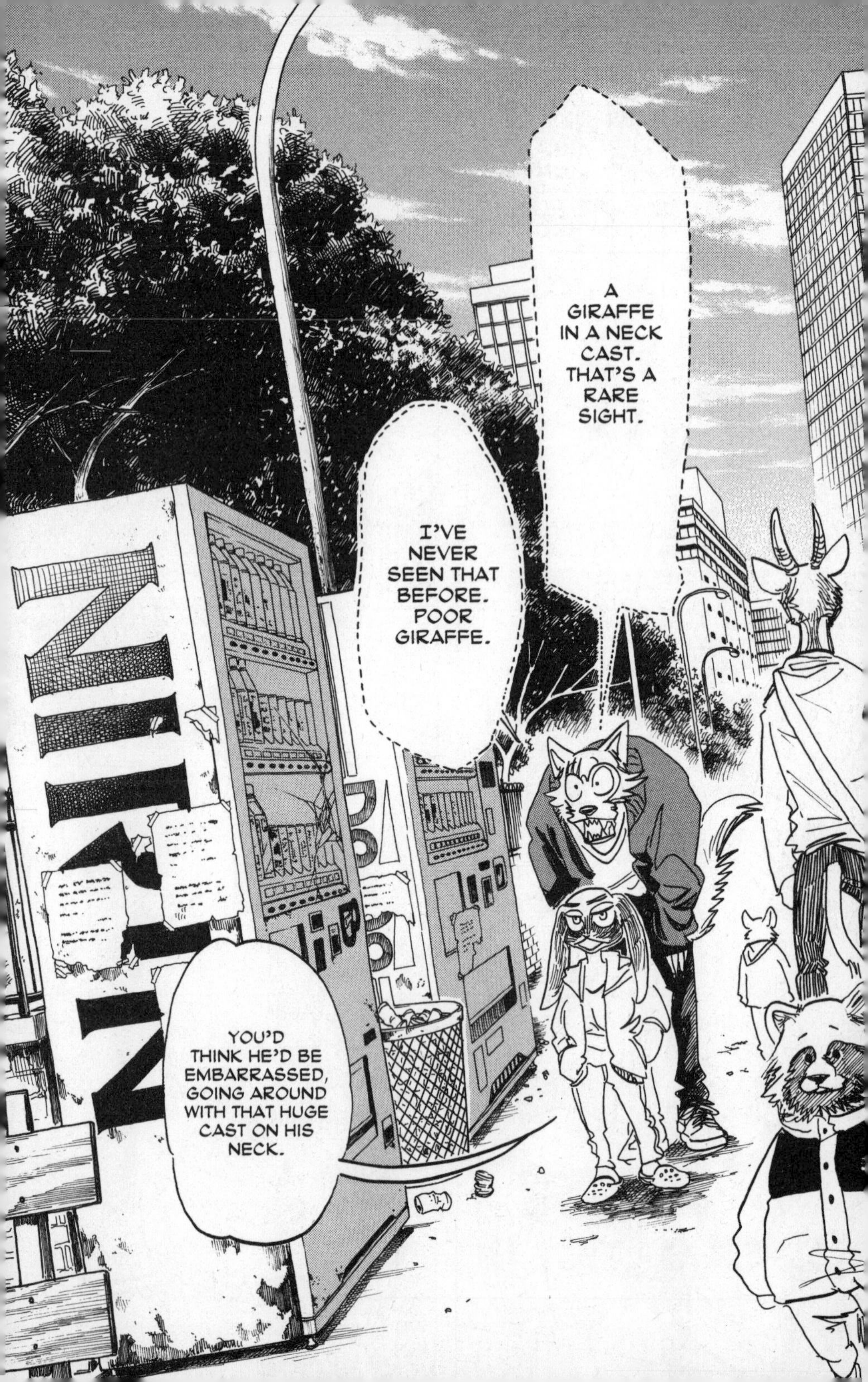
A GIRAFFE IN A NECK CAST. THAT'S A RARE SIGHT.
I'VE NEVER SEEN THAT BEFORE. POOR GIRAFFE.
YOU'D THINK HE'D BE EMBARRASSED, GOING AROUND WITH THAT HUGE CAST ON HIS NECK.

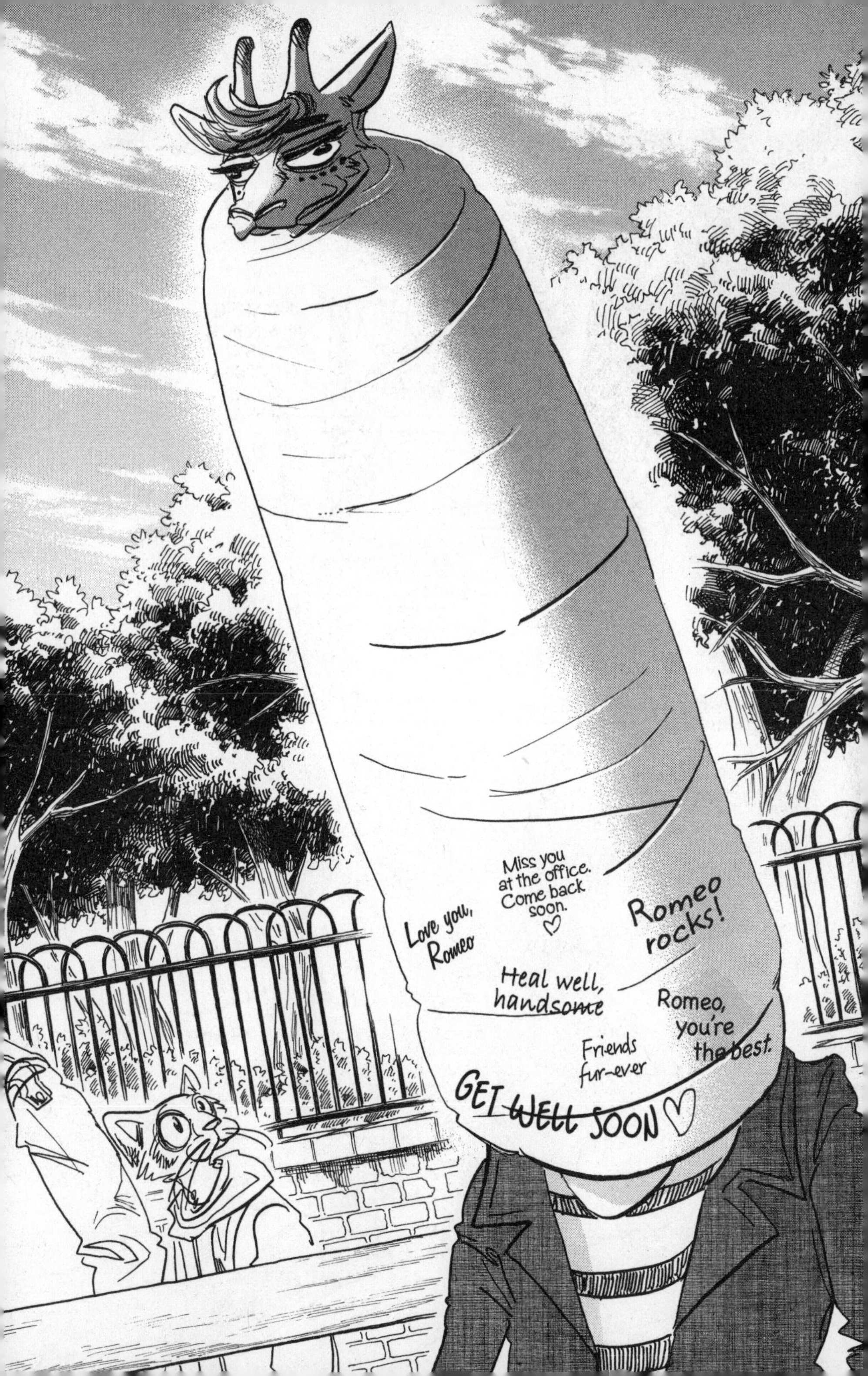
Miss you at the office. Come back soon. ♡
Romeo rocks!
Love you, Romeo
Heal well, handsome
Romeo, you're the best.
Friends fur-ever
GET WELL SOON ♡

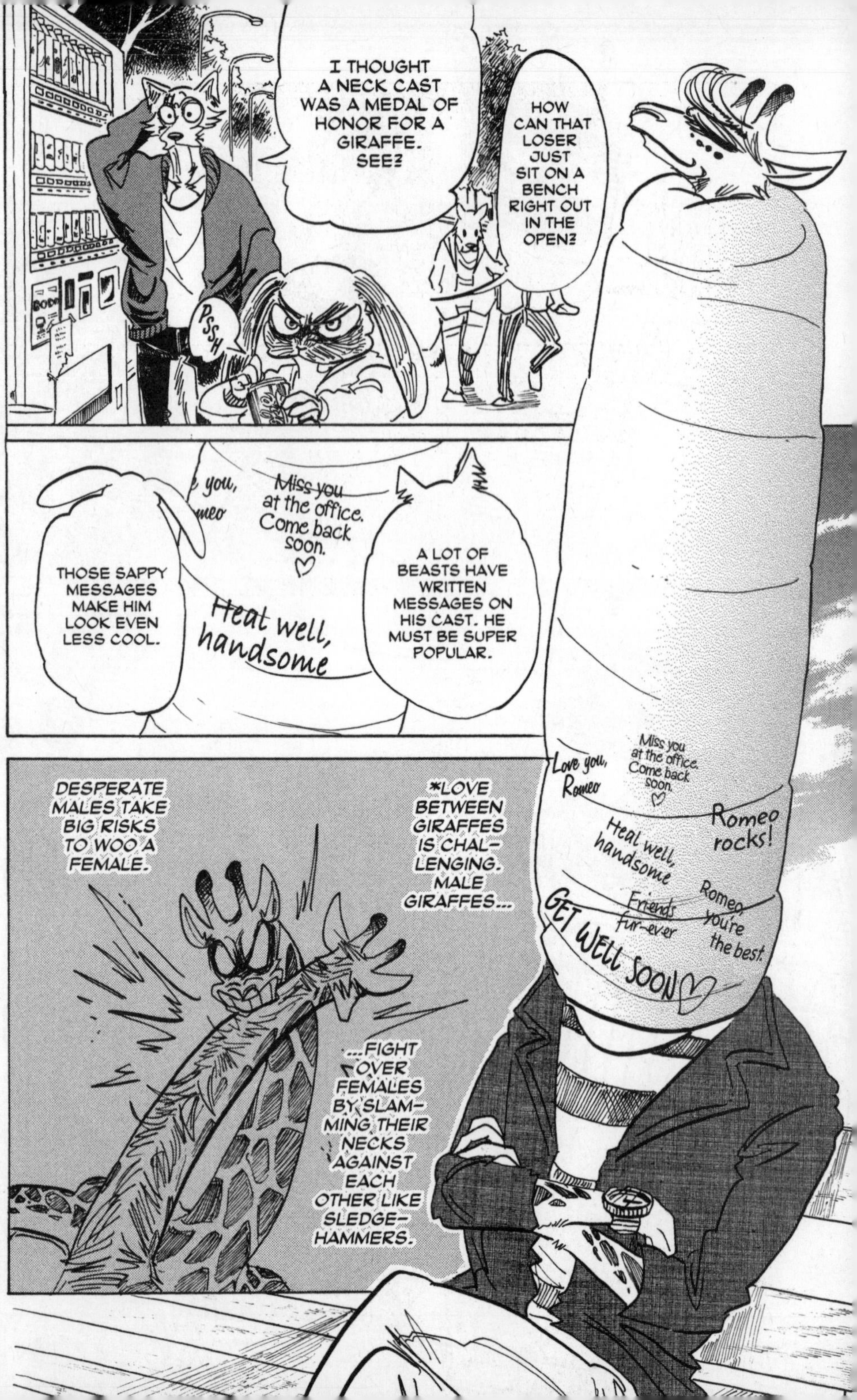
HOW CAN THAT LOSER JUST SIT ON A BENCH RIGHT OUT IN THE OPEN?
I THOUGHT A NECK CAST WAS A MEDAL OF HONOR FOR A GIRAFFE. SEE?
PSSH
A LOT OF BEASTS HAVE WRITTEN MESSAGES ON HIS CAST. HE MUST BE SUPER POPULAR.
Miss you at the office. Come back soon. ♡
you, meo
Heal well, handsome
THOSE SAPPY MESSAGES MAKE HIM LOOK EVEN LESS COOL.
Miss you at the office. Come back soon. ♡
Love you, Romeo
Romeo rocks!
Heal well, handsome
Romeo, you're the best.
Friends fur-ever
GET WELL SOON ♡
*LOVE BETWEEN GIRAFFES IS CHAL-LENGING. MALE GIRAFFES...
...FIGHT OVER FEMALES BY SLAM-MING THEIR NECKS AGAINST EACH OTHER LIKE SLEDGE-HAMMERS.
DESPERATE MALES TAKE BIG RISKS TO WOO A FEMALE.

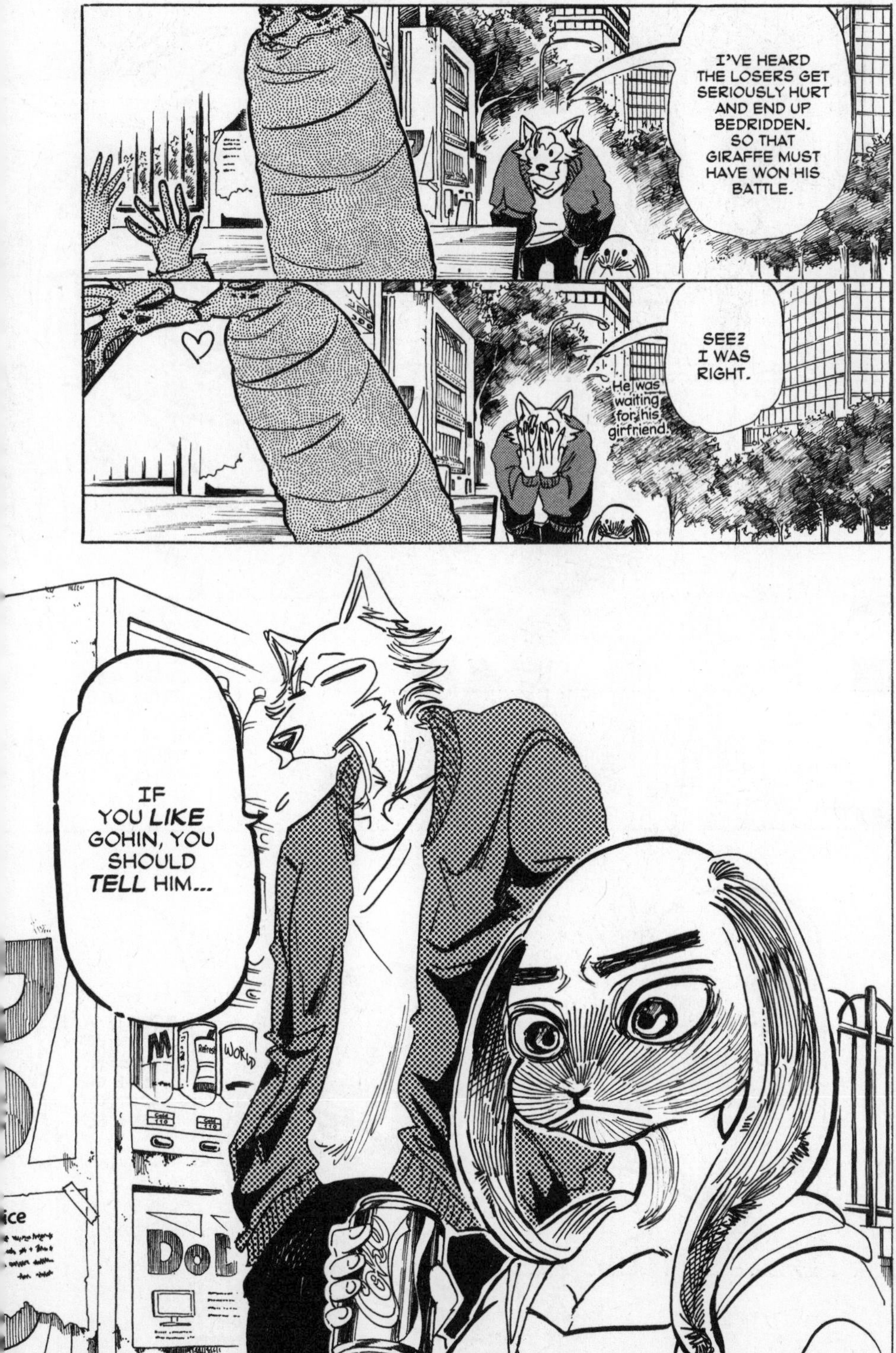
I'VE HEARD THE LOSERS GET SERIOUSLY HURT AND END UP BEDRIDDEN. SO THAT GIRAFFE MUST HAVE WON HIS BATTLE.
SEE? I WAS RIGHT.
He was waiting for his girlfriend.
IF YOU ***LIKE*** GOHIN, YOU SHOULD ***TELL*** HIM...

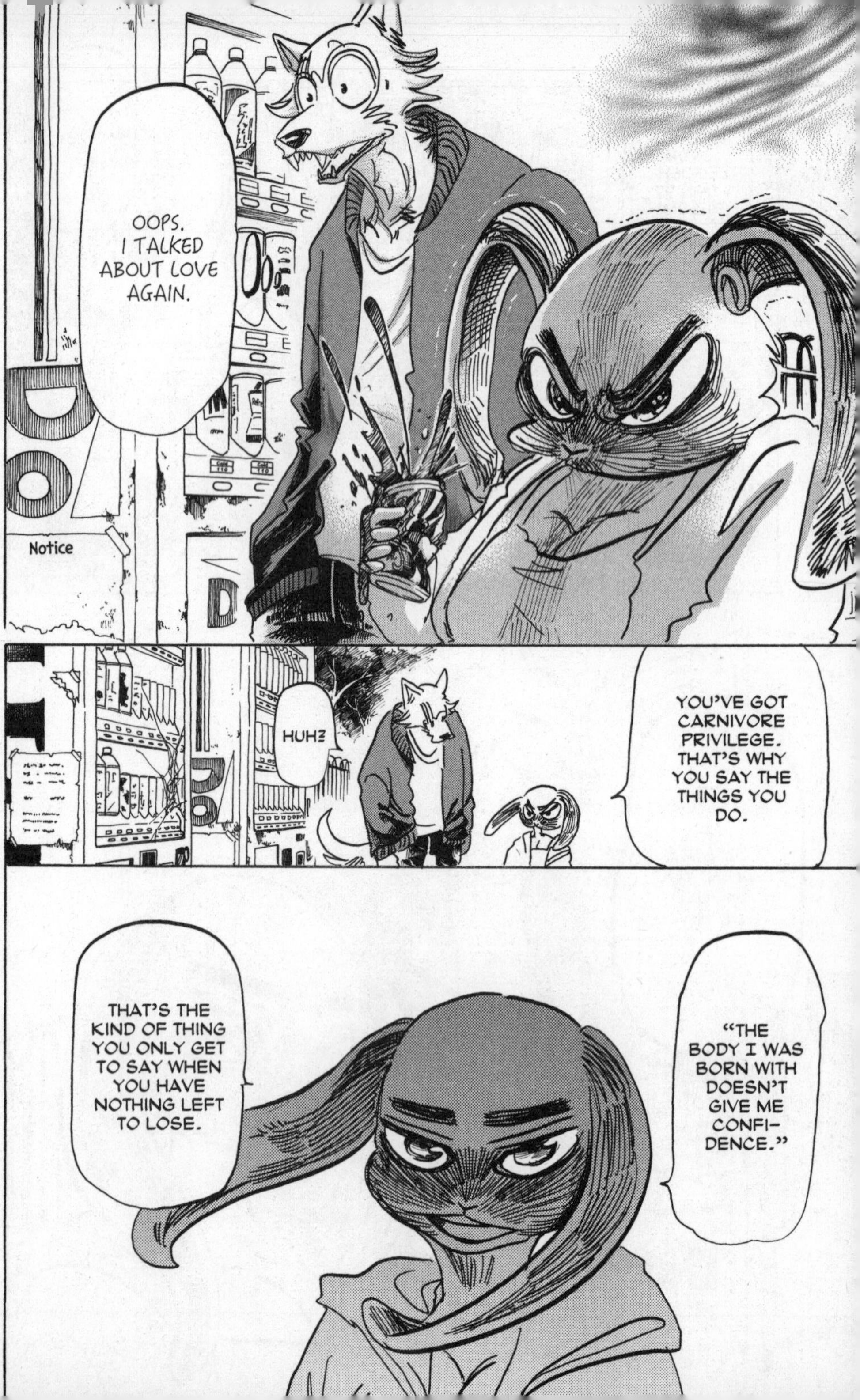
OOPS. I TALKED ABOUT LOVE AGAIN.
Notice
YOU'VE GOT CARNIVORE PRIVILEGE. THAT'S WHY YOU SAY THE THINGS YOU DO.
HUH?
"THE BODY I WAS BORN WITH DOESN'T GIVE ME CONFIDENCE."
THAT'S THE KIND OF THING YOU ONLY GET TO SAY WHEN YOU HAVE NOTHING LEFT TO LOSE.

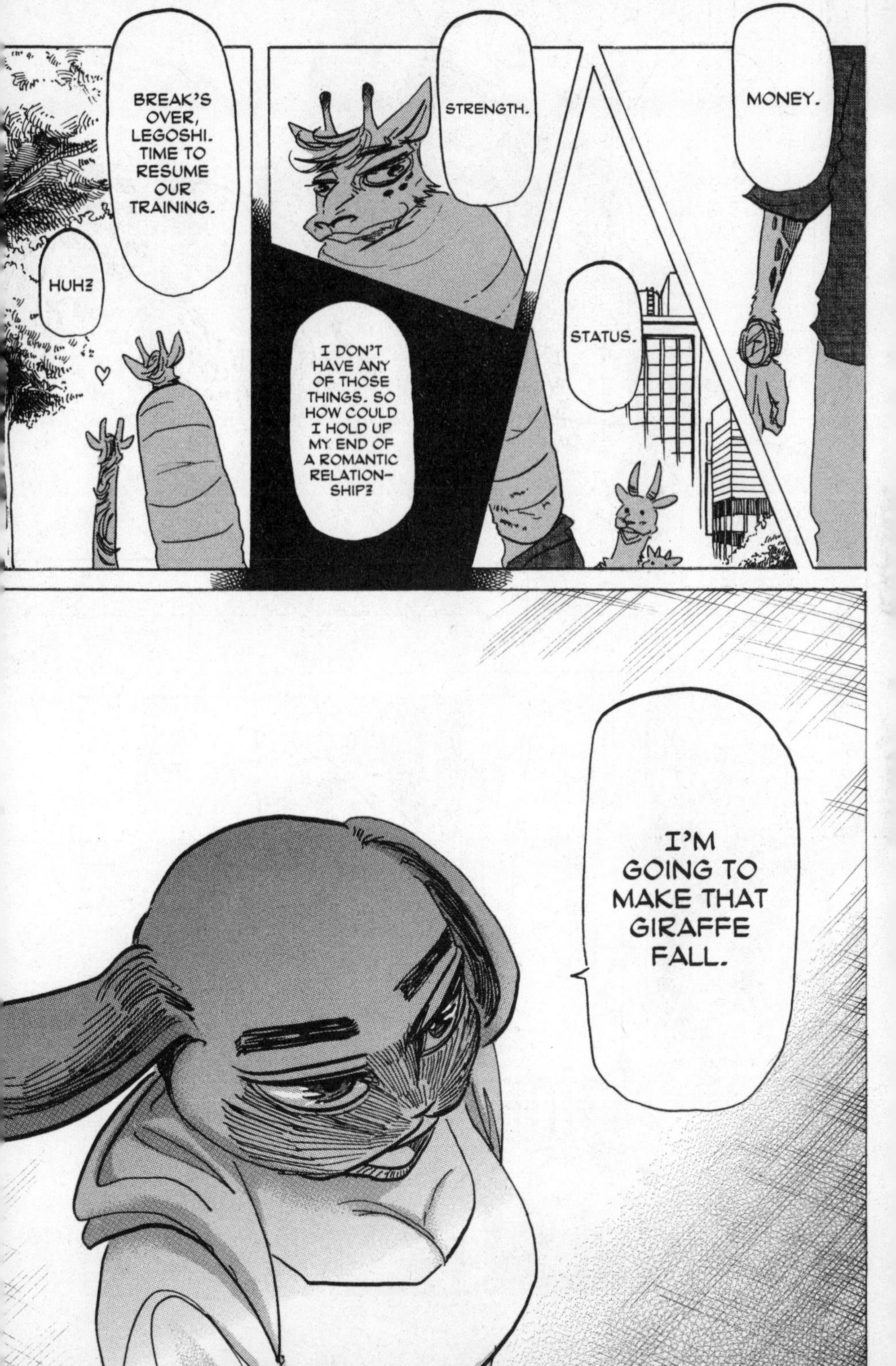
MONEY.
STATUS.
STRENGTH.
I DON'T HAVE ANY OF THOSE THINGS. SO HOW COULD I HOLD UP MY END OF A ROMANTIC RELATION-SHIP?
BREAK'S OVER, LEGOSHI. TIME TO RESUME OUR TRAINING.
HUH?
I'M GOING TO MAKE THAT GIRAFFE FALL.

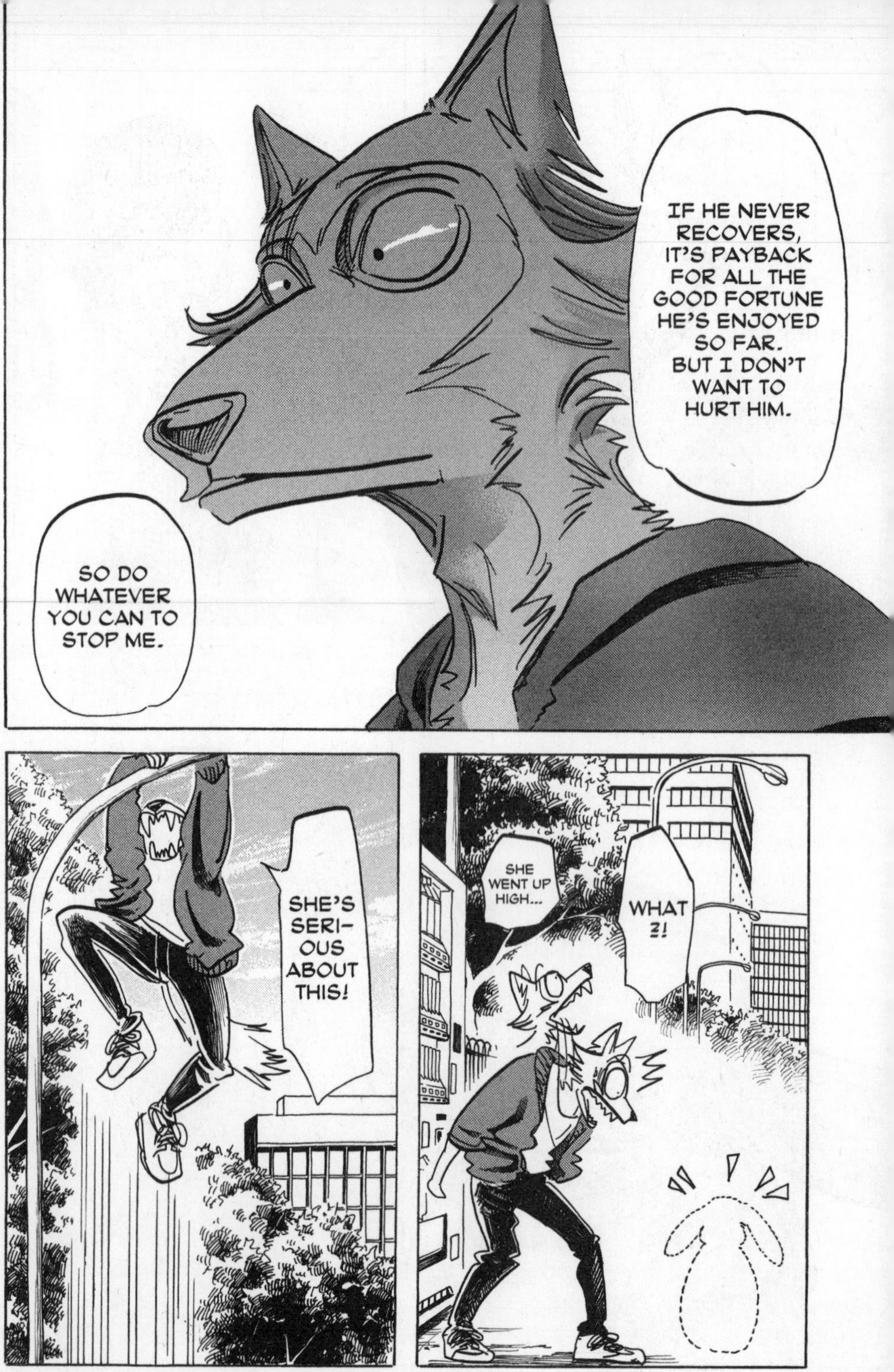
IF HE NEVER RECOVERS, IT'S PAYBACK FOR ALL THE GOOD FORTUNE HE'S ENJOYED SO FAR. BUT I DON'T WANT TO HURT HIM.
SO DO WHATEVER YOU CAN TO STOP ME.
WHAT ?!
SHE WENT UP HIGH...
SHE'S SERI-OUS ABOUT THIS!

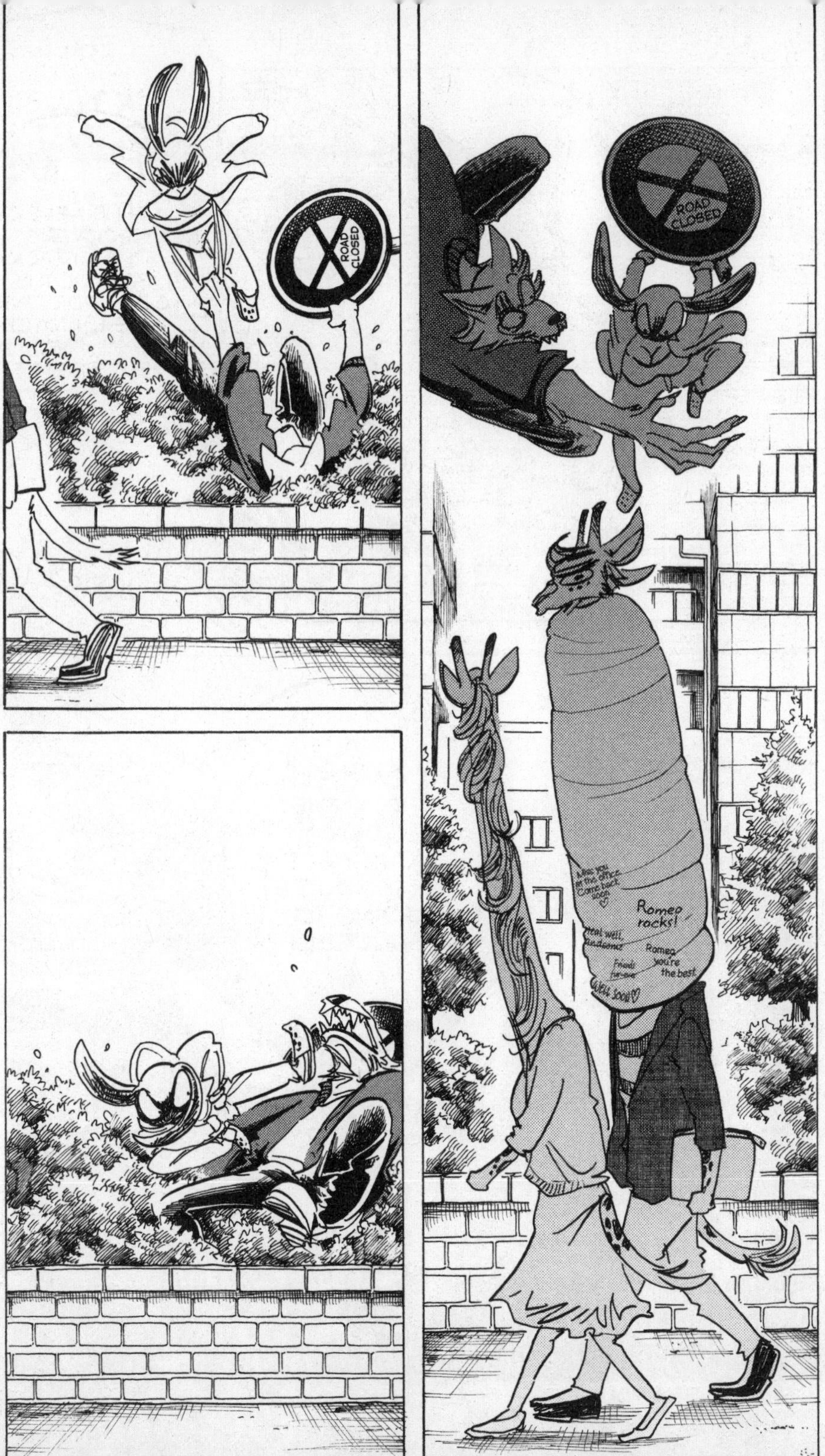

ROAD CLOSED
Miss you at the office. Come back soon ♡
Romeo rocks!
Romeo you're the best
ROAD CLOSED

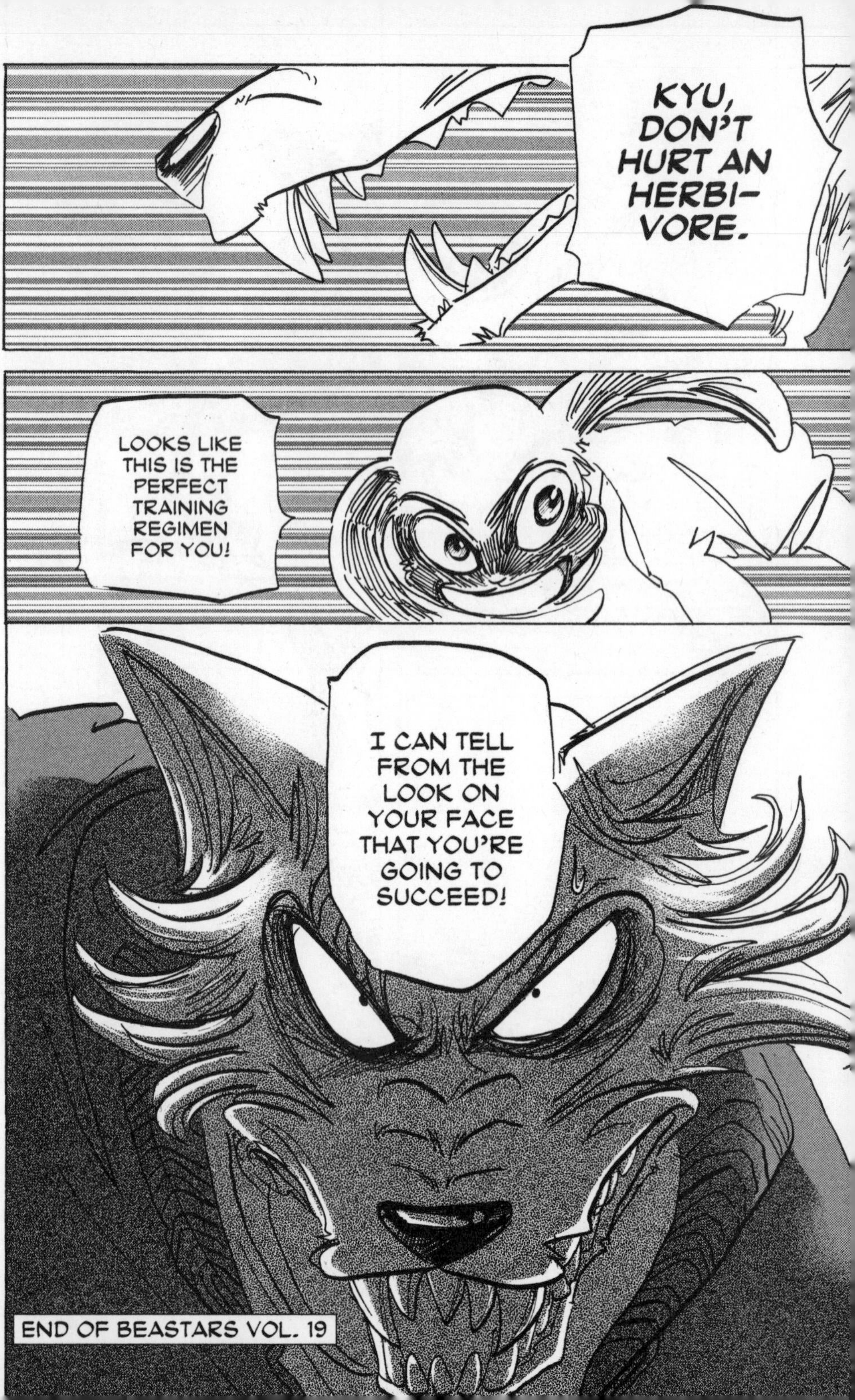
KYU, DON'T HURT AN HERBI-VORE.
LOOKS LIKE THIS IS THE PERFECT TRAINING REGIMEN FOR YOU!
I CAN TELL FROM THE LOOK ON YOUR FACE THAT YOU'RE GOING TO SUCCEED!
END OF BEASTARS VOL. 19

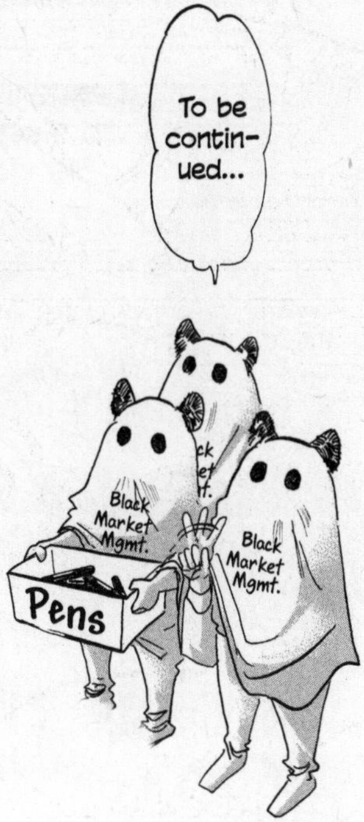
To be contin-ued...
Black Market Mgmt.
Black Market Mgmt.
Pens

Legoshi's sideburns

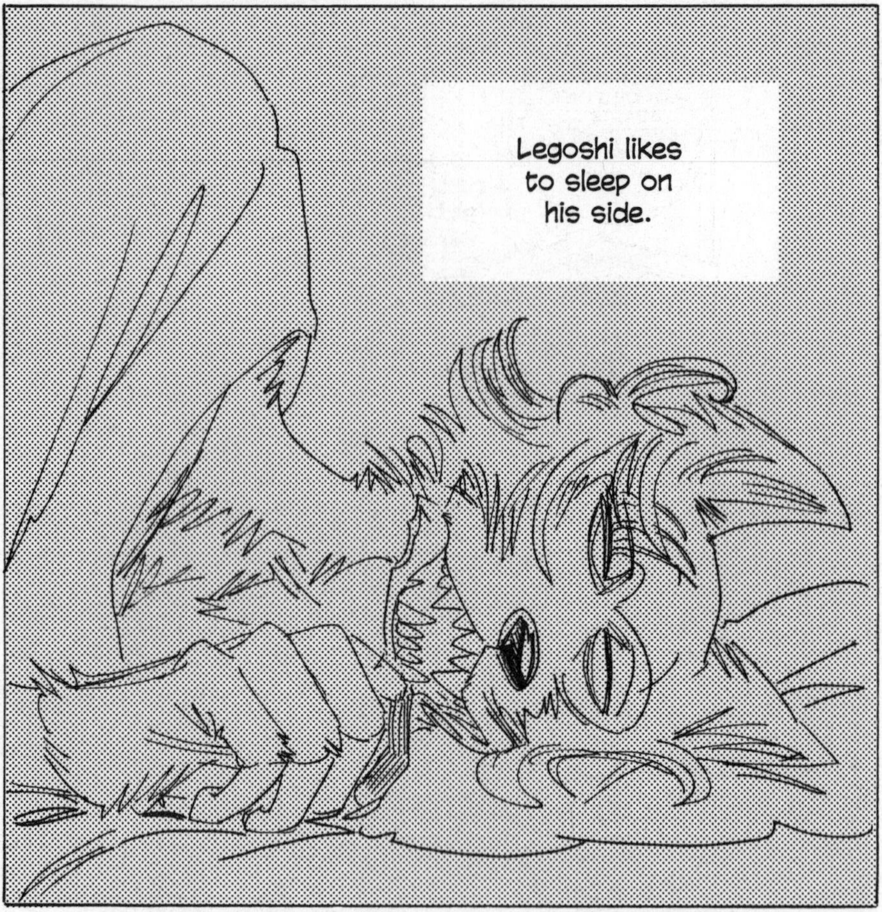
Legoshi likes to sleep on his side.

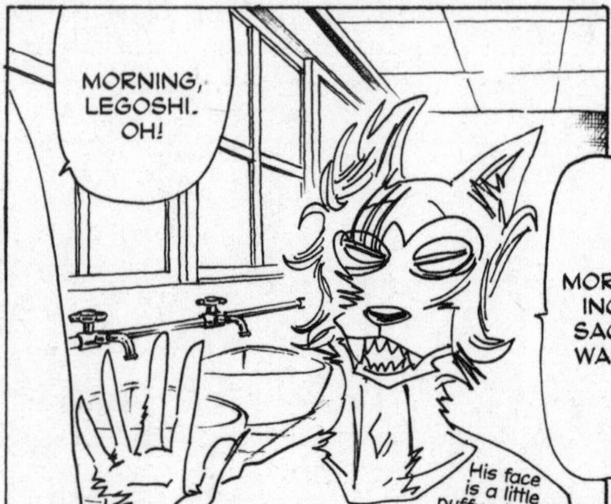
MORNING, LEGOSHI. OH!
MORNING, SAGWAN!
His face is a little puffy when he gets out of bed.

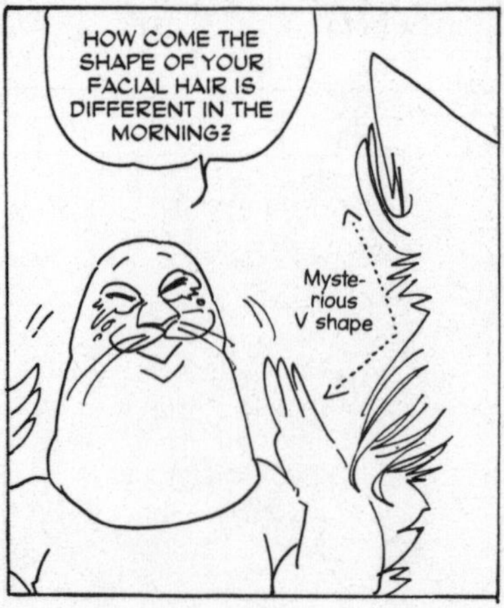
HOW COME THE SHAPE OF YOUR FACIAL HAIR IS DIFFERENT IN THE MORNING?
Mysterious V shape

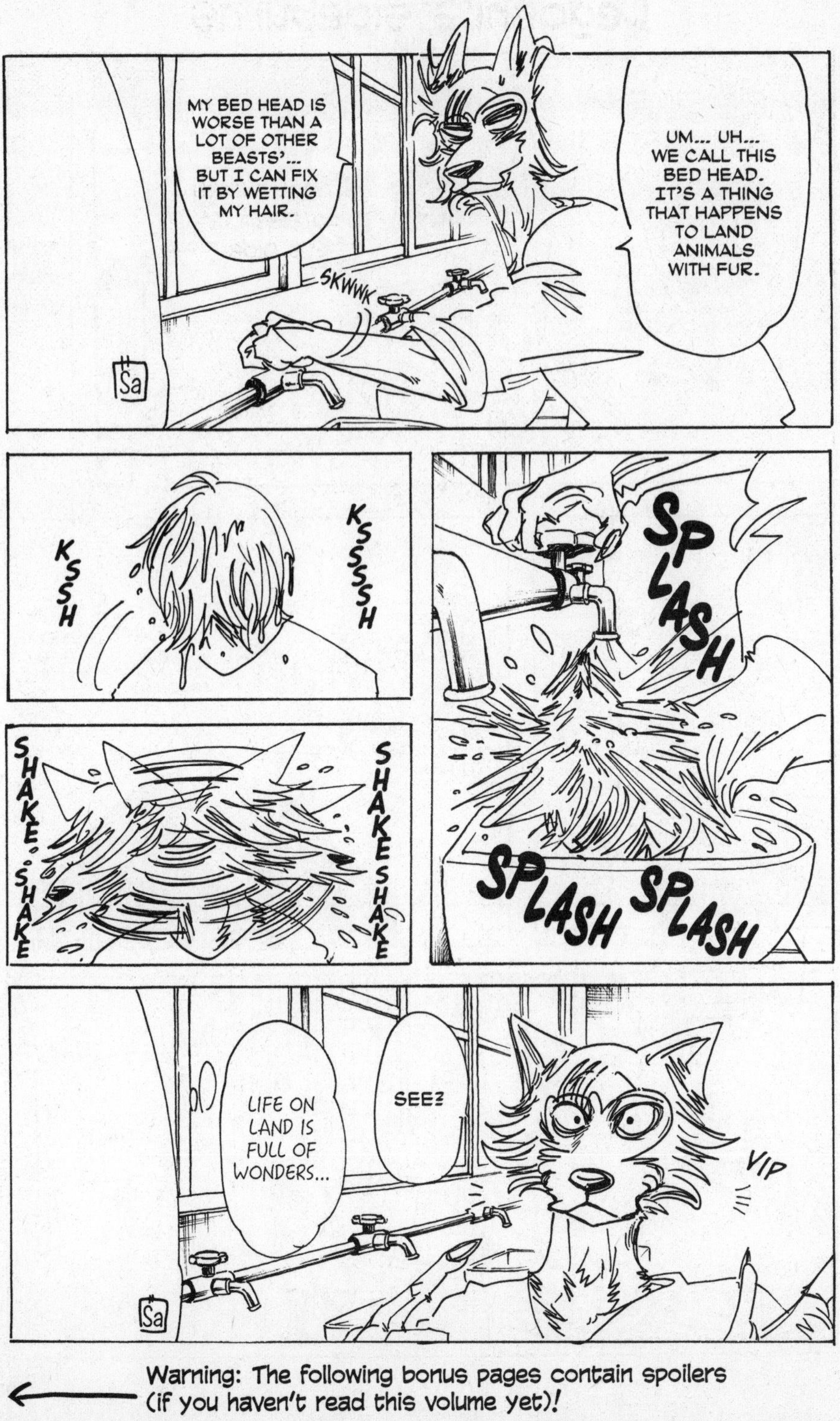
UM... UH... WE CALL THIS BED HEAD. IT'S A THING THAT HAPPENS TO LAND ANIMALS WITH FUR.
MY BED HEAD IS WORSE THAN A LOT OF OTHER BEASTS'... BUT I CAN FIX IT BY WETTING MY HAIR.
SKWWK
SPLASH
SPLASH
SPLASH
KSSSSH
KSSH
SHAKE SHAKE
SHAKE SHAKE
VIP
SEE?
LIFE ON LAND IS FULL OF WONDERS...

Warning: The following bonus pages contain spoilers (if you haven't read this volume yet)!

*Contains spoilers

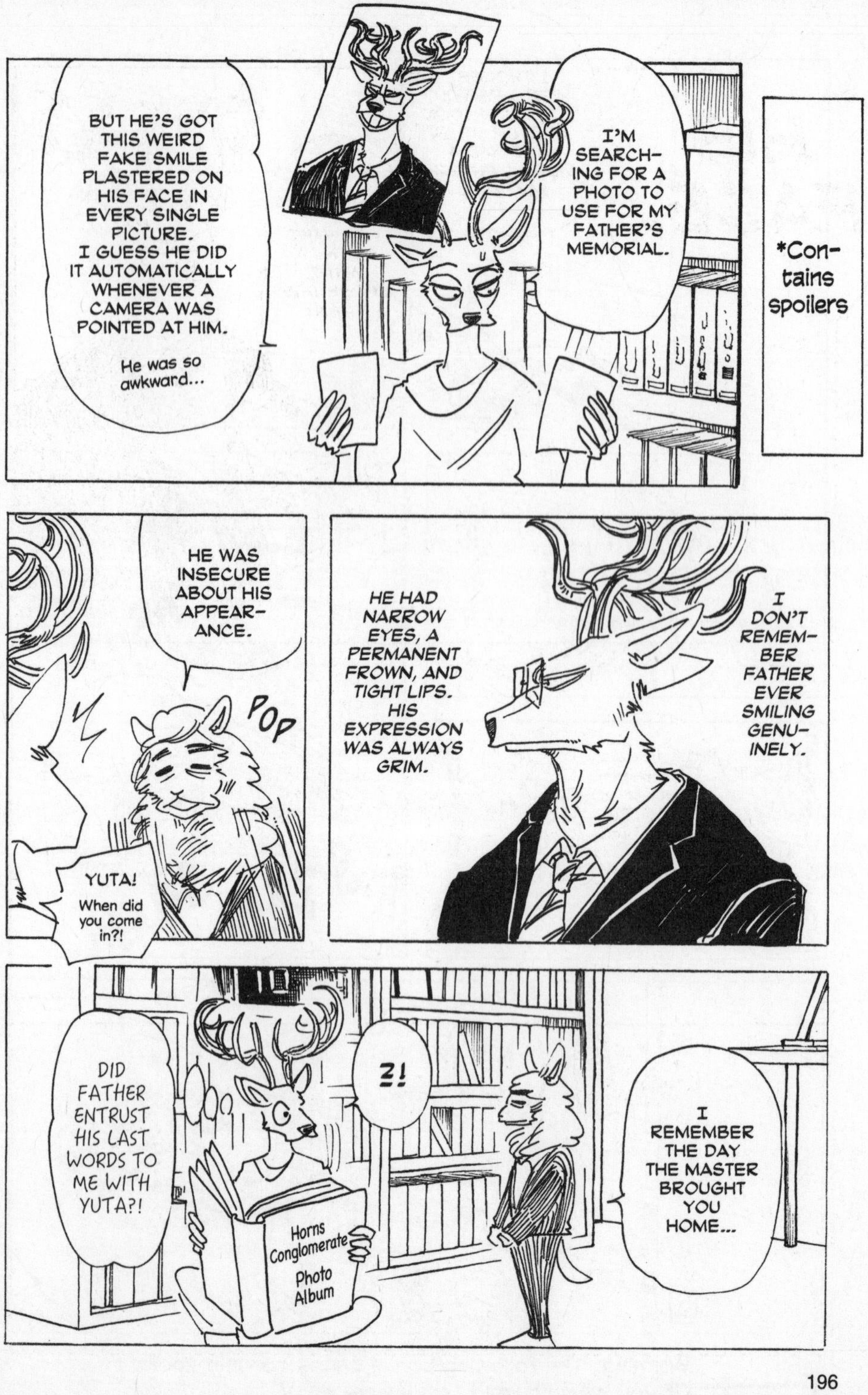

I'M SEARCHING FOR A PHOTO TO USE FOR MY FATHER'S MEMORIAL.
BUT HE'S GOT THIS WEIRD FAKE SMILE PLASTERED ON HIS FACE IN EVERY SINGLE PICTURE. I GUESS HE DID IT AUTOMATICALLY WHENEVER A CAMERA WAS POINTED AT HIM.
He was so awkward...
I DON'T REMEMBER FATHER EVER SMILING GENUINELY.
HE HAD NARROW EYES, A PERMANENT FROWN, AND TIGHT LIPS. HIS EXPRESSION WAS ALWAYS GRIM.
HE WAS INSECURE ABOUT HIS APPEARANCE.
POP
YUTA!
When did you come in?!
I REMEMBER THE DAY THE MASTER BROUGHT YOU HOME...
Z!
DID FATHER ENTRUST HIS LAST WORDS TO ME WITH YUTA?!
Horns Conglomerate Photo Album

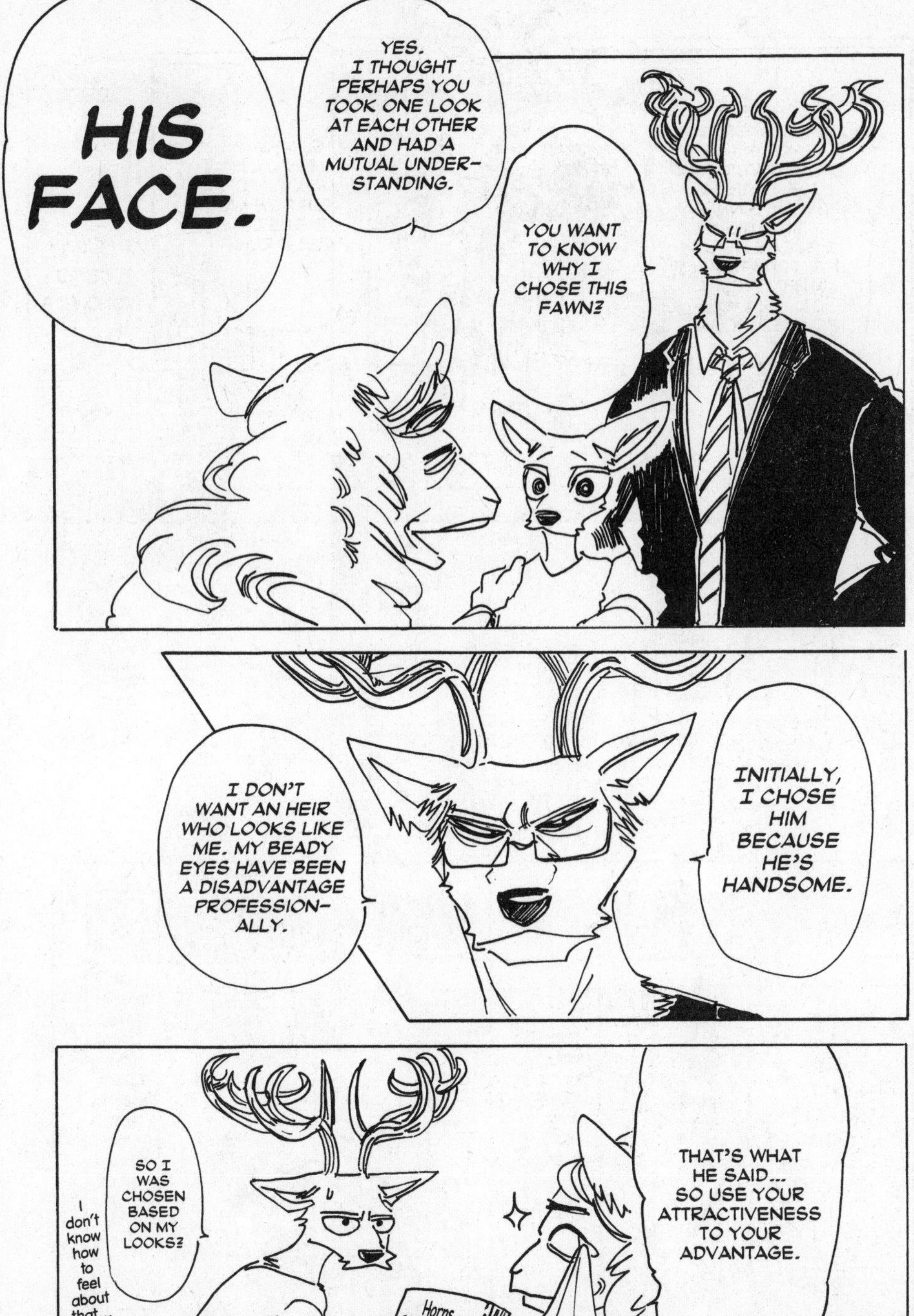
YOU WANT TO KNOW WHY I CHOSE THIS FAWN?
YES. I THOUGHT PERHAPS YOU TOOK ONE LOOK AT EACH OTHER AND HAD A MUTUAL UNDER-STANDING.
HIS FACE.
INITIALLY, I CHOSE HIM BECAUSE HE'S HANDSOME.
I DON'T WANT AN HEIR WHO LOOKS LIKE ME. MY BEADY EYES HAVE BEEN A DISADVANTAGE PROFESSION-ALLY.
THAT'S WHAT HE SAID... SO USE YOUR ATTRACTIVENESS TO YOUR ADVANTAGE.
SO I WAS CHOSEN BASED ON MY LOOKS?
I don't know how to feel about that...
Horns Conglomerate Photo Album

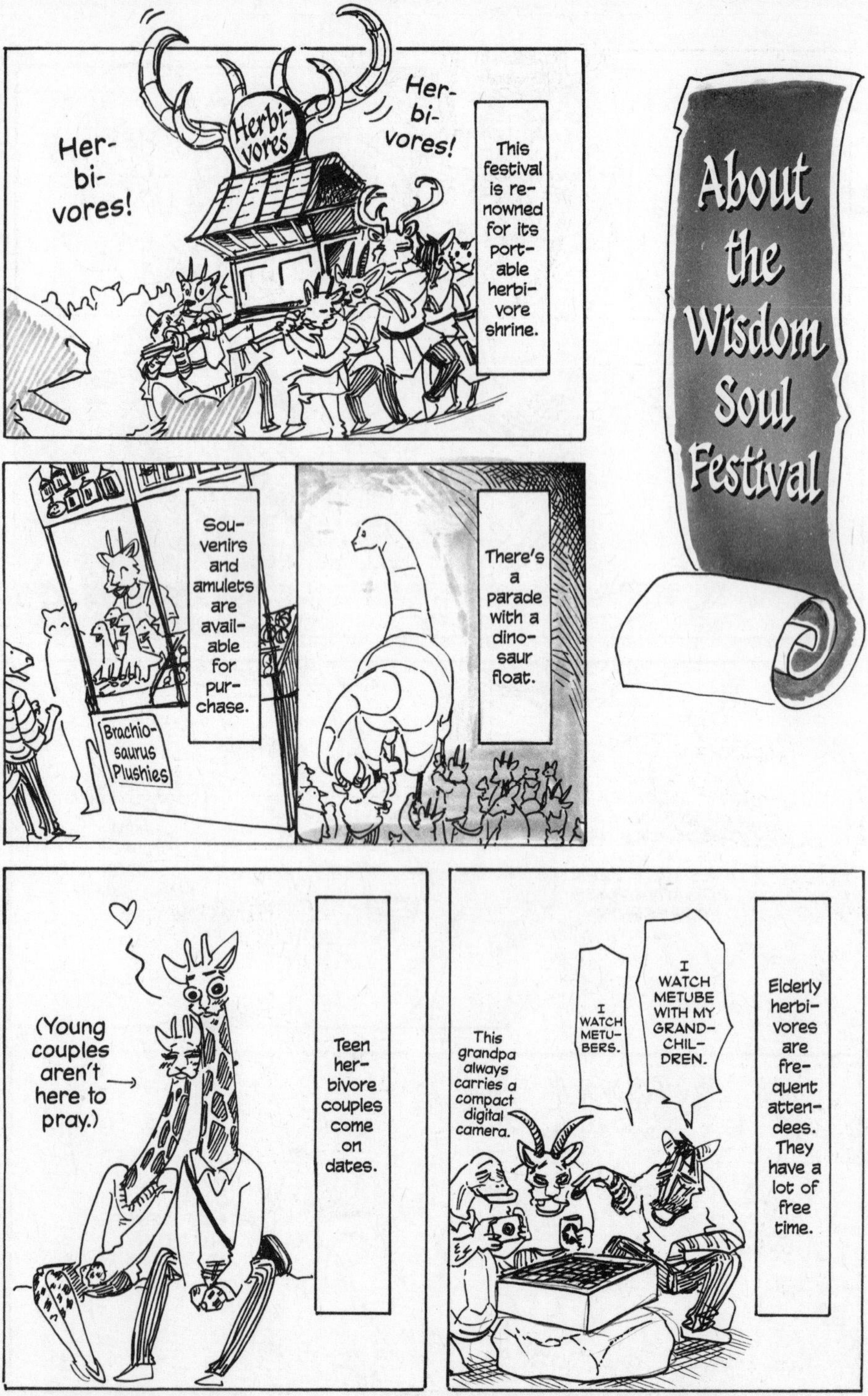
About the Wisdom Soul Festival
This festival is re-nowned for its port-able herbi-vore shrine.
Her-bi-vores!
Herbi-vores
Her-bi-vores!
There's a parade with a dino-saur float.
Sou-venirs and amulets are avail-able for pur-chase.
Brachio-saurus Plushies
Elderly herbi-vores are fre-quent atten-dees. They have a lot of free time.
I WATCH METUBE WITH MY GRAND-CHIL-DREN.
I WATCH METU-BERS.
This grandpa always carries a compact digital camera.
Teen her-bivore couples come on dates.
(Young couples aren't here to pray.)

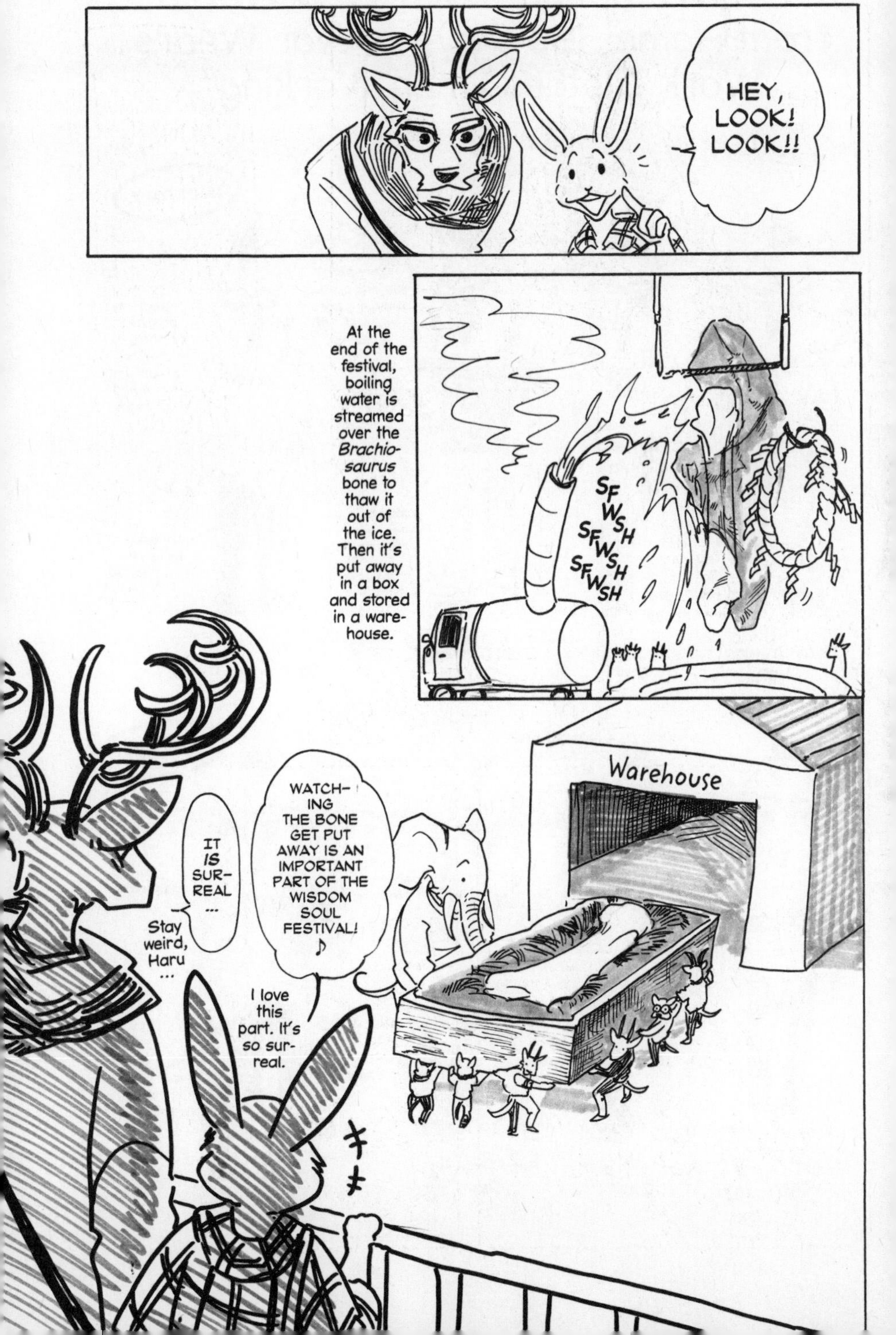
HEY, LOOK! LOOK!!
At the end of the festival, boiling water is streamed over the *Brachiosaurus* bone to thaw it out of the ice. Then it's put away in a box and stored in a warehouse.
SFWSH SFWSH SFWSH
Warehouse
WATCHING THE BONE GET PUT AWAY IS AN IMPORTANT PART OF THE WISDOM SOUL FESTIVAL! ♪
I love this part. It's so surreal.
IT *IS* SURREAL...
Stay weird, Haru...

"Even a Manga Artist Who Works from Home 365 Days a Year Wears Work Clothes when Working"

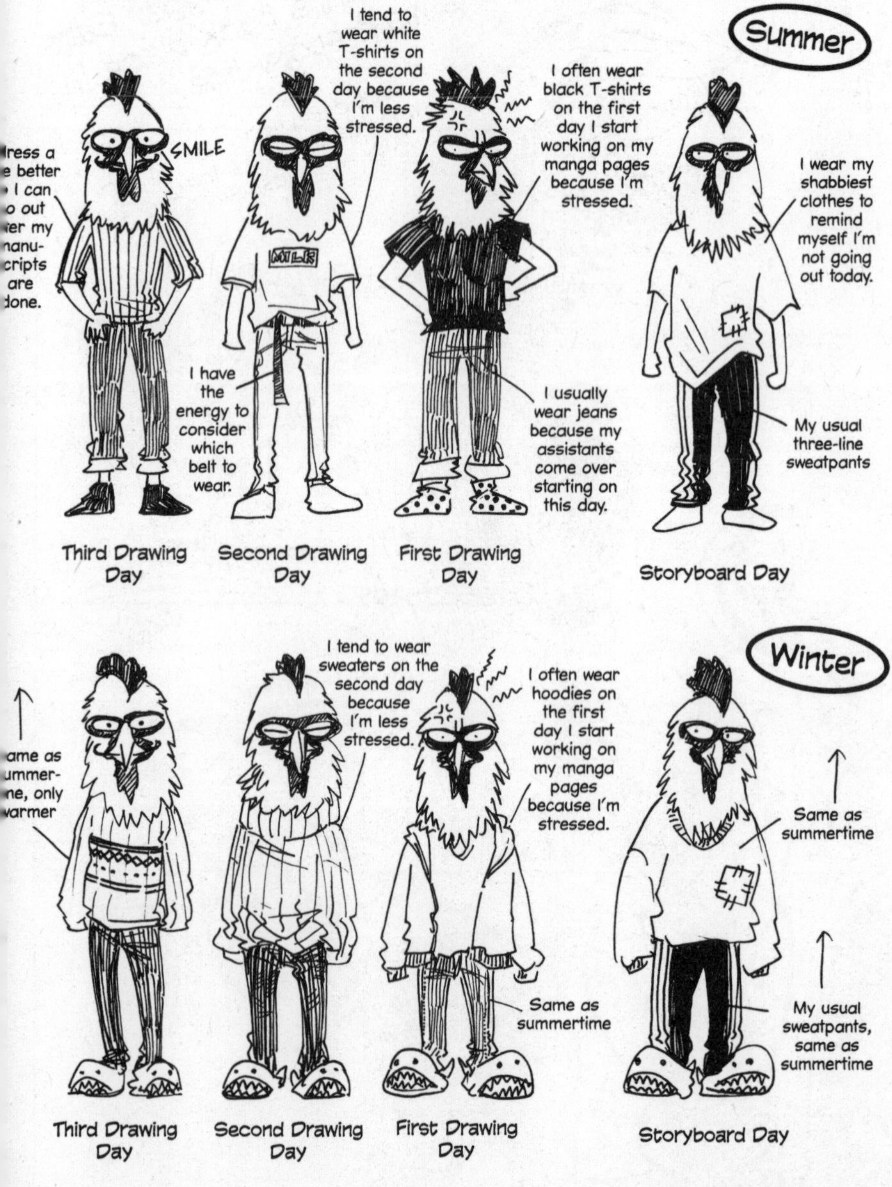

Summer
I wear my shabbiest clothes to remind myself I'm not going out today.
My usual three-line sweatpants
Storyboard Day
I often wear black T-shirts on the first day I start working on my manga pages because I'm stressed.
I usually wear jeans because my assistants come over starting on this day.
First Drawing Day
I tend to wear white T-shirts on the second day because I'm less stressed.
MILK
I have the energy to consider which belt to wear.
Second Drawing Day
SMILE
ress a e better I can o out er my nanu- cripts are done.
Third Drawing Day
Winter
Same as summertime
My usual sweatpants, same as summertime
Storyboard Day
I often wear hoodies on the first day I start working on my manga pages because I'm stressed.
Same as summertime
First Drawing Day
I tend to wear sweaters on the second day because I'm less stressed.
Second Drawing Day
ame as ummer- ne, only varmer
Third Drawing Day

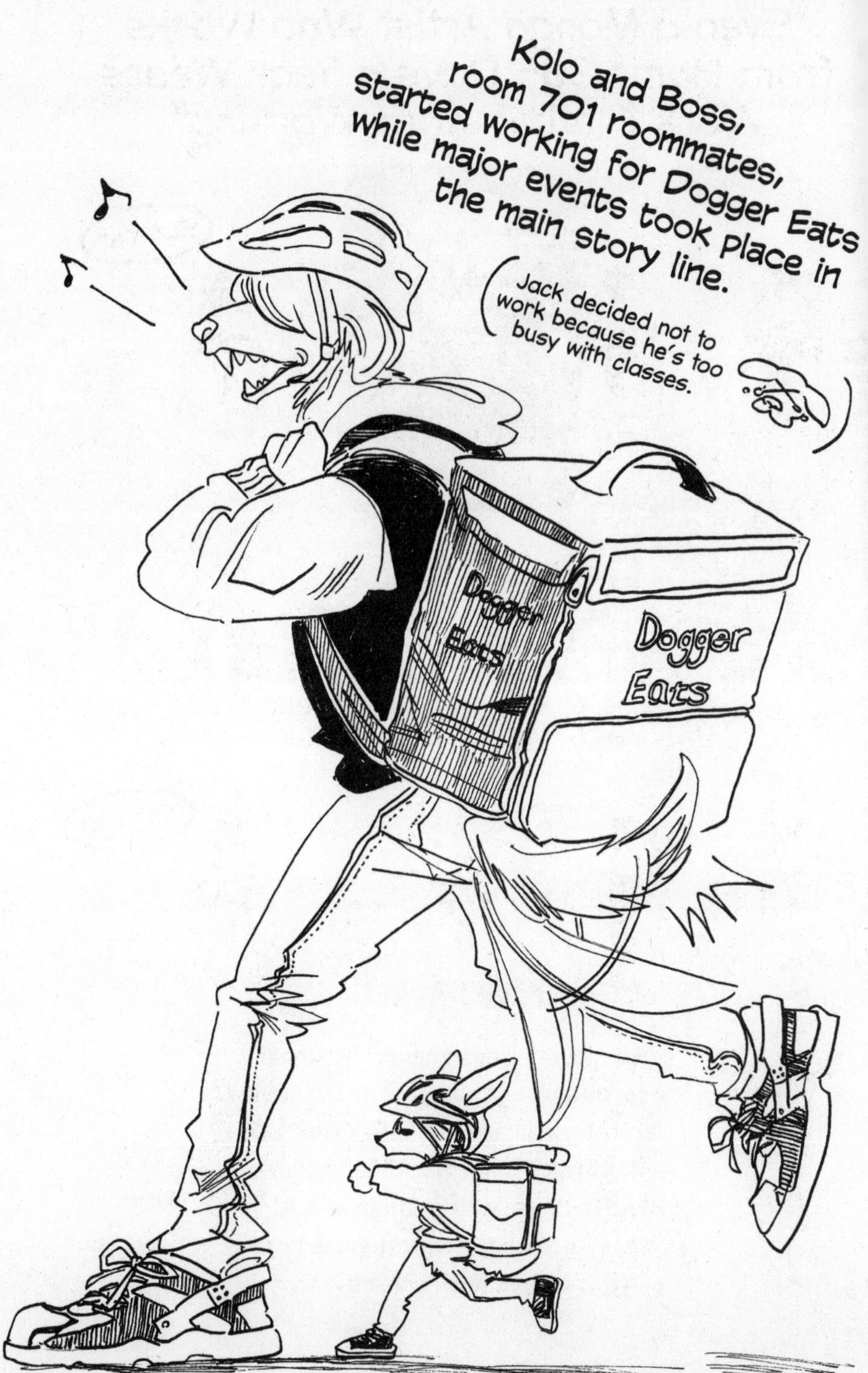
Kolo and Boss, room 701 roommates, started working for Dogger Eats while major events took place in the main story line.
(Jack decided not to work because he's too busy with classes.)
Dogger Eats
Dogger Eats

I EAT ICE CREAM WHEN I TAKE A BREAK. I START WORKING ON MY MANGA PAGES AFTER I EAT ICE CREAM. I EAT ICE CREAM BEFORE I GO TO BED. *BEASTARS* PAGES ARE MADE OF ICE CREAM.

PARU ITAGAKI

Paru Itagaki began her professional career as a manga author in 2016 with the short story collection **BEAST COMPLEX**. **BEASTARS** is her first serialization. **BEASTARS** has won multiple awards in Japan, including the prestigious 2018 Manga Taisho Award.

BEASTARS

VOL. 19
VIZ Signature Edition

Story & Art by
Paru Itagaki

Translation/Tomo Kimura
English Adaptation/Annette Roman
Touch-Up Art & Lettering/Susan Daigle-Leach
Cover & Interior Design/Yukiko Whitley
Editor/Annette Roman

Printed in Canada

Published by VIZ Media, LLC
P.O. Box 77010
San Francisco, CA 94107

10 9 8 7 6 5 4 3 2 1
First printing, July 2022

VIZ MEDIA
viz.com

VIZ SIGNATURE
vizsignature.com

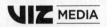

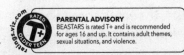

OMING IN
OLUME 20...

Gray wolf Legoshi trains and fasts in preparation for the monthly black market battles, where he plans to duel mixed-species psychopath Melon. What is red deer Louis willing to sacrifice this ime to help Legoshi triumph? Regardless, it seems that Legoshi's oft heart may be his biggest obstacle. And first, Legoshi must efeat a gang boss who reminds him of someone he loves...

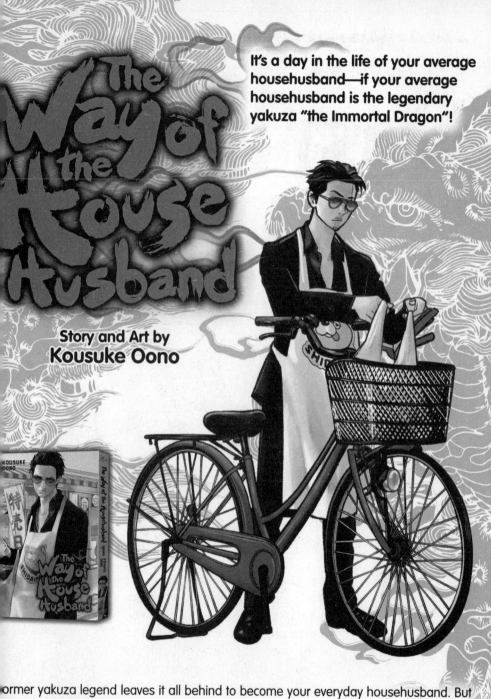

The Way of the House Husband

It's a day in the life of your average househusband—if your average househusband is the legendary yakuza "the Immortal Dragon"!

Story and Art by
Kousuke Oono

ormer yakuza legend leaves it all behind to become your everyday househusband. But not easy to walk away from the gangster life, and what should be mundane household ks are anything but!

A deadly typhoon, a mysterious creature and a girl who won't quit.

ASADORA!

Story and Art by NAOKI URASAW

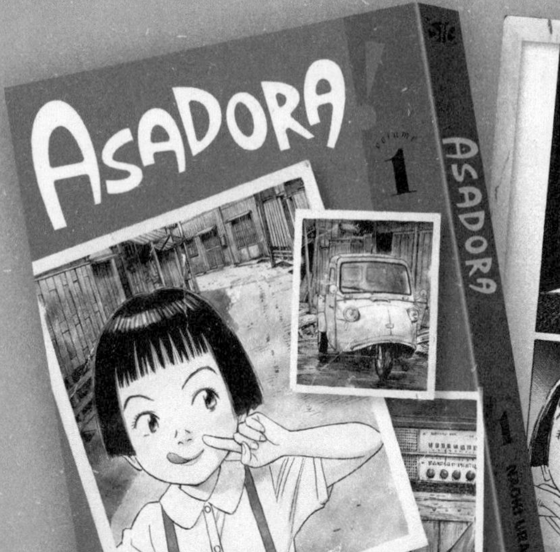
ASADORA
volume 1
ASADORA
1
NAOKI URASAWA
VIZ
NAOKI URASAWA

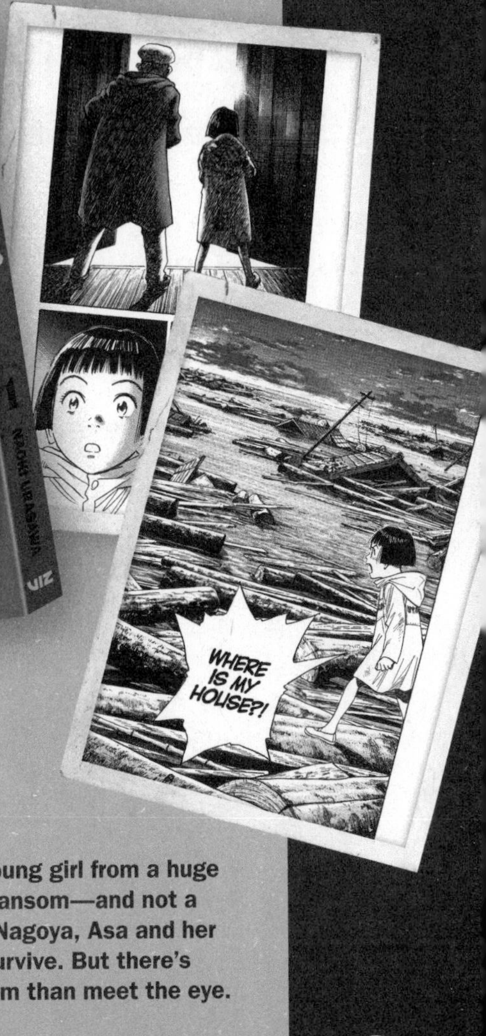
WHERE IS MY HOUSE?!

In 2020, a large creature rampages through Tokyo, destroying everything in its path.

In 1959, Asa Asada, a spunky young girl from a huge family in Nagoya, is kidnapped for ransom—and not a soul notices. When a typhoon hits Nagoya, Asa and her kidnapper must work together to survive. But there's more to her kidnapper and this storm than meet the eye.

This is the last page.

BEASTARS reads from right to left to preserve the orientation of the original Japanese artwork.